Study

PSYCHOLOGY

BRIDGET SCHOPPERT
DOUGLAS A. BERNSTEIN

Study Guide

PSYCHOLOGY

Douglas A. Bernstein
Edward J. Roy
Thomas K. Srull
Christopher D. Wickens

University of Illinois at Urbana-Champaign

HOUGHTON MIFFLIN COMPANY   **BOSTON**

Dallas   Geneva, Ill.   Palo Alto   Princeton, N. J.

Cover photograph by James Scherer

Printed in the U.S.A.

Library of Congress Catalog Card Number: 87–80237

ISBN: 0–395–35507–9

DEFGHIJ-WC-9543210/89

Contents

Chapter 4   Sensation   61
OUTLINE 61
KEY TERMS 65
LEARNING OBJECTIVES 70
CONCEPTS AND EXERCISES 71
MULTIPLE CHOICE QUESTIONS 73

Chapter 5   Perception   81
OUTLINE 81
KEY TERMS 84
LEARNING OBJECTIVES 89
CONCEPTS AND EXERCISES 90
MULTIPLE CHOICE QUESTIONS 93

Chapter 6   Consciousness   103
OUTLINE 103
KEY TERMS 105
LEARNING OBJECTIVES 110
CONCEPTS AND EXERCISES 111
MULTIPLE CHOICE QUESTIONS 112

Chapter 7   Learning   121
OUTLINE 121
KEY TERMS 123
LEARNING OBJECTIVES 129
CONCEPTS AND EXERCISES 130
MULTIPLE CHOICE QUESTIONS 133

Chapter 8   Memory   143
OUTLINE 143
KEY TERMS 145
LEARNING OBJECTIVES 150
CONCEPTS AND EXERCISES 151
MULTIPLE CHOICE QUESTIONS 155

Chapter 9   Thought and Language   163
OUTLINE 163
KEY TERMS 166

Preface   vii

Chapter 1   The World of Psychology   1
OUTLINE 1
KEY TERMS 3
LEARNING OBJECTIVES 8
CONCEPTS AND EXERCISES 8
MULTIPLE CHOICE QUESTIONS 12

Chapter 2   Human Development   21
OUTLINE 21
KEY TERMS 25
LEARNING OBJECTIVES 29
CONCEPTS AND EXERCISES 30
MULTIPLE CHOICE QUESTIONS 32

Chapter 3   Biological Bases of Behavior   41
OUTLINE 41
KEY TERMS 43
LEARNING OBJECTIVES 49
CONCEPTS AND EXERCISES 50
MULTIPLE CHOICE QUESTIONS 53

LEARNING OBJECTIVES 170
CONCEPTS AND EXERCISES 171
MULTIPLE CHOICE QUESTIONS 174

Chapter 10 Mental Abilities   183
OUTLINE 183
KEY TERMS 185
LEARNING OBJECTIVES 190
CONCEPTS AND EXERCISES 190
MULTIPLE CHOICE QUESTIONS 193

Chapter 11 Motivation   201
OUTLINE 201
KEY TERMS 203
LEARNING OBJECTIVES 206
CONCEPTS AND EXERCISES 207
MULTIPLE CHOICE QUESTIONS 210

Chapter 12 Emotion   219
OUTLINE 219
KEY TERMS 221
LEARNING OBJECTIVES 223
CONCEPTS AND EXERCISES 223
MULTIPLE CHOICE QUESTIONS 226

Chapter 13 Stress and Coping   235
OUTLINE 235
KEY TERMS 237
LEARNING OBJECTIVES 239
CONCEPTS AND EXERCISES 240
MULTIPLE CHOICE QUESTIONS 242

Chapter 14 Personality   251
OUTLINE 251
KEY TERMS 255
LEARNING OBJECTIVES 260
CONCEPTS AND EXERCISES 261
MULTIPLE CHOICE QUESTIONS 263

Chapter 15 Abnormal Behavior   273
OUTLINE 273
KEY TERMS 277
LEARNING OBJECTIVES 282
CONCEPTS AND EXERCISES 283
MULTIPLE CHOICE QUESTIONS 286

Chapter 16 Treatment of Psychological
**   Disorders   295**
OUTLINE 295
KEY TERMS 299
LEARNING OBJECTIVES 303
CONCEPTS AND EXERCISES 304
MULTIPLE CHOICE QUESTIONS 305

Chapter 17 The Individual in the
**   Social World   315**
OUTLINE 315
KEY TERMS 317
LEARNING OBJECTIVES 321
CONCEPTS AND EXERCISES 321
MULTIPLE CHOICE QUESTIONS 324

Chapter 18 Group Influences and
**   Interpersonal Behavior   333**
OUTLINE 333
KEY TERMS 336
LEARNING OBJECTIVES 337
CONCEPTS AND EXERCISES 338
MULTIPLE CHOICE QUESTIONS 340

Appendix   Statistics in Psychological
**   Research   349**
OUTLINE 349
KEY TERMS 350
LEARNING OBJECTIVES 352
CONCEPTS AND EXERCISES 352
MULTIPLE CHOICE QUESTIONS 356

Preface

TO THE STUDENT

This *Study Guide* was designed to help you master the material in *Psychology* by Bernstein/Roy/Srull/Wickens. The *Study Guide* supplements the textbook but does not replace it. If used properly, the *Guide* should help you to not merely memorize but to *take command of* key facts, concepts, and issues discussed in the text.

We, the authors, want you to succeed in your introductory psychology course. We also want to help you deepen your understanding of how psychological principles can illuminate and enrich your life. These two desires steered us as we created this *Guide*.

Each *Study Guide* chapter corresponds to a text chapter and is divided into five sections: Chapter Outline, Key Terms, Learning Objectives, Concepts and Exercises, and Multiple Choice Questions.

1. *Chapter Outline.* The outline presents the major topics and ideas from the text chapter. It reveals in handy fashion the organizational logic underlying each chapter—that is, the way each chapter's components fit together. Reviewing the Chapter Outlines may prove especially useful before a quiz or an exam.

2. *Key Terms.* Terms that are underlined in the Chapter Outlines are also defined in the Key Terms section. We have tried to help you fix these terms in your memory: for many of them, we provide an illustrative example. For others, we present a "remember" statement. For further reference, you will find a number in parentheses at the end of each definition. It identifies the *textbook* page on which the term is first defined and explained in the book.

Note: We urge you to create your own examples of key terms as part of your study program. If you do so successfully, you will have taken a giant step toward mastering the material.

3. *Learning Objectives.* The Chapter Outline and Key Terms sections provide a basic overview of the contents of your textbook. The next section of each *Study Guide* chapter, Learning Objectives, will further strengthen your command of textbook material so that you will be able to discuss, describe, and explain the important information in each chapter. To help you master these learning objectives, we have identified the textbook pages to which each objective corresponds.

4. *Concepts and Exercises.* This section will help you achieve selected learning objectives stated in the preceding section. The exercises apply key psychological concepts to situations from everyday life. You are asked to identify the concepts being applied. At the end of the exercises we provide not only the correct answer to each exercise but also an explanation of why the answer is correct and why the other answers are wrong.

5. *Multiple Choice Questions.* Once you have carefully worked through the first four sections, you will be ready to test your comprehension of the material covered. Every *Study Guide* chapter contains two multiple choice self-tests, each consisting of fifteen questions. In the first, you can test your knowledge of facts and definitions. In the second, you can judge your ability to apply concepts to everyday situations. At the end of these tests we once again provide the cor-

rect answers—and again explain *why* each answer is correct or incorrect.

We suggest that you begin your self-quiz by taking the test on Facts and Definitions. Next, check your answers against ours. If you get a question wrong, turn to the text pages listed next to the answers and reread the relevant sections. Also look back over sections of the *Study Guide*'s Chapter Outline and the appropriate Key Terms. Then retest on questions you missed in the Facts and Definitions section. When you are in control of that material, take the complete test on Applications and score that test, noting our explanations of right and wrong answers. Finally, restudy textbook and *Study Guide* materials as necessary. By following this procedure you build incrementally toward mastering the contents of your text.

The self-test sections will also serve a second purpose. If multiple choice exams are part of your instructor's program, the multiple choice tests in the *Study Guide* will provide a valuable way to prepare for exams.

As you can see, we have designed each chapter of this *Guide* as a sequenced program of study, and each section builds on the last. However, if you believe that a different sequencing of sections will work better for you, we hope you will give it a try.

Here's to your success!

B.S.
D.A.B.

Chapter 1

The World of Psychology

OUTLINE

I. FROM CELL TO SOCIETY: THE SCOPE OF PSYCHOLOGY (pp. 2–12)

Psychology is the science of behavior and mental processes.

A. Subfields of Psychology

Each subfield or area of specialization is defined by the types of questions, problems, and issues associated with it.

1. *Biological or Physiological Psychology.* The biological factors underlying our behavior are the concern of biological or physiological psychology. How do nerve cells communicate with each other? What parts of the brain are activated when people engage in different behaviors?

2. *Experimental and Cognitive Psychology.* How do we learn? How do we think? Experimental and cognitive psychology involve questions about the processes underlying perception, memory, and other aspects of human thought.

3. *Personality Psychology.* What characteristics make individuals unique? Personality psychology focuses on the characteristics that make people unique and studies the relationship between personality characteristics and behavior and mental processes.

4. *Social Psychology.* How do groups influence the behavior and attitudes of individuals? Social psychology research focuses on how people influence one another, especially in groups of two or more.

5. *Clinical Psychology.* What causes abnormal behavior? How can abnormal behavior be corrected? Clinical psychology seeks to understand and correct abnormal functioning, using tests, interviews, and observations.

6. *Developmental Psychology.* How do we change and grow over the life span? Developmental psychology describes and explores the effects of changes in behavior and mental processes that occur over the course of a lifetime.

7. *Quantitative Psychology.* How can behavior and mental processes be measured and analyzed? Quantitative psychology provides the means by which data can be summarized and analyzed.

B. Psychological Approaches

Each theoretical approach makes different assumptions about the factors that cause, maintain, and alter behavior and mental processes.

1. *The Biological Approach.* According to the biological approach, physiological factors determine behavior and mental processes.

2. *The Psychodynamic Approach.* According to the psychodynamic approach, behavior reflects

1

internal conflict between people's instincts and society's behavioral rules.

3. *The Behavioral Approach.* According to the behavioral approach, the rewards and punishments people experience determine behavior.

4. *The Humanistic Approach.* According to the humanistic approach, people choose how to behave, based on their perceptions of the world, in order to grow toward their potential.

5. *The Cognitive Approach.* According to the cognitive approach, our various mental processes, such as perception, memory, thought, judgment, and decision making, guide and generate behavior.

C. Unity Within Diversity

Despite the wide variety of interests, opinions, and approaches in psychology, shared knowledge and the use of empirical research to study behavior and mental processes unify the field.

II. THE GOALS OF RESEARCH (pp. 12–18)

Psychological research, like research in any other science, is gradual and cumulative, always adding new information to knowledge provided by others in the past. This process is guided by the four basic goals of any science: description, prediction, control, and explanation.

A. Description

Description involves gathering information about the phenomenon of interest.

B. Prediction

Prediction involves exploring hypotheses, specific, testable propositions about the behaviors and mental processes underlying a phenomenon of interest. Research aimed at prediction tests hypotheses by

analyzing correlations, which represent the degree to which one variable is related to another.

C. Control

Control eliminates factors that might interfere with understanding a cause-effect relationship. Controlled research uses experimental methods to test predictions.

D. Explanations

Explanations of behavior and mental processes, based on research, are used to form general rules about behavior or mental processes. Explanations and general rules are used to form psychological theories.

III. SOME RESEARCH METHODS (pp. 18–24)

A. Surveys

Surveys use questionnaires or special interviews to obtain information about people's behavior, attitudes, beliefs, opinions, and intentions.

B. Case Studies

Case studies involve the intensive examination of a phenomenon in a particular individual, group, or situation.

C. Naturalistic Observation

Naturalistic observation entails observing a phenomenon as it occurs in its own environment.

D. Experiments

Experiments allow the researcher to manipulate or control one variable in order to observe the effect of that manipulation on another variable.

1. *The Structure of Experiments.* In an experiment the variable that the researcher manipu-

lates or controls is called the independent variable. The variable observed to assess the effect of that manipulation is called the dependent variable. Any differences in the dependent variable observed between the control and experimental groups is caused by the independent variable.

2. *Selecting the Subjects.* When each member of a particular population has an equal chance of being chosen for study, the individuals selected constitute a random sample. Experiments that use random samples provide information *only* about the particular population from which the sample was selected.

3. *Flaws in Experiments.* Flaws in experimental control might account for the results of an experiment. Confounding variables confuse the interpretation of experimental data. Random variables, placebos, the Hawthorne effect, and experimenter bias are all confounding variables.

KEY TERMS

1. **Psychology** is the science of behavior and mental processes. (p. 2)

2. **Behavior** is any action an organism performs. Behavior includes not only actions that you can see, but also many activities that you cannot. (p. 2)

Examples: heart rate, nervous system activity, blood pressure, jogging, eating, laughing

3. **Mental processes** are activities involved in thinking. (p. 2)

Examples: remembering, dreaming, forming opinions, imagining

4. **Biological psychology** is the study of the biological factors that provide the basis of behavior and mental processes. (p. 4)

Example: Eating certain foods changes the chemical interactions within and between nerve cells in your brain, which can induce drowsiness.

5. **Experimental psychology** and **cognitive psychology** involve studying perception, learning, memory, thinking, language, and phenomena related to these basic mental and behavioral processes. (pp. 5–6)

Example: Is remembering how to tie our shoes the same as remembering a friend's telephone number?

6. **Personality psychology** is the study of what makes one person different from others, and looks at the relationship between personality characteristics and behavior and mental processes. (pp. 6–7)

Example: Why are some people eternal optimists and others are consistently pessimistic?

7. **Social psychology** is the study of how people influence one another and of the interactions between people in groups of two or more. (p. 7)

Example: An anonymous crowd member may be boisterous but the same person may be quiet when recognized as an individual. For example, Joe is rowdy when he and his friends go out on the weekends. In a classroom, Joe is quiet and obeys all the rules.

8. **Industrial-organizational psychology** is the study of group behavior in a business or some other organizational setting. (p. 7)

Example: Do large or small groups make faster or better decisions? What skills help an employer lead a group of employees to maximum production?

9. **Clinical psychology** is the study of abnormal behavior and mental processes: what causes them and how to treat them. Clinical psychologists also evaluate how well and why a treatment works. (pp. 7–8)

Example: Is schizophrenia hereditary? What therapy produces the best results with schizophrenic patients? Why is one particular therapy more effective than another?

10. **Community psychology** involves the development of local facilities offering programs that try to prevent psychological problems. (p. 8)

Example: A community psychologist may create a local hotline for people who are in crisis situations and need someone to talk to.

11. **Developmental psychology** is the study of changes in behavior and mental processes over the life span. (p. 8)

Example: How do people develop morals, social skills, and intellectual abilities?

12. **Quantitative psychology** is the study and application of mathematical methods designed to measure phenomena, analyze data, and describe or predict complex behavior. (pp. 8–9)

Example: Psychologists are interested in many behaviors that are difficult to measure. How should happiness be measured? Suppose you measure happiness by recording how often a person laughs. Can you be sure that two people who are equally happy will laugh for the same amount of time or with the same intensity?

REMEMBER: The word *quantitative* pertains to the number or amount of something. Measuring psychological phenomena involves creating ways to quantify behavior and mental processes.

13. **Statistical analyses** are mathematical methods used to summarize and analyze research data. (p. 9)

14. The **biological approach** assumes that biological factors, such as genetics, the electrical and chemical activity in the brain, or the actions of hormones, are the most important factors determining behavior and mental processes. (p. 10)

Example: People who are chronically depressed may have abnormal levels of norepinephrine, an important chemical in brain activity.

15. The **psychodynamic approach** assumes that our behavior results from our struggle to fulfill instinctive desires and wishes despite society's restrictions concerning these activities. (p. 10)

Example: Freud might have said that surgeons display aggressive instincts in a manner that is approved of by society.

16. The **behavioral approach** assumes that the rewards and punishments that each person experiences determine most behaviors and ways of thinking. (pp. 10–11)

Example: Doctors become surgeons because they are rewarded for doing so, possibly by their salaries or by the respect their positions receive.

17. The **humanistic approach** assumes that people control their own behaviors. This approach is unlike other models, which assume that biology, instincts, or the presence of rewards and punishments in the environment control behavior. The humanistic approach also assumes that each person has an inborn tendency to grow toward his or her unique potential. (p. 11)

Example: The innate tendency to grow toward one's unique potential is analagous to a flower that will bloom if it receives adequate light, water, and nourishment. People, too, will achieve their potential if their environments provide the correct psychological and physical nourishment.

18. The **cognitive approach** assumes that mental processes cause behavior. The brain takes in information; processes it through perception, memory, thought, judgment, and decision making; and generates integrated behavior patterns. (p. 11)

REMEMBER: Cognition means thinking. The cognitive approach assumes that our thoughts cause our behavior.

19. **Description,** the first research goal that scientists must meet, involves gathering information regarding all aspects of a phenomenon through surveys, case studies, and observation. (p. 13)

Example: A developmental psychologist interested in finding out the age at which children begin to walk must carefully *observe* infants' motor behavior in many situations (such as walking aided or unaided) and under many conditions (such as receiving normal or abnormal nutrition) in order to *describe* the phenomenon as it naturally occurs.

20. **Predictions** are usually based on descriptive information and are stated as hypotheses that propose something testable about a phenomenon (a behavior or a mental process) being studied. Researchers usually collect more data to test hypotheses once they are generated. (pp. 13–14)

Example: Knowing that rats raised in a toy-filled environment learn mazes faster than rats raised without access to toys may lead a researcher to form a hypothesis. *If* rats have access to toys *then* they can practice behaviors similar to those required to run a maze, and therefore be able to learn more quickly than rats raised without access to toys.

21. **Variables** are specific factors or characteristics that can vary. Researchers examine relationships between variables when testing hypotheses. (p. 13)

Example: Moods, decision-making processes, emotions, eating behaviors, chemical activity in the brain, heart rate, or types of clothing worn are just some examples of the many possible variables that would interest psychologists.

22. A **hypothesis** is a prediction stated as a specific, testable proposition, usually in the form of an if-then statement. (p. 13)

Example: If rats have access to toys, *then* they can practice behaviors similar to those used in running a maze and perform better than rats raised without access to toys.

23. A **correlation** is an indication of the relationship between two variables (X and Y). A *correlation coefficient* (r, a number between -1 and $+1$) is a mathematical representation of the strength and direction of a correlation. A *positive correlation* (r varies from 0 to $+1$) describes two variables that change in the same direction: as X increases so does Y; as X decreases so does Y. A *negative correlation* (r varies from -1 to 0) describes an inverse relationship: as X increases Y decreases; as X decreases Y increases. A *perfect correlation,* positive or negative (r equals ± 1), describes a perfect relationship; knowing the value of X allows the certain prediction of Y. Correlations *do not indicate causation.* (pp. 13–16)

Example: In a small English town, the seasonal appearance of a large number of storks is positively correlated with the number of human births; as X (the number of storks) increases, Y (the number of births) increases. If correlations indicated causation we could say that the storks cause babies to appear. But correlations *do not* imply causation, and storks do not bring babies.

24. **Scatterplots** are graphs that provide pictures of the strength and direction of a correlation. (p. 15)

Example: See Figure 1.2 in the text.

25. **Statistical significance** allows a researcher to know if the data collected from a sample accurately represent the kinds of behaviors and mental processes that exist in the population of interest or if the data occurred by chance—possibly because of an unrepresentative sample or the presence of confounding variables. (p. 14)

26. **Control** is achieved when researchers use the experimental method; the researcher can manipulate an independent variable, hold all other variables constant, and observe the effect on the dependent variable. Control and experimentation allow a researcher to establish a cause-effect relationship, because the independent variable produces any change found in the other variable. (p. 16)

Example: A researcher hypothesizes that caffeine causes an increase in physiological arousal. To test this hypothesis, the researcher gives one group of people caffeinated coffee and another group of people decaffeinated coffee. Then the researcher measures the physiological arousal of both groups. Because the two groups are identical in every way except for the type of coffee they drank, any differences in physiological arousal can be caused only by the caffeine in the drinks.

27. **Explanations,** based on data gathered at the descriptive, predictive, and control levels of research, lead to the formation of general rules and then *theories,* integrated sets of principles that can be used to explain or predict phenomena. (pp. 16–17)

28. **Surveys** are questionnaires or special interviews administered to a large group of people. Surveys are designed to obtain *descriptions* of people's attitudes, beliefs, opinions, or behavioral intentions. (p. 18)

Example: Social psychologists are interested in learning what teenagers from families of varying income levels think of marriage. They can administer a questionnaire to a sample of teenagers to obtain this descriptive information.

29. **Case studies** are used to collect *descriptive* data through the intensive examination of a phenomenon in a particular individual, group, or situation. Case studies are particularly useful for studying rare or complex phenomena. (p. 19)

Example: Biological psychologists cannot alter a person's brain in the laboratory for the purposes of study. Hence, there is intense interest in people who have, by an unfortunate accident, an injured area of the brain. Researchers would examine these patients intensively over a long period of time.

30. **Naturalistic observation,** a method of gathering descriptive information, involves watching behaviors of interest as they occur in their natural environments. (pp. 19–20)

Example: A researcher interested in how much time children of different ages play alone could observe children at a playground.

REMEMBER: A researcher is *observing* a phenomenon in its *natural* environment.

31. **An experiment** allows a researcher to control the data-collection process. A random sample of subjects is selected and divided into the *control* group and the *experimental* group. Both groups are identical in every way except for the administration of the independent variable to the experimental group. The dependent variable is then measured. Any differences in the dependent variable between the two groups is caused by the independent variable. Experiments indicate causation. (p. 20)

REMEMBER: An experiment is a trial or test of a hypothesis.

32. **Independent variables** are manipulated or controlled by the researcher in an experiment. They are administered to the experimental group. (p. 20)

Example: An experiment is conducted to test the effects of alcohol on reflex speed. Two groups of subjects are randomly selected. One group, the experimental group, is given alcohol (alcohol is the independent variable), and the other group, the control group, is given a nonalcoholic beverage.

33. **Dependent variables** are the behaviors or mental processes affected by the independent variable. They are observed and measured before and after the administration of the independent variable. (p. 20)

Example: In the experiment examining the effects of alcohol on reflex speed, reflex speed is the dependent variable.

REMEMBER: The measure or value of the dependent variable *depends* on the independent variable.

34. **Sampling** is a procedure used to choose subjects for research. Ideally, subjects chosen should be representative of the population being studied. (p. 21)

Example: If you are studying the behavior of gifted children, your sample should be drawn from this group of children.

35. **Random samples** are groups of subjects selected from the population of interest. A sample is random if every person in the population has an equal chance of being selected for the sample. If a sample is not random it is *biased.* (p. 21)

Example: A social psychologist is interested in the influence of parents on the career choice of college freshmen in the United States. For the sample to be random, every college freshman must have an equal chance of being selected as a subject. The researcher draws the sample from lists of freshmen from colleges located all over the United States, not just from schools in one state.

36. **Confounding variables** are any factors affecting the dependent variable in an experiment instead of or along with the independent variable. Several types of confounding variables are the random variable, an experimenter bias, the Hawthorne effect, and the placebo effect. (p. 21)

37. **Random variables** are uncontrolled or uncontrollable factors that could affect the dependent variable in an experiment. (p. 22)

Example: An experimenter wishes to test the effects of a teaching technique on test performance. The subjects are chosen and assigned randomly to the control and experimental group. The researcher does not know it, but most of the students in the experimental group are much brighter than the students in the control group. The data may suggest that the students who received the teaching technique performed at a higher level than those who did not. However, the level of intelligence is a random variable

that, instead of the independent variable, could be responsible for the results.

38. The **Hawthorne effect** occurs when the subjects' behavior changes, not because of the independent variable, but because the subjects know they are being observed. (p. 22)

Example: An experimenter wishes to test the effects of a teaching technique on the incidence of classroom behavior problems. To measure the level of problem behavior, the researcher decides to sit in the classroom and observe the students' behavior. All of the subjects are quiet and attentive and ask pertinent questions throughout the lecture. The experimenter's presence, not the teaching technique, may have caused the students to behave properly.

39. A **placebo** is a physical or psychological treatment that contains no active ingredient but produces an effect because the person receiving it believes it will. (p. 22)

Example: In an experiment on the effects of alcohol, a researcher may find that people who have been given a nonalcoholic beverage behave as though they are drunk if they *believe* they have been given an alcoholic drink.

40. In a **double-blind design** neither the experimenter nor the subjects know who has received the independent variable. (p. 23)

Example: The experiment on the effects of alcohol (described in key term 39) is repeated using a double-blind design. Neither the subjects nor the experimenter knows who has received alcohol and who has not. This will prevent the subjects from changing their behavior because they think they have been given alcohol. This will also prevent the experimenter from inadvertently biasing the behavior or mental processes of the subjects.

41. **Experimenter bias** occurs when a researcher inadvertently encourages subjects to respond in a way that supports his hypothesis. (p. 23)

Example: An experimenter hypothesizes that an expert will be able to persuade a group of people that decision A is better than decision B. After the expert has spoken to the subjects, the researcher asks them which decision they prefer. He can ask the question in a number of ways. Asking "Now, don't you think A is better than B?" will bias his data much more than if he asks "Which do you think is better, decision A or decision B?" The bias is caused by something the experimenter has done.

LEARNING OBJECTIVES

1. Define psychology and give examples of each component. (p. 2)

2. Know the names of the different subfields of psychology. Be able to give examples of the kinds of questions and issues associated with each subfield. (pp. 4–10)

3. Compare and contrast the basic assumptions that define the five approaches to psychological phenomena: biological, psychodynamic, behavioral, humanistic, and cognitive. (pp. 10–12)

4. Explain why the field of psychology is unified, despite its many areas of specialization and the numerous approaches to psychological phenomena. (p. 12)

5. Name the four scientific goals of psychology. Know the research methods and activities involved in the pursuit of each goal. (pp. 12–18)

6. Define hypothesis and know the research goals associated with it. (p. 13)

7. Define correlation and know the research goals associated with it. (p. 13)

8. Describe the relationship between hypotheses and correlations. (pp. 13–14)

9. Be able to interpret a correlation coefficient. (Highlight, p. 14)

10. Know why correlations do not imply causation. Describe the role of alternative hypotheses in the interpretation of a correlation. (pp. 14–16)

11. Describe the four basic research methods and give examples of each. Know the advantages and disadvantages of using each method. (pp. 18–23)

12. Name and define the two classes of variables used in an experiment. (p. 20)

13. Explain why an experiment allows investigation of causation. (pp. 20–21)

14. Define sampling, random sample, and biased sample. Discuss the importance of sampling in data collection. (p. 21)

15. Define confounding variables. Discuss the problems presented by confounding variables in the interpretation of experimental results. Define the four types of confounding variables and be able to give an example of each. (pp. 21–23)

16. Describe the relationship between a double-blind experimental design and the placebo effect and experimenter bias. (pp. 22–23)

17. Discuss the ethical standards by which psychologists must abide. (Highlight, pp. 23–24)

CONCEPTS AND EXERCISES

No. 1 The Problem of Obesity

Completing this exercise should help you to achieve the following learning objective.

(2) *Know the names of the different subfields of psychology. Be able to give examples of the kinds of questions and issues associated with each subfield. (pp. 4–10)*

QUESTION

Select an area (listed below) to fill in the blanks in the following questions.

1. What is the effect of peer pressure on the eating patterns of obese people? _____

2. Is there a common pattern of weight gain throughout the life span of an obese person? _____

3. Do obese people have an external or internal locus of control? _____

4. How should a mathematical model of decision making concerning dieting be constructed? _____

5. Is obesity correlated with any other disorder, such as depression? _____

6. Do obese people use food as a reward more often than those of normal weight? _____

7. Do fat cells in obese people differ in number or size from those in normal-weight people? _____

AREA

A. Biological   E. Personality

B. Experimental   F. Developmental

C. Clinical   G. Quantitative

D. Social

No. 2 Career Choices in Psychology

Completing this exercise should help you to achieve the following learning objective.

(2) *Know the names of the subfields of psychology. Be able to give examples of the kinds of questions and issues associated with each subfield. (pp. 4–10)*

Six high school seniors are waiting for appointments outside a counselor's office. Each student wants advice from the counselor concerning what to major in at college. Below you will find a description of each person's career objectives. In the space provided write what you think the counselor should suggest.

1. Joe is a dog lover. Eventually he wants to open a school for dogs and train them to perform many different tasks such as defense, narcotics location, and leading blind people. Joe should study _____ psychology.

2. Jill wants to provide a personal service offering nannies for small children, a big-brother and big-sister program for adolescents, and companions for the elderly. Therefore, Jill must be able to teach her employees how to fulfill the psychological needs of every age group. Jill should study _____ psychology.

3. Richard grew up in a close-knit family and is very happy and well adjusted. He knows many people, however, who have problems with school, parents, and making friends, or who are just uncomfortable with adolescence. He wants to open a center in the community where troubled teenagers can find help. Richard should study _____ psychology.

4. Susan has belonged to many clubs and been president of a few of them. She is a leader and can usually choose the right people to perform organizational tasks. She wants to work in a large corporation's personnel department. Susan should study _____ psychology.

5. Laura does not really have a job in mind, but for the past six months she has been listening to her friends discuss their career plans. She has become curious about how people find out what makes them unique, what jobs they would do well, and whether this changes over time. Laura should study _____ psychology.

No. 3 Research Methods

Completing this exercise should help you to achieve the following learning objectives.

(6) *Define hypothesis and know the research goals associated with it. (p. 13)*

(7) *Define correlation and know the research goals associated with it. (p. 13)*

(8) *Describe the relationship between hypotheses and correlations. (pp. 13–14)*

(11) *Describe the four basic research methods and give examples of each. Know the advantages and disadvantages of using each method. (pp. 18–23)*

(12) *Name and define the two classes of variables used in an experiment. (p. 20)*

(14) *Define sampling, random sample, and biased sample. Discuss the importance of sampling in data collection. (p. 21)*

As a study aid for her final exam in a research-methods course, Susan has made note cards listing the procedures followed for each method. As she sat down to study, she knocked the cards to the floor and they scattered. Your job is to put the cards back in order. From the jumbled list below pick out the steps necessary to carry out a survey and an experiment. Separate the steps by method and put them in order. You may use some items more than once in order to use them for both methods.

A. Look for patterns or relationships among variables.

B. Calculate a correlation to test your hypothesis.

C. Choose the independent and dependent variables.

D. Manipulate the independent variable.

E. Administer the questionnaire.

F. Choose a random sample.

G. Form a hypothesis based on descriptive and predictive information.

H. Decide how to measure the dependent variable.

I. Form a hypothesis based on descriptive information.

J. Measure the dependent variable.

K. A researcher, curious about a phenomenon, decides to describe it.

L. A researcher, curious about a phenomenon, decides to study it in a controlled environment.

Survey	Experiment
1. ___	1. ___
2. ___	2. ___
3. ___	3. ___
4. ___	4. ___
5. ___	5. ___
6. ___	6. ___
	7. ___

No. 4 Choose Your Method

Completing this exercise should help you to achieve the following learning objective.

(11) *Describe the four basic research methods and give examples of each. Know the advantages and disadvantages of using each method. (pp. 18–23)*

From the list below, choose the best research method for obtaining the answer to each of the following questions.

1. Does a lack of sleep cause changes in problem-solving ability? _____

2. Throughout history very young children have occasionally been lost in the wild and found several years later. Recently another child has been discovered. Has growing up in the wild affected his cognitive development? _____

3. What is the average five-year-old's attention span at a playground? _____

4. How do people residing near nuclear reactors feel about the nuclear arms race? Are their opinions different from those of people living far from nuclear facilities? _____

Research Methods

A. survey

B. experiment

C. naturalistic observation

D. case study

ANSWERS TO CONCEPTS AND EXERCISES

No. 1 The Problem of Obesity

1. *D* Social psychologists are interested in group behavior and how it influences individual group members. (p. 7)

2. *F* Developmental psychologists are interested in people's physical, behavioral, and mental growth over the life span. (p. 8)

3. *E* Personality psychologists are interested in locus of control—whether people think that external events or internal abilities control their behavior. (pp. 6–7)

4. *G* Quantitative psychologists make mathematical models to describe and predict behavior such as decision making. (pp. 8–10)

5. *C* Clinicians would be interested in finding out if depressed people tend to be obese. Further research would be done to understand the relationship between depression and obesity. (pp. 7–8)

6. *B* Experimental psychologists study the learning process. Some types of learning involve the use of rewards. An experimental psychologist might wonder whether obese people reward themselves with food for learning or performing a behavior. (pp. 5–6)

7. *A* Biological psychologists study the physiological factors that guide or control our behavior. Having fat cells that are larger in size or number may cause altered eating patterns and possibly weight increase. (pp. 4–5)

No. 2 Careers in Psychology

1. Studying *experimental* psychology will help Joe learn about the principles of learning. (pp. 5–6)

2. Studying *developmental* psychology will help Jill learn about the psychological needs of every age group. (p. 8)

3. Studying *community or clinical* psychology will help Richard learn about the development of programs designed to prevent psychological problems in the community. (pp. 7–8)

4. Studying *industrial-organizational* psychology will help Susan learn the psychology of group interaction in a business setting. (p. 7)

5. Studying *personality* psychology will help Laura learn about the characteristics that make people's actions, thoughts, and feelings unique. (pp. 6–7)

No. 3 Research Methods

Survey

1. *K* Researchers use survey results to describe a phenomenon.

2. *F* It is usually impossible to administer surveys to an entire population because it is too big. Therefore, a random sample must be selected.

3. *E* The questionnaire must be administered to the random sample.

4. *A* Survey responses are actually descriptions of the variables related to the phenomenon in question. A researcher looks for patterns or relationships among these variables.

5. *I* Based on descriptive information showing several possible patterns or relationships among variables, hypotheses are formed concerning the consistency of these relationships.

6. *B* A correlation tests the hypothesis by measuring the consistency of the relationship between the variables. (A correlation coefficient or *r* ranges from −1 to +1.)

Experiment

1. *L* Experiments involve studying a phenomenon in a controlled environment.

2. *G* Researchers usually conduct experiments after gathering descriptive (survey, naturalistic observation, and case studies) and predictive (correlational) information. Remember, correla-

tions do not imply causation. They only indicate how consistently two variables occur together: they both increase at the same time, or as one increases the other decreases. Experimental results *can* indicate whether one variable causes the other.

3. *C* A researcher must decide what form of the variables to use in an experiment. For example, the hypothesis states that consuming alcohol causes slower and less efficient thinking. The independent variable is alcohol, but what kind should be used—beer, gin, wine, or liqueur? Should the kind of thinking be mathematical problem solving, or understanding a joke at a party?

4. *H* Using the example above, the dependent variable is mathematical problem solving. We must decide how to measure the ability to solve math problems.

5. *F* As in a survey, it is usually impossible to use the entire population in an experiment. A random sample must be chosen.

6. *D* The researcher must decide which subjects will receive the independent variable and when they will receive it. Some of the subjects, the experimental group, are given the independent variable.

7. *J* The dependent variable is measured in both the experimental and control groups.

No. 4 Choose Your Method

1. *B* Experiments indicate causation. This question asks if sleep loss *causes* changes in problem solving. No other method indicates causation. (pp. 20–23)

2. *D* This is a rare phenomenon, which requires much information from one person (the child). Researchers conduct a case study in these circumstances. (p. 19)

3. *C* Naturalistic observation would provide the data necessary to answer this question. The re-

searcher would observe children's attention spans at the playground, *not* ask them about it. (pp. 19–20)

4. *A* Surveys are used to find out people's opinions. (p. 18)

MULTIPLE CHOICE QUESTIONS

Facts and Definitions

1. The personality subfield can be distinguished from all other subfields of psychology because personality psychologists

   a. study the differences between people; other psychologists look for the similarities between people.
   b. never use surveys as a research method.
   c. conduct field research but not laboratory research.
   d. develop therapies to treat abnormal personalities.

2. Statistical analyses provide a means to

   a. summarize and analyze research data.
   b. measure the dependent variable.
   c. measure the independent variable.
   d. examine correlations for cause-effect relationships.

3. Psychologists who assume that genetics, nervous system activity, and hormones determine behavior follow the _____ approach to studying psychological phenomena.

   a. humanistic
   b. psychodynamic
   c. biological
   d. cognitive

4. The four scientific goals associated with any research program are

   a. measurement, prediction, control, and explanation.

b. explanation, understanding, reasoning, and control.

c. description, reasoning, control, and explanation.

d. description, prediction, control, and explanation.

5. A hypothesis is a

a. method of control used in experiments.

b. method of describing a psychological phenomenon.

c. prediction in the form of an if-then statement.

d. theory in its final form.

6. A positive correlation indicates that there is a relationship between two variables such that

a. one variable increases as the other decreases.

b. one variable increases as the other increases.

c. one variable causes an increase in the other.

d. one variable causes a decrease in the other.

7. Choose the strongest correlation coefficient.

a. +.89

b. −.99

c. +.01

d. −.01

8. A psychologist interested in controlling his research would use which of the following methods?

a. Naturalistic observation

b. Multilevel surveys

c. An experiment

d. A case study

9. Methods for collecting descriptive data include

a. naturalistic observation.

b. multilevel experiments.

c. multifactor experiments.

d. correlations.

10. Questionnaires or special interviews designed to obtain descriptions of people's attitudes, beliefs, opinions, and behavioral intentions are

a. experiments.

b. surveys.

c. case studies.

d. naturalistic observations.

11. Before using survey results to support a hypothesis, one must be sure that

a. the questions were properly worded.

b. the sample used is representative of the population being studied.

c. the responses were not biased by "socially acceptable" standards.

d. All of the above

12. Case studies are used to

a. collect psychological data from many people.

b. determine the effects of an independent variable on a dependent variable.

c. collect descriptive data.

d. provide control in an experiment.

13. Studying individuals in their own environments for the purpose of collecting data is called

a. experimentation.

b. naturalistic observation.

c. personal observation.

d. statistical analysis.

14. In an experiment the _____ variable is manipulated and the _____ variable is measured.

a. dependent, independent

b. confounding, dependent

c. independent, confounding

d. independent, dependent

15. The experimental design that prevents placebos or experimenter bias from confounding a study's results is

a. Hawthorne's design.

b. naturalistic observation.

c. random.

d. double-blind.

MULTIPLE CHOICE QUESTIONS

Application of Concepts

1. Psychology is defined as the science of behavior and mental processes. Therefore, a psychologist may be concerned with which of the following questions?

    a. Do schizophrenics have biochemical processes different from those of normal individuals?

    b. Does urban crowding cause higher crime rates?

    c. Does the decision-making process vary with the number of factors involved in the decision?

    d. All of the above

2. Herman, a freshman at the University of Illinois, wants to become a biological psychologist. His counselor will probably tell him to take which of the following courses?

    a. Cognitive development

    b. Physiology of behavior

    c. The history of Freud

    d. Community medical prevention programs

3. Francis majors in education because he wants to become an excellent teacher. Which of the following courses will best help Francis reach his goal?

    a. Experimental psychology

    b. Neurobiology

    c. Clinical psychology

    d. Social psychology

4. You are a clinical psychologist studying the effects of diet on depression. You want your results to be reliable and valid. Hence, you are concerned about measuring depression as accurately as possible. You would probably ask a _____ psychologist for advice.

    a. biological

    b. experimental

    c. quantitative

    d. community

5. Sari's psychology class is team taught. Sari is confused because Dr. Miller told her that behavior is determined by the rewards and punishments a person experiences. Dr. Musselman has told her that behavior is caused by activity in the nervous system, genetic inheritance, and hormones. Dr. Miller takes a _____ approach and Dr. Musselman takes a _____ approach to psychological phenomena.

    a. cognitive, biological

    b. psychodynamic, humanistic

    c. behavioral, biological

    d. cognitive, humanistic

6. Bill's therapist has told him that his thought patterns cause his depression. Bill's therapist follows the _____ approach to psychological phenomena.

    a. biological

    b. psychodynamic

    c. cognitive

    d. behavioral

7. Recently, several states implemented laws requiring drivers and passengers to wear seat belts. Since the laws' implementation the number of accident-related deaths has decreased. Therefore a negative correlation exists, which indicates that

    a. wearing seat belts causes fewer car accidents.

    b. wearing seat belts prevents accident fatalities.

    c. when the number of people wearing seat belts increases, the number of accident-related deaths decreases.

    d. enforcing the law has caused fewer accidents to occur.

8. As you withdraw money from your checking account, your account balance decreases. Which of the following best describes the relationship between your checking account balance and the amount of cash you have withdrawn?

a. A strong negative correlation
b. A perfect negative correlation
c. A strong positive correlation
d. A perfect positive correlation

9. You are studying the effects of alcohol consumption on decision-making time. Your hypothesis states that if alcohol consumption increases, then decision-making time will also increase. You would need to find a _____ correlation to provide evidence supporting your hypothesis.

    a. negative
    b. curvilinear Spearman's
    c. positive
    d. statistically significant negative

10. Matt and George both present data supporting the same hypothesis. Matt reports correlations and George reports experimental data. Matt's work is at the _____ level, whereas George's work is at the _____ level.

    a. predictive, descriptive
    b. descriptive, explanatory
    c. predictive, controlled
    d. controlled, explanatory

11. Dr. McMarty has collected data via surveys, case studies, and naturalistic observation. Her next step will probably be to

    a. design an experiment.
    b. examine the data for patterns or relationships among the variables.
    c. check for statistical significance.
    d. form an explanation that will lead to a theory.

12. Susan wants to study the effects of peer pressure on study habits in college freshmen at her university. She needs to obtain a random sample. How should she choose the subjects for her experiment?

    a. Select one dormitory and ask all its freshmen to participate in the experiment.
    b. Randomly select names from the introductory psychology course roster.

c. Randomly select names from the dormitory phone book.
d. Randomly select names from a list of all freshmen at the university.

13. The Food and Drug Administration (FDA) has tested fluoxetine, a new drug thought to decrease depression without causing weight gain. The experiment consisted of a random sample of depressed patients split into two groups. The experimental group received the drug; the control group received no treatment. The results were very clear: those patients receiving fluoxetine experienced a decrease in depression without weight gain; those in the control group reported no change in depression or weight. Based on these results, should the FDA allow marketing of fluoxetine?

    a. No, results may have been due to the placebo effect.
    b. No, the study should be repeated using a case study.
    c. Yes, the experimental design is appropriate and the results are clear-cut.
    d. No, results may have been due to the Hawthorne effect.

14. Which of the following is a possible random variable?

    a. Level of intelligence
    b. State of health
    c. Prior experience with the independent variable
    d. All of the above

15. Sabrina has decided to employ the naturalistic observation method to study the negotiation behavior of gang members. What type of confounding variables might she encounter?

    a. The placebo effect
    b. Experimenter prophecy
    c. The Hawthorne effect
    d. Naturalistic bias

ANSWERS TO MULTIPLE CHOICE QUESTIONS

Facts and Definitions

1. *a* is the answer. Most psychologists look for general rules or theories governing behavior and mental processes. However, personality psychologists look for the characteristics that make an individual unique. (pp. 6–7)

b. Surveys are one of several research methods personality psychologists use.

c. Personality psychologists conduct research in the field and the laboratory.

d. Although psychologists from all areas of psychology can contribute information regarding the causes and treatment of abnormal behavior, clinicians usually focus their research in this area.

2. *a* is the answer. Two types of statistics are used: one describes or summarizes the data and the other analyzes it. (p. 9)

b. Measuring the dependent variable occurs before using statistics to summarize or analyze the data.

c. Manipulating the independent variable occurs before using statistics to summarize or analyze the data.

d. Correlations do not yield cause-effect relationships.

3. *c* is the answer. The biological approach assumes that biological or physiological factors such as genetic inheritance, nervous system activity, or hormones determine behavior. (p. 10)

a. The humanistic approach assumes that behavior is determined by each person's perception of reality and by an innate tendency to grow toward the individual's unique potential.

b. The psychodynamic approach assumes that behavior is determined by the combination of unconscious internal conflicts and external (parents', peers', or society's) reactions to those conflicts.

d. The cognitive approach assumes that any behavior is determined by the thought processes involved in producing that behavior.

4. *d* is the answer. Description, prediction, control and explanation are the scientific goals researchers attempt to achieve. (pp. 12–18)

a. Measurement is a process involved in pursuing scientific goals, but it is not a goal *per se*.

b. & c. Reasoning is a process involved in pursuing scientific goals, but it is not a goal *per se*.

5. *c* is correct. A hypothesis is a predictive statement based on patterns or relationships found in descriptive data. (p. 13)

a. Control is obtained through the use of the experimental method.

b. Hypotheses, although based on descriptive information about psychological variables, are predictions, not descriptions about the relationship between variables.

d. Tested hypotheses can contribute information to the formation of a theory. However, theories are broader, more general rules of behavior than hypotheses, and theories are never considered final. Theories are repeatedly tested in new ways and added to or amended as researchers collect new data.

6. *b* is the answer. (pp. 30–38)

a. A negative correlation tells us that as one variable increases, the other decreases.

c. & d. Correlations do not imply causation. One can never conclude that one variable *causes* the other to change in any direction based on a correlation—regardless of its positive or negative direction.

7. *b* is the answer. The strongest correlation coefficient possible is ±1.00. No other coefficient listed is closer to a perfect correlation than −.99. (pp. 14–15)

a. The strength and direction of a correlation are independent of each other. The positive or negative sign indicates the direction. The number indicates the strength—the closer to ±1, the stronger the correlation. For example, −.99 is closer to −1.00 than +.89 is to +1.00 and, therefore, is the stronger correlation.

c. & d. You may have thought that a positive or negative .01 correlation coefficient represented a perfect correlation. A perfect correlation is ±1.00 (not ±.01).

8. *c* is the answer. Experiments are used to conduct controlled research. Experimental and control groups are formed and both groups are treated identically except for the presence of the independent variable in the experimental group. If there is a difference between the two groups on the dependent variable, the difference can only have been caused by the independent variable. (p. 16)

a. Naturalistic observation is a descriptive method.

b. There is no such thing as a multilevel survey.

d. A case study is a descriptive method.

9. *a* is the answer. Methods for collecting descriptive data include naturalistic observation, surveys, and case studies. (pp. 18–20)

b. & c. Experiments are used to conduct controlled research.

d. Correlations are mathematical representations of the relationship between two variables. Correlations are usually based on descriptive data but are not a descriptive method of data collection.

10. *b* is the answer. Surveys are used to collect descriptive data on people's attitudes, beliefs, opinions, and behavioral intentions. (p. 18)

a. Experiments are controlled methods of establishing a cause-effect relationship.

c. Case studies are used to collect descriptive information from a particular individual, group, or situation.

d. Naturalistic observation is used to collect behavioral information in the subjects' natural environment.

11. *d* is the answer. A subject may misinterpret an improperly worded question. This will bias the data. If the question is embarrassing the subject may simply lie, which will also bias the data. Representative samples are important when using any research method. A sample unrepresentative of the population of interest will prevent data from being useful in the formation of a theory regarding that population's behavior. (p. 18)

12. *c* is the answer. Case studies are one method of collecting descriptive data. (p. 19)

a. Case studies gather data from one individual.

b. Independent and dependent variables are used in experiments.

d. Case studies do not provide control; experiments do.

13. *b* is the answer. Studying individuals (observation) in their own environments (naturalistic) is called naturalistic observation. (pp. 19–20)

a. Experiments are often conducted in a laboratory, which is not a subject's natural environment.

c. Personal observation is not a research method.

d. Studying individuals is a data collection method. Statistical analysis is a method of summarizing or analyzing collected data.

14. *d* is the answer. (p. 20)

a. The independent variable is manipulated; the dependent variable is measured.

b. & c. A confounding variable is any aspect of the experiment that affects the dependent variable instead of or along with the independent variable. Researchers try to prevent the presence of confounding variables.

15. *d* is the answer. In a double-blind experimental design, neither the subjects nor the experimenter know who has received the independent variable. The subjects are less likely to react to the independent variable if they don't know whether they have received it. Also, the experimenter cannot bias

the data in favor of his hypothesis, because he will not know which subjects received the independent variable. (p. 23)

a. There is no such thing as the Hawthorne design. You may have been thinking of the Hawthorne effect, a confounding variable.

b. Naturalistic observation is a research method but not an experimental design.

c. Random refers to how the subjects were selected for a study. It is not an experimental method.

ANSWERS TO MULTIPLE CHOICE QUESTIONS

Application of Concepts

1. *d* is the answer. Psychologists are concerned with any behavior or mental process. Aberrant biochemical processes are a possible cause of schizophrenic behavior. Crime is a behavior. Decision making is a mental process. (p. 2)

2. *b* is the answer. Herman will learn which physiological processes affect behavior. (p. 4)

a. Cognitive development is the study of the development of thinking.

c. Clinical, personality, and developmental psychologists may incorporate Freud's ideas in the generation and testing of hypotheses, but biological psychologists probably would not.

d. Clinicians specializing in community psychology develop and operate prevention programs.

3. *a* is the answer. Experimental psychologists study the processes of learning and memory. (pp. 5–6)

b. Neurobiological research may include studies on the neurological changes accompanying learning. However, Francis would have difficulty directly applying most of this knowledge to teaching his students.

c. Although clinical psychologists may have patients whose learning problems result from disorders, they do not focus their research in this area.

d. Social psychologists study interactions between people. This information will help Francis understand students' social behaviors. However, his first priority as a teacher will be to present material in such a way that students can easily learn and remember it.

4. *c* is the answer. Quantitative psychologists develop mathematical models of psychological phenomena, methods of measurement, and statistical techniques. This case requires a method of measuring depression. (pp. 8–9)

a., b., & d. Biological psychologists may be interested in depression (possibly as a function of the physiological changes induced by different diets). However, they too would need a reliable, valid measure of depression and might consult a quantitative psychologist. This is also true of experimental and community psychologists.

5. *c* is the answer. Behavioral psychologists assume that behavior is caused by the rewards and punishments individuals experience in response to their behaviors. Biological psychologists assume that nervous-system activity, hormones, and genetic inheritance cause behavior. (pp. 10–11)

a., b., & d. The cognitive approach assumes that behavior is caused by the thoughts involved with that behavior. The psychodynamic approach assumes that behavior results from our struggle to fulfill instinctive desires despite society's restrictions. The humanistic approach assumes that behavior is caused by people's perception of reality and their innate tendency to work toward their fullest potential.

6. *c* is the answer. The cognitive approach assumes that behavior results from the thoughts involved in that behavior. (pp. 5–6)

a. The biological approach assumes that genetic inheritance, nervous-system activity, and hormones cause behaviors.

b. The psychodynamic approach assumes that behavior is a result of our struggle to fulfill instinctive desires despite society's restrictions.

d. The behavioral approach assumes that behavior is caused by the rewards and punishments individuals experience in response to their behaviors.

7. *c* is the answer. A negative correlation tells us that as one variable (seat-belt use) increases the other variable (accident-related deaths) decreases. This correlation does not imply that changes in seat-belt use cause a change in the number of accident-related deaths; because correlations do not imply causation. (pp. 14–16)

a. Correlations do not imply causation. Also, the variables here are the number of seat belts worn and the number of accident-related deaths, not the number of accidents.

b. Correlations do not imply causation. The word *prevents* implies causation.

d. Correlations do not imply causation. Also, the variable is the number of accident-related deaths, not the number of accidents.

8. *b* is the answer. The money withdrawn represents an increasing variable. The amount of money left in your account represents a decreasing variable. Therefore, this is a negative correlation. In a perfect correlation, knowing the value of one variable allows you to predict the exact value of the second variable. Here, knowing the amount of money you have withdrawn allows you to predict the exact amount of money you have left in your account. (pp. 14–16)

a. The correlation described is not merely strong; it is perfect.

c. & d. A positive relationship between variables indicates that as one variable increases the other increases. Unfortunately, your account balance will not increase every time you withdraw money.

9. *c* is the answer. A positive correlation indicates that as one variable increases the other variable increases. This type of relationship supports the data;

as alcohol consumption increases so does decision-making time. (pp. 14–16)

a. & d. A negative correlation indicates that as one variable increases the other decreases. This relationship does not fit our data.

b. There is no such thing as a curvilinear Spearman's correlation. Curvilinear correlations do not exist.

10. *c* is the answer. Correlations are tests of hypotheses at the predictive level. An experiment is a controlled research method. (pp. 13–16)

a. Experimental data are not just descriptive; they are controlled and therefore demonstrate cause-effect relationships.

b. Correlations are predictive, although they test hypotheses generated from descriptive information. Explanations are derived from information collected at all levels of research: descriptive, predictive, and controlled.

d. Correlations are not controlled and do not yield cause-effect relationships. Explanations are derived from information collected at all levels of research: descriptive, predictive, and controlled.

11. *b* is the answer. Dr. McMarty should examine the data for patterns or relationships between variables. (pp. 13–14)

a. In order to design an experiment one must have a hypothesis to test. Hypotheses are usually based on descriptive data; hence, Dr. McMarty must examine the data before forming a hypothesis.

c. Statistics are used to test the significance of correlational and experimental data. Dr. McMarty must examine the data to find patterns or relationships between variables to form a hypothesis. Then she can check for statistical significance.

d. Explanations are based not only on descriptive data but also on experimental data. Dr. McMarty has only descriptive data. She should form a hypothesis based on relationships between variables in the data set, complete an experiment, and *then* she may have information that will contribute to a theory.

12. *d* is the answer. Following this procedure will ensure that every student in the population Susan wishes to study (freshmen) will have an equal chance of being selected for participation in the experiment. (p. 21)

a. The use of one dorm will not allow every freshman to have an equal chance of being selected. Also, a particular dorm might house a certain kind of student. For example, a dorm located next to the College of Agriculture may house a majority of agriculture majors who live there because of the convenient location. Susan is interested in *all* freshmen, not just agriculture students.

b. Some freshmen may not take introductory psychology. Therefore, every freshman does not have an equal chance of being selected for the study.

c. Some freshmen may not have a phone.

13. *a* is the answer. The subjects in the experimental group may report less depression because they think fluoxetine has medicinal value. (p. 22)

b. A case study usually involves one subject. Using only one subject to test a drug that will be used by many is dangerous; perhaps the subject's physiological system is different from most people's. Therefore, the results of a case study may not apply to the general population.

c. The experimental design is incorrect. Both the experimental and control groups should have been given pills. The experiment should be repeated using a double-blind design.

d. The results of the experiment could have occurred because the subjects realized they were being observed or treated differently. However, when the independent variable is a medical or psychological treatment, the confound is called a placebo effect.

14. *d* is the answer. Levels of intelligence, states of health, and prior experience with the independent variable could all have an effect on the dependent variable, making it difficult to know whether the results of the experiment were due to the independent variable or to random variables. (p. 22)

15. *c* is the answer. Gang members may change their negotiating behavior if they know that they are being observed. (pp. 22–23)

a. A placebo effect may occur in an experiment using some kind of medical treatment (for example, a pill) or psychological treatment (for example, therapy).

b. There is no such thing as experimenter prophecy.

d. There is no such thing as naturalistic bias. You may be confusing the terms *naturalistic observation* and *experimenter bias.*

Chapter 2

Human Development

OUTLINE

I. THE STUDY OF DEVELOPMENT (pp. 30–35)

Developmental psychology is the psychological specialty that documents the course of people's social, emotional, moral, and intellectual development throughout the life span.

A. Philosophical Roots

Two questions have motivated the study of development: 1) Is a person's development determined by the environment or by heredity? 2) Does development occur in distinct stages that differ qualitatively from each other?

B. Scientific Observation

Development has been studied via several scientific methods: surveys, IQ tests, naturalistic observation, and laboratory experiments.

C. Theories of Development

1. Several theories incorporate some combination of the influence of nature (genes) and nurture (environment), as well as the idea that development occurs in distinct stages.

2. Freud's psychodynamic theory states that development, occurring in stages, is an interaction of nature (sexual urges) and nurture (parental reactions to the child's sexual impulses).

3. Gesell's maturational theory states that development, occurring in stages, is influenced by nature (natural growth) only.

4. Watson's behavioral theory states that development is influenced by nurture (external conditions) only.

5. Piaget's cognitive theory states that development, occurring in stages, is the ongoing interaction of nature (mental images) and nurture (experience with surroundings).

D. Nature and Nurture Today

Today, psychologists recognize that both nature and nurture interact to influence the developmental process. The environment (nurture) can determine if a genetic tendency (nature) is expressed, and genetic tendencies (nature) can evoke particular responses from the environment (nurture).

II. BEGINNINGS (pp. 36–41)

A. Genetic Building Blocks

The forty-six chromosomes, twenty-three from the sperm and twenty-three from the ovum, constitute an individual's genetic make-up or genotype. The resulting phenotype—how a person looks or acts—will depend on how dominant and recessive genes interact with the environment.

B. Prenatal Development

1. *Germinal Stage*. During the germinal stage, the first two weeks after fertilization, the zygote divides rapidly.

2. *Embryonic Stage*. The embryonic stage, lasting until the eighth week of pregnancy, is a critical period, during which the basic plan for the body emerges and the organs develop.

3. *Fetal Stage*. This stage lasts until birth. During the fetal stage, systems become integrated and organs grow and function more efficiently. The fetus is sensitive to certain sounds, lights, touch, and may be able to learn. The effect of adverse environmental conditions depends on the fetus's genetic constitution, the stage at which the fetus is exposed to harm, and the intensity of the harmful factor.

III. INFANCY (pp. 41–51)

A. Birth

The birth process is a better physical and emotional experience for the mother and a better physical experience for the infant if drugs and anesthesia are minimal and if both parents are actively involved in the process.

B. Capacities of the Newborn

1. *Vision*. Newborns have 20:600 sight. They prefer to look at objects that have contour, contrast, complexity, and movement.

2. *Hearing*. Within two to three days infants can hear soft voices and differentiate tones. At four weeks they can differentiate similar verbal sounds and locate them in space.

3. *Smell and Taste*. Newborns have a good sense of smell and taste. They can distinguish among sugar water, salt water, milk, and water.

4. *Reflexes*. These are swift, automatic, and finely coordinated movements that occur in response to external stimuli. Infants have more than twenty reflexes, including the rooting and sucking reflexes.

C. Sensorimotor Development (or Period)

During the first stage of cognitive development proposed by Piaget, the sensorimotor period, the infant's mental activity is confined to sensory and motor functions. Behaviors, such as looking at an object and then grasping it, are called object-action schemes.

1. *The Elaboration of Schemes*.
 a. Organization involves combining and integrating simple schemes.

 b. Adaptation consists of assimilation, which means adding information to existing schemes; and accommodation, which means modifying existing schemes according to environmental information.

2. *The Concept of Object Permanence*. Infants learn that an object exists even when they cannot see or touch it. Piaget called this knowledge object permanence.

D. Early Social Interactions

1. *Parent-Infant Interaction*. Parents and infants become coordinated social partners, each responding to the other's laughs, smiles, cries, and verbal communication.

2. *The Infant Grows Attached*. By six- or seven-months of age, the infant can discriminate among people and will seek out its mother. Infants also form attachments to their fathers.

E. Individual Temperament

Individual temperaments are obvious in infants at birth. If the child's temperament matches the parents' expectations, their interaction most likely will be positive.

F. Learning to Talk: First Words

Infants can hear speech sounds and prefer those that are exaggerated, expressive, and friendly. They also prefer rising tones. Babblings—the first sounds babies make—will then be shortened to specific, sometimes meaningful, syllables. Infants understand some words, but also rely on accompanying gestures to interpret their verbal world. At twelve to eighteen months, the one-word stage begins when children communicate by using single words, sometimes overextending their use.

IV. COGNITIVE DEVELOPMENT IN CHILDHOOD (pp. 51–58)

A. Logical Thought

1. *The Preoperational Period.* Lasting from ages two to seven, the preoperational period is characterized by intuitive and egocentric thought. Symbol usage appears during this period.

2. *Concrete Operations.* The concrete operations stage, from age seven to adolescence, is marked by the ability to conserve number and amount.

3. *Criticisms of Piaget's Theory.* Studies show that children are capable of many tasks, such as conservation and nonegocentric thinking, at earlier ages than Piaget predicts, providing that tasks are presented in simpler terms or that the children are trained.

B. Learning Theory and Information Processing

Learning theory suggests that children will think in ways that have been rewarded. From an information-processing approach, children are viewed as more able to absorb, remember, and store more information in more organized ways as they grow older. Memory improves as children learn memory strategies, improve metamemories, and increase their knowledge.

C. Variations in the Pace of Cognitive Development

Activities that affect cognitive development include reading, conversation, watching television, and the social interactions available to a child.

V. SOCIAL AND EMOTIONAL DEVELOPMENT IN CHILDHOOD (pp. 58–63)

A. Relationships with Parents and Siblings

From ages two to four, children become more autonomous, but the emotional bond to their parents is still great. By age five, siblings play with each other, imitate one another, and have strong positive feelings for one another.

B. Relationships with Peers

1. *Changing Play Patterns.* Two-year-olds engage in parallel play, using the same toys as playmates but not interacting socially. By age four, associative play is seen; children begin to socially interact through play. As they get older, children learn to cooperate and compete.

2. *Conformity and Friendship.* School children are influenced by peers and try to imitate their dress, interests, and lifestyle. Their company is preferred and friendships based on feelings and loyalty are long-lasting.

C. Social Skills and Understanding

1. *Interpreting Situations and Signals.* Social competence increases with the ability to detect and interpret emotional signals, understand the basis and complexity of emotion, and recognize consistencies in others' personalities.

2. *Social Rules and Roles.* Children learn the social norms governing behavior and role-appropriate behavior.

D. Socialization

1. *Socialization Styles* (used by parents).
   a. Authoritarian parents are firm, punitive, and unsympathetic.

   b. Permissive parents give children complete freedom and use lax discipline.

   c. Authoritative parents are firm but understanding, increase children's responsibility as they grow older, and reason with their children.

2. *Socialization Outcomes.*
   a. Authoritarian parents tend to have children who are unfriendly, distrustful, and withdrawn.

   b. Permissive parents tend to have children who are immature, dependent, unhappy, and have little self-control.

   c. Authoritative parents tend to have children who are friendly, cooperative, self-reliant, and socially responsible.

VI. ADOLESCENCE (pp. 63–70)

Owing to the interplay of nature and nurture, adolescents experience changes in physical size, shape, and capacities.

A. The Big Shakeup

Sudden growth spurts are seen, sexual characteristics develop, moods swing wildly, sexual interest stirs, and opportunities to experience drugs and alcohol arise. Self-esteem, highly dependent on self-perceptions of attractiveness and rate of physical maturation, is challenged.

B. Social Relationships with Parents and Peers

Conflicts between parents and teens develop as a result of the adolescent's attempt to become independent and cope with the challenges of adolescence. Friends become more important than family.

C. Identity

According to Erikson, teens must develop a unique and integrated image of themselves. If they have experienced trust, admiration, and autonomy during infancy and childhood, they will resolve their identity crisis positively.

D. Abstract Thought

Piaget's formal operational period first occurs during adolescence. Hypothetical thinking, hypothesis generation, and consideration of abstract concepts are now possible.

VII. ADULTHOOD (pp. 70–76)

Development is a lifelong process. Adults also experience transitions of physical and cognitive change.

A. Physical Changes

Growth continues until the forties or fifties, when fat increases and sensory acuity begins to decrease. Susceptibility to disease increases.

B. Cognitive Changes

Cognitive abilities continue to improve until late adulthood. At that time, speed of information absorption slows and memory declines. However, if mental faculties are used throughout the life span, these skills are less apt to diminish.

C. Social and Psychological Changes

1. *Early Adulthood* (ages twenty to forty). Many people marry, keeping in step with their culture's social clock, and become concerned with the crisis of generativity: producing something

that will outlast them, usually through children or job achievements.

2. *Middle Adulthood* (ages forty to fifty-five). Around age forty, people may experience a mid-life transition and reappraise or modify their life in some way.

3. *Late Adulthood* (ages fifty-five to seventy-five). Although basic personalities are stable, people become more reflective, cautious, conforming, and androgynous. Eventually they must confront death both psychologically and physically.

KEY TERMS

1. **Developmental psychology** is the area of specialization that documents the course of people's social, emotional, moral, and intellectual development throughout the life span. (p. 28)

Example: How do children learn to use language? Do infants respond to parents' emotional cues? Do cognitive changes occur during old age?

2. **Maturation** refers to any developmental process (such as walking) that is guided by biological or genetic factors (nature). These processes occur in a fixed sequence and are usually unaffected by environmental conditions (nurture). (p. 32)

Example: The development of secondary sexual characteristics occurs in a fixed sequence and is rarely affected by environmental conditions.

3. The **psychodynamic theory of development** was proposed by Freud. Development, occurring in stages, is characterized by sexual urges focused on different zones of the body. Development is a product of the interaction between internal sexual impulses (nature) and parental reactions (nurture) to those impulses. (p. 34)

4. The **maturational theory of development** holds that development is a biological unfolding of physical, behavioral, and cognitive abilities. (p. 32)

REMEMBER: This is a *nature* point of view, which claims that we develop according to the biological instructions of our genetic make-up or genotype.

5. The **behavioral theory of development** is supported by behaviorists, who believe that behaviors and abilities develop because they are learned, either by being rewarded or by being paired with a stimulus. (p. 33)

Example: If parents reward a child with praise for learning to read some of the words in a storybook, then the child may strive to learn to read more words in order to receive another reward.

6. **Piaget's theory of development** supports the idea that development of thought and knowledge occurs because of the interaction of nature and experience (nurture). Development occurs in distinct stages in a fixed order, characterized by increasingly sophisticated modes of thought. The four stages are *sensorimotor, preoperational, concrete operations* and *formal operations*. These are discussed throughout the chapter and each is listed as a key term. (p. 34)

7. **Chromosomes** are structures made of genes. Each sperm and ovum carries twenty-three single chromosomes. Fertilization results in twenty-three pairs of chromosomes. (p. 37)

8. **Deoxyribonucleic acid (DNA)** is composed of molecules that make up a gene. The arrangement of these molecules determines which protein a gene will produce. Thus, DNA provides the individual's genetic code, a blueprint for constructing the entire human being. (p. 37)

9. A **genotype** is the full set of genes that individuals inherit from their parents. (p. 37)

REMEMBER: A genotype will tell you what *type* of *genes* someone has.

10. A **phenotype** is the result of a person's genotype (nature) and environment (nurture) interacting to determine how he or she looks and acts. (p. 37)

REMEMBER: You cannot see a person's genotype but you can see a person's phenotype. A photograph gives the same kind of information as a phenotype. Photograph and phenotype both begin with *ph*.

11. **Dominant genes** are expressed in an individual's phenotype whenever they are present in the genotype. (p. 37)

REMEMBER: To be dominant means to have power. Dominant genes have power over recessive genes.

12. **Recessive genes** are expressed in an individual's phenotype only when they are paired with a similar recessive gene. (pp. 37–38)

Example: To have blue eyes, two recessive genes for the color blue must be present. If a dominant gene—say for brown eyes—is present, the person will have brown eyes. People with blue eyes do not have any brown-eye genes to pass on to their offspring. Therefore, their children cannot have brown eyes.

13. **Polygenic traits** are characteristics controlled by more than one gene. (p. 38)

Example: Several different genes interact to determine height.

14. A **zygote** is the new cell produced during conception, the merging of a sperm and an ovum. (p. 38)

15. The **germinal stage** occurs during the first two weeks after fertilization. The cells making up the zygote divide rapidly, creating the embryo, placenta, amniotic fluid, and the yolk sac. (p. 38)

16. An **embryo** is the developing individual after the germinal stage. (p. 38)

REMEMBER: Embryo comes from the Greek word *embryon,* which means *thing newly born.*

17. The **embryonic stage** lasts from the end of the second week to the eighth week after conception, during which time the organs and nervous system develop. (pp. 38–39)

18. **Critical period** refers to any time period during which some developmental process must occur or it never will. (p. 39)

Example: If the heart, eyes, ears, hands, and feet do not appear during the embryonic period, they will not be formed later.

19. The **fetal stage** extends from the eighth week after conception to birth. Systems become integrated and organs grow and function more efficiently. (pp. 39–41)

20. **Fetal alcohol syndrome** occurs in infants born to alcoholic mothers. The resulting defects include physical malformations of the face and mental retardation. (p. 40)

21. The **rooting reflex** causes an infant to turn its mouth toward any object that touches its cheek. It is a swift, automatic, and finely coordinated movement that the infant makes for the first three or four months of life. (p. 43)

22. The **sucking reflex,** a swift, automatic, and finely coordinated movement exhibited for the first three to four months of life, causes the newborn to suck on any object that touches its lips. (p. 43)

23. The **sensorimotor period** is Piaget's first stage of cognitive development. The infant's mental activity is confined to sensory and motor functions such as looking and reaching. (p. 43)

REMEMBER: Sensor equals sensory: vision, hearing, tasting, and so on. Motor equals movement: reaching, grasping, pulling, and so on.

24. **Schemes** are basic units of knowledge, which may be a pattern of action, an image of an object, or a complex idea. (p. 43)

Example: Sucking on a pacifier is a scheme composed of a pattern of action.

25. **Assimilation** is the process of taking in information that adds to an existing scheme. (p. 44)

Example: An infant who has learned to suck milk from a bottle will use the same sucking motion or scheme when a pacifier is put in its mouth for the first time.

26. **Accommodation** is the process of taking in information that causes the infant to modify an existing scheme. (p. 44)

Example: Infants who have become very good at sucking milk from a bottle are given a cup. They must learn new patterns of motor behavior (modify the old sucking scheme) to get the liquid out of the cup and into their mouth. Watch small children just learning how to drink out of a cup. They suck and slurp up the liquid instead of pouring it into their mouth and swallowing.

27. **Object permanence** is acquired during the sensorimotor period. Children form mental representations of objects and actions. Hence, they do not have to rely on sensory information to know that an object exists even when they cannot see or touch it. (p. 44)

Example: A child knows that a rattle exists when you put it behind your back, out of sight.

28. **Attachment** is the close emotional relationship between an infant and his or her caretaker. For a secure attachment to develop, the caretaker must provide not only adequate, consistent care, but also be loving, supportive, helpful, sensitive, and responsive. When the caretaker fails to do this the child may develop an insecure ambivalent attachment or an insecure avoidant attachment. (pp. 46–49)

Example: Johnny has an insecure avoidant attachment; he ignores or avoids his mother when she returns after a separation. Andy has an insecure ambivalent attachment; he is very upset when his mother leaves but reacts in an angry fashion and rejects her when she returns after a brief separation. Carl's attachment to his mother is secure; he may or may not protest when she leaves, but will greet her enthusiastically when she returns.

29. **Temperament** is the style of emotional reactivity an infant displays in response to the environment; it is the basic, natural disposition of an individual. (pp. 49–50)

Example: When Sarah takes a bath, she squeals with delight, splashes in the water, and eagerly reaches for new toys. She has a very predictable schedule of eating and sleeping. Sarah is an easy baby. Franny, on the other hand, fusses all the time, does not have a set schedule, and cries very loudly whenever she meets a new situation, person, or toy. Franny is a difficult baby.

30. **Babblings,** the first sounds a child makes that resemble speech, are repetitions of syllables. (p. 50)

31. The **one-word stage** lasts from approximately twelve to eighteen months. Children speak in one-word "sentences" and use their words for more than one object. (p. 51)

Example: Brenda has just learned the word *cookie.* She calls bread, rolls, mashed potatoes, and apples *cookie,* and will do so until she learns the words for these objects.

32. The **preoperational period** is Piaget's second stage of cognitive development, lasting from age two to seven. Children learn to use symbols allowing them to talk, pretend, and draw. Thinking during this time is intuitive, egocentric; children are incapable of viewing anything from a perspective other than their own. (pp. 52–53)

Example: If an angry adult is present, a child in this period will often assume that he or she has done something wrong. He or she cannot understand that the source of an adult's anger may be something other than the child.

33. **Conservation** (conserve), a skill first accomplished during the concrete operations period, is the knowledge that a substance's number or amount does not change when its shape or form does. (pp. 53–54)

Example: Ellen is babysitting for a nine-year-old and a four-year-old. She gives each child a glass of lemonade. She gives the older child a tall skinny glass and the younger child a short fat glass. The four-year-old insists that the short fat glass does not contain as much lemonade as the tall skinny glass, even after Ellen has poured the contents of the tall skinny glass into the short glass and back again. The younger child, still in the preoperational period, cannot conserve.

34. **Concrete operations** is Piaget's third stage of cognitive development, occurring between age seven and eleven (approximately). Children can now perform such operations as addition, subtraction, and conservation; visual appearances no longer dominate thinking. (p. 54)

35. **Information processing** is a cognitive approach to studying the development of cognitive activities, such as how information is taken in, how it is remembered or forgotten, and how it is used. This approach differs from Piaget's because the focus is on the quantitative changes that take place in the child's mental abilities, not on the qualitative changes that occur at different stages. (pp. 55–56)

36. **Parallel play** is characteristic of two-year-olds. Children playing with the same toy focus their attention on the toy, not on interacting with each other. (p. 59)

REMEMBER: Parallel lines run alongside each other but never touch. Two-year-olds play alongside each other but do not interact.

37. **Associative play** is characteristic of four-year-olds. Children discuss their activities with each other as they play. (p. 59)

REMEMBER: One of the definitions of *associate* is *a companion*. Children's playmates are now companions.

38. **Gender roles** are the general patterns of work, appearance, and behavior associated with being male or female. (p. 61)

Example: In our society some occupations have been considered more appropriate for men and others have been considered more appropriate for women. Men have been encouraged to become doctors and women to become nurses; men have been encouraged to become police officers and women have not. These gender roles are beginning to break down, but they still exist.

39. **Authoritarian parents** are firm, punitive, and unsympathetic. They demand obedience from their children and value being authority figures. They do not encourage independence and infrequently offer praise. (pp. 62–63)

40. **Permissive parents** give their children complete freedom and their use of discipline is lax. (p. 63)

41. **Authoritative parents** reason with their children, are firm but understanding, and encourage give-and-take. As children get older, parents allow them increasing responsibility. These parents set limits, but also encourage independence. (p. 63)

42. The **formal operational period** is Piaget's fourth stage of cognitive development, which begins, on the average, at age eleven. Children can think and reason about abstract concepts, generate hypotheses, and think logically. (p. 67)

Example: Children can think about abstract moral issues such as whether animals should be killed for fur or what the consequences of nuclear war might be.

43. An **identity crisis** usually occurs during adolescence. By combining bits and pieces of self-knowledge learned in childhood, the individual must develop an integrated image of himself or herself as a unique person. (p. 66)

44. **External morality,** exhibited at five to ten years of age, involves considering rules as sacred and unalterable. (p. 68)

45. **Internal morality,** exhibited after age ten, involves the realization that rules are alterable, reasoned out, and are agreed upon by equal participants. (p. 68)

46. A **social clock** is a timeline of major or significant events in a person's life. The events and when they are supposed to occur depend on the culture and class of the individual. (p. 72)

> *Example:* In this culture, people generally marry between the ages of eighteen and twenty-six. In other cultures people may marry as young as thirteen or fourteen. The social clocks of these cultures are different.

47. A **crisis of generativity** usually occurs during a person's thirties. People become concerned with producing something that they consider worthwhile. To resolve this crisis people usually have children or decide to achieve an occupational goal. (pp. 72–73)

48. A **midlife transition** usually occurs during a person's forties, at which time people usually reevaluate the decisions they have made concerning their goals and social relationships. (p. 73)

LEARNING OBJECTIVES

1. State the definition of developmental psychology. (p. 28)

2. Discuss the differences between the maturational, behavioral, and psychodynamic views of development. (p. 34)

3. Describe the influence of nature and nurture on development. (pp. 34–35)

4. Define dominant gene, recessive gene, genotype, and phenotype. (p. 37–38)

5. Describe the process of development in each of the prenatal stages. Define critical period and know the stage associated with it. (pp. 38–41)

6. Describe the capacities of a newborn. (pp. 42–43)

7. Describe the development of mental abilities in the sensorimotor period. Define object permanence, scheme, adaptation, assimilation, and accommodation. (pp. 43–44)

8. Define attachment. Discuss the behaviors required of both infant and mother for a secure attachment to develop. (pp. 46–49)

9. Know the characteristics that define temperament. (pp. 49–50)

10. Describe the development of language and communication from birth to eighteen months. (pp. 50–51)

11. Describe the changes in cognition during the preoperational period. Discuss the importance of symbol usage during this period. (pp. 52–54)

12. Describe the changes in cognition in Piaget's concrete operations stage. Know the criticisms of Piaget's theories and the alternatives to Piaget's theory of cognitive development. (pp. 54–58)

13. Describe the different kinds of relationships that children of two to twelve years have with parents, siblings, and peers. (pp. 58–60)

14. Describe the development of social skills and gender roles from ages two to twelve years. (pp. 60–62)
15. Describe the three parenting styles discussed in the text. Describe the characteristics of children who have grown up with each parenting style. (pp. 62–63)
16. Know the physical and psychological changes that occur during adolescence. Describe the relationship adolescents have with their parents and peers. (pp. 63–65)
17. Discuss the problems an American adolescent faces in forming or finding an identity. (pp. 86–89)
18. Describe the changes in cognition during the formal operations period. (pp. 67–68)
19. Know the five stages of moral reasoning suggested by Kohlberg. Discuss the relationship between gender, cognitive changes, and moral decision making. (pp. 68–70)
20. Describe the physical, cognitive, social, and psychosocial changes during adulthood. (pp. 70–76)

CONCEPTS AND EXERCISES

No. 1 Nature or Nurture

Completing this exercise should help you to achieve the following learning objectives.

(2) *Discuss the differences between the maturational, behavioral, and psychodynamic views of development. (p. 34)*

(3) *Describe the influence of nature and nurture on development. (pp. 34–35)*

Today, developmental psychologists think that nature (genetic factors) and nurture (environmental factors) interact to produce an individual's phenotype. Below is a list of situations. After each one, decide whether nature or nurture has had more influence on the final phenotype.

1. Even though Pauline and Beth have spent just about the same amount of time lying in the sun, Pauline's tan is very dark and Beth's is a light brown. Pauline's ability to tan so darkly is probably a result of _____.

2. Jane and Isabelle, piano majors, are very dedicated to practicing, and both work at it eight hours a day. Isabelle is very frustrated because her playing is not as musical as Jane's despite her long hours at the piano. Jane's ability to play so musically is probably a result of _____.

3. Tom and Jim are identical twins. Their parents died in a car accident when they were nine weeks old. They had no other relatives, and separate adoptions were arranged. Tom's adoptive parents are language professors at a large university, and Jim's parents are both advertising executives. At age twelve, Tom can speak three languages other than English; Jim is getting a *D* in English. The difference in their language abilities is probably due to _____.

4. Tony was always slight of build and all through high school had very thin arms and legs. When he entered college, he started working out. The first time he went home, Tony's mother was surprised to see his well-developed muscles. Tony's new physique is probably due to _____.

No. 2 The Toy Industry

Completing this exercise should help you to achieve the following learning objectives.

(6) *Describe the capacities of a newborn. (pp. 42–43)*

(7) *Describe the development of mental abilities in the sensorimotor period. Define object permanence, scheme, adaptation, assimilation, and accommodation. (pp. 43–44)*

(11) *Describe the changes in cognition during the preoperational period. Discuss the importance of symbol usage during this period. (pp. 52–54)*

(12) *Describe the changes in cognition in Piaget's concrete operations stage. Know the criticisms of Piaget's theories and the alternatives to Piaget's theory of cognitive development. (pp. 54–58)*

(18) *Describe the changes in cognition during the formal operations period. (pp. 67–68)*

Bill has just landed a job with a large toy company. His first assignment is to develop a new line of toys designed for children in each of Piaget's stages of cognitive development. Match each of Bill's ideas (listed below) to the appropriate stage of cognitive development.

1. A simple board game: The first player to move a token completely around the board, wins. The board itself is made of squares with pictures of animals, foods, family members (grandma, uncle, sister), and toys. Some of the squares have instructions to move ahead or fall back to the nearest square with a picture of a certain type of animal, toy, food, or relative. For example, one square might say to move ahead to the nearest picture of a horn, and another might say to move back to the nearest picture of a cow. To play the game, players roll a die and move the appropriate number of squares. The player's turn ends if he lands on a square with a picture. If the player lands on a square with instructions, he or she must follow them. The game is designed so that the players practice counting and recognizing different classes of objects. _____

2. A set of edible paints: The paints come with a set of canvases that will not absorb paint. However, paint will adhere to the surface enough to remain in place. Each canvas contains an outline of a picture. The idea is for the child to paint a picture, and then peel it off the board and eat it. _____

3. A mobile of clown faces painted in vibrant primary colors. Via batteries, each clown face will,

when pulled, emit a different melody or laugh, and the eyes in each face will light up. _____

4. A board game called Planet Wars: Each player receives his or her own planet. Some planets are more desirable than others and a roll of the dice decides who gets which planet. Each planet comes with an army, several nearby star systems with arsenals, an assortment of special weapons, and spy devices. The winner is the player who conquers the most planets. The players must generate hypotheses to help them form strategies for attack and must be able to logically anticipate the consequences of their own and their opponents' moves. _____

ANSWERS TO CONCEPTS AND EXERCISES

No. 1 Nature or Nurture

1. *Nature.* Pauline tans better than Beth, despite their spending the same amount of time in the sun, because Pauline's genotype causes her pigmentation to be more reactive to the sun.

2. *Nature.* Jane plays well because she has a genotype that predisposes her to be musical.

3. *Nurture.* Neither Tom nor Jim have a genetic predisposition for languages or both would excel in this area. Jim may not have been exposed to other languages in school or at home, but his poor performance in English indicates that he does not have a natural talent for languages. Tom's parents have provided a multilingual environment for him and this is a likely reason why he can speak three languages.

4. *Nurture.* Tony's genotype guided his physical development throughout high school. However, working out in the gym (an environmental factor, or nurture) was responsible for the changes in his muscles.

No. 2 The Toy Industry

1. *Concrete operations*. In this stage of cognitive development children learn how to do simple operations such as addition, subtraction, and conservation and to place objects into classes—for example, cows, dogs, and rabbits are grouped as animals. The board game lets the child practice counting and putting objects into classes.

2. *Preoperational*. The ability to use symbols introduces the child to many new activities. Drawing is creating a symbol of something in the real world.

3. *Sensorimotor*. An infant in this period loves to look at large objects that move and have lots of contrast and complexity, especially smiling faces. The mobile is perfect for this age; it moves, is made of faces, and the colors, lights, and sounds provide contrast.

4. *Formal operations*. In this stage, adolescents learn to generate hypotheses and think logically about the outcome of events. To develop a strategy for the Planet Wars game, each player must create a plan (hypothesis) and think logically about the consequences of the plan's moves.

MULTIPLE CHOICE QUESTIONS

Facts and Definitions

1. In the context of the nature-nurture debate, nurture could be defined as

   a. a child's education.
   b. the sensitivity of the parents' care.
   c. a healthy diet.
   d. All of the above.

2. A behaviorist believes that development is a result of

   a. maturational processes.
   b. natural growth guided by genetic factors.
   c. sexual impulses.
   d. the influence of external conditions.

3. A dominant gene is expressed

   a. when present in the genotype.
   b. only when paired with a similar recessive gene.
   c. only when paired with a similar dominant gene.
   d. only when paired with a polygenic gene.

4. The development of the cardiovascular and nervous systems and the organs occurs during which stage of prenatal development?

   a. Germinal
   b. Embryonic
   c. Fertile
   d. Fetal

5. Touching an infant's _____ results in a rooting reflex.

   a. nose
   b. lips
   c. cheek
   d. palm

6. Object permanence is acquired during Piaget's _____ period of cognitive development.

   a. formal operations
   b. concrete operations
   c. preoperational
   d. sensorimotor

7. Infants respond to their parents' overt emotions. Studies have shown that infants respond

   a. to smiling faces, because they think their mothers are happy.
   b. to smiling faces, because they are more interesting.
   c. negatively to frowns, because infants are egocentric and think they have done something wrong.
   d. to the differences in subtle facial expressions.

8. What types of sounds do infants prefer?
   a. soothing descending tones
   b. low pitches
   c. monotones
   d. female voices

9. The thinking of children who cannot yet conserve is dominated by
   a. auditory cues (hearing).
   b. visual cues.
   c. textural cues.
   d. verbal cues.

10. Children engaged in parallel play
    a. will talk to each other about what they are doing.
    b. ask to borrow a toy instead of grabbing it away from another child.
    c. cooperate with each other.
    d. use the same toys but do not interact with each other.

11. An authoritative parent is
    a. firm, punitive, and unsympathetic.
    b. very lax about discipline and gives the child complete freedom.
    c. firm but reasonable and explains why a child's behavior is incorrect.
    d. one who demands obedience to authority.

12. Bulimia and anorexia nervosa are eating disorders characteristic of
    a. teenage boys with good bodies.
    b. teenage girls with low self-esteem.
    c. males in early adulthood who are late bloomers.
    d. females in the preoperational period.

13. Preschool children identify themselves by
    a. giving their name, sex, and age.
    b. describing their physical appearance.
    c. stating stable psychological characteristics.
    d. listing their favorite activities.

14. In the second stage of Kohlberg's model of moral reasoning, children will
    a. consider what they will gain by the moral decision.
    b. choose an action that will bring approval.
    c. make decisions from a human rights perspective.
    d. make decisions based on their personal standards.

15. Which of the following is characteristic of an older adult's (over sixty-five) thinking?
    a. Information is registered at a faster pace.
    b. Mathematical ability increases due to practice in everyday life.
    c. Memory for complicated stories or situations decreases.
    d. Verbal ability increases as a result of a larger vocabulary.

MULTIPLE CHOICE QUESTIONS

Application of Concepts

1. Jane is pregnant and has been reading about different activities that she can do with her new baby to improve the baby's intellectual skills. Jane is behaving according to what viewpoint?
   a. Nature
   b. Maturational
   c. Psychodynamic
   d. Nurture

2. Karen drinks heavily and smokes almost two packs of cigarettes a day. Her doctor told her that she must abstain from these activities at least during the _____ stage of her baby's prenatal development.
   a. germane
   b. embryonic
   c. fetal
   d. gestation

3. Colleen is five years old. She is mentally retarded and her face is malformed. Her mother most likely

    a. took thalidomide during pregnancy.
    b. is a heroin addict.
    c. drinks heavily.
    d. experienced severe stress during pregnancy.

4. Penny is going to decorate her newborn's room and wants the baby to enjoy looking all around it. Which of the following will meet her decorating needs?

    a. Wallpaper covered with very small blue flowers
    b. A mobile with very small butterflies for the far end of the room
    c. Curtains with large smiling clown faces for the window right next to the baby's bed
    d. A wall hanging of gray-and-white-checked fabric

5. Joey is six months old and loves to play a mini tug-of-war game. When his dad leans over the crib with a toy in his hand, Joey grasps and pulls on it. Joey's mom just got him a new toy, a little string of colored animals, to hang across his crib. She does not understand why Joey always reaches up and pulls down the string of colored animals. Joey is elaborating his scheme of grasping and pulling by

    a. accommodation.
    b. integration.
    c. assimilation.
    d. anticipation.

6. Sherri babysits for Peter every afternoon and has noticed that he cries and fusses when his mother leaves. When his mother returns, Peter squirms and refuses to be held by her. Peter most likely has

    a. an insecure avoidant attachment.
    b. an insecure ambivalent attachment.
    c. a secure avoidant attachment.
    d. a secure ambivalent attachment.

7. It is interesting to watch nine-month-old P. J. react to a new object. He holds on to his mother very tightly for several long moments, and then, using the furniture to steady himself, walks toward the object and warily checks it out. P. J. has a temperament that is typical of

    a. easy babies.
    b. difficult babies.
    c. slow-to-warm-up babies.
    d. exploratory babies.

8. Susie is crying because her teddy bear, Roger, has fallen off the kitchen table and landed on its face. Susie insists that her mother put a bandage on Roger's nose. Susie is in Piaget's _____ stage of cognitive development.

    a. sensorimotor
    b. preoperational
    c. formal operations
    d. concrete operations

9. Two mothers are assessing their children's abilities. One turns to the other and says, "Of course Johnny is doing better at math. Now that he is older, his concentration is better and he can hold more chunks of information in his memory at the same time." _____ would agree with Johnny's mom.

    a. Piaget
    b. A learning theorist
    c. An information processing theorist
    d. Kohlberg

10. Child X is between five and seven years old. The parents of child X, in accordance with the *typical* socialization behavior of most American parents, are encouraging X to achieve, act independently, explore, and assume personal responsibility. What sex is child X?

    a. Male
    b. Female
    c. These traits are encouraged in both sexes.
    d. Cannot be determined

11. Sam and Alex want to attend a rock concert in New York City on July 4. Sam's parents have told him that, although they understand his frustration, it is too dangerous for a fourteen-year-old to go to the city by himself on a big holiday. Alex's parents have decided that he may go to the concert. Sam's parents are _____ and Alex's parents are _____.

    a. permissive, authoritative
    b. authoritarian, permissive
    c. authoritative, authoritarian
    d. authoritative, permissive

12. Steve has grown 5 inches in the past year and gained 20 pounds. He is depressed over the sudden appearance of acne on his face and elated a moment later as he tears out the door to go play football with his buddies. How old is he?

    a. eight to ten years old
    b. ten to twelve years old
    c. twelve to fifteen years old
    d. eighteen to twenty years old

13. Gary's parents are constantly amazed at how their son has changed over the past year. Suddenly, he loves to study science, is a feminist, and wants to participate in an anti-nuclear power demonstration. Gary has moved into the _____ stage of cognitive development.

    a. sensorimotor
    b. preoperational
    c. consequential operations
    d. formal operations

14. Jeanene and Helen are in a drugstore spending several weeks' allowances on penny candy. Helen decides she wants to steal the candy but Jeanene argues that they might get caught and put in jail. According to Kohlberg, Jeanene is at which stage of moral reasoning?

    a. One
    b. Three
    c. Four
    d. Five

15. In the past ten years, Vernon has gained weight, especially around his middle. He has a slight hearing loss and has just found out that he needs glasses. How old is Vernon?

    a. Fifteen
    b. Twenty-five
    c. Fifty
    d. Seventy-five

ANSWERS TO MULTIPLE CHOICE QUESTIONS

Facts and Definitions

1. *d* is the answer. Nurture is *anything* in the environment that influences an organism; education, parents' care, physical exercise, and diet. Nature is any characteristic resulting from inherited genetic material; eye color or a physical predisposition toward a disease, body type, or temperament. (pp. 32–34, 34–35)

2. *d* is the answer. A behaviorist believes that external conditions are responsible for the developmental process. For example, transferring to a better educational setting will alter the development of cognitive abilities. (pp. 33–34)

    a. & b. A maturationalist believes that abilities unfold with age in a fixed sequence and are determined by nature, which is equivalent to saying that genetics controls development.

    c. A psychodynamic theorist believes that a child's natural sexual impulses and the parental reaction to those impulses guide development.

3. *a* is the answer. A dominant gene is always expressed when it is present in the genotype unless a genetic mutation occurs. (p. 37)

    b. A dominant gene is expressed when paired with a recessive gene, but this is not the *only* situation in which it will be expressed.

c. A dominant gene is expressed when paired with another dominant gene, but this is not the *only* situation in which it will be expressed.

d. There is no such thing as a polygenic gene. Polygenic traits are those controlled by more than one gene.

4. *b* is the answer. It is during the embryonic stage that the cardiovascular and nervous systems develop. A critical period exists; if certain systems and organs do not develop properly at this time, they never will. (p. 39)

a. The germinal stage begins with fertilization and lasts for two weeks. The zygote divides rapidly and travels down the fallopian tubes to attach itself to the uterine wall.

c. & *d.* There is no such thing as the fertile stage in prenatal development. You may be thinking of the fetal stage. During this stage, systems integrate and the organs grow and function more efficiently.

5. *c* is the answer. If you touch an infant's cheek, the infant will automatically turn his or her head toward your hand. This is called a rooting reflex. (p. 43)

a. There is no reflex associated with touching an infant's nose.

b. If you put an object, such as a nipple or your finger, to an infant's lips, the infant will automatically try to suck on it. However, this is called the sucking reflex, not the rooting reflex.

d. Brushing an infant's palm or ball of the foot results in the infant grasping with his or her hands or curling his or her toes with quite a bit of strength. However, this is called a grasping reflex, not a rooting reflex.

6. *d* is the answer. Object permanence is the ability to know that an object exists even when it is out of sight. Children acquire this ability during the sensorimotor period, the first stage of cognitive development. (pp. 44–45)

a. An adolescent acquires the ability to think hypothetically and imagine events' logical consequences.

b. A child learns to perform simple operations—subtraction, addition, classification, seriation, and conservation—during the concrete operations period.

c. A child acquires the ability to use symbols during the preoperational period.

7. *b* is the answer. Research shows that infants are unable to distinguish subtle facial expressions of emotion. They simply seem to respond to faces that have the most interesting features. To an infant, a toothy grin is much more interesting than a frown. (p. 45)

a. Research does not indicate that infants can recognize and enjoy happy emotions.

c. This type of thinking is egocentric. Infants do not think egocentrically; children in the preoperational period of cognitive development (ages two to seven) do.

d. Research has shown that infants cannot recognize the differences between subtle facial expressions.

8. *d* is the answer. (p. 50)

a., b., & *c.* Infants prefer ascending tones, spoken by a woman or a child. They like speech that is friendly, high-pitched, exaggerated, and expressive.

9. *b* is the answer. The ability to conserve involves realizing that a substance does not change in amount or number when its form changes. Thinking dominated by visual appearances makes conservation impossible. A child incapable of conserving would say that a tall skinny glass contains more liquid than does a short fat glass, even when both glasses contain the same amount of liquid. (pp. 48–49)

a., c., & *d.* There is no period during which hearing, texture, or verbal cues dominate children's thinking.

10. *d* is the answer. Children engaged in parallel play focus most of their attention on the toys they are using instead of on each other. (p. 59)

a., b., & c. Children engaged in associative play talk about their activities, cooperate with each other, and lend and borrow toys instead of grabbing them away from each other.

11. *c* is the answer. Authoritative parents are firm but reasonable and explain why a child's behavior is incorrect. They encourage the child to take responsibility and be independent. (p. 63)

a. Authoritarian parents are firm, punitive, and unsympathetic.

b. Permissive parents are very lax about discipline and give their children complete freedom.

d. Authoritarian parents demand obedience to authority figures.

12. *b* is the answer. For teenagers, personal appearance is correlated with self-esteem. Girls with low self-esteem frequently experience problems with eating disorders, such as bulimia and anorexia nervosa, in attempts to improve their personal appearance. (pp. 64–65)

a. & c. Boys, even if they have low self-esteem, usually do not have anorexia nervosa or bulimia. This may be because girls usually want to be thin, whereas boys usually want to be muscular, which requires not only physical exertion but also a good diet.

d. Females in the preoperational period are between the ages of two and seven years old. This is not a period when personal appearance is extremely important or correlated with self-esteem.

13. *d* is the answer. When asked who they are, preschool children will tell you about their favorite activities. (p. 66)

a. & b. Children eight or nine years old will give their name, sex, and age, and will describe their physical appearance.

c. Adolescents use general, stable, psychological characteristics to describe themselves.

14. *a* is the answer. Stage two, moral reasoning, is basically selfish. Decisions are based on the potential for personal gain. (p. 69)

b. Children in stage three make moral decisions based on the potential for others' approval.

c. Children in stage six consider human rights or other universal ethical principles when making a moral decision.

d. Children in stage five make moral decisions based on their own personal standards.

15. *c* is the answer. Memory for complicated stories or situations decreases. However, with support or training, performance does rise to the level of a younger adult. (p. 71)

a., b., & d. Verbal and mathematical skills decline after the mid-sixties and the brain registers information at a slower pace.

ANSWERS TO MULTIPLE CHOICE QUESTIONS

Application of Concepts

1. *d* is the answer. Jane's behavior implies that she believes that her infant's environment will affect his or her intellectual development. This is in accordance with a nurture viewpoint. (p. 32)

a. & b. A maturationalist would say that the development of a phenotype (how the individual looks and acts) is guided by biological or genetic factors, which are not generally altered by changes in the environment.

c. From a psychodynamic viewpoint, development is the product of an individual's sexual impulses and the parents' reactions to them.

2. *b* is the answer. There is a critical period in the embryonic stage during which systems and organs must develop or they never will. Drugs and alcohol negatively affect this process. (p. 39)

a. & d. There is no such thing as the germane stage. You may have been thinking of the germinal stage. There is no such thing as the gestation stage.

c. Alcohol and nicotine in the mother's system do affect development in the fetal stage, but not as severely as they do in the embryonic stage.

3. *c* is the answer. Mental retardation and facial malformations are symptoms of fetal alcohol syndrome, which occurs in infants of alcoholic mothers. (p. 40)

a., b., & d. Drug use of any kind (whether recreational or medicinal) and stress levels can affect prenatal development. However, the combination of symptoms listed can be linked to one specific abuse: drinking alcohol.

4. *c* is the answer. Infants can see large objects with lots of contrast, contour, complexity, and movement. They enjoy looking at faces. The clown faces are large and smiling and may move as the curtains flutter in the breeze. (pp. 42–43)

a. This wallpaper design may appeal to Penny, but her infant will not have the visual capability to see the small pattern.

b. A mobile is a good idea because the parts move, but the infant will be unable to see it in the far corner.

d. A wall hanging of brightly colored checks may provide enough contrast for the infant to see it. However, grey and white are not as different as, say, blue and red. Also, infants prefer looking at faces, which makes *c* the one best response for this question.

5. *c* is the answer. Joey is assimilating because he is using the *same* scheme of reaching and grasping to investigate a new object. (p. 44)

a. Accommodation occurs when a scheme is *modified* or *changed* in response to acquiring information about a new object or situation. If the question stated that Joey had learned to push the animals back and forth in the air instead of always reaching,

grasping, and pulling them down, accommodation would have been the answer.

b. Integration is the process of putting two schemes together. If the question stated that Joey had learned that reaching and grasping can become a sequence of movements, this would be the correct answer.

d. There is no anticipatory process in the elaboration of schemes.

6. *b* is the answer. A child who is upset when his mother leaves and when she returns has an insecure ambivalent attachment. (p. 48)

a. A child who is content with the care and comfort of a person aside from his or her mother, but who avoids contact or ignores the mother when she returns, has an insecure avoidant attachment.

c. There is no such thing as a secure avoidant attachment.

d. There is no such thing as a secure ambivalent attachment.

7. *c* is the answer. Children who fuss a bit or hesitate when they approach a new situation or object but then enjoy the new activity are known as slow-to-warm-up babies. (p. 50)

a. An easy baby has predictable cycles of eating and sleeping, reacts cheerfully to a new situation, and seldom fusses.

b. A difficult baby is irritable and irregular.

d. Although some infants are more exploratory than others, there is no category or classification called exploratory.

8. *b* is the answer. Susie is probably between the ages of four and six and thinks that her bear, an inanimate (nonliving) object, is alive and feels pain because he fell on his face. Mom puts a bandage on Susie's cuts and bruises, and Susie wants the same treatment for Roger. This is characteristic of the preoperational stage. (p. 53)

a. Children in the sensorimotor stage do not recognize or label their own emotions, and therefore cannot assume that their bears have emotions.

c. Adolescents realize that inanimate (nonliving) objects do not feel pain.

d. Children in the concrete operational stage realize that inanimate (nonliving) objects do not feel pain.

9. *c* is the answer. Developmental research based on information processing theory focuses on the *quantitative* changes in children's mental capacities, rather than looking for qualitative advances or changes as Piaget did. A *bigger* vocabulary, *more* concentration, and holding *more* chunks of information in memory at one time are all quantitative changes. Therefore, Johnny's mother is explaining her son's improvement as an information processing theorist would. (pp. 55–56)

REMEMBER: This approach focuses on quantitative changes. Quantitative pertains to *number* or *amounts;* so *bigger* or *more* ability accounts for a change or advance in ability according to this view of cognitive development.

a. Piaget explained cognitive development in terms of qualitative changes. Each stage of cognitive development contains a *different* kind of mental ability, not just an improved capacity for the same cognitive ability. The ability to use symbols (acquired in the preoperational period) is an ability that is different from being able to generate hypotheses (acquired in the formal operation period).

REMEMBER: The definition of the noun *quality* is a distinguishing element or characteristic. Therefore, each stage of Piaget's cognitive development theory is distinguished by a *unique* characteristic or type of thinking.

b. According to a learning theorist, children will repeat behaviors if they are rewarded for them in some way. Rewards can be food or favorite activities or any number of things the child finds pleasant. Therefore, a child will acquire new mental abilities if he or she is rewarded for it.

d. Kohlberg was interested in moral decision-making. This is only one type of cognitive activity.

His work does not provide a general theory about the development of cognitive abilities.

10. *a* is the answer. Boys are encouraged to achieve, act independently, explore, and assume personal responsibility. (pp. 61–62)

b. Girls are encouraged to be expressive, nurturant, reflective, dependent, obedient, helpful, and kind.

c. The traits listed in the question are encouraged only in males.

d. Research has shown that boys are encouraged to achieve, act independently, explore, and assume personal responsibility. Therefore, *a* is the answer.

11. *d* is the answer. Authoritative parents would be sympathetic and be sorry that Sam has to miss the concert, but they would also be firm in their decision. Alex's parents have given him complete freedom and are therefore permissive. Neither set of parents are authoritarian (firmly upholding rules with no explanation). (pp. 62–63)

12. *c* is the answer. The beginning and middle of adolescence are marked by large growth spurts and sudden mood changes. (p. 64)

a., b., & d. None of the other age groups correspond to the beginning and middle of the adolescent period.

13. *d* is the answer. Studying science involves thinking logically and being able to generate hypotheses. Being involved with feminist movements and nuclear demonstrations requires the ability to question social institutions and to think about the world as it might be or as it ought to be. (pp. 67–68)

a. & b. Children in the sensorimotor or preoperational periods do not have the ability to question social institutions. They may have some knowledge of feminism or nuclear power plants, but they cannot think about or accurately imagine the consequences of nuclear war or of treating women as inferior.

c. There is no cognitive stage called consequential operations. You may have been thinking of concrete operations.

14. *a* is the answer. Jeanene is thinking about the painful experience of going to jail. That is why she decides against stealing the candy. This is characteristic of stage one moral reasoning. (pp. 68–69)

b. Stage three moral reasoning is characterized by a concern for pleasing others. If Jeanene said she did not want her mother to think badly of her, this would have been the correct answer.

c. Stage four moral reasoning is characterized by a concern for following rules and regulations. If Jeanene had said that it would be breaking the law

to steal the candy, this would have been the correct answer.

d. Stage five moral reasoning is characterized by following one's own personal standards. If Jeanene said that *she* does not think it is right to steal from someone, this would have been the correct answer.

15. *c* is the answer. Weight gain (especially around the middle), hearing loss, and decreased visual ability begin to occur in the forties. Since the question refers to the past ten years, Vernon must be about fifty years old. (p. 73)

a. & b. Weight gain is common in the beginning of adolescence, but hearing and vision loss are not.

d. People at seventy-five do experience hearing and vision losses, but this generally begins before age sixty-five. Also, weight gain is not common at age seventy-five.

Chapter 3

Biological Bases of Behavior

OUTLINE

I. INTRODUCTION (p. 80)

Biological Psychology is the study of the physical and chemical factors that influence or cause behavior and mental processes. The nervous system, made up of cells that can communicate with each other, is one of the most important biological factors involved in behavior.

II. THE NERVOUS SYSTEM: AN OVERVIEW (pp. 82–85)

The nervous system allows us to gain information about the environment, make decisions concerning that information, and carry out responses based on those decisions.

III. COMMUNICATION IN THE NERVOUS SYSTEM (pp. 85–91)

A. Neurons: The Basic Unit of the Nervous System

1. *The Structure of Neurons: Axons and Dendrites*. Neurons, like all other cells, have a nucleus, an outer membrane, and a cell body. However, they also possess unique structures that allow them to communicate with other cells.

   a. Axons carry signals from the cell body of a neuron to the synapse.

   b. Dendrites receive and carry information from other nerve cells to the cell body.

2. *Membranes and Action Potentials*. The selective permeability of the neuronal membrane keeps sodium from freely entering the axon through the sodium gates. This allows the inside of the axon to become negatively charged or polarized. When an action potential occurs, some part of the axon becomes depolarized, which causes a sodium gate to open. Sodium rushes into the axon which, in turn, causes the neighboring sodium gates to open, and more sodium rushes in. This chain of events occurs along the entire length of the axon. The speed of the action potential is affected by the presence of myelin. The length of the refractory period determines the number of action potentials that occur per time unit.

3. *Synapses and Communication Between Cells*. Neurotransmitters are chemicals that carry the signal from the axon (presynaptic cell) of one neuron, across the synapse to the dendrite (postsynaptic cell) of the next neuron.

B. Neurotransmitters and Receptors

Neurotransmitters stimulate receptors predominantly on the postsynaptic cell. The resulting activity depends on the excitatory or inhibitory nature of the neurotransmitter and the receptor. After a brief

41

time, the neurotransmitters are either broken down by enzymes or transported back into the presynaptic cell where they are housed in vesicles.

C. Pathways and Nuclei

Nuclei are collections of cell bodies. Fiber tracts are composed of bundles of axons and form pathways.

IV. STRUCTURES AND FUNCTIONS OF THE CENTRAL NERVOUS SYSTEM (pp. 91–105)

A. The Spinal Cord

The spinal cord carries messages to and from the brain.

1. *Reflexes.* The behaviors called reflexes are quick, involuntary muscular responses to incoming sensory information and occur completely within the spinal cord.

2. *Four Principles of Nervous System Functioning.*
   a. Central coordination of opposing actions.

   b. Complicated behaviors are created from simple behaviors.

   c. Smooth functioning depends on feedback systems.

   d. Coordination of several levels of central nervous system organization.

B. Studying the Brain

Several techniques are used to study the brain: studies of animals, surgical procedures, studying behavioral deficits in brain damaged people, autopsies, electroencephalograms (EEGs), computer-assisted tomography (CT scanning), positron emission tomography (PET scanning), and magnetic resonance imaging (MRI).

C. The Structure of the Brain

1. *The Hindbrain.* Nuclei that control vital functions are located in the hindbrain. One of these nuclei is the medulla. The cerebellum is also located in the hindbrain, and it controls finely coordinated movements.

2. *The Midbrain.* Located between the hindbrain and forebrain, the midbrain serves as a relay station for information from the eyes, ears, and skin, and controls certain automatic behaviors. The substantia nigra is a nucleus in the midbrain and is involved in initiating smooth movement.

3. *The Reticular Formation.* Running throughout the hindbrain and midbrain, the reticular formation is a network of cells, and alters the activity of the rest of the brain.

4. *The Forebrain.*
   a. The diencephalon includes the hypothalamus and thalamus, which are involved in emotion, basic drives, and sensation.

   b. The telencephalon, or cerebrum, includes the striatum and parts of the limbic system, which includes the hippocampus, the septum, and the cerebral cortex. The striatum is involved in initiation of smooth movement. The limbic system plays an important role in regulating emotion and is involved in memory and other thought processes.

D. The Cerebral Cortex

The cerbral cortex is the outer surface of the cerebrum or cerebral hemispheres. It includes the frontal, parietal, temporal, and occipital lobes.

1. *Sensory and Motor Cortex.* The sensory cortex receives sensory information. The motor cortex neurons control the onset of voluntary movement.

2. *Association Cortex.* These areas receive information from more than one sense or combine sensory and motor information. Deficits in un-

derstanding and producing language are caused by damage to Broca's or Wernicke's areas.

E. The Divided Brain in a Unified Self.

1. *Split-Brain Studies*. Sometimes, people with severe epilepsy have their cerebral hemispheres functionally separated by severing the corpus callosum. Data collected from these patients demonstrate that each hemisphere is superior in certain abilities. The left hemisphere controls spoken language and the right is superior at recognizing faces and on tasks dealing with spatial relations, such as drawing three-dimensional shapes. Also, the left hemisphere controls the right side of the body and the right hemisphere controls the left side.

2. *Lateralization of Normal Brains*. Data collected from people with intact brains demonstrate the superiority of the left hemisphere in logical thinking and language abilities. The right hemisphere has better spatial, artistic, and musical abilities.

V. THE CHEMISTRY OF PSYCHOLOGY (pp. 105–111)

Neurons communicate by releasing neurotransmitters at their synapses. A neurotransmitter system is a group of neurons that all use the same neurotransmitter. A neurotransmitter can be excitatory or inhibitory, depending on the type and location of the receptor it fits into.

A. Five Neurotransmitters

1. *Acetylcholine*. Muscle contractions are controlled by acetylcholine.

2. *Norepinephrine*. Arousal, learning, and mood are regulated by norepinephrine.

3. *Serotonin*. Sleep, moods, and pain are regulated by serotonin.

4. *Dopamine*. Movement and complex cognitive abilities are regulated by dopamine.

5. *GABA (gamma-amino butyric acid)*. The major inhibitory neurotransmitter is GABA.

B. Drugs, Neurotransmitters, and Behavior

Psychopharmacology is the study of psychoactive drugs, which alter neurotransmission in one of four ways:

1. *Altering the Amount of Neurotransmitter (NT) Released*. Drugs can cause more NT to be synthesized or released at the synapse.

2. *Mimicking Neurotransmitters*. These drugs, called agonists, fit snugly into receptors and imitate the NT's activity.

3. *Blocking Receptors*. Drugs called antagonists occupy receptor sites but do not fit snugly, and thus do not initiate activity in the receptors that NTs normally occupy.

4. *Blocking Reuptake*. Some drugs can prevent the removal of an NT from the synapse or the return of the neurotransmitter to the presynaptic terminal. Consequently, the drug stays in the synapse and the NT is active for a longer time.

VI. ENDOCRINE SYSTEMS (pp. 111–113)

The endocrine system, like the nervous system, controls a wide variety of behaviors. Glands secrete hormones, which travel via the bloodstream and affect coordinated systems of target tissues and organs, producing such responses as the fight-or-flight syndrome. Feedback systems involving the brain regulate the amount of hormone released.

KEY TERMS

1. **Biological** or **physiological psychology** is the study of the role of physical and chemical factors in behavior and mental processes. The nervous system, composed of cells that can communicate with each other, is one of the most important biological factors involved in behavior. (p. 80)

Example: Depression is associated with various biochemical changes in the brain.

2. The **nervous system** is a complex combination of cells that has three basic functions: receiving information, integrating it with previous information to generate choices and decisions, and guiding actions based on those decisions. (p. 82)

Example: When we stand at the curb of a busy street, our nervous system takes in sensory information about oncoming traffic, makes a decision to cross the street at a particular moment, and controls the movement of stepping off the curb and crossing the street.

3. **Sensory systems,** which include vision, hearing, touch, taste, and smell, provide us with information about the environment. (p. 82)

Example: When you walk into your grandmother's house on Thanksgiving Day, your nose provides information about the food she has prepared for the family.

4. **Motor systems** influence muscles and other organs to respond to the environment in some way. (p. 82)

Example: After you have smelled the food in your grandmother's house on Thanksgiving, and have decided that you want to eat it, your motor system allows you to walk to the table, sit down, and manipulate the fork, knife, and spoon.

5. The **central nervous system** is one of the two major units of the nervous system and includes the brain and spinal cord. Its primary function is to process the information provided by the sensory systems and decide on an appropriate course of action for the motor system. (p. 83)

REMEMBER: The brain and spinal cord are centrally located. Your spinal cord is in the center of your torso; the brain is *centered* over your shoulders (see Figure 3.2 in the text).

6. The **peripheral nervous system** is the only major unit of the nervous system that is not encased in bone. It has two major subdivisions, the somatic and autonomic nervous systems. (p. 84)

REMEMBER: Peri means around. The peripheral nervous system is located around the center of your body (see Figure 3.2 in your text).

7. The **somatic nervous system** transmits information from the senses to the central nervous system and carries signals from the central nervous system to the muscles that move the skeleton. (p. 84)

Example: When you dance, the somatic nervous system transmits the sound of the music to your brain and carries the signals from your brain to the muscles that move your arms and legs.

REMEMBER: Soma means body. The somatic nervous system is involved with taking sensory information from the body parts, such as the ears, and sending signals back to the body, such as movement instructions to coordinate dance steps.

8. The **autonomic nervous system** carries messages back and forth between the central nervous system and the various organs and glands. (p. 84)

Example: While you dance, your peripheral nervous system may alter the expansion of your lungs so that you can breathe in more oxygen. Also, your heartbeat increases so that more blood reaches your muscles.

REMEMBER: The autonomic nervous system regulates the automatic functions of your body, such as breathing and blood pressure. You do not normally think about these functions.

9. **Neurons** are the cells that make up the nervous system. Neurons can communicate with one another, which makes these cells different from most other cells found in the body. (p. 85)

10. **Axons,** which are part of the neuron, carry signals from the cell body out to the synapse, where

communication with other nerve cells takes place. Each neuron usually has only one axon. (p. 86)

REMEMBER: Axons carry signals <u>a</u>way from the cell body.

11. **Dendrites** are part of the neuron. They receive signals from the axons of other neurons and carry those signals to the cell body. Each neuron can have up to several thousand dendrites. (p. 86)

REMEMBER: <u>D</u>endrites <u>d</u>etect signals from other neurons.

12. **Polarization** occurs when the selective permeability of a neuronal membrane prevents positively charged molecules, such as sodium, from entering a cell. This allows the inside of the cell to have more negative charge than the outside of the cell. (p. 86)

REMEMBER: The membrane's selective permeability allows it to become polarized. Polarized means to <u>separate</u> into two <u>opposed</u> groups. Positive and negative charges are <u>opposed</u>. The membrane <u>separates</u> the negatively charged molecules inside the cell from the positively charged molecules outside the cell.

13. **Sodium gates,** which are distributed along the axon, keep the positively charged sodium molecules outside the membrane. When the axon's membrane becomes less polarized (or depolarized), the sodium gates open and sodium rushes into the axon. (p. 87)

14. **Action potentials** occur when the neuron becomes depolarized and sodium rushes into the axon. Opening one sodium gate causes the gate next to it to open, which causes the next one to open, and so forth all the way down the length of the axon. Action potentials are all-or-none activities; the cell either fires at full strength or it does not fire at all. (p. 87)

REMEMBER: Electrical potentials occur when there is a difference in charge between the outside and inside of the cell. When there is an *active* change in the electrical *potential,* which

happens when sodium rushes into the axon and makes the inside less negative, an *action potential* occurs.

15. **Myelin,** a fatty substance that wraps around some axons, causes an action potential to travel very quickly down the length of the axon. (p.87)

Example: When a stray object flies toward your face, the sensory nerves must quickly transmit the information to the brain, and the motor nerves must carry the signal to your muscles to move very rapidly. These sensory and motor nerves are covered with myelin.

16. A **refractory period** is a rest period between action potentials. After an action potential has been fired, the axon must become repolarized before another action potential can occur. The time required for the axon to become repolarized is called a refractory period. (p. 89)

REMEMBER: An axon <u>ref</u>rains from firing an action potential during a <u>ref</u>ractory period.

17. A **synapse** is the very small gap between an axon sending a message and the dendrite receiving that message. The axon is the presynaptic cell, and the dendrite is the postsynaptic cell. The neurotransmitters released from the presynaptic cell cross the synapse and fit into the receptors on the postsynaptic cell. (p. 89)

REMEMBER: Pre means before. The presynaptic cell comes before the synapse. *Post* means after. The postsynaptic cell comes after the synapse (see Figure 3.5 in your text).

18. The **postsynaptic cell** follows the gap (synapse) between an axon sending a message and the dendrite (the postsynaptic cell) receiving it (see Figure 3.6 in your text). (p. 89)

19. The **presynaptic cell** precedes the gap (synapse) between an axon (or presynaptic cell) sending a message and the dendrite receiving it (see Figure 3.6 in your text). (p.89)

20. **Neurotransmitters** are chemicals that carry a signal from the axon (of the presynaptic cell) across the synapse to the receptors on the dendrite (of the postsynaptic cell). (p. 89)

REMEMBER: Neuro refers to neuron. *Transmit* means to send something across space. Neurotransmitters <u>send</u> the signal or message <u>across</u> the synapse to the dendrite of the postsynaptic <u>neuron.</u>

21. **Receptors,** located on the dendrites of the postsynaptic cell, are stimulated when neurotransmitters fit into them, like a key fits a lock. A stimulated excitatory receptor will make the postsynaptic cell more likely to fire, whereas an inhibitory receptor will make the presynaptic cell less likely to fire. (p. 89)

REMEMBER: A <u>receptor</u> is something that <u>receives</u>. <u>Receptors receive</u> neurotransmitters.

22. **Nuclei** are collections of cell bodies. (p. 91)

23. **Fiber tracts** (pathways or nerves) are collections of axons that travel together in bundles. (p. 91)

24. The **spinal cord,** part of the central nervous system, receives signals from the somatic system in the periphery, such as vision, and relays them to the brain via fiber tracts within the spinal cord. The brain relays signals to the muscles via fiber tracts in the spinal cord. (p. 91)

Example: The sensory information from feeling the fur on a kitten travels through the spinal cord's fiber tracts on its way to the brain. When your brain makes the decision to pick up the kitten, it sends signals through the fiber tracts in the spinal cord on the way to the muscles in your hands and arms.

25. **Reflexes** are quick, involuntary responses to incoming sensory information. The reflex arc consists of an afferent (or incoming) sensory neuron, an interneuron, and an efferent (or motor) neuron. Reflexes take place only in the spinal cord; the brain is not immediately involved. (p. 91)

Example: If you accidentally step on a pin embedded in your carpet, a withdrawal reflex occurs. The afferent sensory neuron will take the information from your foot to the spinal cord, the message will pass through an interneuron, and the efferent motor neuron will send the signal back to the foot to make it withdraw from the floor.

26. **Feedback systems** allow for automatic adjustment. They send information about the consequences of an act to the source of the action so that adjustments can be made. (p. 92)

Example: As soon as you move a muscle (act), stretch receptors in the muscle <u>feed</u> information about the movement (consequence) <u>back</u> to the spinal cord (action source). A reflex pathway in the spinal cord can send more signals to the muscle if adjustment is necessary.

27. **Electroencephalograms (EEG)** are measurements of the collective electrical activity of many nerve cells in the brain. (p. 94)

Example: Through electrodes placed on a person's head, the patterns of the brain's electrical activity can be measured. Some patterns are so similar from person to person that any major change usually indicates a medical problem.

28. The **hindbrain,** a major subdivision of the brain, includes the medulla and the cerebellum. The hindbrain is an extension of the spinal cord, is housed in the skull, and is involved in controlling vital functions. (p. 96)

29. The **medulla** is located in the hindbrain. It helps to regulate blood pressure, heart rate, and breathing. (p. 96)

30. The **cerebellum** is located in the hindbrain. It controls fine motor coordination. (p. 97)

Example: Performing brain surgery requires delicate precision of movement so as to avoid damaging fragile tissue. A surgeon's cerebellum would be very active during an operation.

31. The **midbrain,** which includes the *substantia nigra,* is located between the hindbrain and the forebrain. Sensory information is relayed through the midbrain. The substantia nigra assists in the smooth initiation of movement. (p. 97)

32. The **substantia nigra** is part of the midbrain and assists in the smooth initiation of movement. (p. 97)

33. The **reticular formation** is not a well-defined area of brain tissue but a collection of nuclei and fibers that form a network of cells throughout the hindbrain and midbrain. The reticular formation is involved in arousal and attention. (p. 97)

34. The **forebrain,** which is composed of the diencephalon and the telencephalon, is the most highly developed part of the brain. It is responsible for the most complex aspects of behavior and mental processes. (p. 97)

> *Example:* Many years ago a surgical procedure called a lobotomy was used to treat several types of mental disorders. The surgery involved destroying large parts of the forebrain. Patients who had this surgery often could not perform complex cognitive tasks.

35. The **hypothalamus** is a part of the diencephalon, located in the forebrain. The hypothalamus regulates hunger, thirst, sex drives, and is involved in emotion. (p. 97)

> *Example:* Destroying certain parts of the hypothalamus results in an animal's ceasing to eat or drink. It will eventually die if not force-fed.

36. The **thalamus** is a part of the diencephalon, located in the forebrain, above the hypothalamus. This region processes and relays sensory information on its way to higher centers of the brain. (p. 97)

37. The **cerebrum,** also called the telencephalon, is part of the forebrain. Many structures are located within the cerebrum: the striatum, the limbic system, and the cerebral cortex. (p. 98)

38. The **cerebral hemispheres** are the outermost part of the cerebrum. Each hemisphere makes up one half of the top of the brain. To understand how the cerebrum is split into hemispheres, do the following: place your finger right between your eyes, lift it straight over your forehead and trace an imaginary part in the middle of your hair to the back of your head. The line that you have just traced is the dividing line of the two cerebral hemispheres. For an illustration of this division, see Figure 3.17. (p. 98)

> *REMEMBER:* The cerebrum is round like a sphere. *Hemi* means half. A cerebral hemisphere means half of the sphere of the cerebrum.

39. The **striatum** is part of the cerebrum and is responsible for smooth initiation of movement (like the substantia nigra). (p. 98)

40. The **limbic system** is contained in several brain areas. Two of the limbic system's structures, the hippocampus and the septum, are located in the cerebrum. The limbic system is involved in emotion, memory, and some thought processes. (p. 98)

41. The **hippocampus,** part of the limbic system, is involved in learning and storing new pieces of information. (p. 98)

42. The **cerebral cortex,** the outer surface of the cerebral hemispheres, is divided into four lobes: frontal, parietal, occipital, and temporal. The cortex is also divided into three functional areas: the sensory cortex, the motor cortex, and the association cortex. (p. 98)

43. The **sensory cortex,** located in the parietal, occipital, and temporal lobes, receives information from different senses, including touch, hearing, and vision. (p. 98)

44. The **motor cortex,** located in the frontal lobe, controls all voluntary movement. (p. 99)

45. The **association cortex** is in *all* lobes of the cortex. These regions of cortex receive information from more than one sense or combine sensory and motor information. These are the areas that perform such complex cognitive tasks as associating words with images and other abstract thinking. (p. 99)

46. The **corpus callosum** connects the two cerebral hemispheres. Many important skills are *lateralized* within the cerebral hemispheres; one hemisphere performs certain tasks much better than the other. The left hemisphere is better at logical reasoning and language skills, while the right hemisphere is superior in musical and artistic abilities and spatial reasoning. Without the corpus callosum, the two hemispheres could not communicate about their respective activities. (p. 102)

47. A **neurotransmitter system** is a collection of neurons using the same neurotransmitter. Some of the systems are related to specific behaviors and mental processes. (p. 105)

   Example: Neurons that use the neurotransmitter dopamine are involved in movement.

48. **Acetylcholine,** the neurotransmitter found in the cholinergic system, is used in the periphery, where neurons contact muscles. In the central nervous system, acetylcholine is involved in movement control and memory. (p. 105)

49. **Norepinephrine** is the neurotransmitter used in the adrenergic system. The cells of the locus coeruleus, which project to many areas of the brain, contain half of the brain's norepinephrine. This neurotransmitter helps to regulate sleep, learning, and mood. (p. 106)

   Example: Depressed people may have low levels of norepinephrine.

50. **Serotonin** is found in cells in the hindbrain which branch to areas in the forebrain. This neuro-transmitter affects sleep, mood, and the sensation of pain. (p. 106)

51. **Dopamine** is a neurotransmitter. Dopaminergic neurons found in the substantia nigra are involved in movement. Others, located in the midbrain and extending into the cerebral cortex, are involved in movement and complex cognitive abilities. (p. 107)

   Example: The degeneration of cell bodies in the substantia nigra causes Parkinson's disease. The symptoms include shakiness and difficulty in initiating movement. Also, it is believed that problems in the dopaminergic system cause schizophrenia.

52. **GABA (gamma-amino butyric acid)** is an inhibitory neurotransmitter which reduces the likelihood that the postsynaptic neuron will fire an action potential. GABA, found in widespread regions of the brain, is involved in a variety of behaviors and mental processes. (p. 107)

   Example: Dysfunctions in the GABA system are associated with epilepsy and Huntington's disease.

53. **Psychoactive drugs** are chemicals that affect behavior and mental processes, usually by altering neurotransmitter activity in one of four ways: modifying the amount of neurotransmitter released from the presynaptic neuron, mimicking neurotransmitters, blocking the attachment of neurotransmitters to receptors, and blocking reuptake. (p. 108)

   Example: Cocaine blocks reuptake in noradrenergic and serotonergic neurons. The neurotransmitter is usually taken back into the presynaptic terminal. Cocaine slows this process, resulting in the prolonged presence and activity of the neurotransmitter in the synapse.

54. **Psychopharmacology** is the study of psychoactive drugs and their effects. (p. 108)

   Example: Psychopharmacologists would be interested in how amphetamines (speed), LSD, marijuana, and opium affect neurotransmitter activity in the brain and consequently alter behavior.

55. Agonists are drugs that mimic neurotransmitter activity. They fit into the receptors normally occupied by neurotransmitters and stimulate the cell. (p. 109)

> *REMEMBER:* The Greek word *agon* means a contest. You can think of these drugs and neurotransmitters as being in a contest as they race to fit into a receptor and stimulate it.

56. Antagonists block neurotransmitters. Antagonists, like agonists, compete with neurotransmitters for receptors. However, the antagonists do not fit the receptors tightly enough to cause stimulation in the postsynaptic cell. Therefore, an antagonist's presence decreases the number of receptors that can be activated by a neurotransmitter. (p. 109)

57. An **endorphin,** a naturally occurring neurotransmitter, acts just as morphine does to block the sensation of pain. Endorphins may cause the placebo effect. (p. 111)

> *Example:* It is believed that "runner's high," the absence of pain and a euphoric feeling that many runners report after covering long distances, is due to the release of endorphins.

58. The **endocrine system** controls a wide variety of behaviors just as the nervous system does. Glands secrete *hormones* which, traveling via the bloodstream, affect coordinated systems of target tissues and organs by producing such responses as the *fight-or-flight syndrome. Feedback systems* involving the brain regulate the amount of hormone released. (p. 111)

59. Hormones are chemicals that, when released by the glands of the endocrine system, travel via the bloodstream and communicate with other cells. (p. 111)

> *Example:* A woman's menstrual cycle is governed by the timed release of several different hormones.

60. The **fight-or-flight syndrome,** caused by the release of hormones, is a coordinated set of responses to danger that prepares the organism for action. The heart beats faster, the liver releases glucose to be used as energy, and the organism is placed in a state of high arousal. In short, the organism is prepared to stay and fight or to flee very quickly. (p. 112)

> *Example:* Any scary experience will induce the fight-or-flight syndrome. Hearing strange noises at night, giving your first speech in college, or almost being hit by a car can be very frightening. If you have been in any of these situations, you may recall how your heart suddenly thudded.

LEARNING OBJECTIVES

1. Be able to state the definition of biological or physiological psychology. (p. 80)

2. Describe the organization and the three basic functions of the nervous system. (pp. 82–85)

3. Compare and contrast neurons with other body cells. Name and describe the function of those parts of neurons that allow them to communicate with each other. (pp. 85–89)

4. Describe the electrical and chemical changes that lead to an action potential. Define polarization and refractory period. (pp. 86–89)

5. Describe the role of neurotransmitters and receptors in the communication process between neurons. (pp. 89–90)

6. Define nuclei and fiber tracts. (p. 91)

7. Define reflex. Describe the type of neurons found in a reflex pathway. (pp. 91–92)

8. Describe the four principles of central nervous system functioning. (pp. 92–93)

9. Define and describe the methods used to study the brain. (pp. 93–95)

10. Name and define the three major subdivisions of the brain and describe their functions. (pp. 96–98)

11. Define cerebral cortex. Name the four lobes that make up the cortex. Name the functional divisions of the cortex and their locations. (p. 98)

12. Name and describe the role of the areas in the association cortex involved in understanding and producing language. (pp. 99–101)

13. Describe the lateralization of the cerebral hemispheres. Describe the function of the corpus callosum. (pp. 102–105)

14. Define neurotransmitter systems. Name and describe the location of the five neurotransmitters. Discuss the behaviors and mental processes associated with them. (pp. 105–108)

15. Define psychopharmacology, psychoactive drugs, agonists, and antagonists. Discuss the four ways that psychoactive drugs affect neurotransmission. (pp. 108–110)

16. Describe the endocrine system. Discuss the differences between the communication processes in the nervous system and the endocrine system. (pp. 111–113)

CONCEPTS AND EXERCISES

No. 1 The Organization of the Nervous System

Completing this exercise should help you to achieve the following learning objective.

(2) *Describe the organization and the three basic functions of the nervous system. (pp. 82–85)*

The following organizational chart is all mixed up. Correct the mistakes.

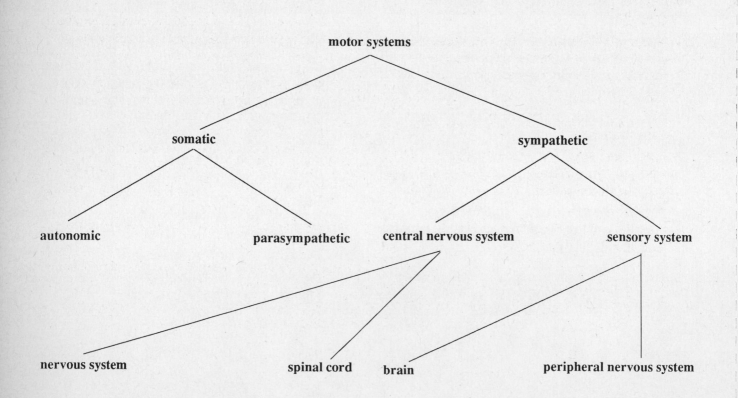

No. 2 The Functions of the Brain

Completing this exercise should help you to achieve the following learning objectives.

(10) *Name and define the three major subdivisions of the brain and describe their functions. (pp. 96–98)*

(11) *Define cerebral cortex. Name the four lobes that make up the cortex. Name the functional divisions of the cortex and their locations. (p. 98)*

(12) *Name and describe the role of the areas in the association cortex involved in understanding and producing language. (pp. 99–101)*

(13) *Define the lateralization of the cerebral hemispheres. Describe the function of the corpus callosum. (pp. 102–105)*

In the year 3000, parents can decide what kind of special talents their children will have. The doctor makes changes in the genetic coding for the child's brain structure. Below are instructions from several sets of parents. Pick the part of the brain (from the list that follows) that the doctor must manipulate. Answers may be used more than once or not at all.

1. Victor and Cynthia want their child to be a dancer who can move across the floor as smoothly and easily as Fred Astaire once did. _____

2. Rob and Laura want their son to have the manual dexterity necessary to become a world famous pianist. _____

3. Frank and Jean want their daughter to be a translator for the United Nations. This will require her to understand the subtle inflections of many languages. _____

4. Stewart and Lori want their daughter to have enough artistic ability to become a great painter. _____

5. Joanna and Richard want their daughter to become a rock star. She will need extensive musical abilities. _____

6. Colleen and Tim want their son to have the mathematical ability required of an accountant. _____

Parts of the brain
A. Striatum or substantia nigra
B. Left cerebral hemisphere
C. Right cerebral hemisphere
D. Cerebellum
E. Wernicke's area

No. 3 Neurochemistry

Completing this exercise should help you to achieve the following learning objectives.

(14) *Define neurotransmitter systems. Name and describe the location of the five neurotransmitters. Discuss the behaviors and mental processes associated with them. (pp. 105–108)*

(15) *Define psychopharmacology, psychoactive drugs, agonists, and antagonists. Discuss the four ways that psychoactive drugs affect neurotransmission. (pp. 108–110)*

Match each of the following medical problems with the psychoactive drug that helps alleviate it.
1. Parkinson's disease
2. Schizophrenia
3. Narcolepsy
4. Alzheimer's disease
5. Depression

A. L-dopa, a drug that increases the amount of dopamine available for release into synapses

B. Ephedrine is an agonist that mimics norepinephrine

C. An antagonist that interacts with the dopamine system

D. An agonist that interacts with the acetylcholine system

E. A drug that blocks the reuptake of norepinephrine and serotonin

ANSWERS TO CONCEPTS AND EXERCISES

No. 1 The Organization of the Nervous System

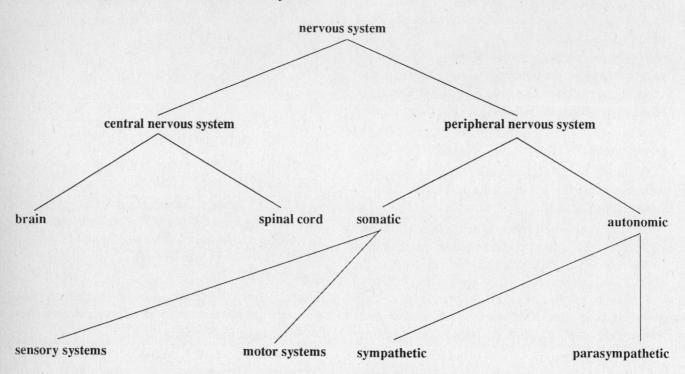

No. 2 The Functions of the Brain

1. *A* The substantia nigra or the striatum is responsible for the smooth initiation of movement. (pp. 97 & 98)

2. *D* The cerebellum is involved in fine motor movement. (p. 97)

3. *E* Wernicke's area is responsible for understanding language. (p. 100)

4. *C* The right cerebral hemisphere is superior at artistic tasks. (p. 104)

5. *C* The right cerebral hemisphere is superior at musical tasks. (p. 104)

6. *B* The left cerebral hemisphere is superior in mathematical ability. (p. 104)

No. 3 Neurochemistry

1. *A* L-dopa increases the amount of dopamine available for release into synapses, which alleviates the symptoms of Parkinson's disease. (p. 108)

2. *C* An antagonist that blocks dopamine activity decreases the activity of dopaminergic neurons,

which alleviates the symptoms of schizophrenia. (p. 109)

3. *E* Ephedrine is an agonist that mimics norepinephrine. This increases the activity of the noradrenergic neurons and alleviates the symptoms of narcolepsy. (p. 109)

4. *D* An agonist that increases the activity of acetylcholine neurons relieves the symptoms of Alzheimer's disease. (p. 109)

5. *E* Drugs that block the reuptake of norepinephrine and serotonin relieve depression. (p. 110)

MULTIPLE CHOICE QUESTIONS

Facts and Definitions

1. The spinal cord is a part of the _____ system.
   a. peripheral nervous
   b. somatic
   c. autonomic
   d. central nervous

2. Which of the following characteristics distinguishes neurons from other cells?
   a. Turning oxygen and glucose into usable energy
   b. A nucleus that carries genetic information
   c. A cell body
   d. An excitable surface membrane

3. During an action potential,
   a. a neuron becomes polarized.
   b. large amounts of sodium enter the dendrite.
   c. large amounts of sodium enter the axon.
   d. a neuron is at rest.

4. When coming into contact with a postsynaptic cell, a neurotransmitter
   a. always causes a polarization wave.
   b. fits snugly into a receptor.

c. causes an action potential.
d. All of the above.

5. A reflex
   a. can occur entirely within the spinal cord.
   b. involves the activity of afferent and efferent neurons and interneurons.
   c. is involuntary.
   d. All of the above.

6. The _____ is located in the hindbrain and helps to regulate blood pressure, breathing, and heart rate.
   a. medulla
   b. hypothalamus
   c. thalamus
   d. cerebellum

7. The cerebellum controls
   a. breathing and blood pressure.
   b. emotional response.
   c. arousal.
   d. fine motor coordination.

8. The reticular formation is
   a. a well-defined structure.
   b. located in the forebrain.
   c. involved in arousal.
   d. part of the telencephalon.

9. The occipital lobe receives sensory information concerning
   a. pain.
   b. body movement.
   c. vision.
   d. body temperature.

10. Broca's area and Wernicke's area are located in the _____ cerebral hemisphere and are involved in _____ .
   a. right, language
   b. left, language
   c. right, movement
   d. left, movement

11. Which of the following is not true? The corpus callosum

    a. connects the two cerebral hemispheres.
    b. contains many fibers.
    c. is enlarged in cases of severe epilepsy.
    d. allows the brain to function as a whole.

12. A dysfunctional cholinergic system is associated with which disease?

    a. Parkinson's
    b. Alzheimer's
    c. Schizophrenia
    d. Epilepsy

13. Serotonin is involved in

    a. sleep.
    b. mood.
    c. pain.
    d. All of the above.

14. An agonist

    a. blocks the actions of a neurotransmitter.
    b. mimics the actions of a neurotransmitter.
    c. accelerates the reuptake of a neurotransmitter.
    d. always depolarizes the postsynaptic membrane.

15. Drugs that partially relieve schizophrenic symptoms

    a. are called dopamine antagonists.
    b. are also used to treat depression.
    c. are called dopamine agonists.
    d. block reuptake of neurotransmitters.

MULTIPLE CHOICE QUESTIONS

Application of Concepts

1. A woman was rushed into an emergency room with severely burned hands. She said that she could not feel pain in her hands then or when she picked up the iron after it had been on for a long time. The neurologist who examined her concluded that the woman's _____ system was dysfunctional.

    a. sensory
    b. motor
    c. autonomic
    d. parasympathetic

2. You are watching your favorite soap opera. A doctor charges through the emergency room doors and tells a worried spouse that her husband has a neurological problem. The nerves that carry signals to the muscles are not functioning. The _____ system has been damaged.

    a. central
    b. autonomic
    c. sympathetic
    d. somatic

3. Dr. Frankenstein has given up on creating a human and is trying to build King Kong's cousin. He forgot to install the motor nerves of the somatic system. What will Kong's kin be unable to do?

    a. Lift skyscrapers
    b. Hear people scream
    c. Digest skyscrapers
    d. See people run from him

4. Julie is running a marathon. Her hindbrain is informing her _____ system to make the lungs take in more oxygen.

    a. central nervous
    b. somatic
    c. occipital
    d. autonomic nervous

5. Scientists have discovered a virus that binds to postsynaptic receptors and prevents the reception of neurotransmitter signals. On which parts of nerve cells would this virus be found?

    a. Dendrites
    b. Axons
    c. Cell bodies
    d. All of the above.

6. Walt Disney has made a new version of the movie "Fantastic Voyage." The main characters are stuck in an axon with a short _____. If they do not find their way back to the cell body quickly, they will soon be hit with a lethal shower of sodium.

   a. nucleus
   b. synapse
   c. refractory period
   d. sodium gate

7. Following is a conversation between two axons. Fill in the blanks.

Axon No. 1: Life is so dull. I have not been _____ all day.

Axon No. 2: Don't complain. I have it rough, too. Even with all of this (these) _____ wrapped around me, I can't seem to get my signals to the synapse fast enough for the boss.

   a. polarized, sodium gates
   b. depolarized, receptors
   c. polarized, vesicles
   d. depolarized, myelin

8. You are setting the table for a romantic dinner. While lighting the candles, you begin to daydream and the match burns your fingers. What path would the information about your singed finger follow first?

   a. Sensory system, spinal cord, sensory cortex, thalamus, motor cortex, and motor system
   b. Sensory system, spinal cord, thalamus, sensory cortex, motor cortex, and motor system
   c. Afferent sensory neuron, efferent motor neuron, and interneuron
   d. Afferent sensory neuron, interneuron, and efferent neuron

9. People with severed spinal cords cannot take in sensory information from or send signals to the muscles below the level of damage because

   a. the brain can no longer decipher incoming sensory information.

b. the information going to and from the brain must travel through the spinal cord.
   c. the thalamus's relay station for sensory information always degenerates after spinal cord injuries.
   d. None of the above are true.

10. You have found an injured cat that cannot move the right side of its body very well. What kind of brain damage might explain the cat's condition?

   a. A severed corpus callosum
   b. Impaired functioning of the motor cortex in the left cerebral hemisphere
   c. A dysfunctional hypothalamus
   d. Impaired functioning of the somatosensory cortex in the right cerebral hemisphere

11. Your younger sister has asked you for help with her history homework. She must be able to recognize and name famous people. Which cerebral hemisphere is she using to do her homework?

   a. Right
   b. Left
   c. Both
   d. Cannot be determined

12. A nurse has mixed up some test results on neurotransmitter function in several patients at the hospital where you work. To help her out, you tell her that the schizophrenic patient's chart will show too much _____ and the depressed patient's chart will show a deficit in _____.

   a. acetylcholine, dopamine.
   b. dopamine, acetylcholine.
   c. dopamine, norepinephrine.
   d. acetylcholine, norepinephrine.

13. You are able to ride on a psychoactive-drug molecule to its destination. It smacks into the receptor on the postsynaptic cell and, without stimulating the dendrite, it prevents other neurotransmitters from fitting into the receptor. What kind of a psychoactive drug is this?

a. An agonist
b. An antagonist
c. An antibiotic
d. None of the above.

14.   Anne Marie is about one month old. Which part of her brain shows the most activity?

a. Thalamus
b. Striatum
c. Cerebellum
d. Frontal cortex

15.   Ted is trying to make a study sheet to help him learn the differences between the neurotransmitter systems and the endocrine system. Which of the following statements on his list is incorrect?

a. Neurotransmitters travel across the synapse, and hormones travel via the bloodstream.
b. Hormones and some neurotransmitters can stimulate cells in the peripheral and central nervous systems.
c. Hormones and neurotransmitters regulate complex behaviors and mental processes.
d. All of the above are correct.

ANSWERS TO MULTIPLE CHOICE QUESTIONS

Facts and Definitions

1. *d* is the answer. The central nervous system includes the brain and the spinal cord. (p. 83)
a., b., & c. The peripheral system includes the somatic and autonomic systems.

2. *d* is the answer. An excitable surface membrane allows a signal to be sent from one end of the axon to the synapse. (p. 86)
a., b., & c. All cells have a nucleus and a cell body, and all cells use glucose for energy.

3. *c* is the answer. During an action potential, large amounts of sodium enter the axon when the membrane becomes depolarized. (p. 87)
a. & d. A neuron is polarized when it is at rest. During an action potential the axon becomes depolarized.
b. Action potentials take place in the axon, not the dendrite. Dendrites *do* carry signals toward the cell body, but the signal weakens as it approaches the cell body. Action potentials maintain their strength as they travel toward the synapse.

4. *b* is the answer. A neurotransmitter fits into a receptor as a key fits into a lock. (p. 89)
a. The consequence of a neurotransmitter fitting into a receptor depends on the excitatory or inhibitory nature of the neurotransmitter *and* the receptor. If the signal is inhibitory, the neuron will remain or become more polarized. If the signal is excitatory, the neuron will become depolarized.
c. Postsynaptic elements are usually dendrites. Action potentials only occur in axons.
d. Only *b* is the answer.

5. *d* is the answer. A reflex can occur entirely within the spinal cord; it involves afferent, efferent, and interneurons; and it is involuntary. (pp. 91–92)

6. *a* is the answer. The medulla, located in the hindbrain, helps to regulate breathing and blood pressure. (p. 96)
b. & c. The hypothalamus and the thalamus are in the diencephalon, which is located in the forebrain.
d. The cerebellum is located in the hindbrain.

7. *d* is the answer. The cerebellum controls fine motor movements, such as those necessary for threading a needle. (p. 97)
a. The medulla regulates breathing and blood pressure.
b. The limbic system and hypothalamus are involved in emotional experiences.
c. The reticular formation is involved in arousal.

8. *c* is the answer. The reticular formation is involved in arousal. (p. 97)

a. The reticular formation is a network of cells, not a well-defined area.

b. The network of cells that makes up the reticular formation can be found in the hind and midbrain.

d. The telencephalon is in the forebrain. The reticular formation is in the hindbrain and the midbrain.

9. *c* is the answer. The sensory cortex, found in the occipital lobe, receives sensory information concerning vision. (pp. 98–99)

a. There is no one specific brain structure involved in pain perception.

b. The motor cortex, found in the frontal lobe, is involved in movement.

d. The hypothalamus, found in the diencephalon, is involved in body temperature regulation.

10. *b* is the answer. Broca's and Wernicke's areas are in the left cerebral hemisphere and are responsible for the mental organization, production and comprehension of language. (pp. 100–101)

a. The right side of the brain is not very good at tasks involving language.

c. The right side of the brain is not very good at language tasks. The motor cortex, found in the frontal lobe in *both* hemispheres, is involved in movement.

d. The left hemisphere does include Broca's and Wernicke's areas, but they do not regulate motor movement.

11. *c* is the answer. The corpus callosum, a massive bundle of fibers, connects the two cerebral hemispheres. It has been surgically severed, not enlarged, in cases of severe epilepsy to decrease the spread of electrical seizures. (p. 102)

a., b., & d. are all true.

12. *b* is the answer. People with Alzheimer's disease have degenerating acetylcholine neurons in the basal forebrain. (p. 106)

a. Parkinson's disease is associated with a dopamine deficiency.

c. Schizophrenia is associated with a dopamine surplus.

d. Epilepsy is associated with dysfunctions in GABA systems.

13. *d* is the answer. Serotonin is associated with sleep, mood, and pain. (p. 107)

14. *b* is the answer. An agonist binds to receptors and mimics the normal neurotransmitter's actions. (p. 109)

a. A drug that blocks a neurotransmitter's actions is an antagonist.

c. Neurotransmitters are rendered inactive by reuptake; accelerating reuptake makes the neurotransmitter *less* effective. Agonists mimic the neurotransmitter's actions.

d. An agonist does whatever the neurotransmitter normally does; it depolarizes the membrane or it hyperpolarizes the membrane.

15. *a* is the answer. Schizophrenia is thought to be caused by an excess of dopamine in the neurons that send axons to the frontal lobes of the cerebral cortex. An antagonist, instead of dopamine, will bind to the receptors but will not stimulate them. This is equivalent to decreasing dopamine activity. (p. 109)

b. & d. Drugs used to treat depression block the reuptake of norepinephrine and serotonin.

c. An agonist will fit into dopamine receptors and stimulate them. This serves to increase the overall activity of the dopamine receptors, causing a possible increase in schizophrenic behavior.

ANSWERS TO MULTIPLE CHOICE QUESTIONS

Application of Concepts

1. *a* is the answer. The sensory systems, such as vision, touch, pain, taste, hearing, and smell, provide information about the environment. (p. 82)

   b. The motor system causes muscle movement.

   c. The autonomic system carries messages back and forth between the central nervous system and the body's organs and glands.

   d. The parasympathetic system is part of the autonomic system.

2. *d* is the answer. The somatic system carries information from the senses to the central nervous system and carries signals from the central nervous system to the muscles that move the skeleton. (p. 84)

   a. The central nervous system includes the brain and spinal cord. The brain makes decisions about how to move, and the somatic nervous system carries these signals to the muscles.

   b. The autonomic system carries messages back and forth between the central nervous system and the body's organs and glands.

   c. The sympathetic system is part of the autonomic system.

3. *a* is the answer. Without motor nerves to move the skeletal muscles, King Kong's cousin will not be able to move or pick up a rock, let alone lift a skyscraper. (p. 82)

   b. The somatic system's sensory nerves will be able to carry auditory information to the brain.

   c. The autonomic nervous system will allow King Kong's cousin to digest skyscrapers. The autonomic system carries messages to the organs of the body, such as the stomach.

   d. The somatic system's sensory nerves will be able to carry visual information to the brain.

4. *d* is the answer. The autonomic nervous system carries messages back and forth between the central nervous system and the heart, lungs, and other organs and glands in the body. (p. 84)

   a. The hindbrain is part of the central nervous system. The message must travel from the central nervous system to the autonomic part of the peripheral nervous system and then to the muscles that expand the lungs.

   b. The somatic nervous system sends messages to the skeletal muscles. This system allows you to wiggle your toes, wave your arms, stand up, and sit down. The autonomic system moves the muscles that are connected with your organs, such as the lungs, digestive muscles, and heart.

   c. There is no such thing as an occipital system. The occipital lobe is in the forebrain and receives visual information.

5. *d* is the answer. Axons release neurotransmitters at synapses, and the most common arrangement is to have postsynaptic receptors on dendrites. However, postsynaptic receptors are also found on cell bodies and on axons (the axon of a second neuron can be postsynaptic to a presynaptic axon). (p. 86)

6. *c* is the answer. An axon with a very short refractory period has very little time between action potentials. During the next action potential, sodium will rush into the cell. If the refractory period were longer, the characters in the axon would have more time to make an escape. (pp. 87–89)

   a. Axons do not have a nucleus.

   b. The size of a synapse does not affect the rate of action potentials.

   d. The length of a sodium gate will not affect the length of time between action potentials.

7. *d* is the answer. When an axon is at rest, it is polarized. Depolarization leads to action potentials. The bored axon with no action is polarized. Myelin

speeds the action potential on its way. The second neuron, despite the myelin wrapped around its axon, cannot seem to get action potentials down the length of the axon to the synapse fast enough for the boss. (pp. 86–87)

a. An axon at rest is polarized. All axons have sodium gates. They do not affect the speed at which the action potential travels down the axon.

b. This is a conversation between axons. Axons may have receptors, but they do not affect conduction speed.

c. An axon at rest is polarized. Vesicles are located at the very tip of the axon and do not influence the speed of an action potential.

8. *d* is the answer. When you burn your hand, a withdrawal reflex causes your hand to jerk away from the heat source. The information will travel through an afferent sensory neuron and go through an interneuron in the spinal cord. The signal to withdraw will travel back down to the hand muscles via efferent motor neurons. (p. 92)

a. & b. Both of these answers involve brain structures. A reflex pathway does not involve the brain. Information goes to the brain *while* the reflex is initiated.

c. The order of neurons is mixed up. The information will go from an afferent neuron, to an interneuron and, finally, to an efferent neuron.

9. *b* is the answer. Information about the environment travels through the spinal cord on its way to the brain. Also, any directions that the brain sends to the skeletal muscles must pass through the spinal cord. If the spinal cord is severed, information cannot travel between the brain and any destination below the severed section of the spinal cord. (pp. 91–92)

a. & c. Damage to the spinal cord will not injure the brain. The brain may not be as active because it does not receive as much information as it did prior to the spinal cord's injury, but it would still be capable of handling that information.

d. Only *b* is the answer.

10. *b* is the answer. The motor cortex in the left hemisphere controls the movement of the body's right side. (p. 102)

a. A severed corpus callosum will only prevent the right hemisphere from communicating with the left hemisphere.

c. A damaged hypothalamus causes malfunctions in eating, drinking, sex drives, and, possibly, emotional responses.

d. The right somatosensory cortex receives sensory information from the body's left side. This will not impair motor functioning.

11. *c* is the answer. (pp. 102–105)

a., b., & d. The right hemisphere would help your younger sister recognize the famous people's faces, and the left hemisphere would enable her to recite their names.

12. *c* is the answer. Increased levels of dopamine are associated with schizophrenia, and decreased levels of norepinephrine are associated with depression. (pp. 106–107)

a. & b. Degenerating acetylcholine neurons are associated with Alzheimer's disease, and high levels of dopamine are associated with schizophrenia.

d. Degenerating acetylcholine neurons are associated with Alzheimer's disease, and a low norepinephrine level is associated with depression.

13. *b* is the answer. An antagonist fits into a receptor and blocks other neurotransmitters from fitting into it but does not stimulate the receptor. (p. 109)

a. An agonist fits into the receptor and stimulates it.

c. Antibiotics fight bacterial infections. They do not fit into neuronal receptors.

d. Only *b* is the answer.

14. *a* is the answer. Newborns have relatively high neural activity in the thalamus. (p. 114)

b. & c. The striatum and the cerebellum are not very active in newborns, which may explain their uncoordinated movement.

d. The frontal cortex begins to show increased activity at eight or nine months, when an infant's cognitive abilities begin to appear.

15. *d* is the answer. *a., b.,* & *c.* are all true. (pp. 111–113)

Chapter 4

Sensation

OUTLINE

I. INTRODUCTION (pp. 118–120)

Our knowledge of the world comes through our senses. This chapter will explain how our senses pick up information and convert it into forms that our brains can interpret.

II. SENSORY SYSTEMS (pp. 120–124)

A. Steps in Sensation

The first step in some systems occurs when the stimulus is modified in some way by an accessory structure (the lens of the eye or the outer part of the ear). Transduction, the transformation of incoming energy into neural energy, takes place at the receptors. Each nerve that carries sensory information responds to the energy of only a small portion of the environment, its receptive field.

B. The Problem of Coding

Coding is the translation of the distinguishing characteristics of an object into a pattern of neural activity that identifies only those characteristics.

C. Representing Stimuli in the Brain

Visual, auditory, and tactile information travels through the thalamus to a primary area of sensory cortex, is contralaterally represented, and is mapped out in topographical representation. The density of neurons in the sense organ determines the extent of its representation in the brain. Regions of primary sensory cortex are divided into columns of cells that respond to similar stimuli in the environment. More complex processing of sensory information occurs in association cortex areas.

III. HEARING (pp. 124–131)

Sound is a repetitive fluctuation in the pressure of a medium like air.

A. Sounds

1. *The Physical Characteristics of Sound.* Vibrating objects create the fluctuations in pressure that create sound. A repetitive fluctuation or change in pressure is a wave. Waves have three important characteristics: amplitude, wavelength, and frequency.

2. *Psychological Dimensions of Sound.* The frequency of sound waves determines pitch, how high or low a tone is. The amplitude of the sound wave determines loudness. The mixture of frequencies and amplitudes that make up a sound wave produce timbre, a sound's quality.

B. The Ear

1. *Auditory Accessory Structure.* The pinna collects the sound waves, which then strike the tympanic membrane, which produces a vibra-

61

tion that causes the malleus (hammer), incus (anvil), and stapes (stirrup) to vibrate.

2. *Auditory Transduction*. Vibrations pass through the oval window and the fluid in the cochlea to move the basilar membrane, which stretches along the floor of the cochlea. Movement of the basilar membrane causes tiny hair cells which touch it to move. Movement of the hair cells causes neuron activity in the auditory nerve, which carries auditory information to the brain. This process is known as auditory transduction.

C. The Coding of Intensity

The firing rate of neurons within the auditory nerve increases as sound intensity increases.

D. Frequency Coding

1. *Place Theory*. Hair cells at a particular place on the basilar membrane respond most to a particular frequency of sound. A characteristic frequency is one that most effectively causes a particular neuron in the auditory nerve to fire. High frequencies are coded exclusively by the place where a traveling wave peaks.

2. *Frequency Matching: The Volley Theory*. The firing rate of a neuron in the auditory nerve matches the frequency of a sound wave. The lowest frequencies are coded by frequency matching. Low to moderate frequencies are coded both by frequency matching and the place on the basilar membrane where the traveling wave peaks.

E. Auditory Pathways and the Auditory Cortex

Information from the right auditory nerve crosses to the left side of the brain and passes through the thalamus on its way to the auditory cortex. Cells in the primary auditory cortex, arranged in a tonotopic organization, are the first to receive information about the sounds we hear.

IV. VISION (pp. 131–147)

A. Light

Visible light is electromagnetic radiation that has a wavelength from about 400–700 nanometers. We cannot see electromagnetic radiation, or wavelengths of light, that are outside of this range. Our sensation of light depends on its intensity and wavelength.

B. Focusing Light: Accessory Structures of the Eye

Light waves travel through the cornea, then the pupil, and through the lens which bends the light rays by accommodation and focuses them on the retina.

C. Converting Light into Images: Visual Transduction

The photoreceptors in the retina carry out transduction.

1. *Photoreceptors*. The photoreceptors, called rods and cones, contain photopigments which react to light and cause changes in membrane potential of the photoreceptors. The rods are more sensitive to light but cannot discriminate between colors. In very bright light, the cones, which can detect color, are more active. Cones are most concentrated in the fovea, where acuity is highest.

2. *Dark Adaptation*. The increasing ability to see in a darkened room is called dark adaptation. The cones adapt more quickly than the rods, but are not nearly as sensitive to light. The rods adapt completely to darkness in about fifteen to forty-five minutes.

3. *Interactions of Cells in the Retina*. Convergence is a process in which many signals from photoreceptors converge onto the bipolar cells and then on to the ganglion cells. The axons of ganglion cells form the optic nerve that extends into the brain. In lateral inhibition, photorecep-

tors connect with horizontal cells and amacrine cells, which make lateral connections between bipolar cells. Convergence and lateral inhibition increase our sensitivity and acuity.

4. *Ganglion Cells and Their Receptive Fields.* Most ganglion cells have center-surround receptive fields.

D. Color Vision

1. *Wavelengths and Color Sensation.* Hue, saturation, and brightness are three psychological aspects of color sensation. Mixing different wavelengths of light is called additive color mixing and always produces a lighter color.

2. *The Trichromatic Theory of Color Vision.* According to the trichromatic theory, there are three visual elements, each of which responds best to a different wavelength.

3. *The Opponent-Process Theory of Color Vision.* The opponent-process theory states that the visual elements sensitive to color occur in three pairs and the members of each pair inhibit each other. Each element signals one or the other color in a pair, but never both. The three element pairs are red-green, blue-yellow, and black-white.

4. *A Synthesis.* The two theories of color vision, together, can explain color vision. There are three types of cones that pick up information about red, green, and blue color. This conforms with the trichromatic theory. The center-surround receptive fields of the ganglion cells are color coded in pairs which correspond to the three element pairs of the opponent-process theory.

5. *Color Blindness.* People who are color blind discriminate fewer colors than other people. The most common form of color blindness involves red and green; the cones lack the color sensitive pigments that respond to red and green.

E. Visual Pathways to the Brain

The axons of all the ganglion cells combine to form the optic nerve, which travels to the brain. There are no photoreceptors at the point where the optic nerve leaves the eye, creating a blind spot. At the optic chiasm, fibers carrying information about the right side of the visual field cross over to the left side of the brain (see Figure 4.23 in your text). Beyond the optic chiasm the fibers synapse in the lateral geniculate nucleus (LGN); from the LGN, fibers go to the primary visual cortex, located in the occipital lobe.

1. *Feature Detectors.* The hierarchical feature-detection model states that anything we see is a compilation of features. Cells in the cortex respond to specific features of objects and are called feature detectors. Complex feature detectors are built out of more complex connections of simpler feature detectors.

2. *Organization of the Cortex.* The cells in the cortex, arranged in columns, form topographical representations of the visual world. Larger areas of the cortex are devoted to areas of the retina that have many photoreceptors.

V. THE CHEMICAL SENSES: TASTE AND SMELL (pp. 147–150)

A. Olfaction (Sense of Smell)

Olfaction occurs when airborne chemicals or those in the mouth are detected by receptor cells in the upper part of the nose. Axons from the nose travel to the olfactory bulb, and from there axons spread to many areas of the brain, especially the amygdala. Chemicals called pheromones can shape the behavior or physiology of another animal. Although no solid evidence exists for the action of pheromones in humans, people learn to associate smells with sexual activity or certain people.

B. Gustation (Sense of Taste)

Papillae contain receptors for taste, which can only detect sweet, sour, bitter, and salty flavors. Each taste bud in the papillae responds best to one or two of these categories, and also responds weakly to other categories. This is how gustation; or our sense of taste, operates.

C. Smell, Taste and Flavor

Flavor is a combination of smell and taste. The temperature and texture of food also add to its flavor.

VI. SOMATIC SENSES AND THE VESTIBULAR SYSTEM (pp. 150–158)

The somatic senses or the somatosensory systems include the skin senses of touch, temperature, and pain. Also included is kinesthesia, the sense that tells the brain where the parts of the body are. The vestibular system tells the brain about the position of the body in space and about its general movements.

A. Touch and Temperature

1. *The Stimulus and Receptors for Touch*. There are many types of receptors in or somewhere near the skin that respond to mechanical deformation of the skin. The fingers, mouth, and lips have many receptors for touch.

2. *Adaptation of Touch Receptors*. We are most sensitive to *changes* in touch. When in constant contact with a stimulus, the touch receptors show adaptation by decreasing the rate at which they fire.

3. *The Coding of Touch Information*. Information about the weight and the vibration of a stimulus is coded by the number of nerves stimulated and the frequency at which individual nerves fire. Location is coded by the organization of the information, which is called

somatotopic; it tells the brain where you have been touched.

4. *Temperature*. There are skin receptors that are sensitive to warmth and cold. Many receptors that respond to temperature also respond to touch.

B. Pain

1. *Pain as an Information Sense*. Painful stimuli cause the release of bradykinin, which causes pain nerves to fire. A-delta fibers and C fibers carry information about different types of pain to the spinal cord.

2. *Emotional Aspects of Pain*. Specific pathways carry an emotional component of the painful stimulus to areas of the medulla and reticular formation, activating aversion. Our expectations of the onset and intensity of pain affect our evaluation of it.

3. *Modulation of Pain: The Gate Theory*. According to the gate theory, pain can be blocked in several ways at the spinal cord. Other sensory information can compete and take over pain pathways. The brain can produce analgesia by sending signals down the spinal cord.

4. *Natural Analgesics*. Serotonin, endorphins, enkephalins, and dynorphins are naturally occurring chemicals that block the pain sensation.

C. Proprioception

We know where we are and what each part of our body is doing through information provided by proprioceptive sensory systems.

1. *Kinesthesia*. The ability to know where the parts of your body are with respect to each other is called kinesthesia. It operates through information received from the joint receptors and receptors in muscle fibers.

2. *Vestibular Sense*. Often called balance, the vestibular sense tells the brain about the body's

position in space and about general movement. Fluid within the vestibular sacs and the semicircular canals located near the inner ear shifts as our position changes, moving hair cells, which then stimulate neurons. The vestibular system has connections to the cerebellum, parts of the autonomic nervous system, and the eyes.

KEY TERMS

1. A **sense** is a system that translates information about the world into neural activity, which provides the brain with information about the environment. (p. 118)

2. **Accessory structures** modify stimuli prior to transduction. (p. 121)

Example: The lens in the eye bends light before it is picked up by photoreceptors in the retina and transduced into neural activity.

3. **Transduction** is the process whereby receptors convert stimulus energy into neural energy that the brain can interpret. (p. 121)

Example: Photoreceptors in the eye pick up information about light and change it into neural energy, which tells the brain about what is in the visual field.

4. **Receptors** are specialized cells that detect certain types of energy (such as light or sound) and convert it into neural energy through transduction. (p. 121)

REMEMBER: Just as a receptionist <u>receives</u> people, the receptors in the sensory systems <u>receive</u> information about the world.

5. A **receptive field** is a specific area of the environment that stimulates a neuron. Each neuron in a sensory system carries information about its own receptive field to the brain. (p. 121)

Example: One of the neurons in your visual system has the job of carrying information about light that is in a small area on the right side of whatever you look at. That small area on the right is a receptive field for that neuron.

REMEMBER: Each member in the outfield of a baseball team is responsible for covering a certain area of the field. A neuron that receives information from a particular area in the environment is like a baseball player who catches balls when they enter the field area for which he is responsible.

6. **Coding** is the translation of information into a specific pattern of neural activity, which represents that information in the brain. (p. 122)

Example: Someone has just touched your cheek. How do the neurons communicate to the brain that your face has been caressed and not pressed? The rate at which the neurons fire is a code that tells the brain about the intensity of the touch. The faster the neurons fire, the harder you have been hit.

REMEMBER: Your brain interprets the firing rate of neurons as if it were a type of Morse <u>code</u>.

7. **Topographical representation** means that any two points that are next to each other in the stimulus are represented next to each other in the brain. (p. 123)

Example: The cells in the brain that receive information about your thumb are right next to the cells that receive information about your index finger. The cells in the brain that represent your nose are close to the cells that represent your mouth. The cells that represent your knees are much farther away.

8. **Sound** is a repetitive fluctuation in the pressure of a medium like air. This activity can be represented in wave form. (p. 124)

Example: When an object vibrates, such as the strings on a violin, molecules in the air move, causing temporary changes in air pressure.

9. **Amplitude** is the difference in air pressure of the peak or top of the wave and the trough or bottom of the wave. Loudness is determined by the amplitude of a sound wave. (p. 124)

REMEMBER: When you amplify something, you make it greater. The greater the amplitude of the sound wave, the greater the loudness of the sound.

10. **Frequency** is the number of complete waves that pass a given point in space in one second. As the wave's frequency increases, so does the sound's pitch. (p. 124)

REMEMBER: Frequency means how often. The frequency of a sound wave tells you how often a complete wave or cycle passes a given point in one second.

11. **Timbre** is the quality of a sound that distinguishes it from other sounds. The mixture of frequencies and amplitudes of the waves that make up a sound determine timbre. (p. 126)

Example: The next time you listen to music, try to identify the instruments that you hear. The sound of each instrument has a unique timbre. A note played on the piano has a much different sound than the same note played on the cello.

12. The **pinna,** an accessory structure of the ear, collects sound waves and channels the sound down through the ear canal. It is the part of the ear that you can see. (p. 126)

REMEMBER: Make a visual image to help yourself remember the name of this structure. You have heard of the game "Pin a tail on the donkey." Simply change the name and the picture in your mind to "Pin a ear on the donkey."

13. The **tympanic membrane**, located at the bottom of the ear canal, vibrates when hit by sound waves. (pp. 126–127)

REMEMBER: The tympanic membrane is stretched tightly across the end of the ear canal, just like the skin stretched tightly across the head of a drum.

14. The **malleus (hammer), incus (anvil), and stapes (stirrup)** are a chain of very small bones located in the ear. Vibrations caused by the movement of the tympanic membrane cause the bones to move. The bones focus the movement of the tympanic membrane onto the oval window. (p. 127)

15. The **oval window** is a membrane situated just behind the three bones in the middle ear and just before the cochlea. It amplifies the changes in air pressure produced by the original sound waves. (p. 127)

REMEMBER: This membrane is like an oval window that affords you a view of the cochlea when you look through it.

16. The **cochlea** is a spiral structure in the inner ear where transduction occurs. (p. 127)

17. The **basilar membrane** is inside the cochlea. When vibrations come through the oval window and into the cochlea, the basilar membrane moves. As this membrane moves, it moves the hair cells that touch it. The hair cells, in turn, stimulate neural activity in the auditory nerve. (p. 127)

18. The **place theory** states that a particular place on the basilar membrane responds most to a particular frequency of sound, determining the pitch of a sound. (p. 130)

REMEMBER: In your mind, make an image of the basilar membrane all curled up inside the cochlea. Along the length of the membrane, mentally write the names of musical notes. Each place on the membrane is associated with one note or pitch.

19. **Frequency matching** states that the firing rate of a neuron (how many times a neuron fires per second) matches the frequency of a sound wave

(how many cycles or complete waves occur in a second). (p. 130)

REMEMBER: The frequency of the neuron's firing <u>matches</u> the frequency of the soundwave.

20. **Tonotopic organization** refers to the map of sound frequencies in the cellular organization of the primary auditory cortex. Neighboring cells have similar preferred frequencies. (p. 131)

REMEMBER: Frequency equals pitch or tone.

21. The **pupil** is an opening, located behind the cornea, that looks like a black spot in the middle of your eye. Light passes through it to get to the retina at the back of the eye. (p. 132)

22. The **lens,** an accessory structure, bends light rays, focusing them on the retina at the back of the eye. The ability to change the shape of the lens to bend light rays so that objects are in focus is called <u>accommodation</u>. (p. 132)

23. The **retina,** a network of several different types of cells, is where transduction takes place in the eye. (p. 132)

REMEMBER: Transduction is the process of converting incoming energy (wavelengths of light) into neural activity.

24. The **photoreceptors** in the retina code light energy into neural energy. The photoreceptors of the eye are called rods, which code light, and cones, which also code color. (pp. 132–133)

REMEMBER: Photo means light and receptors receive. Photoreceptors receive light from the visual environment.

REMEMBER: Cones are photoreceptors that can detect color. The *C* in cones stands for color.

25. **Photopigments** are chemicals inside the photoreceptors. When light strikes a photoreceptor, these chemicals break apart and cause changes in the photoreceptor's membrane potential. Photopig-

ments are necessary for the transduction process. (p. 133)

26. **Rods** are photoreceptors that are located in the retina. They are very sensitive to light, but they cannot distinguish color. (p. 134)

27. **Cones** are photoreceptors that are located in the retina and that can detect color. Cones are less sensitive to light, making it difficult to see color in the dark. (p. 134)

28. The **fovea** is located in the center of the retina. A very high concentration of cones in the fovea makes spatial discrimination (visual accuracy) or acuity greatest in the fovea. (p. 134)

REMEMBER: Use the following sentence to help you remember the definition of fovea: *FO*cusing *V*ery *E*asy in this *A*rea.

29. **Dark adaptation** is the adjustment that our eyes make when the amount of light in our environment decreases. In the dark, photoreceptors synthesize more photopigments, and people can begin to see more and more. The cones adapt to dark more quickly than rods, but are not as sensitive to light. The rods adapt to dark completely in about forty-five minutes and allow us to see with greater acuity in dim light. (p. 134)

30. **Bipolar cells** are located in the retina and stimulate ganglion cells. Each bipolar cell receives information from many rods and cones. Bipolar cells also receive information from horizontal cells and amacrine cells that have been stimulated by the rods and cones. (p. 135)

31. **Convergence** is the reception of information by one bipolar cell from many photoreceptors. This capacity allows bipolar cells to compare the amount of light on larger regions of the retina and enhances our sensation of contrast in visual stimuli. (p. 135)

32. **Lateral inhibition** occurs when the greater activity in one cell suppresses the activity in neighboring cells. Lateral inhibition exaggerates the differences or contrast in light hitting the photoreceptors. (p. 135)

33. **Hue** is the essential "color" and is determined by the dominant wavelength of the light. (p. 138)

Example: Red and green are two different hues with two different wavelengths. Also read the example for key term 34, saturation.

REMEMBER: Black, white, and gray are not considered colors because they do not have their own dominant wavelengths.

34. **Saturation** is the purity of a color. If many waves of the same length are present, the color is more pure or saturated. (p. 139)

Example: The next time you go to a fast food restaurant, compare the pictures of food on the wall with the actual food you buy. The colors or hues are the same. However, the picture looks very colorful and vibrant. This is because the picture is saturated with wavelengths of similar lengths whereas the food you get has a broad variety of wavelengths in it.

35. The **trichromatic theory** states that since any color can be made by combining red, green and blue, there must be three types of visual elements, each of which is most sensitive to one of these three colors. Indeed, there are three types of cones that are most sensitive to red, green, and blue wavelengths. (p. 140)

REMEMBER: Tri means three and *chromo* means color. The trichromatic theory is concerned with the sensation of three colors.

36. The **opponent-process theory** states that visual elements sensitive to color are grouped into three pairs, and that each pair member opposes or inhibits the other. The pairs are red-green, blue-yellow, and black-white. Each element signals one color or the other, but not both. The ganglion cells in the retina have color coded center-surround receptive fields. (p. 141)

Example: One ganglion cell may have a red-green center-surround receptive field. If red light causes the center to be stimulated, the surround is inhibited. If green light causes the surround to be stimulated, the center is inhibited. If both the center and the surround are stimulated, we see grey because the opponent colors cancel each other out.

37. The **optic nerve.** The axons of all the ganglion cells come together at one point in the back of the retina to make up the optic nerve. There are no photoreceptor cells at the point where this nerve leaves the eye, creating a blind spot. (p. 143)

38. The **hierarchical feature-detection model** states that cells in the cortex, which detect features, such as lines, combine their input to create the sensation of an object. (p. 145)

Example: Suppose you are looking at a suitcase. According to this model, how would the cells in your cortex "see" the suitcase? First, the cells that detect lines would "see" the sides, top and bottom of the suitcase. These cells would stimulate cells that "see" spatial orientation, so your brain would know if the suitcase were standing upright, lying flat on the floor, or balanced on one of its corners. The spatial orientation cells would stimulate more complicated detector cells, possibly a "box detector." This process would go on until your brain recognized the object as a suitcase.

39. **Olfaction** is our sense of smell. Receptors in the upper part of the nose detect chemicals in the air or in our mouths. (p. 147)

REMEMBER: Olere means to smell and *facere* means to make. Olfaction literally means to make a smell. If you prefer, you can use the following story to help you remember this word. My grandfather worked in a paper mill that was very old and produced an incredibly awful smell. Just remember that the OL' FACTory smells.

40. The **olfactory bulb** is a structure in the brain that receives information from nerves in the nose. Neural connections from the olfactory bulb travel to many parts of the brain, especially the amygdala. (p. 148)

41. **Pheromones** are chemicals that animals release into the air. Other animals may experience behavioral and physiological changes as a result of smelling the pheromones. There is no evidence that people give off or can smell pheromones. (p. 147)

Example: Female pigs immediately assume a mating stance after smelling a pheromone called androstenone in a boar's saliva.

42. **Gustation** is our sense of taste. Receptors in the taste buds pick up chemical information from substances inside the mouth. (p. 148)

REMEMBER: The first letters of the words in the following sentence spell gustation. Gus's Uncle Sam Tasted All The Indian's ONions.

43. **Papillae** are groups of taste buds. Each taste bud responds to all four categories: sweet, sour, bitter, and salty. However, each taste bud responds best to only one or two of them. (p. 149)

44. The **somatic senses** or the **somatosensory systems** are distributed throughout the body instead of residing in a single structure. The senses include touch, temperature, pain, and kinesthesia. (p. 150)

REMEMBER: Soma means body. The somatosensory system senses what happens to the body in terms of touch, pain, temperature and kinesthesia.

45. **Adaptation** occurs when a constant stimulus is applied to the body. Initially, the receptors in the skin fire rapidly, but their activity decreases over time. (p. 150)

Example: Try to feel your underwear. You probably had to concentrate to feel it against your skin, if you felt it at all. That is because the skin receptors that are in contact with your underwear may have fired rapidly when you got dressed this morning, but now have decreased their activity.

46. **Somatotopic organization** is the topographical representation of the somatosensory system. There is a map of the body in the somatosensory cortex. (p. 151)

Example: See example for key term 7, topographical representation.

47. The **gate theory** states that the nervous system has two methods of preventing pain information from reaching the brain. Other sensory information from the skin may take over the pathways the pain impulses would use to travel up the spinal cord to the brain. Alternatively, the brain can send signals down the spinal cord and prevent pain signals from ascending the spinal cord and entering the brain. (p. 153)

REMEMBER: The nervous system can use the spinal cord as a gate that will allow only so much information to go through it in either direction. To understand this, think of what happens when a movie lets out. There are so many people coming out the doors (or gate in the spinal cord) that nobody can get into the theater for a few minutes. This is similar to what the brain does to prevent pain information from reaching its destination. The brain sends information down the spinal cord that blocks the pain information from ascending the spinal cord.

Or think of what happens when people have been standing in line for a long time and suddenly the doors (or gate in the spinal cord) open. So many people try to shove through the door that some individuals cannot enter. This is similar to another method of preventing pain information from reaching its destination. There can be so much information trying to ascend the spinal cord that there is not enough room for pain information.

48. **Analgesia** is the absence of pain sensation in the presence of painful stimuli. (p. 154)

Example: Aspirin is an analgesic drug. Our bodies naturally make chemicals, called natural analgesics, that can reduce pain sensation. These include endorphins, enkephalins, and dynorphins. Serotonin, a neurotransmitter, also plays a role in blocking pain sensation.

49. **Proprioceptive sensory systems** provide us with the ability to know where we are in space and what each of our body parts is doing relative to all other body parts. Kinesthesia, which is part of the somatosensory system, and the vestibular system provide proprioceptive information to the brain. (pp. 154–155)

50. **Kinesthesia** is the sense that tells you where your body parts are in relation to each other. (p. 155)

Example: You must know where your head is in relation to your hands to be able to touch the tip of your finger to your nose while your eyes are shut.

51. The **vestibular system** or sense tells the brain about the position of the body in space and its general movements. The vestibular sacs and the semicircular canals in the inner ear provide vestibular information. (p. 155)

Example: Doing something as simple as a handstand requires vestibular information. If your vestibular senses were not working, you would not know if you were upside-down or right-side-up.

LEARNING OBJECTIVES

1. Define sense and sensation. (pp. 118–120)
2. Define accessory structure, receptor, transduction, and receptive field. Give an example of receptive field. (pp. 121–122)
3. Define coding. Explain why sensory information must be coded before it reaches the brain. Define the doctrine of specific nerve energies. (pp. 122–123)
4. Describe the five characteristics of sensory representation for vision, hearing, and the skin senses. Define topographical representation. (pp. 123–124)
5. Define sound. Describe the physical characteristics of sound, including waveform, amplitude, wavelength, and frequency. (pp. 124–125)
6. Describe the psychological characteristics of sound, including pitch, loudness, and timbre. Discuss the relationship between pitch and frequency and that between amplitude and loudness. (pp. 125–126)
7. Name and describe the accessory structures of the ear. (pp. 126–127)
8. Describe the roles of the cochlea, the basilar membrane, the hair cells, and the auditory nerve in the process of auditory transduction. (pp. 127–128)
9. Describe the process of coding auditory information. Discuss the relationship between place theory and the volley theory (frequency matching) in frequency coding. (pp. 129–130)
10. Define and describe the tonotopic organization of the primary auditory cortex. (p. 131)
11. Define visible light. Explain the psychological component of vision that is determined by the wavelength of light. (p. 131)
12. Define and describe the accessory structures of the eye, including the cornea, pupil, and lens. (p. 132)
13. Define retina, photoreceptors, photopigments, rods, cones, and fovea. Describe the relationship between these structures and light transduction. (pp. 132–134)

14. Describe the process of dark adaptation and the role that rods and cones play in it. (pp. 134–135)

15. Define convergence and lateral inhibition. Describe the role of the bipolar, horizontal, amacrine, and ganglion cells in convergence and lateral inhibition. (pp. 135–136)

16. Describe the center-surround receptive field of ganglion cells. (pp. 136–137)

17. Define hue, saturation, and brightness. (pp. 138–139)

18. Describe the trichromatic and opponent-process theories of color vision. Explain why each theory is correct. (pp. 140–143)

19. Describe the physical problem that causes color blindness. (p. 143)

20. Describe the path that visual information follows on its way to the brain, including the roles of the optic nerve, the optic chiasm, the lateral geniculate nucleus, and the primary visual cortex. (pp. 143–144)

21. Describe the hierarchical feature-detection model of vision. Give an example of how you would see an object, such as a box, according to this model. Describe the spatial frequency filter model of vision. Describe the topographical representation of visual cortical cells. (pp. 144–147)

22. Define olfaction and pheromones. Describe the transduction process in the olfactory system. Describe the path that olfactory information follows to the brain. (pp. 147–149)

23. Define gustation and papillae. Describe the relationship between taste, smell, and flavor. (p. 150)

24. Define somatic sense or somatosensory system. Describe the transduction process in the skin senses, including touch, pain, and temperature. Define adaptation. (pp. 150–152)

25. Describe the gate theory of pain sensation. Define analgesia. Know the names of the body's natural analgesics. (pp. 153–154)

26. Define proprioception and kinesthesia. Name the source of kinesthetic information. (pp. 154–155)

27. Describe the types of information that the vestibular senses provide. Describe the role of the vestibular sacs and the semicircular canals in the sensation of vestibular information. (pp. 155–158)

CONCEPTS AND EXERCISES

No. 1 Frankenstein's Senses

Completing this exercise should help you to achieve the following learning objectives.

(8) *Describe the roles of the cochlea, the basilar membrane, the hair cells, and the auditory nerve in the process of auditory transduction. (pp. 127–128)*

(13) *Define retina, photoreceptors, photopigments, rods, cones, and fovea. Describe the relationship between these structures and light transduction. (pp. 132–134)*

(22) *Define olfaction and pheromones. Describe the transduction process in the olfactory system. Describe the path that olfactory information follows to the brain. (pp. 147–149)*

(23) *Define gustation and papillae. Describe the relationship between taste, smell, and flavor. (p. 150)*

(24) *Define somatic sense or somatosensory system. Describe the transduction process in the skin senses, including touch, pain, and temperature. Define adaptation. (pp. 150 152)*

(25) *Describe the gate theory of pain sensation. Define analgesia. Know the names of the body's natural analgesics. (pp. 153–154)*

Dr. Frankenstein is constructing the senses in his monster. He has forgotten to include several features. Describe the deficits that would occur in sensation without the following physical structures.

Iodopsin

_____

_____

_____

Hair cells on the basilar membrane

_____

_____

_____

Spinal cord

_____

_____

_____

Papillae

_____

_____

_____

Amygdala

_____

_____

_____

No. 2 Life Without Your Senses

There are no right or wrong answers to the following exercise. Rather, it is meant to impress upon you how important your senses are to your daily existence. One by one, pretend that each of your sensory systems has stopped working. Simply think of ten activities that you would no longer be able to do without each sensory system.

No. 3 Processes in Sensation

Completing this exercise should help you to achieve the following learning objectives.

(3) *Define coding. Explain why sensory information must be coded before it reaches the brain. Define the doctrine of specific nerve energies. (pp. 122–123)*

(14) *Describe the process of dark adaptation and the role that rods and cones play in it. (pp. 134–135)*

(15) *Define convergence and lateral inhibition. Describe the role of the bipolar, horizontal, amacrine, and ganglion cells in convergence and lateral inhibition. (pp. 135–136)*

(24) *Define somatic sense or somatosensory system. Describe the transduction process in the skin senses, including touch, pain, and temperature. Define adaptation. (pp. 150–152)*

Name the sensory process demonstrated in each of the following incidents.

1. Lori has just stepped into the shower with her watch on. She did not realize the watch was on her arm until it was wet. _____

2. Dr. Malpeli is recording the activity of horizontal, amacrine, and bipolar cells in the retinas of cats. Whenever he places a complex figure in the visual field, the recordings show a large increase in neuronal firing. _____

3. In general, the faster a neuron fires the more intense the stimulus is. _____

4. Jill is six years old. She awakens with a bad dream in the middle of the night. She decides to play with her crayons and coloring book. She becomes frustrated, however, because she cannot see the colors in the dim light. _____

ANSWERS TO CONCEPTS AND EXERCISES

No. 1 Frankenstein's Senses

1. Iodopsin is the photopigment in the cones that allows transduction to occur. Without it, you would not be able to see color. Also, the fovea has many cones and very few rods. If iodopsin were missing, your cones would not work and the fovea would no longer have a high degree of acuity. (pp. 133–134)

2. The hair cells on the basilar membrane cause changes in auditory-nerve activity. This is the point where transduction occurs. If sound could not be converted to neural energy, you would be deaf. (pp. 127–128)

3. The information from all of the skin senses, including touch, pain, and temperature, reaches the brain after ascending the spinal cord. If there were no spinal cord you would not be able to detect touch, pain, and temperature. (pp. 151–154)

4. The taste buds are located in the papillae, bumps on the tongue. Transduction takes place in these structures. Without them, you would not be able to taste anything. (p. 149)

5. The amygdala, which plays a large role in emotion, receives olfactory information. Without your amygdala, smells would probably not have any emotional meaning for you. (p. 148)

No. 2 Living Without Your Senses

This exercise has no right or wrong answers.

No. 3 Processes in Sensation

1. Being unable to feel a watch on your wrist occurs because of the adaptation process. When you put on your watch, the cells in the skin begin to fire rapidly and then decrease their activity back to a baseline rate. When Lori stepped into the shower, the cells that would detect the presence of her watch had long ago returned to a baseline firing rate.

   If you think about it, you will realize that the process of adaptation is very necessary. For just a moment make yourself notice everything that is touching you. Without adaptation, all of the information would feel as though it were new; as if you had just put on all of your clothes, had just sat down, and had just put on your makeup and jewelry. Without adaptation, we would be overloaded with sensory information. (p. 151)

2. Complex stimuli have many contrasting features: light or dark, edges, or lines. When presented with these kinds of stimuli, the horizontal, amacrine, and bipolar cells engage in lateral inhibition so that the brain receives exaggerated information regarding these contrasts. The exaggerated information makes it easier for the brain to "see." (pp. 135–136)

3. A neuron's firing rate tells the brain how intense a stimulus is. This is the process of coding. (pp. 123–124)

4. Jill is experiencing dark adaptation. Her cone and rod cells have adapted so that she can see shapes and images. However, the rods, which work best in dim light, cannot pick up color information. That is why Jill cannot see the colors of her crayons. (pp. 134–135)

MULTIPLE CHOICE QUESTIONS

Facts and Definitions

1. An accessory structure
   a. is where transduction occurs.
   b. functions as a receptor.
   c. modifies incoming stimuli prior to transduction.
   d. changes stimulus energy into neural energy.

2. A receptive field

   a. is the area where receptors are located.
   b. is an area in the environment to which a neuron responds.
   c. is where transduction occurs.
   d. is that part of a neuron that is sensitive to stimulation.

3. The frequency of a sound determines

   a. pitch.
   b. loudness.
   c. the wavelength of sound.
   d. amplitude.

4. Conduction deafness is related to problems with

   a. the hair cells of the basilar membrane.
   b. the auditory nerve.
   c. the malleus (hammer), incus (anvil), and stapes (stirrup).
   d. the pinna.

5. Which theory suggests that pitch is determined by the location of movement along the basilar membrane?

   a. The place theory
   b. The characteristic frequency theory
   c. The frequency matching theory
   d. The volley theory

6. Wavelengths of visible light are

   a. 100–400 nanometers long.
   b. 400–700 nanometers long.
   c. 700–1000 nanometers long.
   d. 1000–1200 nanometers long.

7. Which of the following structures is not necessary for the transduction of light energy?

   a. Photoreceptors
   b. Rods and cones
   c. Visual cortical cells
   d. Photopigments

8. The process of lateral inhibition allows the brain to see

   a. color.
   b. black and white.
   c. more distinct contrasts in stimuli.
   d. movement.

9. Which of these lights would be sensed as the most saturated color?

   a. Wavelengths ranging from 400–700 nanometers
   b. Wavelengths that have a very high intensity
   c. Wavelengths that are all 600 nanometers
   d. Wavelengths ranging from 600–700 nanometers

10. Which of the following is true?

   a. Fibers from the inside half of each retina cross to the right side of the brain.
   b. Fibers from the outside half of each retina cross to the right side of the brain.
   c. Fibers from the inside half of each retina cross to the opposite side of the brain.
   d. Fibers from the outside half of each retina cross to the opposite side of the brain.

11. Which sense does not send information through the thalamus on its way to the cortex?

   a. Hearing
   b. Vision
   c. Olfaction
   d. Somatosensory

12. Which taste is most strongly responded to by the tip of the tongue?

   a. Sweet
   b. Salty
   c. Bitter
   d. Sour

13. Which of the following can alter the flavor of food?

   a. Texture
   b. Smell

c. Temperature

d. All of the above.

14. Proprioception is the ability to

   a. block the sensation of pain.

   b. tell where body parts are in relation to each other.

   c. determine the temperature of a stimulus.

   d. determine the intensity of a touch.

15. According to the gate theory, the nervous system can block pain sensation by

   a. preventing pain information from ascending the spinal cord.

   b. releasing endorphins.

   c. releasing bradykinin.

   d. All of the above.

MULTIPLE CHOICE QUESTIONS

Application of Concepts

1. The pitch of a dog whistle is so high that humans cannot hear it. What physical dimension of sound would describe such a high pitch?

   a. A waveform with a very high frequency

   b. A waveform with a very low frequency

   c. A waveform with a very high amplitude

   d. A waveform with a very low amplitude

2. If the place theory is true, which of the following would cause the least amount of auditory impairment?

   a. Sitting in front of the speakers at a rock concert

   b. Hearing a pure tone with a very high amplitude

   c. Working in a factory where there are many noisy machines

   d. Listening to Bach at full volume over your headphones

3. There is a villain working feverishly in his laboratory to devise a way to prevent visual transduction. Which of the following methods would work?

   a. Destroy all the photopigments in a person's eye.

   b. Remove the lateral geniculate nucleus.

   c. Uncross the optic nerve at the optic chiasm.

   d. All of the above will prevent transduction.

4. Rhoda, who is visiting her sister, has just turned out the bathroom light and is returning to bed. She has to grope for the wall to feel her way back to the bedroom. After being in bed again for about forty-five minutes, she realizes that she can see well. Why?

   a. The photopigments in her cones have finally been synthesized.

   b. The photopigments in her rods have finally been synthesized.

   c. The muscles that control her lenses have adapted to the dark.

   d. The dendrites in her optic nerve have finally resynthesized.

5. Which of the following would cause the least amount of lateral inhibition to occur?

   a. Looking at a spider web covered with dew in the morning sun

   b. Looking at a zebra's black and white stripes

   c. Looking at a green refrigerator's surface

   d. Looking at the pattern of light coming through the blinds

6. Roxanne is responsible for teaching a new student how to do the stage lighting for their school's play. What should Roxanne tell the student?

   a. Mixing colors for lights is identical to the process used for mixing paint.

   b. Mixing two colors of light produces a darker color.

c. Mixing two different colors of light is called subtractive color mixing.

d. Mixing all possible colors of lights together produces a white light.

7. Another villain is trying to destroy the visual system. If he destroys _____, his enemy will be unable to see color.

a. rhodopsin
b. rods
c. iodopsin
d. photoreceptors outside the fovea

8. Cindy is an advertising executive. She wants her creative staff to create purer colors in the print ad they are working on. What will they have to do?

a. Alter the ad's hue.
b. Saturate the ad's colors.
c. Increase the ad's brightness.
d. Add a red tint to all green objects in the ad.

9. Your right visual cortex can "see" a mosquito biting one of your hands. If your right hand is only in your right visual field, and the left is in only the left visual field, which hand will swat the mosquito?

a. The right
b. The left
c. Cannot be determined

10. Mr. Bothfield has just learned about pheromones and has a brilliant idea for a new perfume. He is going to put sexual pheromones in the fragrance. Of what is Mr. Bothfield unaware?

a. Humans do not produce pheromones.
b. Humans learn to associate smells with certain people and activities.
c. Smells do not cause reflexive behavior in humans.
d. All of the above.

11. P.J. complains that his medicine is very bitter. His mother has put his medicine in a dropper and gently squeezes drops of the liquid onto his tongue.

Where should his mother not put the medicine in order to reduce the bitter sensation?

a. On the tip of his tongue
b. On the back of his tongue
c. On the right side of his tongue
d. On the left side of his tongue

12. Excellent proprioception would be required for which of the following careers?

a. A chef
b. A wine taster
c. An acrobat
d. A musician

13. Many of the nerves that determine what is touching Gary's face are firing very rapidly. Which of the following most likely happened?

a. He was just punched in the mouth.
b. He was just kissed on the cheek.
c. He just took a drink of water.
d. A fly just landed on his nose.

14. Jim's girlfriend has informed him that he must buy her a ring that is heavy with gold. Jim has bought a phony ring but wants to convince his girlfriend that it is heavy. What can he do just before she comes over to get the ring?

a. Keep the ring in the refrigerator until just before giving it to her.
b. Keep the ring wrapped in a very warm heating pad until just before giving it to her.
c. There is nothing that Jim can do.
d. Both *a* and *b* will work.

15. Our villain is at it again. Now he wants to wipe out feelings of pain in his enemies, so that they will not know when they have hurt themselves. To do this, he should deplete the body's supply of

a. endorphins.
b. bradykinin.
c. enkephalins.
d. dynorphins.

ANSWERS TO MULTIPLE CHOICE QUESTIONS

Facts and Definitions

1. *c* is the answer. An accessory structure modifies the stimulus in some way prior to transduction. For example, the pinna of the ear collects sounds to be funneled into the ear canal. (p. 121)

a. Transduction takes place in the receptors.

b. Receptors are involved in transduction. Accessory structures modify a stimulus in some way prior to transduction.

d. Transduction is the process of changing stimulus energy into neural energy. Transduction takes place at the receptors.

2. *b* is the answer. Every neuron that carries sensory information responds to a particular area of that sense environment. In vision, the receptive field is some small part of the world that you see. (p. 121)

a. There is no general name for all locations of the receptors. Each sense has its own location. For example, visual receptors are located in the retina.

c. Transduction occurs at the receptors. A receptive field is some area of the environment.

d. The part of a neuron that is sensitive to stimulation is the dendrite.

3. *a* is the answer. The frequency of a waveform determines pitch. (p. 125)

b. The amplitude of a waveform determines loudness.

c. The wavelength is the distance from one peak to the next in a waveform.

d. The amplitude of a waveform determines loudness.

4. *c* is the answer. Conduction deafness is caused by improper vibration in the malleus (hammer), incus (anvil), and stapes (stirrup). This usually occurs with increasing age when the bones begin to fuse together, preventing their movement. (p. 127)

a. Damage to the hair cells of the basilar membrane results in nerve deafness.

b. Damage to the auditory nerve results in nerve deafness.

d. Damage to the pinna, depending on its severity, may not harm hearing.

5. *a* is the answer. According to place theory, the location of movement along the basilar membrane determines the pitch that we hear. (p. 129)

b. There is no such thing as the characteristic frequency theory. A neuron's characteristic frequency is the frequency that will cause the greatest response in neurons in the auditory nerve.

c. & d. The volley theory or frequency matching suggests that the rate of neuronal firing in the auditory nerve matches the frequency of the sound.

6. *b* is the answer. The wavelengths of visible light are between 400 and 700 nanometers. (p. 131)

7. *c* is the answer. Transduction is the conversion of stimulus energy into neural energy. This process occurs before information reaches the central nervous system so that brain cells receive information about the world in a code that they can decipher. That code is neural activity. (pp. 132–133)

a., b., & d. Visual transduction takes place at the photoreceptors or rods and cones in the retina. Photopigments in the rods and cones break apart when stimulated by light, causing changes in membrane potential. A change in membrane potential is the first step toward neural activity.

8. *c* is the answer. Lateral inhibition occurs when a cell with the greatest stimulation (cell 1) causes a reduction in activity in the surrounding cells (cells 2–5). This will cause the brain to receive information that says the receptive field of cell 1 contains much more light than the receptive fields of cells 2–5. That means there is a light region next to a dark region. Therefore, lateral inhibition codes for contrast in the environment. (p. 135)

a. Cones pick up color information.

b. Rods pick up black-and-white information.

d. Specialized cells in the cortex detect movement.

9. *c* is the answer. Saturation refers to the purity of a color. If a light contains a single wavelength that is relatively more dominant than other wavelengths, the color is saturated and it will appear to be pure and vibrant. Since there is only one wavelength in *c,* it is clearly dominant. Therefore the light is sensed as saturated. (p. 139)

a. Waves of visible light range from 400–700 nanometers. If all the waves of visible light were present, you would see white.

b. Waves that have a very high intensity would appear to be very bright.

d. Waves that range from 600–700 nanometers in length would be a reddish brown.

10. *c* is the answer. Fibers from the inside half of each retina cross to the opposite side of the brain at the optic chiasm. (p. 144)

a. Only fibers from the inside half of the left retina cross to the right side of the brain.

b. & *d.* Fibers from the outside half of the retinas never cross to the opposite side of the brain.

11. *c* is the answer. Nerves that carry information about smell leave the nose and travel to the olfactory bulb. Axons leaving the olfactory bulb travel to many parts of the brain, especially the amygdala. (p. 148)

a., *b.*, & *d.* Nerves carrying information about vision, hearing, and touch do travel through the thalamus.

12. *a* is the answer. The tip of the tongue is most sensitive to sweetness. Remember that all taste buds respond to all taste categories, but each taste bud responds most to one or two categories. (p. 149)

b. The entire tongue is responsive to saltiness.

c. The back of the tongue responds most to bitterness.

d. The tongue's edges respond most to sourness.

13. *d* is the answer. Texture, smell, and heat all contribute to food's flavor. (p. 150)

14. *b* is the answer. Proprioception is the ability to determine one's body location in space and where the body parts are in relation to each other. (pp. 154–155)

a. Pain sensation is part of the somatosensory system but is not called proprioception.

c. Temperature sensation is part of the somatosensory system but is not called proprioception.

d. Touch sensation is part of the somatosensory system but is not called proprioception.

15. *a* is the answer. According to the gate theory, information can be prevented from passing through the "gate" or spinal cord. (pp. 153–154)

b. The release of endorphins will reduce pain sensation but is not part of the gate theory.

c. The release of bradykinin stimulates the nerve fibers that carry pain information and cause pain sensation.

d. Only *a* is the answer.

ANSWERS TO MULTIPLE CHOICE QUESTIONS

Application of Concepts

1. *a* is the answer. A very high frequency will produce a very high-pitched sound. (p. 125)

b. A very low frequency will produce a very low-pitched sound.

c. A very high amplitude will produce a very loud sound.

d. A very low amplitude will produce a very soft sound.

2. *b* is the answer. A very pure tone has only one frequency. According to the place theory, a specific frequency will cause a specific place on the basilar membrane to move. A damaging pure tone would, therefore, cause damage to only one location. (pp. 129–130)

a. & d. Rock music and orchestral music would be made up of many frequencies, causing damage all along the basilar membrane.

c. Machinery noise consists of many frequencies. This would cause damage all along the basilar membrane.

3. *a* is the answer. Visual transduction occurs at the retina's receptors, called rods and cones. Photopigments in the rods and cones break apart when stimulated by light and cause changes in membrane potential. (pp. 132–133)

b. Removal of the lateral geniculate nucleus would impair vision, but not the transduction process.

c. Uncrossing the optic nerve at the optic chiasm would change the way we see the world but it would not impair transduction.

d. Only *a* is the answer.

4. *b* is the answer. The rods, photoreceptors in the retina, allow us to see well in the dark. When the lights are first turned out the rods must synthesize photopigments. This process takes approximately forty-five minutes. (pp. 134–135)

a. The resynthesis of photopigments takes less time in the cones than in the rods, but cones provide very low acuity in the dark. The question states that Rhoda can see well in the dark.

c. The muscles of the lens do help us to focus on objects in the environment. However, the level of light in the environment does not affect these muscles' efficiency.

d. Dendrites are permanent fixtures. They do not have to be resynthesized or remade in any way.

5. *c* is the answer. Lateral inhibition occurs when there are many contrasts in visual stimuli, such as stripes or patterns of light and dark. The surface of a refrigerator does not have much contrast. (p. 135)

a. The edges of the lines in the web would be seen as differences between light and dark, causing a great deal of lateral inhibition.

b. The edges of a zebra's stripes would be seen as differences between light and dark, causing a great deal of lateral inhibition.

d. The pattern of light coming through the blinds would create strips of dark next to strips of light on the floor. The contrast would cause a great deal of lateral inhibition.

6. *d* is the answer. Mixing lights is called additive color mixing. The more colors of light you add, the closer the resulting color is to white. (pp. 139–140)

a. Mixing paint is called subtractive color mixing. The more colors of paint you add, the darker the color becomes. This occurs because the two paints absorb, or subtract, more wavelengths of light than either color can alone.

b. Mixing two colors of light will always produce a lighter, not a darker, color.

c. Mixing paint, not light, is called subtractive color mixing.

7. *c* is the answer. Iodopsin is the photopigment in cones that initiates the transduction process. If this substance were destroyed, transduction would not occur and color vision would be impossible. (pp. 133–134)

a. & b. Rods contain the photopigment rhodopsin. Rods see black and white. Destroying rhodopsin would not destroy color vision.

d. The photoreceptors outside of the fovea are rods, which detect black and white.

8. *b* is the answer. A saturated color will appear pure and vibrant. (p. 139)

a. If Cindy changes the hues, she will change the colors but not necessarily their pureness.

c. Increasing the ad's brightness will not increase the colors' pureness.

d. Adding two opponent colors will produce grey.

9. *a* is the answer. Your right hand will swat the mosquito. Information in the right visual cortex comes from the right sides of both eyes after coming from the left environment. Therefore, the mosquito is on your left hand and the right hand will swat it. (p. 144)

b. If the mosquito were on your right hand, then the left visual cortex, not the right, would receive the information.

c. Only *a* is the answer.

10. *d* is the answer. First, there are no human pheromones so Mr. Bothfield would have to use an animal pheremone. Secondly, humans learn to associate smells with people and objects. (For example, my grandmother always carried spearmint chewing gum in her purse. Every time I smell that kind of gum, I think of her.) Finally, smells do not cause reflexive behavior in humans as they do in animals. (pp. 147–148)

11. *b* is the answer. The back of the tongue responds most to bitterness. (p. 149)

a. The tip of the tongue responds most to sweetness.

c. & d. The sides of the tongue respond most to sourness.

12. *c* is the answer. Proprioception is the ability to know where the body parts are in space and in relation to each other. An acrobat would need excellent proprioception. (pp. 154–155)

a. & b. A chef would need very discriminating taste buds, as would a wine taster.

d. A musician would require an ability to discriminate sounds.

13. *a* is the answer. The intensity or heaviness of an object touching the skin is coded by the number of active neurons as well as how rapidly they fire. Many of Gary's neurons are firing rapidly, so the touch must be heavy. Getting punched in the mouth is the heaviest touch among the choices. (p. 151)

b., c., & d. A kiss on the cheek, the feel of a glass against one's lips, and the feel of a fly on one's nose would cause few neurons to be active and they would not fire very rapidly.

14. *d* is the answer. Objects that are warm or cold feel heavier than those that are thermally neutral. (p. 152)

a. Only *d* is the answer.

b. Only *d* is the answer.

c. Jim can either heat or cool the ring so that it will feel heavier.

15. *b* is the answer. Painful stimuli cause the release of bradykinin, which causes pain-fiber activity. Decreasing the supply of bradykinin would decrease pain sensation. (p. 152)

a. Increasing, not decreasing, the endorphin level would reduce pain sensation. Endorphins are one of the body's natural painkillers.

c. Increasing, not decreasing, the enkephalin level would reduce pain sensation. Enkephalins are one of the body's natural painkillers.

d. Increasing, not decreasing, the dynorphin level would reduce pain sensation. Dynorphins are one of the body's natural painkillers.

Chapter 5

Perception

OUTLINE

I. FROM SENSATION TO PERCEPTION: AN OVERVIEW (pp. 164–168)

Perception is the process by which we take raw sensations from the environment and interpret them, using knowledge and understanding of the world, so that they become meaningful experiences.

A. Some Features of Perception

Perception is knowledge-based, inferential, categorical, relational, and adaptive. Many perceptual processes operate automatically.

B. Relating Sensation and Perception

Proponents of the constructionist view argue that the perceptual system must often make a reality out of bits of sensory information, whereas proponents of the ecological view argue that the environment provides plenty of information and construction is not necessary.

II. PSYCHOPHYSICS (pp. 168–174)

Those who study psychophysics are interested in understanding the relationship between the environment's physical characteristics and the psychological experience that stimuli produce.

A. Absolute Thresholds: Is Something Out There?

1. *Determining thresholds.* Subjects are presented with stimuli of varying intensity, such as lights of varying brightness levels, and asked if they can see them. Absolute threshold is the minimum amount of energy that can be detected 50 percent of the time.

2. *Sources of Variation.* Internal noise and response bias can cause variation in an absolute threshold.

B. Going Beyond the Threshold: Signal Detection Theory

Signal Detection Theory is a mathematical model of what determines whether a person perceives a stimulus. It assumes that sensitivity to the stimulus and response criterion determine this perception.

C. Judging Differences Between Stimuli: Weber's Law

Weber's law states that the amount of stimulus you must add to detect a change in the stimulus is proportional to the original amount of the stimulus. The just noticeable difference (JND) is the smallest difference in stimulus energy that can be detected. JND = *KI;* where *K* is a constant and I is the intensity of the stimulus.

D. Judging Stimulus Magnitude: Fechner's and Stevens's Laws

Fechner's law describes the amount of stimulus change necessary to psychologically perceive the stimulus as being twice or three times (and so on) as much as the original stimulus. However, Fechner's law does not apply to all sensory stimuli (pain is one example). Stevens's power law is a more general law that describes psychological magnitude for all sensory stimuli.

III. ORGANIZING THE PERCEPTUAL WORLD (pp. 175–186)

A. Principles of Perceptual Organization

1. *Figure and Ground*. Our perceptual processes actively try to assign some stimuli to the foreground (figure) and some to background (ground).

2. *Grouping*. According to Gestalt psychologists, we see a figure via principles of grouping. These principles include proximity, similarity, continuity, closure, orientation, and simplicity.

B. Perceptual Constancy

Perceptual constancy is the ability to perceive sameness even when the image on the retina changes.

1. *Size Constancy*. Our perception of an object's size is based on the size of our retinal image and how far away we think the object is: the retinal image is interpreted in relation to perceived distance.

2. *Shape Constancy*. The brain automatically puts together information about retinal images and distance as movement occurs. Take a square object, turn it in all different directions (movement and distance cues) and see if you perceive anything other than a square.

3. *Brightness Constancy*. How bright we perceive an object to be is based on real world knowledge and the brightness of that object relative to its background.

4. *Constancy and the Nature of Perception*. Constancy is knowledge-based, relative, adap-

tive, and simplifies our perceptions of the world.

C. Depth Perception

Depth perception, the perception of distance, allows people to experience the world in three dimensions.

1. *Stimulus Cues*. Relative size, height in the visual field, interposition, linear perspective, reduced clarity, textural gradients, and movement gradients all provide depth cues.

2. *Cues Based on Properties of the Visual System*. The brain can evaluate binocular disparity to determine an object's distance. The brain receives and processes information about the convergence of the eyeballs and the accommodation of the lens muscles in order to determine distance. The brain processes information about the difference in timing of sounds reaching the right and left ears, and the intensity of sound to determine the distance of the sound source.

D. Watching the World Go By: The Perception of Motion

Our brains decide if something is moving by evaluating movement cues in the retinal image (such as those produced by looming) and the movement of the eyes and head.

E. Perceptual Illusions

An illusion is a distortion of reality.

1. *Illusions of Movement*. Stroboscopic motion, the phi phenomenon, and induced motion are illusions of motion. Induced motion demonstrates visual dominance. The information from the visual system is given more weight in perceptual decisions than information from other senses.

2. *Illusions of Shape, Size and Depth.* The Ebbinghaus, Ponzo, moon, and Müller-Lyer illusions seem to be due to the misinterpretation of depth cues.

IV. RECOGNIZING THE PERCEPTUAL WORLD (pp. 186–190)

Perception is a result of top-down processing and bottom-up processing.

A. Feature Analysis

We can recognize an object because we perform feature analysis. This is bottom-up processing.

B. Top-Down Processing

1. *Expectancy.* What we expect to perceive creates a perceptual set, which is a readiness or predisposition to perceive a stimulus in a certain way. Expectancies are influenced by context and past experience.

2. *Motivation.* In short, what we want (food when we are hungry, for instance) will be perceived.

C. Top-Down Processing and Bottom-Up Processing Together

These two types of processing interact to produce perception. When one kind of processing is impaired, the other "fills in" and completes the perception.

V. ATTENTION (pp. 191–195)

A. Selective Attention.

Selective attention is our tendency to focus on some stimuli in our environment while ignoring others. Our attention is drawn by novel stimuli and guided by our motivations and expectancies.

B. Focused and Divided Attention

It is very difficult to focus on one of two stimuli that are close together or on two aspects of a stimulus at the same time, as demonstrated by the Stroop task. It is also difficult to divide attention between two different tasks, as demonstrated by dichotic listening tasks.

1. *Practice.* People who are experienced at dividing their attention perform these types of tasks better than those of us with no practice.

2. *Nature of the Stimuli.* It is easier to divide attention when stimuli are very similar or when different sensory systems are used to perceive them.

3. *Stress.* Stress reduces our ability to divide attention.

VI. SOME APPLICATIONS OF RESEARCH ON PERCEPTION (pp. 195–199)

A. Aviation Psychology

At night, pilots may misinterpret their distance and height from the ground when the ground surface slopes upward. Psychologists have advised pilots to rely on their instruments extensively during night flight to compensate for this problem.

1. *Illusory Movement.* A single light, when surrounded by darkness, may appear to be moving. This illusion, called the autokinetic effect, has led to the use of two adjacent lights or flashing lights on the wings of aircraft.

2. *Divided Attention.* Stress can reduce a pilot's ability to pay attention to many different stimuli, even when the stimuli are sensed at the same time.

B. Reading

1. *From Letters to Text.* Our eyes make little jumps or saccadic movements, from point to point on the page we are reading.

2. *Speed Reading and Reading Problems.* Adaptive reading is the ability to slow down or speed up, depending on the difficulty of the material. Reading problems, such as dyslexia, are due to perceptual problems, not to speed deficits. Dyslexia may be due to abnormal persistence of the sensory memory for visual stimuli.

KEY TERMS

1. **Perception** is the process by which we take raw sensations from the environment and interpret them, using our knowledge and understanding of the world, so that they become meaningful experiences. (p. 162)

Example: We use our knowledge and understanding of the world to perceive objects in our environment. After being in school for years, you will recognize the sign +. You know what it is, what it is used for, and in what situations you will encounter it. However, when you were one year old you would have been unable to understand this sign.

2. The **constructionist view** of perception holds that we construct reality by putting together the raw bits of information provided by our senses. Our ability to construct reality is dependent on top-down processing. (pp. 166–167)

Example: Many children's books contain connect-the-dot tasks. On the page are a series of dots and some features, such as eyes, ears, or a mouth. A constructionist would say that we can make pretty good guesses as to what the picture is going to be by putting together all the bits of information from the dots and the features. Since eyes and ears go with a face, the completed drawing will probably have a person in it.

3. The **ecological view** of perception argues that perception is automatically carried out at the sensory level. A psychologist who espouses the ecological view would argue that the environment holds many clues that allow us to perceive. Bottom-up processing is important to perception according to this view. (p. 167)

Example: A far-away object projects a very small image on our retina. The relative size of this retinal image tells us about depth. This example is an illustration of bottom-up processing; our sensory systems have built-in mechanisms that help us to perceive our world.

4. **Psychophysics** is the study of the relationship between the physical characteristics of environmental stimuli and the conscious psychological experiences those stimuli produce. (p. 168)

Example: How do you decide how many people have to get on an already crowded elevator before you notice that the elevator is more crowded? The number of people on the elevator is the physical characteristic of your visual and somatosensory sensations of the environment. Your realization that the elevator is more crowded is a conscious psychological experience.

REMEMBER: Psych is part of the word *psychological* and *physics* is part of the word *physical.* Psychophysics is the study of the relationship between perception's psychological and physical aspects.

5. **Absolute threshold** is the amount of stimulus energy necessary for a stimulus to be detected 50 percent of the time. (p. 169)

6. **Internal noise** is the spontaneous, random firing of nerve cells. Sometimes, when internal noise is "loud" enough, we perceive a nonexistent stimulus. This can cause variation in the amount of stimulus energy necessary for an absolute threshold. (p. 169)

Example: The noise of the nervous system resembles that of static on a radio. It is meaningless, background activity that is internal to the nervous system.

7. **Response bias** is a person's willingness or reluctance to respond to a stimulus. The bias is created by changes in expectancy and motivation. (p. 170)

Example: Dr. Charles, a cancer specialist, sees cancer patients who have been referred to him by other physicians. Therefore, when he looks at these patients' x-rays for the first time, he *expects* to perceive shadows that indicate a tumor. Suppose a new patient shows an extremely faint shadow on his x-ray. Because Charles expects to see a tumor, he will perceive the faint shadows as cancer when, in reality, none may exist.

8. **Signal detection theory** is a mathematical model that can help explain why a person detects or does not detect a stimulus. This model attributes perception to stimulus sensitivity and a person's response criterion. (p. 170)

REMEMBER: This model talks about the <u>detection</u> of <u>signals</u> in the environment.

9. **Sensitivity** is the ability to detect a stimulus. This is influenced by internal neural noise, the intensity of the stimulus, and how well a person's nervous system is working. (p. 170)

Example: In the chapter on sensation, you learned how the effects of age can affect the capabilities of the three bones in the inner-ear to conduct sound. A person with a decrease in bone conductivity would be less sensitive to external auditory stimuli.

REMEMBER: In contrast to response criterion (influenced by a person's motivation and expectancies), sensitivity reflects physical changes in the nervous system, sensory system, or stimulus.

10. **Response criterion** is the amount of energy necessary for a person to justify reporting that a signal has occurred. A person's motivation and expectancies influence the response criterion. (p. 170)

Example: If you are sailing a boat at night, you are more likely to detect the lighthouse's faint glimmer if you know that you are close to shore

than if you think you are 100 miles from the coast. Knowing you are close to shore increases your expectations of seeing lights and, therefore, decreases your response criterion (the amount of stimulus—light—necessary for perception to occur).

REMEMBER: In contrast to sensitivity (influenced by physical changes), the response criterion reflects a person's judgment, which is influenced by motivation and expectations.

11. A **just noticeable difference (JND)** is the smallest difference in stimulus energy that can be detected. (p. 173)

Example: During a power outage you put your roommate in charge of lighting candles. She lights twenty candles while you are downstairs coping with the fuse box. When you get back, you tell her that the room is still too dark and ask her to light another candle. She replies that she just did, but that you did not notice the difference. Then your roommate comments that she will have to light several more candles before you can "just notice a difference" in the light in the room.

12. **Receiver operating characteristic (ROC) curves** provide a measure of a subject's sensitivity in a signal detection task. The curve depicts the overall pattern of hits and false alarms that occurs as the response criterion changes. (See Figure 5.7 in your text.) (p. 171)

13. **Weber's law** states that the amount of stimulus that you have to add before just noticing a difference or change in the stimulus depends on and is proportional to the original amount of the stimulus. (p. 173)

Example: Imagine that a book weighing 10 pounds is in your knapsack. You notice a change in the weight of your knapsack after adding 2 pounds of books. According to Weber's law, if you started out with 20 pounds of books, then you would need to add 4 pounds of books before you would notice a difference. The proportion of 2 to 10 is the same as the proportion of 4 to 20.

14. **Fechner's law** is easiest to understand if you begin by thinking about Weber's just noticeable difference (JND). (p. 174)

a. According to Weber, you have to add a proportional amount of stimulus to get a JND. The larger the original stimulus, the more you have to add to get *one* JND.

b. If you have to add more and more stimulus to get a JND as the stimulus gets larger, then to perceive, for example, the brightness of a light as three times as bright, you would have to add more brightness than you did to get the light to be twice as bright.

c. As your perception of the light increases from twice as bright to three times as bright, to four times as bright, the stimulus added will have to be much more than twice, three times, or four times as large as the original stimulus.

15. **Stevens's power law** explains more accurately than Fechner's law the change in stimulus needed (for any type of stimulus) to produce the psychological perception of stimulus change. Fechner's law says that for successive increases in the perceived intensity of a stimulus, more and more of a stimulus change is required. This is not the case, however, for painful stimuli. (p. 174)

Example: For each successive increase in the perceived intensity of light, more and more light must be added. But, contrary to Fechner's law, it takes less and less of an increase in the intensity of an electric shock to perceive each successive increase.

16. **Figure-ground** is a principle of perceptual organization. A figure is that part of the visual field which has meaning and stands out from the rest of the stimulus. The perception of what is a figure and what is ground (background) is influenced by grouping. (p. 175)

17. **Gestalt psychologists** believe that our perception of a whole object is more than just the sum of an object's various parts. (p. 175)

Example: What do you see at the end of this sentence?   •

Now what do you see below this sentence?

• • • • • • • • • • • •

If you are like most people you probably responded to the first question with "dot" and to the second question with "line." A Gestalt psychologist would argue that there is nothing about a dot that tells you about the characteristics of a line. Therefore, perception of the line must have something more to it than just the sum of the properties of many dots.

18. **Proximity** is a Gestalt principle of perception stating that objects that are close together are perceived as a whole. (p. 176)

Example: You would be more likely to call the dots in (a) a line

(a) • • • • • • • • • • • •

than you would be to call the dots in (b).

(b)   •   •   •   •

19. **Similarity** is a Gestalt principle of perception stating that similar objects are perceived as part of the same group. (p. 176)

Example: When you watch basketball or some other sports game on television, the players on one team are perceived as similar because they are all dressed the same way.

20. **Continuity** is a Gestalt principle of perception, stating that sensations that appear to create a continuous form are perceived as belonging together. (p. 176)

21. **Closure** is a Gestalt principle of perception stating that we tend to fill in missing contours or bits of data to form a complete object. (p. 176)

Example: As Sally was walking through her childhood neighborhood, she came upon a fence that she had painted one summer for the elderly gentleman who owned it. The paint had faded and many slats were missing. Despite the missing pieces of wood, Sally's perception was of a complete fence.

22. **Orientation** is a Gestalt principle of perception stating that objects with the same orientation are seen as part of a group. (p. 176)

Example: If you go to a park in nice weather you will notice that it is easy to determine which people are with what group. Some of the people may be lying on the grass, while others may be sitting in a circle, and still others may be standing and talking to each other. Even if those standing are close to those seated, you will probably perceive them as two different groups.

23. **Simplicity** is a Gestalt principle of perception stating that we tend to group stimulus features in a way that provides the simplest interpretation of the world. (p. 176)

Example: When you look at a picture of the structure in which you grew up, you probably perceive a house. You do not perceive a collection of separate objects, such as the door, windows, chimney, and front steps. It is much simpler for you to <u>group</u> these sensations into one object, the house.

24. **Perceptual constancy** is the ability to perceive sameness even when the image on the retina changes. We have perceptual constancy for size, shape, and brightness. (p. 177)

Example: When you get poor seats at a concert, you may end up sitting very far from the stage. As you look at the band, you perceive them as being the size of adults, rather than children, because of the perceptual constancy of size.

25. **Depth perception** is the perception of distance and allows people to experience the world in three dimensions. (pp. 178–179)

26. **Relative size** is a stimulus cue for depth perception. Objects that are larger are perceived as being nearer. (p. 179)

Example: Monica and her twin daughters are in the backyard. Monica hears a sudden noise and looks up from reading her book. Her retinal image of Jackie is much larger than her retinal image of Jessica. She knows that Jackie is closer because she seems bigger. Jessica, who is playing at the farthest end of the yard seems farther away, not tiny.

27. **Interposition** is a stimulus cue for depth perception. Objects that are closer block a complete view of objects that are farther away. (p. 180)

Example: Stand in your driveway and look at your residence. You know the bushes standing in front of your house, dorm, or apartment are closer than the building is to you because they block your complete view of the building.

28. **Linear perspective** is a stimulus cue for depth perception. Parallel lines that stretch out into the distance seem to converge or come together at a point. A stimulus is farther away as it approaches the point of convergence. (p. 180)

Example: Stand in the middle of railroad tracks and look far into the distance. The tracks seem to come together to make a point. Objects that are close to the point are perceived as far away.

29. **Reduced clarity** is a stimulus cue for depth perception. Objects that are far away are hazy and more difficult to see. (p. 180)

Example: As you drive toward the skyline of a city on a smoggy day, notice the way the details of the buildings become clearer as they become closer.

30. **Textural gradients** are stimulus cues for depth perception. A graduated change in the texture or "grain" of the visual field indicates distance. (p. 180)

Example: Try and find the biggest, steepest, classroom on campus. Go to the front of the class and look up at the empty seats. Your view should form a texture. As your eyes look toward the back of the classroom, you will notice that the texture is gradually changing as the chairs get smaller and smaller. The amount of change in texture indicates how far away the chairs are.

31. A **movement gradient** is a stimulus cue for depth perception. The rate of an object's movement tells you how close or far away it is. (p. 180)

Example: The next time you ride in a car, you will notice that objects close to you will whiz by, but that those farther away seem to move more slowly. If you have a pet in the car, you can tell how close the objects it is tracking are by how fast your pet turns its head.

32. **Binocular disparity** is the difference between the two retinal images and tells the brain about depth. The greater the difference between the two images, the closer an object is. (p. 180)

Example: Hold your arm straight out in front of your face and focus on the tip of one finger. To see the disparity in the images that your eyes see, look at your finger first with one eye and then with the other. Now focus on an object at the far end of the room. Again, shut one eye and then the other. There should be a greater difference between the images your eyes saw when you focused on your finger than between those your eyes saw when focused on the object far away from you.

33. **Convergence** is a depth perception cue. The closer an object is, the more your eyes must turn inward to focus on it. Your brain uses information from the muscles that move your eyes inward to perceive depth. (p. 181)

Example: Try to focus on the end of your nose. You will feel your eyes strain as they attempt to "find" your nose. Slowly shift your focus to an object across the room and you will feel your muscles relax.

34. **Accommodation** is a depth cue. The closer an object is, the more convex, or round, the lens must become to focus on it. Your brain receives messages about an object's distance from the muscles that control the shape of the lens. (p. 182)

35. **Looming** is a motion cue. Objects that enlarge quickly are perceived as moving toward the viewer instead of just growing in size. (p. 182)

Example: Ted is in a fight on the playground. He knows that the fist that is quickly getting bigger and bigger is moving toward his face. He doesn't perceive the fist as simply growing in size.

36. **Visual dominance** is the tendency to rely on visual information even when the other senses provide us with discrepant information. (p. 183)

Example: You are in a parked car that is parallel to railroad tracks on which a train slowly starts to move backward. You will probably think for a second that you, not the train, are moving. Your vestibular sense has not provided you with any information about movement. Your visual sense, which sees movement, dominates your perceptions.

37. **Top-down processing** refers to aspects of recognition that begin at the "top" (the brain), guided by higher-level cognitive processes and by psychological factors like expectations and motivation. (p. 186)

38. **Bottom-up processing** refers to aspects of recognition that depend first on the information about the stimulus that the brain receives from the sensory receptors. (p. 186)

39. **Feature analysis** is the process whereby a stimulus is recognized first by analysis of its basic features. (p. 187)

40. A **perceptual set,** created by past experience and context, is a readiness or predisposition to perceive a stimulus in a certain way. (p. 189)

Example: Three people—an interior designer, an architect, and a professional dancer—go to an abstract art exhibit. They all stand in front of a sculpture for several minutes. When asked what the sculpture represents, the interior designer says that she sees a couch from the art deco period, the architect says that he sees the leaning tower of Pisa, and the dancer says that he sees Ginger Rogers and Fred Astaire dancing. Their past occupational experience has influenced their perceptions of the sculpture.

41. **Selective attention** is our tendency to focus on some stimuli and ignore others. (p. 190)

Example: Selective attention allows us to shut out some of the stimuli in the environment. If you work at home during the day with the windows open, you are likely to hear children shouting and playing outside. Through selective attention, you will be able to ignore these stimuli and pay attention to your work.

42. **Adaptive reading** is the ability to increase or decrease reading speed depending on the difficulty of the material. (p. 198)

Example: Dig out your first-grade reader and your most difficult textbook. Your goal is to comprehend and remember the gist of the text in each book. Now, read a paragraph from each book. Even if both paragraphs are the same length, you will find that it takes much less time to read your first-grade reader than it takes to read your most difficult textbook.

43. **Dyslexia** is the reading problem exhibited by people who have normal intelligence and full comprehension of spoken words but who cannot understand written words. The causes of dyslexia are not well understood. One theory holds that people who are dyslexic may retain material in sensory memory for too long, causing letters on the page to appear scrambled. (p. 198)

Example: Read the following sentence. "The cats are hungry and crying for food." A dyslexic person may see: "The stca are nuhgry and cyrngi rof odof."

LEARNING OBJECTIVES

1. Define perception. Compare and contrast perception and sensation. (pp. 162–165)

2. Name and give an example of each feature of perception. (pp. 165–166)

3. Discuss the debate between the constructionist and ecological viewpoints as to how perception works. (pp. 166–168)

4. Define psychophysics. Define absolute threshold. Explain the influence of internal noise and response bias on perception. (pp. 168–170)

5. Define and describe signal detection theory. Be sure to include sensitivity to stimuli and response criterion in your answer. Explain the data graphed on a receiver operating characteristic curve (ROC curve). (pp. 170–171)

6. Describe Weber's law. Explain the equation $JND = KI$. Define just noticeable difference (JND). (pp. 172–174)

7. Describe Fechner's law and Stevens's power law. (p. 174)

8. Describe the two basic principles of perceptual organization, figure-ground and grouping. Define and give examples of the six properties that influence figure-ground and grouping. (pp. 175–176)

9. Define perceptual constancy. Explain the influences that allow us to perceive constant size, shape, and brightness. (pp. 177–178)

10. Define and describe depth perception. (pp. 178–179)

11. Describe the stimulus cues that influence depth perception. Your answer should include relative size, height in the plane, interposition, linear perspective, reduced clarity, textural gradient, and movement gradient. (pp. 179–180)

12. Describe the cues provided by the visual system that influence depth perception. Your answer should include binocular disparity, convergence, auditory clues, and accommodation. (pp. 180–182)

13. Describe the cues used to perceive movement. Your answer should include looming and the brain's ability to sense the position of the eyes and head. (pp. 182–183)

14. Explain the basis for the perceptual illusions of stroboscopic motion, phi phenomenon, induced motion, and the Ebbinghaus, Ponzo, moon, and Müller-Lyer illusions. Describe the influence of visual dominance on the illusion of induced motion. (pp. 183–186)

15. Define feature analysis and bottom-up processing. Describe the perceptions for which feature analysis cannot account. (pp. 186–188)

16. Define top-down processing. Define perceptual set. Describe the influences on top-down processing. Your answer should include expectancy, motivation, and context. (pp. 188–190)

17. Describe the interaction between top-down processing and bottom-up processing. (pp. 190–191)

18. Define attention and selective attention. Describe the type of stimuli and influences that direct our selective attention. (pp. 191–192)

19. Describe the influences that determine the ease of dividing our attention. (p. 192)

20. Explain the effect of practice, the nature of a stimulus, and stress on the ability to divide attention. (pp. 192–194)

21. Discuss the effects of research findings on the development of aviation equipment. (pp. 195–197)

22. Explain the effect of saccadic eye movements on reading. Define adaptive reading. Define dyslexia. (pp. 197–199)

CONCEPTS AND EXERCISES

No. 1 James Bond's Psychological Secrets

Completing this exercise should help you to achieve the following learning objectives.

(4) *Define psychophysics. Define absolute threshold. Explain the influence of internal noise and response bias on perception. (pp. 168–170)*

(6) *Describe Weber's law. Explain the equation JND = KI. Define just noticeable difference (JND). (pp. 172–174)*

(7) *Describe Fechner's law and Stevens's power law. (p. 174)*

James Bond needs to have some weapons and equipment made for a new assignment. He has hired you to make them. After reading the description of each, decide whether you will need to know the absolute threshold or difference threshold in order to make the device.

1. A lipstick with a deadly poison in it

2. A poison that can be added to a spice

3. A pen that is really a silent gun

4. An alcoholic drink containing a powerful tranquilizer

5. A watch that is really a radio. When the watch beeps a little louder than usual, Bond will know that his accomplices are trying to get in touch with him.

No. 2 Perception on the Playground

Completing this exercise should help you to achieve the following learning objectives.

(8) *Describe the two basic principles of perceptual organization, figure-ground and grouping. Define and give examples of the six properties that influence figure-ground and grouping. (pp. 175–176)*

(9) *Define perceptual constancy. Explain the influences that allow us to perceive constant size, shape, and brightness. (pp. 177–178)*

(10) *Define and describe depth perception. (pp. 178–179)*

(11) *Describe the stimulus cues that influence depth perception. Your answer should include relative size, height in the plane, interposition, linear perspective, reduced clarity, textural gradient, and movement gradient. (pp. 179–180)*

Many childhood activities and games require the ability to perceive figure-ground, grouping, and depth. Match the grade school activities listed below with the appropriate cues or principles of perception (from the list that follows). Answers may be used once or not at all. Each problem may have more than one answer.

1. One hundred children are to participate in a spelling bee. The audience knows that only those children left standing are part of the group that has not misspelled a word. _____

2. As Alice runs to get in the line progressing back into the building after recess, she sees a line of students instead of individuals. _____

3. Roy is playing softball. He knows that he has hit the ball very far, because he can barely see it as it soars through the air. _____

4. Sally is calling to Penny and Ali, who are across the playground. She knows that Ali is closer because she is blocking part of Penny from Sally's view. _____

5. The fifth graders are performing a play in the gym. Mark, a fourth grader, wants to sit with his pals. As he looks for them among the sea of faces in the bleachers, the heads of people seem to be getting smaller and smaller, creating a difference in texture on his retina. _____

6. Children play a game called "Duck, Duck, Goose." Everyone stands in a circle. One or two people are chosen to leave the circle. They walk around the circle, touching each person as they go and saying, "Duck." Eventually, they touch someone and say "Goose." The "goose" must chase the person all the way around the circle and try to catch him or her. Even though there are always two to four individuals missing from the circle, everyone still perceives a circle. _____

7. Ted likes to ride on the playground merry-go-round. He loves to try and look at the objects that are close to the merry-go-round because they seem to move so fast. _____

Cues/principles of perception

similarity

reduced clarity

simplicity

proximity

texture gradient

orientation

linear perspective

motion gradient

interposition

relative size

No. 3 Top-Down and Bottom-Up Processing

Completing this exercise should help you to achieve the following learning objectives.

(15) *Define feature analysis and bottom-up processing. Describe the perceptions for which feature analysis cannot account. (pp. 186–188)*

(16) *Define top-down processing. Define perceptual set. Describe the influences on top-down processing. Your answer should include expectancy, motivation and context. (pp. 188–190)*

(17) *Describe the interaction between top-down processing and bottom-up processing. (pp. 190–191)*

Each type of processing contributes to our ability to perceive the world around us. Some activities require more of one type of processing than the other. Match the activities below with the appropriate type of processing.

1. Marla was treated very badly while she was in a concentration camp during World War II. She is sure that the Nazis will someday return. She is constantly mistaking plus signs and crosses for swastikas. _____

2. Brian's brain is receiving two different pictures of his environment, one picture from each of his eyes.

3. Linda knows that the fly buzzing in front of her head is very close because her eyes are almost crossed._____

4. Vinny misses his girlfriend very much. He is constantly smelling her perfume even though she is not in his apartment. _____

ANSWERS TO CONCEPTS AND EXERCISES

No. 1 James Bond's Psychological Secrets

1. *Absolute threshold.* You would need to know the absolute threshold for the taste of the poison so that the person using the lipstick would not be able to taste it. (pp. 168–169)

2. *Difference threshold.* Spices already have a flavor. Therefore, you need to know how much poison you can add before someone just notices a difference in the taste. (p. 173)

3. *Absolute threshold.* You would have to know the absolute threshold for the gunshots. The amount of auditory stimulus that the gunshot would make would have to be below the absolute threshold so that nobody could hear it. (pp. 168–169)

4. *Difference threshold.* Most alcohol already has a taste. You would have to find out what amount of tranquilizer you could add before someone would just notice a difference. (p. 173)

5. *Difference threshold.* Bond must be able to just notice a difference in the amplitude of the beep of the watch/radio. (p. 173)

No. 2 Perception on the Playground

1. *Orientation.* This is a grouping principle. Those children who are standing all have the same orientation. This will tell the audience which children belong to the group of disqualified people and which children are still in the spelling bee. (p. 176)

2. *Simplicity.* This is a grouping principle. We perceive the most simple pattern in an object. Seeing many individual students would be much more complicated than just seeing a line of people. Continuity would be an equally good answer. Sensations that

appear to create a continuous form (a line) are perceived as belonging together. (p. 176)

3. *Reduced clarity*. This is a depth cue. The clarity with which Roy can see the ball is reduced as it gets farther and farther away. Relative size, also a depth cue, would be an equally good answer. As the size of the ball gets smaller, Roy perceives it as being farther away. (p. 180)

4. *Interposition*. This is a depth cue. Objects that block the view of other objects are closer to us. Ali is blocking the view of Penny; therefore, Ali is closer to Sally. (p. 180)

5. *Texture gradient*. This is a depth cue. Mark knows that the objects that create a smaller image and different texture on his retina are farther away. (p. 180)

6. *Closure*. This is a grouping principle. Even though parts of the circle are missing, the children still perceive the group of students as a circle. Their perceptual abilities allow them to fill in the gaps. (p. 176)

7. *Movement gradient*. This is a depth cue. Ted knows that the objects that are closer to him seem to be moving much faster than those objects that are farther away. (p. 180)

No. 3 Top-Down and Bottom-Up Processing

1. *Top-down processing*. Marla is expecting to see Nazi soldiers again. Her expectations, part of top-down processing, lead her to perceive swastikas instead of plus signs and crosses. (p. 186)

2. *Bottom-up processing*. Perception based solely on information provided by the sensory systems is bottom-up processing. Brian's brain is interpreting the difference between the pictures that his eyes are picking up from the environment. His expectation,

the context that he is in, and his motivation are not altering his perceptions. (pp. 186–187)

3. *Bottom-up processing*. The brain interprets the amount of convergence for information about depth or, in this case, how close the fly is to Linda. Perception that is based solely on the information provided by the sensory systems is bottom-up processing. (pp. 186–187)

4. *Top-down processing*. Vinny would very much like to see his girlfriend. His past experience and motivation to see her are altering his perception of smell. She is not in his apartment, but he still smells her perfume due to top-down processing. (p. 186)

MULTIPLE CHOICE QUESTIONS

Facts and Definitions

1. Expectations and motivation affect which perceptual process?

   a. Bottom-up processing
   b. Internal noise
   c. Top-down processing
   d. Sensitivity

2. Knowing that an object is closer to you because it blocks out part of the background is called

   a. linear perspective.
   b. reduced clarity.
   c. interposition.
   d. movement gradient.

3. Psychophysics is the study of

   a. perceptual illusions.
   b. the psychological perception of physical stimuli.
   c. depth perception.
   d. movement perception.

4. Sensitivity refers to the ability to detect a stimulus. Which of the following would not affect a person's sensitivity?

    a. The level of neural noise in the nervous system

    b. The person's motivation

    c. The condition of a person's sensory system

    d. The intensity of a stimulus

5. JND = KI. The I stands for

    a. absolute threshold.

    b. a constant that varies among different senses.

    c. the intensity of the stimulus.

    d. difference threshold.

6. Fechner's law does not work with which of the following types of stimuli?

    a. Pain

    b. Light

    c. Sound

    d. All of the above.

7. Which of the following is not a principle of grouping?

    a. Interposition

    b. Similarity

    c. Closure

    d. Continuity

8. Which of the following is not a clue for depth perception?

    a. Interposition

    b. Orientation

    c. Linear perspective

    d. Reduced clarity

9. Feature analysis cannot explain the categorization of objects that

    a. are similar to each other.

    b. have slightly different features.

    c. are ambiguous in nature.

    d. share common features.

10. Dyslexia is

    a. a form of speed reading.

    b. possibly due to abnormal sensory memory encoding.

    c. due to problems with attention span.

    d. an indication of mental retardation.

11. Which of the following does not contribute to the creation of a perceptual set?

    a. Context

    b. Expectancy

    c. Past experience

    d. Sensitivity

12. Expecting to see a stimulus will _____ a person's response bias and _____ their response criterion.

    a. increase, decrease

    b. decrease, decrease

    c. increase, increase

    d. decrease, increase

13. Signal detection theory allows psychologists to determine

    a. the ability to detect stimuli.

    b. the effect of expectancy on response bias.

    c. sensitivity.

    d. All of the above.

14. A proponent of the ecological view of perception would say,

    a. "Our sensory systems are capable of gathering all the information necessary for perception."

    b. "Top-down processing is important in the perceptual process."

    c. "Bottom-up processing is important in the perceptual process."

    d. Both a and c.

15. _____ allow(s) us to perceive an object as being the same size despite a change in the size of the retinal image.

    a. Looming

b. Proximity

c. Size constancy

d. Movement gradients

MULTIPLE CHOICE QUESTIONS

Application of Concepts

1. John, a newlywed, is expecting his wife home from work in ten minutes. Suddenly, he hears her footstep on the stair. He jumps up and runs out the door, ready to scoop up his wife in his arms. To his embarrassment, he almost kisses the landlord. What type of processing caused John's close call?

   a. Feature analysis

   b. Bottom-up processing

   c. Perceptual set

   d. Auditory gradients

2. A Cyclops has only one eye. What depth cue would a Cyclops not have?

   a. Linear perspective

   b. Motion gradient

   c. Convergence

   d. Reduced clarity

3. Joey is bored in class. He takes his notebook and draws little pictures on the bottom corners of all the pages. He can then make the pictures "move" by flipping the corners of the pages. This is an example of

   a. phi phenomenon.

   b. stroboscopic motion.

   c. continuity.

   d. proximity.

4. Billy, who is rather lazy, pretends that he cannot carry much wood from the woodpile. His brother Mike has just learned about Weber's law at school. Mike gives Billy 10 pounds of wood to start out with. How much wood should Mike be able to add before Billy notices a difference?

   a. .2 pounds

   b. .5 pounds

   c. 1 pound

   d. 2 pounds

5. Pretty Boy, a Persian cat, is stepping out for the first time all spring. He bounds across the yard after a mouse, only to watch it crawl under the fence. Pretty Boy steps up to the fence and peers through a hole with one eye. He realizes that the mouse is already far away because it looks very small. This is an example of

   a. convergence.

   b. binocular disparity.

   c. relative size.

   d. looming.

6. Renada is on a trip to China with her parents. To keep her occupied while traveling, Renada is given a book, which is written in Chinese. She immediately returns the book to her mother and says "Someone was naughty and scribbled in this book." The fact that Renada saw scribbles instead of words demonstrates that perception is

   a. knowledge-based.

   b. inferential.

   c. relational.

   d. adaptive.

7. Jake is a detective. He is usually very good at his job but has been making mistakes lately. Last night, he was on a stakeout and let Mugsy slip away. Which of the following explanations would point to inadequate sensitivity as the reason for Jake's mistake?

   a. Jake was sure that Mugsy was going to sleep that night instead of making a break for it.

   b. Jake fell asleep in the car at about 5 A.M.

   c. Jake knew that Mugsy's partner was across the street aiming a gun at Jake. If Jake had made a move, he would have been shot.

   d. Jake knows that he is going to retire soon, and a few mistakes will not mar his record.

8. Paul and John love to sneak out of their houses at night. Paul shines a dim light when he cannot leave the house. When John sees a light twice as bright, he knows that he should meet Paul behind his garage. Which law will give a description of how much light is necessary for John to perceive it as being twice as bright?

    a. Weber's law
    b. Fechner's law
    c. Gestalt's law
    d. Ebbinghaus's Law

9. A burglar will paint his face black and wear dark clothing in order to violate which principle of perceptual organization or grouping?

    a. Proximity
    b. Figure-ground
    c. Closure
    d. Similarity

10. Nina, age three, is traveling with her family through the mountains of West Virginia for the first time. At one point she peers over the edge of a cliff and sees another road far below her. The absence of linear perspective cues causes Nina to exclaim, "Look, Dad, all the cars down there are really small. Where do the small people driving them come from?" What explains Nina's perceptions?

    a. Perceptual constancies
    b. Stroboscopic motion
    c. Similarity in grouping
    d. Binocular disparity

11. Harriet Greene is going to take her Brownie troop on a field trip to Chicago. She wants all the children to wear the same T-shirt. That way, a stray child will still be recognized as part of the troop. This demonstrates the principle of

    a. similarity.
    b. proximity.
    c. orientation.
    d. texture gradients.

12. A group of pygmies living in a very thick forest in a preindustrial country probably would not understand

    a. perceptual size constancy.
    b. perceptual brightness constancy.
    c. perceptual shape constancy.
    d. perceptual complexity.

13. An advertising agency has produced an ad for a delivery pizza place. When should they show the ad on television so that people will selectively attend to the ad?

    a. 9 a.m.
    b. 2 p.m.
    c. 7 p.m.
    d. 10 p.m.

14. Rina can knit intricately designed sweaters while she watches movies in the theatre. Her ability to perform this feat is probably a result of

    a. motivation.
    b. practice.
    c. shadowing.
    d. the nature of the stimuli.

15. Wanda leads séances. She completely darkens the room, lights only one candle, and says that spirits will make the candle move. Wanda is using the _____ illusion to fool people.

    a. Autokinketic effect
    b. Ebbinghaus
    c. Moon
    e. Ponzo

ANSWERS TO MULTIPLE CHOICE QUESTIONS

Facts and Definitions

1. *c* is the answer. Expectations and motivation affect top-down processing. Past experience and context can create a perceptual set, which is a readiness to perceive a stimulus in a certain way. (p. 188)

a. The contribution of our sensory systems to the process of perception is called bottom-up processing. For example, lateral inhibition causes us to see edges and contrasts quite clearly. Our expectations and motivations do not alter lateral inhibition.

b. Internal noise is the random firing of nerve cells. Our expectations and motivations will not change this.

d. Sensitivity, the ability to detect a stimulus, is influenced by neural noise, stimulus intensity and the health of the sensory systems. Expectations and motivation will not alter any of these.

2. *c* is the answer. Knowing that an object is closer to you because it blocks out part of the background is called interposition, which is a depth perception cue. (p. 180)

a. Linear perspective is a depth cue. As parallel lines get farther and farther away, they seem to converge at a point.

b. Reduced clarity is a depth cue. As objects get very far away, we see them less clearly.

d. Movement gradients are depth cues. As you move forward—for example, in a car—the objects that are close to you seem to move more quickly than those that are far away.

3. *b* is the answer. Psychophysics is the study of the relationship between the physical energy of environmental stimuli and the conscious psychological experience that those stimuli produce. (p. 168)

a., c., & d. Perceptual illusions, depth perceptions, and movement perception do not involve the amount of stimulus energy. Psychophysics studies the relationship between the amount of stimulus energy and the perception of those stimuli.

4. *b* is the answer. Sensitivity is the ability to detect a stimulus. Motivation affects whether or not we do

perceive a stimulus, but it does not affect our *ability* to perceive a stimulus. (p. 170)

a. A very high level of neural noise may be mistaken for a very faint stimulus. This will alter sensitivity or our ability to detect a stimulus.

c. The sensory system's physical condition can affect its ability to perceive a stimulus. For example, a person who has burned much of the skin on his or her fingers will be unable to detect slight pressure very well.

d. The intensity of a stimulus will affect our ability to detect it. If the stimulus is below absolute threshold it will be undetectable.

5. *c* is the answer. *I* stands for the stimulus intensity. (p. 173)

a. This formula will tell you the amount of stimulus that must be added before a just <u>n</u>oticeable <u>d</u>ifference is detected. An absolute threshold is the amount of stimulus necessary before a stimulus can be detected.

b. *K* is the constant that varies with each sensory system.

d. The entire formula will tell you the amount of stimulus that must be added before a just <u>n</u>oticeable <u>d</u>ifference is detected. *I,* representing stimulus intensity, is only part of the formula.

6. *a* is the answer. Fechner's law predicts that one must add more stimulus to produce the psychological effect of a threefold change in stimulus intensity than that required to produce the psychological effect of a twofold change in intensity. However, for painful stimuli, less and less of an increase is necessary to psychologically detect more and more of a stimulus. (p. 174)

b. & c. Fechner's law will work with light and sound.

d. Only *a* is the answer.

7. *a* is the answer. Interposition is a depth cue. (p. 175)

b., c., & d. Similarity, closure and continuity are principles of grouping.

8. *b* is the answer. Orientation is a grouping principle. Objects that have the same orientation are perceived as members of the same group. (p. 180)

a. Interposition is a depth cue. Closer objects block the view of objects that are farther away.

c. Linear perspective is a depth cue. Parallel lines seem to converge at a point in the distance.

d. Reduced clarity is a depth cue. Objects that are far away are less clear or, in other words, more difficult to see.

9. *c* is the answer. Feature analysis allows us to place objects, after analyzing their features, into one category or another, but never both. Ambiguous objects, by definition, are sometimes part of one category and sometimes part of another category because their features are difficult to detect. (p. 187)

a. Objects that are similar to each other are placed in the same category. For example, the feature of four legs beneath a flat surface describes the category of table. Both a kitchen table and a dining room table share this feature.

b. Objects that have slightly different features may still be placed in the same category. For example, Persian cats have long hair, and other cats have no hair. However, the two types of cats share enough features to be placed in the same category.

d. Objects that share features are placed in the same category. For example, most cats meow, have four legs, a long tail, and fur.

10. *b* is the answer. The sensory memory for visual stimuli appears to persist longer for dyslexic people than for normal readers. (p. 198)

a. Dyslexia is not a form of speed reading.

c. People with dyslexia do not have a short attention span.

d. People with dyslexia are of normal intelligence.

11. *d* is the answer. A perceptual set is a readiness to perceive a stimulus in a certain way. Sensitivity is the ability to perceive an object *at all,* not *how* we perceive it. (p. 189)

a. Context can change the way we perceive an object. For example, the sound of "reed" means two different things depending on the context of the sentence. "The oboe contains a reed." "I like to read."

b. Our expectations, based on past experience and context, can create a perceptual set.

c. Our past experiences can create perceptual sets. A person who does not have children may take some time to realize that bloodcurdling screams may not always signify pain. Anyone who has been around children for any length of time knows that they sometimes scream while they play and alarm is not always necessary.

12. *a* is the answer. Response bias is a person's willingness or reluctance to respond to a stimulus. Expecting to see a stimulus increases response bias. Response criterion determines the amount of physical energy needed for a person to justify reporting that a stimulus is present. Expecting to see a stimulus decreases the response criterion. (p. 170)

13. *d* is the answer. Signal detection theory is a mathematical model that allows psychologists to pinpoint the role of sensitivity and response criterion in a person's perception of a near-threshold stimulus. (p. 170)

14. *d* is the answer. Proponents of the ecological view think that our sensory systems, which drive bottom-up processing, are adequate for perceiving our environment. (p. 167)

a. d is the answer. Both *a* and *c* are correct.

b. Constructionists believe that we use top-down processing to construct our environment. For example, context and past experiences (context and past experience influence top-down processing) play a major role in perception.

c. d is the answer. Both *a* and *c* are correct.

15. *c* is the answer. Despite changes in our retinal images, we perceive objects as retaining their same size. (p. 177)

a. Looming is a motion cue. Objects fill the entire retinal space as they get closer and are perceived as moving.

b. Proximity is a grouping principle. The closer objects are the more likely we are to perceive them as part of the same group.

d. Movement gradients help us to perceive depth.

ANSWERS TO MULTIPLE CHOICE QUESTIONS

Application of Concepts

1. *c* is the answer. John has a perceptual set; he expects the sound of footsteps on the stairs to be his wife's. (p. 189)

a. & *b*. Feature analysis is a type of bottom-up processing. If John had analyzed the features of the footsteps in order to determine if they were his wife's, he would not have almost kissed the landlord. John's expectations made him think that he heard his wife.

d. There is no such thing as an auditory gradient.

2. *c* is the answer. The brain receives and processes information from the eye muscles about the amount of muscular activity. The eyes must converge, or rotate inward, to project the image of an object on each retina. The closer the object, the greater the convergence and, thus, the greater the muscular activity reported to the brain. The brain of a Cyclops would receive no information about the convergence since a Cyclops has only one eye. (p. 181)

a. Linear perspective is a depth cue that can be seen with one eye.

b. A motion gradient is a depth cue that can be seen with one eye.

d. Reduced clarity is a depth cue that can be seen with one eye.

3. *b* is the answer. Stroboscopic motion occurs when a series of just slightly different pictures seen in rapid succession creates the illusion of movement (p. 181).

a. The phi phenomenon occurs when a series of lights flashing on and off sequentially at slightly different locations is perceived as just one light moving from one point to the next.

c. Continuity is a grouping principle. Objects are seen as continuous forms and, hence, part of the same group. This does not create the perception of movement.

d. Proximity is a grouping principle. Objects that are seen as close together are perceived as part of the same group.

4. *d* is the answer. JND = *KI*. *K* is equal to .2 for weight and *I* is equal to the original weight of the wood. Therefore, .2 X 10 = 2 pounds. (p. 173)

5. *c* is the answer. Although several of the alternatives are depth cues, the reduced size or relative size of the mouse tells Pretty Boy that his quarry is far away. (p. 179)

a. Convergence is a depth cue, but it requires a visual image from both eyes. The cat is peering through the fence with only one eye.

b. Binocular disparity is a depth cue, but it requires a visual image from both eyes. The cat is peering though the fence with only one eye.

d. Looming is a motion cue. Objects are perceived as moving closer as they take up more and more of our retinal space.

6. *a* is the answer. Renada's lack of knowledge of the Chinese language prevents her from perceiving the marks on the page as words written in another language. (p. 165)

b. Perception is inferential. This means we can fill in the gaps when sensory information is missing. Renada is not missing sensory information; she simply does not have the knowledge to accurately perceive the sensory information with which she has been presented.

c. Perception is relational. This means that we perceive objects because they have features that are related in specific ways. Renada cannot see the relationship between the features of Chinese writing *because* she has no knowledge of Chinese writing.

d. Perception is adaptive. However, Renada's problem is not that she cannot extract information that will help her deal with the situation. She simply does not have the knowledge required to understand Chinese writing.

7. *b* is the answer. Changes in neural noise, stimulus intensity, or the workings of the sensory system alter sensitivity. If Jake is asleep, his visual sensory system is not working. Jake's eyes must be open before he can see Mugsy creep by the car. (p. 170).

a. If Jake thought that Mugsy were in for the night then his expectations of activity would decrease. This would increase the necessary response criterion but would not affect sensitivity.

c. If Jake thought that Mugsy's partner was aiming a gun at him, then his motivation to grab Mugsy may have been lowered. Jake may think he is too close to retirement to take chances. This would affect Jake's motivation, not his sensitivity.

d. If Jake is not concerned about his record, he may not be as attentive at work. This would lower his response bias (he is probably a bit reluctant to hear Mugsy) and increase his response criterion (the amount of noise required before Jake hears Mugsy).

8. *b* is the answer. Fechner's law describes how much stimulus must be added for John to perceive the light as twice as bright. (p. 174)

a. Weber's law describes the amount of stimulus required before a just noticeable difference is perceived.

c. There is no such thing as Gestalt's law.

d. There is no such thing as Ebbinghaus's law.

9. *b* is the answer. Burglars want to fade into the background. Painting their faces black and wearing dark clothing makes it very difficult to see the burglars as separate from the background of the dark sky. (pp. 175-176)

a. Proximity is the tendency to perceive objects that are close together as part of a group.

c. Closure is the ability to fill in the gaps when sensory stimulation is missing. The black paint and dark clothing do not cause a lack of stimuli but do affect our ability to distinguish background and foreground.

d. Things that are similar are perceived as part of the same group. This question deals with just one burglar, not groups of burglars.

10. *a* is the answer. Amy does not understand that objects that are far away stay the same size. (p. 177)

b. Stroboscopic motion is an illusion of movement, not size.

c. Similarity is a grouping principle. Things that have similar appearances are grouped together.

d. Binocular disparity is a depth cue. The brain can interpret the differences between the pictures from each retina for depth information. However, this ability did not prevent Nina from incorrectly assessing the cars' size.

11. *a* is the answer. Mrs. Greene wants to be sure that all of her Brownies look alike so that people will perceive all of them as members of the same group. (p. 176)

b. If one child wanders away from the rest of the Brownies she will *not* be close enough to be perceived as part of the group.

c. Even if one child strays from the group, she will still be in the same orientation (standing up) as everyone else in the museum. Her orientation will not distinguish her as one of Mrs. Greene's Brownies.

d. Texture gradients are a depth cue, not a principle of grouping.

12. *a* is the answer. The pygmies live in a very dense forest; they have probably never seen something far away on the horizon. Therefore, they would not be able to watch a person or animal approach from far away and perceive size as constant. (p. 177)

b. The pygmies are probably very good at perceptual brightness constancy. The pattern of sunlight that filters through the leaves creates patches of varying brightness. The pygmies perceive objects that move through these patches of sunlight as being constant in brightness.

c. To experience shape constancy, one merely needs to pick up an object and hold it at different angles. No matter what the angle, perception of the shape remains constant. The pygmies are not prevented from doing this just because they live in a dense forest.

d. There is no such thing as perceptual complexity.

13. *d* is the answer. Advertisers do show ads for pizza at about 10 P.M. This is long after most people eat dinner, so they are motivated to pay attention to food stimuli. (p. 192)

a., b., & c. All the other times listed are no more than one hour after traditional eating times in this culture. People who are full would probably not be motivated to pay attention to the commercial.

14. *b* is the answer. Rina's ability to split her attention between the movie screen and the knitting in her lap comes from practice. It is similar to the abilities of secretaries who can transcribe a written message and perform an auditory shadowing task simultaneously. (p. 192)

a. Motivation can affect which stimuli catch your attention, but practice is more important when you are trying to split your attention.

c. Shadowing is the verbal repetition of one of two stimuli presented in a dichotic listening task. Rina is not performing a dichotic listening task.

d. Knitting and watching a movie are very different. This would not help Rina be able to both watch the movie and knit the sweater without mistakes.

15. *a* is the answer. The autokinetic effect occurs when one looks at a single point of light in an otherwise dark environment. In the absence of other cues that could provide reference points, the light may seem to move. Wanda has set up this phenomenon but has told her clients that spirits are moving the light. (p. 196)

b. The Ebbinghaus illusion causes us to perceive differences in size, not movement (see Figure 5.18, section d, in your text).

c. The moon illusion causes us to perceive differences in size constancy and distance, not movement (see Figure 5.19 in your text).

d. The Ponzo illusion causes us to see differences in size, not movement (see Figure 5.18, section e, in your text).

Chapter 6

Consciousness

OUTLINE

I. INTRODUCTION (p. 204)

Consciousness is the awareness of both external stimuli and one's own mental activity. In the history of psychology, scientists have approached the study of consciousness from many different directions. Wundt and Titchner were structuralists. Using introspection, they tried to define the elements that make up consciousness. James, a functionalist, wanted to discover not only the structure of consciousness but also the ways in which consciousness helps people adapt to their environments. Watson, a behaviorist, began the study of behavior itself. He thought that consciousness was too private an activity for objective scientific study. Today, consciousness has once again become a main subject of psychological investigation.

II. VARIETIES OF CONSCIOUSNESS (pp. 208–212)

A. Levels of Consciousness

1. The conscious level is an awareness of moment-to-moment activities and thoughts.

2. The preconscious level contains everything that can easily be brought into consciousness.

3. At the nonconscious level, physiological processes that we cannot consciously monitor without the aid of biofeedback occur.

4. According to Freud, at the unconscious level, sexual, aggressive, and other impulses occur, as do unacceptable thoughts and feelings that are kept out of consciousness. Those who reject Freud's view use the term subconscious to describe mental activity that is not usually accessible.

B. States of Consciousness

1. Passive states are characterized by exerting little or no control over one's mental activity.

2. Active states are characterized by active manipulation of one's mental activity.

3. Altered or alternate states are characterized by quantitative and qualitative changes in one's mental processing.

III. DAYDREAMING (pp. 212–213)

Daydreaming, which is the state closest to normal waking consciousness, arises when attention is focused on internal mental events.

IV. SLEEP AND DREAMING (pp. 213–221)

A. Stages of Sleep

1. *Quiet Sleep*. Stages 1 through 4 are progressively deeper stages of quiet sleep. Each stage has a characteristic EEG pattern.

2. *REM (rapid eye movement) Sleep.* Active sleep or REM sleep is a paradoxical state in which brain waves and other physiological functions resemble those of a person awake, but muscle tone decreases.

3. *A Night's Sleep.* We travel through the five stages of quiet and REM sleep four to six times each night. REM sleep is most frequent during the second half of the night. The amount of time spent in stages 1-4 and REM sleep varies with age.

B. Sleep Disorders

1. People with insomnia feel tired during the day because of trouble falling asleep or staying asleep.

2. Sleeping too much at night but feeling tired and taking one or more naps during the daytime is called hypersomnia.

3. People with narcolepsy fall without warning into REM sleep from an active waking state.

4. Frightening dreams during REM sleep are nightmares.

5. Night terrors involve a rapid shift from Stage 4 to REM sleep, often accompanied by frightening dreams.

6. Sleepwalking is walking during non-REM sleep.

C. Why Do People Sleep?

Various answers to this question have been suggested: sleep is necessary for resting and restoring the body, for nervous system development, or for consolidation of what has been learned during the day.

D. Dreams and Dreaming

Dreams are storylike sequences of images, sensations, and perceptions that occur during REM sleep. Recalled dreams usually occur at the beginning and especially the end of the night. Recalled dreams usually occur during light stages of sleep, and are often emotional and vivid. Lucid dreamers know when they are dreaming.

E. Why Do People Dream?

Psychodynamic theory suggests that dreams express unconscious wishes. Physiological theories suggest that dreams represent efforts to decipher random signals sent to the cortex, that dreams are produced by changes in neurotransmitters, or that dreams are a product of checking neural circuits.

V. HYPNOSIS (pp. 221–226)

A. Hypnotic Behavior

Procedures for inducing hypnosis focus people's attention on a restricted, often monotonous set of stimuli while asking them to shut out everything else as they imagine certain feelings. Hypnotized people exhibit reduced planfulness (the ability to initiate action on one's own), redistributed attention, increased ability to fantasize, reduced reality testing, greater susceptibility to suggestion, and enhanced ability to role-take.

B. Who Can Be Hypnotized?

Given the right hypnotist, situation, and time, many people may be somewhat susceptible to hypnosis. A person's willingness to be hypnotized may be more important than general hypnotic susceptibility in determining responsiveness.

C. Explaining Hypnosis

1. *Role Theory.* Subjects merely act in accordance with the hypnotized role. They comply

with the hypnotist because they think that this is what a hypnotized person is supposed to do.

2. *State Theory.* Hypnotized people experience a special state of consciousness.

3. *Dissociation Theory.* Hypnotized subjects dissociate, or split, various aspects of their behavior and perceptions from the "self" that normally controls these functions. When hypnotized, these subjects are sharing some of this control with the hypnotist.

D. Some Uses of Hypnosis

Hypnosis has been used to treat addiction to various substances, and to decrease pain and bleeding during surgery.

VI. MEDITATION (pp. 226–228)

Meditation is an altered state of consciousness characterized by inner peace, calmness, and tranquility.

A. Meditation Methods

All meditation methods share common characteristics that include finding a quiet environment, assuming a comfortable position, using a mental device to organize attention, and taking a passive attitude.

B. The Effects of Meditation

Physiological effects include decreases in respiration rate, heart rate, muscle tension, blood pressure, and oxygen consumption, along with the appearance of alpha wave activity. People report experiencing feelings of inner peace, relaxation, and improvement in various psychological problems.

VII. PSYCHOACTIVE DRUGS (pp. 228–238)

Psychoactive drugs cause psychological changes by altering the functioning of the brain. Many drugs cause physical dependence or addiction, creating tolerance. Others may lead to psychological dependence.

A. Depressants

Depressants reduce central nervous system activity.

1. *Alcohol.*

2. *Barbiturates.* These are also called downers or sleeping pills.

3. *Tranquilizers.*

B. Stimulants

Stimulants increase behavioral activity.

1. *Amphetamines.* These are called uppers.

2. *Cocaine.*

C. Narcotics

Narcotics include opium, morphine, and heroin.

D. Psychedelics and Hallucinogens

Psychedelics and hallucinogens are sometimes referred to as *psychotomimetics.*

1. *LSD.* (Lysergic acid diethylamide)

2. *PCP.* (Phencyclidine)

3. *Marijuana.* (Cannabis sativa)

KEY TERMS

1. **Consciousness** is the awareness of both external stimuli and one's own mental activity. (p. 204)

   Example: At this moment, you are aware of the words printed on this page. You may also be aware of noises around you, such as a radio playing or a jet flying overhead.

2. **Structuralism** is the study of the elements that make up the structure of consciousness. (p. 204)

REMEMBER: Structuralists thought that, just as water is composed of the chemical elements hydrogen and oxygen, consciousness is composed of elements of sensation.

3. **Introspection** is a research method that was used by structuralists. Subjects were presented with a stimulus and asked to report the sensations they experienced. (pp. 204, 206)

Example: A subject is presented with cotton candy and asked to describe the sensations experienced. The person might report experiencing pinkness, softness, stickiness, and sweetness.

4. **Functionalists** were interested in not only the structure but also the functions or workings of consciousness. How does consciousness affect our behavior? How do we form habits or learn not to cross the street in front of oncoming traffic? (p. 206)

REMEMBER: Functionalists were interested in the *function* as well as the structure of consciousness.

5. **Behaviorism** (stimulus-response or S-R psychology) is the study of behavior. Watson, the founder of behaviorism, thought psychologists should study only those things that could be observed and accurately measured. Consciousness was, in Watson's opinion, a phenomenon that no method could penetrate scientifically. (pp. 206–207)

REMEMBER: Behaviorists were interested in *behavior,* not consciousness.

6. The **conscious level** of activity holds the thoughts and mental processes that we are aware of from moment to moment. (p. 208)

Example: You are conscious of the words you are reading at this moment.

7. The **preconscious level** of activity stores sensations, memories, inferences and assumptions that are not at the conscious level but can be easily brought into consciousness. (p. 208)

Example: Before reading this sentence, you probably did not feel your socks or your underwear on your skin. But now that you are attending to them, you can feel these physical sensations. They were at the preconscious level, but were easily brought into consciousness, in this case by a shift in attention.

8. The **nonconscious level** of activity includes physiological processes that we are not conscious of. Training in techniques such as biofeedback can make us conscious of them indirectly. (p. 208)

Example: Your brain is sensing the amount of sugar in your blood, but you cannot consciously experience this activity, even if you try to attend to it.

9. **Biofeedback** is a technique used to help people become aware of the nonconscious level of activity in their bodies. People are connected to a measuring device that shows them their heart rate, blood pressure, or other physiological processes. (pp. 208–209)

REMEMBER: In Chapter 3 we talked about feedback systems in the nervous and endocrine systems. Biofeedback works essentially the same way. Information about a physiological function (blood pressure, for example) is *fed back* with special equipment to a patient. The patient can then use the information to control the function's level.

10. The **unconscious level** of activity, according to Freud, holds our sexual, aggressive, and other impulses as well as once-conscious but unacceptable thoughts and feelings that would cause anxiety if they became conscious again. (p. 209)

Example: A wish to kill your sister is a thought that could cause anxiety. According to Freud, this thought would be kept in the unconscious to prevent it from causing anxiety or guilt.

11. The **subconscious level** of mental activity includes processes such as thinking about a difficult

problem or recognizing certain stimuli without being aware of doing so. Unlike Freud's concept of the unconscious, subconscious material need not be unacceptable. (pp. 209–211)

12. **Passive states of consciousness** involve mental activity that is not directed or actively controlled and manipulated. (p. 211)

Example: Many people let their minds wander when they lie down to take a nap. Thoughts and images or fantasies of the day's activities and events may appear or change without the person's active control.

13. **Active states of consciousness** involve mental activity that is directed and controlled by the individual. (p. 211)

Example: During a math test, you attempt to apply rules of mathematical reasoning to solve problems. This is an active mental process because you are in control of your thoughts.

14. **Altered** or **alternate states of consciousness** occur when changes in the stream of consciousness are noticeably different from normal waking experience. They are characterized by careless or uncritical cognitive processes, distorted perceptions, and a decrease in self-control. (p. 212)

15. **Daydreaming** is the alternate state of consciousness closest to the normal waking state. When a person daydreams, attention shifts from external to internal mental events. (pp. 212–213)

16. **Alpha waves** are found in the electroencephalogram (EEG) of a relaxed but awake person. (p. 214)

17. **Quiet sleep** is a term for the first four stages of sleep, when breathing is slow, the heartbeat is regular, and blood pressure is reduced. Each stage of quiet sleep is differentiated by a change in the EEG. For example, K complexes and sleep spindles appear in stages 2 and 3, while delta waves occur in stage 4 more than 50 percent of the time. (p. 214)

REMEMBER: These four stages are called *quiet sleep* because, in comparison to REM sleep, body and brain activity are relatively calm and quiet.

18. **Active sleep** or **rapid eye movement sleep (REM).** This stage is called active sleep because the EEG and physiological measures (heart rate, respiration, blood pressure) are similar to those that occur during the day. During REM sleep the eyes move rapidly back and forth, and muscle tone decreases to the point of near-paralysis. (p. 215)

REMEMBER: This stage is called *active* because, physiologically, our bodies and brains are very active (except for the muscles).

19. **Insomnia** is the inability to fall asleep or stay asleep. People with insomnia report feeling tired during the day. (p. 217)

REMEMBER: The Latin word *in* means no, not, or without. *Somnus* means sleep. *Insomnia* means without sleep.

20. **Hypersomnia** is a disorder that causes people to sleep too much but still report feeling tired during the day. (pp. 217–218)

REMEMBER: Hyper means above, or excessive. *Somnus* means sleep. *Hypersomnia* means excessive sleep.

21. **Narcolepsy.** People afflicted with this disorder fall directly into REM sleep from an active, waking state. They experience all the physiological changes that occur during REM sleep, including reduced muscle tone. (p. 218)

22. **Nightmares** are frightening dreams that occur during REM sleep. (p. 218)

23. **Night terrors** occur during a rapid shift from stage 4 sleep to REM sleep. Night terrors bring on intense fear that may last for up to half an hour after waking. (p. 218)

24. **Sleepwalking** occurs during non-REM sleep, usually in stage 4, and it is most common during childhood. It is not dangerous to *gently* awaken a sleepwalker. (p. 218)

25. **Lucid dreaming** is the ability to realize that you are dreaming while a dream is occurring. (p. 219)

REMEMBER: The word *lucid* means clear or readily understood. *Lucid dreamers* clearly know, while still asleep, that they are dreaming.

26. **Hypnosis** is an altered state of consciousness brought on by special techniques and characterized by susceptibility to suggestions made by the hypnotist. (p. 221)

Example: Maria, who is hypnotized, believes that she can see a cat sitting on her lap because the hypnotist has suggested to her that a cat is there.

27. **Posthypnotic suggestions** are instructions that are given during hypnosis and that a person follows after the hypnotic state ends. These suggestions wear off in minutes, hours, or days. (p. 222)

Example: Eric, while hypnotized, was told that he would forget the number three. After he awoke, the hypnotist asked Eric to count the number of fingers on his hands. Eric counted eleven because he had skipped the number three.

REMEMBER: Post means after. *Posthypnotic* suggestions are directions to be followed after a person is no longer hypnotized.

28. **Posthypnotic amnesia** is the inability to remember what has happened during hypnosis. (p. 223)

Example: Julia cannot remember anything that happened to her while she was hypnotized, even after the hypnotist told her exactly what occurred.

REMEMBER: Post means after. *Amnesia* is a loss of memory. *Posthypnotic amnesia* is a loss of the memory of what happened under hyp-

nosis. This does not mean a person has amnesia in general. The memory loss is only for what occurred during hypnosis.

29. **Susceptibility** is the degree to which people can become hypnotized and follow a hypnotist's suggestions. (p. 223)

30. **Role theory** of hypnosis states that people play the "role" of being hypnotized, which includes complying with the hypnotist's directions. (p. 224)

31. **State theory** of hypnosis. According to this theory, hypnosis is a special state of consciousness. Supporters of the state theory believe that real, significant changes in basic mental processes take place during hypnosis. (p. 225)

REMEMBER: The *state* theory says hypnosis equals a *state* of consciousness.

32. **Dissociation theory** states that hypnosis is a splitting of central control of thought processes and behavior. The hypnotized person agrees to give some of the control to the hypnotist. (p. 225)

33. **Meditation** is a set of techniques designed to create an altered state of consciousness characterized by inner peace, calmness, and tranquility. The technique involves finding a quiet environment, assuming a comfortable position, using a mental device, and taking a passive attitude. (p. 226)

34. **Psychoactive drugs** bring about psychological changes by affecting the functioning of the brain. (p. 228)

Example: LSD, a psychedelic, changes the perception of sensory information and drastically alters thought processes.

35. **Physical dependence** or addiction exists when the body has a physical need for a drug. Addicts who discontinue drug use typically experience very unpleasant, often dangerous, withdrawal symptoms. (p. 229)

Example: Carol's addiction to a barbiturate became evident when, after attempting to quit using the drug, she experienced restlessness, violent outbursts, convulsions, and hallucinations.

36. **Tolerance** is a by-product of addiction. Repeated use of an addictive substance results in the body's requiring ever-increasing amounts of the drug to achieve the same psychological and physical effects. (p. 229)

Example: After using cocaine daily for several weeks, Jesse began to need more and more of the drug to achieve the "high" he experienced the first few times he used it.

37. **Depressants** include alcohol, barbiturates, and tranquilizers. (p. 229)

REMEMBER: Usually, depressants make a person sedate or calm.

38. **Alcohol** is a depressant. It temporarily decreases activity in the parts of the cerebral cortex that normally tell a person what not to do. (p. 229)

Example: Mary Jane is quiet, shy, wears her hair in a bun, and does not smile very often. However, when she drinks alcohol, she lets her hair down, talks loudly, and loves to tell dirty jokes. This happens because the alcohol has "shut down" the areas in her cerebral cortex that normally inhibit her behavior. Remember that alcohol has different effects on different people, depending on how much they drink, what behaviors they have been inhibiting, and what they expect to feel.

39. **Barbiturates** are also depressants and can create physical dependence. They depress central nervous system activity and produce sleep, relaxation, and mild euphoria. Sometimes problems with muscle coordination and mental concentration occur, depending on the dosage. Overdoses of barbiturates can be fatal. (p. 232)

40. **Tranquilizers** are also depressants. They depress central nervous system activity. Their effects and hazards are similar to those of barbiturates: sleep, relaxation, and disrupted muscle coordination and mental concentration. Overdoses can be fatal. (p. 232)

41. **Stimulants** increase behavioral activity. They include amphetamines and cocaine. Overdoses of cocaine can be fatal. (p. 232)

42. **Amphetamines** include Benzedrine, Dexedrine, and Methadrine. They stimulate the brain and the sympathetic branch of the autonomic nervous system. Amphetamines cause increases in heart rate and blood pressure, constriction of blood vessels, shrinking of mucous membranes, suppression of appetite, and increased alertness. (p. 232)

43. **Cocaine** is a stimulant that causes reduced pain sensations; a heightened level of self-confidence, well-being, and optimism; and, sometimes, increased sexual desire and pleasure. However, long-standing use of cocaine can cause nausea, overactivity, sleeplessness, paranoid thinking, a sudden depressive "crash," and hallucinations. Overdoses can be fatal. (p. 233)

44. **Narcotics,** including opium, morphine, and heroin, produce sleep and pain relief. These substances are highly addictive and overdoses can be fatal. (p. 233)

REMEMBER: In Chapter 3 you learned that your brain produces a class of neurotransmitters called *endorphins* that have effects similar to those of morphine.

45. **Psychedelics,** such as LSD, cause a loss of contact with reality and changes in thought, perception and emotion. Because many of these changes are similar to symptoms of psychotic forms of mental illness, these drugs are sometimes referred to as psychotomimetics; they mimic psychosis. (p. 233–234)

46. **LSD (lysergic acid diethylamide)** is a psychedelic that blocks serotonin receptors in the reticular formation. (If you have forgotten what it means to block a receptor, review page 109 in Chapter 3 of your text.) To understand the changes LSD induces, read the account of Albert Hoffman on page 234 in your text. LSD does not normally produce psychological or physical dependence. (p. 234)

47. **Phencyclidine (PCP)** is a psychedelic that causes agitated excitement, disorientation, hallucinations, insensitivity to pain, and in some cases, an inability to recognize danger. Overdoses can be fatal. (p. 234)

48. **Marijuana (Cannabis sativa)** travels through the bloodstream to the brain and other organs. Its effects include relaxation, increased sensitivity to sensory stimulation, an altered sense of space and time, and feelings of hunger, especially for sweets. (pp. 234–238)

LEARNING OBJECTIVES

1. Define consciousness. (p. 204)

2. Compare and contrast the structuralists' and functionalists' interests in studying consciousness. Describe introspection. Define behaviorism. (pp. 204–208)

3. Distinguish between the various levels of conscious activity: conscious, preconscious, nonconscious, subconscious, and unconscious. Give an example of each. (pp. 208–209)

4. Compare and contrast active and passive states of consciousness. Define altered states of consciousness. (pp. 211–212)

5. Define daydreaming. Discuss possible reasons for daydreaming. (pp. 212–213)

6. Compare and contrast quiet and active sleep. Know the stages of sleep which occur during quiet sleep. (pp. 214–215)

7. Be able to recognize the differences between the EEGs of each stage. Your answer should include descriptions of alpha waves, sleep spindles, K complexes, and delta waves. (p. 215)

8. Define rapid eye movement (REM) sleep. Know the physiological changes that occur during this stage of sleep. (pp. 215–216)

9. Define the various sleep disorders listed in your text. Be able to recognize them by their symptoms and know during which stages of sleep they occur. (pp. 217–218)

10. Define REM rebound. Discuss the various hypotheses on the reasons for quiet sleep and dreaming. (pp. 219–221)

11. Define hypnosis. What kinds of behavior do hypnotized people display? (pp. 221–223)

12. Define posthypnotic suggestions, posthypnotic amnesia, and susceptibility. (pp. 222–223)

13. Compare and contrast the role, state and dissociation theories of hypnosis. (pp. 224–226)

14. List some of the uses of hypnosis. (p. 226)

15. Define meditation. List the common characteristics of meditation techniques. Describe the effects of meditation. (pp. 226–228)

16. Define psychoactive drugs. Define psychological and physical dependence. Define tolerance. (pp. 228–229)

17. Define depressant. Describe the effects of alcohol, barbiturates, and tranquilizers on the nervous system and behavior. (pp. 229–232)

18. Define stimulant. Describe the effects of amphetamines and cocaine on the brain and behavior. (pp. 232–233)

19. Define narcotics. Describe the effects of narcotics, including opium, morphine, and heroin, on the nervous system and behavior. (p. 233)

20. Define psychedelic. Describe the effects of LSD, PCP, and marijuana. (pp. 233–235)

CONCEPTS AND EXERCISES

No. 1 Types of Consciousness

Completing this exercise should help you to achieve the following learning objective.

(3) *Distinguish between the various levels of conscious activity: conscious, preconscious, nonconscious, subconscious, and unconscious. Give an example of each. (pp. 208–209)*

Several types of activities are described in the following list. Decide whether these activities are conscious, preconscious, nonconscious, or unconscious. Answers may be used more than once or not at all.

1. Belinda, enjoying the taste of her favorite food, thanks her mother for preparing it. _____

2. Carmen is putting an adhesive bandage on a cut. She cannot feel the neural activity in her brain which is directing her hand movements. _____

3. Leslie Anne has been in a car accident. She is so busy helping people that she does not feel the pain from her broken collarbone. _____

4. Tom overheard the following piece of conversation: "I stood outside her house holding the candy and flowers for 20 minutes before I rang the doorbell." Tom immediately had a good idea of what had happened. _____

5. Brian was doing his homework in front of the television. He was concentrating on an algebra problem that had him stumped when suddenly he heard his name. One of the characters in the movie he was watching had called his name. _____

No. 2 Stages of Sleep at a Slumber Party

Completing this exercise should help you to achieve the following learning objectives.

(8) *Define rapid eye movement (REM) sleep. Know the physiological changes that occur during this stage of sleep. (pp. 215–216)*

(9) *Define the various sleep disorders listed in your text. Be able to recognize them by their symptoms, and know during which stages of sleep they occur. (pp. 217–218)*

(10) *Define REM rebound. Discuss the various hypotheses on the reasons for quiet sleep and dreaming. (pp. 218–221)*

Joanna's daughter is having a slumber party. The noise died down about one hour ago. Joanna decides to go see if everyone is asleep yet. Match the stages of sleep or disorders listed below with the description of what Joanna found when she went to check on the girls. Answers may be used more than once or not at all.

narcolepsy

hypersomnia

night terrors

insomnia

rapid eye movement (REM) sleep

sleepwalking

1. Diane is perfectly still except for a few twitches of her face and hands. Joanna notices that her eyes are moving rapidly back and forth even though they are closed. _____

2. Joanna spies one little girl in the corner of the room all curled up but clearly still awake. The little girl tells Joanna that it is always hard for her to fall asleep no matter what the time. _____

3. Joanna thinks about the little girl who cannot sleep and wishes that her son, John, had that

problem. Instead, John falls asleep in the middle of the day—sometimes in mid-sentence. _____

4. Suddenly Brenda sits up in her sleeping bag. Staring straight ahead, she lets out a blood-curdling scream. It takes Joanna half an hour to calm her. What has Brenda just experienced? _____

5. Joanna counts only six girls in the room. She knows that there should be seven. She makes a quick search of the house and finds Juliette stumbling around the living room, still asleep. _____

ANSWERS TO CONCEPTS AND EXERCISES

No. 1 Types of Consciousness

1. *Conscious level.* Belinda is aware of the taste of the food in her mouth. (p. 208)

2. *Nonconscious level.* Carmen is not and cannot become aware of the neural activity in her motor cortex. (p. 208)

3. *Preconscious level.* Leslie Anne has her attention focused on the people who need her help. The pain in her collarbone will easily come into consciousness once she attends to it. (p. 208)

4. *Preconscious level.* Tom knew that the man he had overheard was waiting, probably nervously, outside his date's house. The assumptions and inferences he had to make to understand this sentence occurred at the preconscious level. (p. 208)

5. *Subconscious level.* Brian was deep in thought over his algebra homework when he heard his name. This is an example of the *cocktail party phenomenon.* Brian registered hearing his name at the subconscious level. (p. 209)

No. 2 Stages of Sleep at a Slumber Party

1. *Rapid eye movement (REM) sleep.* Diane is not moving because muscle tone decreases to near-paralysis during this stage. The eyes move rapidly back and forth. (p. 215)

2. *Insomnia.* This sleep disorder is characterized by an inability to fall asleep. (p. 217)

3. *Narcolepsy.* This sleep disorder is characterized by the sudden onset of sleep; the person falls directly into REM sleep from an active waking state. (p. 218)

4. *Night terrors.* Night terrors usually involve a rapid shift from stage 4 sleep to REM sleep. The dreams that sometimes accompany these shifts are usually vivid and terrifying. It often takes quite a while to calm people after they have a night terror experience. (p. 218)

5. *Sleepwalking.* Juliette is taking a tour of the house, but she is still asleep. This is sleepwalking. (p. 218)

MULTIPLE CHOICE QUESTIONS

Facts and Definitions

1. Introspection is a research method used primarily by _____ to discover the elements of consciousness.

    a. structuralists
    b. behaviorists
    c. functionalists
    d. psychophysiologists

2. Unacceptable thoughts and sexual and aggressive impulses are in the _____ level.

    a. nonconscious
    b. preconscious
    c. unconscious
    d. active

3. Our memories, assumptions, and inferences seem to operate at the _____ level.

    a. nonconscious
    b. subconscious
    c. preconscious
    d. passive

4. Biofeedback is used to detect activities occurring at the _____ level.

    a. subconscious
    b. unconscious
    c. preconscious
    d. nonconscious

5. Altered states of consciousness are characterized by _____.

    a. uncritical cognitive processes.
    b. changes in perception.
    c. a decrease in self-control.
    d. All of the above.

6. Sleep stages 2 and 3 are distinguished from other stages of sleep by the presence of _____.

    a. reduced blood pressure.
    b. a regular heartbeat.
    c. sleep spindles.
    d. slow breathing.

7. An EEG taken during REM sleep would most resemble which other stage of sleep?

    a. Stage 1
    b. Stage 2
    c. Stage 3
    d. Stage 4

8. REM sleep is most prevalent during _____.

    a. infancy.
    b. puberty.
    c. young adulthood.
    d. old age.

9. Which of the following has *not* been suggested as a reason for dreaming?

    a. As we dream, our nerve connections are developing, checking, and expanding.
    b. REM sleep may be a time of adjustment to new events or problems.
    c. Dreaming allows us to solidify what we have learned the previous day.
    d. Dreaming allows us to remain free of symptoms associated with severe mental disorders.

10. Hypnosis has been used to _____.

    a. help people stop smoking.
    b. help people reduce drug intake.
    c. reduce pain.
    d. all of the above.

11. Which of the following is *not* displayed by hypnotized subjects?

    a. An enhanced ability to fantasize
    b. Reduced reality testing
    c. Increased ability to role-play
    d. Problems remembering events following hypnosis

12. Tolerance is _____.

    a. the abuser's need for larger and larger amounts of a drug to achieve the same effect.
    b. the abuser's physical need for a drug.
    c. the abuser's dependence on the drug to function.
    d. the relief from danger of overdose, no matter how much drug is taken into the system.

13. A mantra is _____.

    a. a person trained in meditation.
    b. the object or sound the meditator focuses on.
    c. the position a person assumes when meditating.
    d. a special form of meditation.

14. Which of the following is a narcotic?

    a. Cocaine
    b. Alcohol
    c. Tranquilizer
    d. Opium

15. There are many myths related to the consumption of alcohol. Which of the following is not true?

    a. Eating prior to excessive drinking will prevent you from getting too drunk.
    b. It is impossible to overdose on alcohol.
    c. Alcohol is a stimulant.
    d. All of the above are false.

MULTIPLE CHOICE QUESTIONS

Application of Concepts

1. Carmen's research involves presenting subjects with various objects and asking them to report the sensations they are experiencing. Carmen is probably a _____.

    a. psychophysiologist.
    b. structuralist.
    c. behaviorist.
    d. hypnotist.

2. Lisa can never seem to remember to take off her watch before she steps into the shower. This is probably because the sensation of the watch on her arm is at the _____ level.

    a. subconscious
    b. conscious
    c. nonconscious
    d. preconscious

3. You are told, "Sue heard the bell ring, grabbed her piggy bank, and ran outside." You know that the little girl went outside to buy ice cream. The knowledge necessary to make this deduction was at the _____ level.

    a. preconscious
    b. nonconscious

    c. subconscious
    d. unconscious

4. Edwin witnessed some gruesome events during World War II. However, he cannot remember much of what occurred. Most of his memories of these events are probably located at the _____ level.

    a. conscious
    b. unconscious
    c. nonconscious
    d. preconscious

5. Snookers the cat has decided that he wants a snack. However, his owner is taking a nap. Despite several minutes of intense tap-dancing on his owner's face, Snookers cannot wake him up. How long has the cat's owner been asleep?

    a. No more than five minutes.
    b. No more than ten minutes.
    c. At least thirty minutes.
    d. This cannot be determined.

6. Miranda, while studying for her midterm in botany, tries to decide what questions the professor is going to ask on the exam. She is experiencing a(n) _____ state of consciousness.

    a. passive
    b. structuralistic
    c. active
    d. functional

7. Last night Sybil woke up screaming. She told her mother that she had dreamed that someone was repeatedly stabbing her. It took her mother almost thirty minutes to calm her down. Sybil was probably in what stage of sleep just before she awoke?

    a. Stage 1
    b. Between stages 2 and 3
    c. Between stage 4 and REM
    d. Stage 3

8. Ruby has had a terrible evening. Just as her boyfriend, Kevin, started to propose to her he fell

asleep. Ruby would feel better if she knew that Kevin has _____.

    a. hypersomnia.
    b. narcolepsy.
    c. insomnia.
    d. night terrors.

9. Benjamin Franklin said "Early to bed, early to rise, makes a man healthy, wealthy, and wise." A psychologist who knew about circadian rhythms would probably say which of the following?

    a. "Whenever you bed, whenever you rise, a change in your rhythm will be your demise."
    b. "Bed when you will, rise when you wish, it just doesn't make that big of a dif."
    c. "Early to bed, early to rise, makes a man grisly, and grumpy, but wise."
    d. None of the above.

10. Mark's hypnotist suggested that Mark saw a big fluffy cat sitting in the chair next to him. Although no cat was present, Mark said that he could see its tail swishing back and forth. This is characteristic of what type of hypnotic behavior?

    a. Reduced planfulness
    b. Role-taking
    c. Reduced reality testing
    d. Redistributed attention

11. Which of the following people would most likely experience the most REM sleep?

    a. A person who goes to bed and gets up at exactly the same time each day
    b. A ninety-year-old person on vacation
    c. A student who has been studying constantly for three days and three nights
    d. A person who has just recovered from hypersomnia

12. Irene is having difficulty falling asleep at night. She could be _____.

    a. an insomniac.
    b. reacting to barbiturates she just took.

    c. abusing cocaine.
    d. either *a* or *c*.

13. Norman has found himself a quiet spot, settled into a comfortable position, started using his mantra, and assumed a passive attitude. He is about to _____.

    a. start meditating.
    b. be hypnotized.
    c. go to sleep.
    d. start daydreaming.

14. One night a young man experiencing hallucinations is brought to a hospital emergency room. Which of the following drugs could his doctor rule out as a possible cause of the hallucinations?

    a. PCP
    b. Cocaine
    c. Valium
    d. LSD

15. Stanley has just taken a drug that alters the activity of the neurotransmitter norepinephrine. Which of the following drugs is it?

    a. Alcohol
    b. LSD
    c. Cocaine
    d. Opium

ANSWERS TO MULTIPLE CHOICE QUESTIONS

Facts and Definitions

1. *a* is the answer. Structuralists used introspection to study the elements that made up the "structure" of consciousness. (pp. 204–206)

    b. Behaviorists do not study consciousness. Watson, the founder of behaviorism, thought that consciousness could not be studied scientifically.

    c. Functionalists were more interested in how our consciousness directed our behavior. They were not as interested in the structure of consciousness.

d. Psychophysiologists are interested in the biological factors that influence consciousness and are not very interested in the elements of sensation that make up consciousness.

2. *c* is the answer. Freud believed that all unacceptable thoughts and impulses were stored in the unconscious. (p. 209)

a. Nonconscious processes are those physiological activities that people cannot become directly aware of. For example, you cannot feel the release of neurotransmitters in your brain.

b. Preconscious activities are those that are easily brought into consciousness. All of our memories and the inferences that we make are stored there.

d. Active states of consciousness are willfully directed and manipulated thought processes.

3. *c* is the answer. Preconscious activities include the inferences that we make. (p. 208)

a. Nonconscious processes are those physiological activities that people cannot become directly aware of.

b. Subconscious activity includes the thoughts that cannot easily be brought into consciousness. This label is used by those who disagree with Freud for what he called "unconscious activity."

d. Passive states of consciousness are undirected thought processes.

4. *d* is the answer. People can learn to be aware of some types of nonconscious activities by using biofeedback. People can become aware of their heart rate and blood pressure. (pp. 208–209)

a. & b. Subconscious and nonconscious activity are thought processes that are unavailable to consciousness. Freud used hypnosis and dream analysis to uncover unconscious thoughts and impulses.

c. Preconscious activity includes all memories and inferences that we are not aware of but that we can easily bring into consciousness.

5. *d* is the answer. *a, b,* and *c* are all true. (p. 212)

6. *c* is the answer. Sleep spindles appear in an EEG during stages 2 and 3. (p. 214)

a., b., & d. Reduced blood pressure, regular heartbeat, and slow breathing are all characteristic of quiet sleep.

7. *a* is the answer. The EEG during REM sleep looks similar to that of stage 1; it appears as though the person is awake. (p. 215)

b. & c. The EEG shows sleep spindles and K complexes during stages 2 and 3.

d. The EEG shows delta waves during the fourth stage of sleep.

8. *a* is the answer. Infants spend more time in REM sleep than any other age group. (p. 216)

b., c., & d. As people get older they spend less and less time asleep. Most of the loss is a decrease in REM sleep.

9. *d* is the answer. People do not show signs of mental illness just because they have been deprived of REM sleep. (pp. 220–221)

a., b., & c. These are all possible explanations of why we dream.

10. *d* is the answer. Hypnosis has been used to help people stop smoking cigarettes and using drugs and to reduce pain. (p. 226)

11. *d* is the answer. Posthypnotic amnesia is an inability to remember what occurred during hypnosis, not what occurs after hypnosis. (p. 223)

a., b., & c. These statements are all true.

12. *a* is the answer. With prolonged drug use, the abuser needs more and more of a substance to achieve the same "high." (p. 229)

b. When there is a physical need for a drug, an abuser is addicted or physically dependent. Physical dependence can lead to tolerance, but they are not the same.

c. Psychological dependence occurs when the abuser relies on a drug in order to function every day. Not taking the drug may cause psychological discomfort.

d. No matter how long people use a drug, they can still overdose if the amount is large enough.

13. *b* is the answer. A mantra is one of several possible points of focus. (p. 227)

a. There is no special name for a person well versed in meditation.

c. Many different types of positions have been used to meditate. Their only common characteristic is that they are comfortable.

d. Several different techniques of meditation exist but none of them is called *mantra*.

14. *d* is the answer. Opium is a narcotic. (p. 233)

a. Cocaine is a stimulant.

b. Alcohol is a depressant.

c. Tranquilizers are depressants.

15. *d* is the answer. All of the above are false. (p. 229)

a. Eating prior to drinking delays the absorption of alcohol and therefore delays its effects, but it does not prevent them from occurring.

b. It is very possible to overdose on alcohol. The alcohol first affects the frontal cortex, then the midbrain, and finally the hindbrain. You will remember from Chapter 3 that the medulla, which controls breathing, heart rate, and blood pressure, is in the hindbrain. It can be dangerously affected by an overdose of alcohol.

c. Alcohol is a depressant, which inhibits central nervous system activity.

ANSWERS TO MULTIPLE CHOICE QUESTIONS

Application of Concepts

1. *b* is the answer. Structuralists used the method of introspection to determine the elements or the structure of consciousness. (p. 204)

a. Psychophysiologists would not use introspection to study consciousness. They would try to determine the biological factors that influence consciousness.

c. Behaviorists study behavior, not consciousness.

d. Introspection is not a technique used in hypnosis.

2. *d* is the answer. Physical sensations, memories, and the inferences we make are at the preconscious level of activity. When Lisa stepped into the shower, the sensation of her watch on her arm was at the preconscious level of activity. (p. 208)

a. Subconscious activity cannot be easily brought into consciousness. The feeling of water between your watch and skin is very easy to bring into consciousness.

b. If Lisa had been conscious of her watch on her arm, she never would have stepped into the shower wearing it.

c. Nonconscious activities are those that cannot reach consciousness. For example, you cannot feel your hair growing. Lisa, although she was a little too late, did feel the watch on her arm.

3. *a* is the answer. Inferences are made at the preconscious level of activity. (p. 208)

b. Nonconscious activities are those biological functions that we cannot become directly conscious of.

c. & *d*. Subconscious and unconscious activity cannot be easily brought into consciousness. Therefore, even if you had figured out what the little girl was doing at these levels of consciousness, you never would have been aware of it.

4. *b* is the answer. Freud would say that unacceptable thoughts and memories are kept in the unconscious to protect a person from anxiety. (p. 209)

a. If Edwin's memories were conscious then he would be thinking of them.

c. Nonconscious activities are those biological activities that we cannot become directly aware of.

d. If Edwin's memories were at the preconscious level, he would be able to bring them into consciousness easily.

5. *c* is the answer. Stage 4, a very deep sleep, occurs about thirty minutes after falling asleep. It is difficult to rouse someone from stage 4 sleep. (p. 214)

a. After five minutes the sleeper would be in stage 1 or just entering stage 2 (not deep sleep).

b. After ten minutes the sleeper would be in stage 2 or 3 (not deep sleep).

d. It *can* be determined. Snooker's owner is taking a nap and, despite all the activity on his face, he has not awakened. He is in a very deep sleep, probably stage 4, which occurs about thirty minutes after falling asleep.

6. *c* is the answer. Purposefully directing one's thoughts as Miranda is doing is an active state of consciousness. (p. 211)

a. Passive states of consciousness are characterized by wandering, nondirected thoughts.

b. There is no such thing as a structuralistic state of consciousness. Structuralists were those psychologists attempting to define the elements or structure of consciousness.

d. There is no such thing as a functional state of consciousness. Functionalists wanted to find out the functions of consciousness in behavior.

7. *c* is the answer. Night terrors, which occur during a rapid shift from stage 4 to REM, are very frightening dreams. It sometimes takes up to thirty minutes to calm a person who has experienced a night terror episode. (p. 218)

a. There are no sleep disorders particularly associated with stage 1.

b. & d. There are no sleep disorders particularly associated with stages 2 and 3.

8. *b* is the answer. People who have narcolepsy often fall asleep in the middle of an active waking state. They immediately shift into REM sleep. Ruby would feel much better if she knew that Kevin had

fallen asleep because of narcolepsy and not because he was bored with the thought of their engagement. (p. 218)

a. People with hypersomnia sleep longer than most people at night, feel tired during the day, and take one or more naps during the daytime. However, they do not fall asleep in the middle of an active waking state.

c. If Kevin had insomnia, he would not be able to fall asleep at all.

d. Night terrors occur during a rapid shift from stage 4 to REM. Ruby is worried about why Kevin fell asleep, not about what happened while he was asleep.

9. *a* is the answer. Disrupting the circadian rhythm can make a person grouchy and less productive and can cause difficulties getting to sleep. It does not really matter what times you choose to go to sleep and wake up, as long as you are consistent. (pp. 216–217)

b. Your sleeping schedule does influence your productivity and happiness. If you go to bed and get up at different times every day, you will disrupt your circadian rhythm. This can make you grouchy and less productive.

c. If you go to bed early and get up early on a consistent basis, your circadian rhythms will not be disrupted.

d. Only *a* is the correct answer.

10. *c* is the answer. The ability to see things that are not there or not to see things that are there is the result of a reduction in reality testing. (p. 223)

a. Hypnotized people do not initiate plans on their own. They usually prefer to wait until the hypnotist tells them what to do. This is not, however, the reason Mark saw the cat when it was not there.

b. An example of role-taking would be acting like a cat or feeling as though you were someone else or a different age.

d. When attention is redistributed, one of the senses may seem to fill one's perceptions. If Mark's head had been described as filled with the sight of the cat, then this would have been the correct answer.

11. *c* is the answer. When people go without REM sleep, they have more REM periods than usual when they finally do sleep. (p. 219)

    a. People who go to sleep and get up at the same time every day will not have their REM periods interrupted. Therefore, their REM periods will not increase in number or length.

    b. The older we get, the less time we spend asleep. Most of the decrease is in REM sleep.

    d. People with hypersomnia have plenty of time to go through REM sleep. Upon recovery, they have no REM deficiency to correct.

12. *d* is the answer. Insomnia is being unable to sleep. Cocaine, a stimulant, would keep Irene awake. (pp. 217, 223)

    a. *d* is the answer.

    b. If Irene were addicted to barbiturates, then she would be very sleepy and relaxed.

    c. *d* is the answer.

13. *a* is the answer. Norman is about to start meditating. Finding a quiet spot, assuming a comfortable position, using a mantra, and taking a passive attitude are all elements of meditation methods. (pp. 227–228)

    b. Hypnotists do not formally use mantras.

    c. You do not use a mantra to go to sleep.

    d. Think about daydreaming. You do not necessarily need a quiet spot; you can be on a busy sidewalk surrounded by hundreds of people and still be lost in a daydream. Also, daydreaming does not require a mantra.

14. *c* is the answer. Valium is a tranquilizer, which does not cause hallucinations. (pp. 232–233)

    a., *b*., & *d*. PCP, prolonged cocaine use, and LSD can all cause hallucinations.

15. *c* is the answer. Cocaine increases norepinephrine activity in the central nervous system. (p. 232)

    a. Alcohol is a central nervous system depressant.

    b. LSD alters activity in serotonergic neurons.

    d. Opium stimulates receptors that normally recognize endorphins, the brain's natural supply of opiate.

Chapter 7

Learning

OUTLINE

I. INTRODUCTION (pp. 242–245)

Learning is a relatively permanent change in an organism or its behavior (response) that results from past experience.

II. CLASSICAL CONDITIONING (pp. 245–256)

A. Pavlov's Discovery

1. *The Initial Experiment*.
a. Phase One: Establishment of natural reflex and neutral stimulus.

b. Phase Two: Repeated pairing of neutral stimulus and stimulus (cause) of natural reflex.

c. Phase Three: The neutral stimulus alone causes some form of the natural reflex to occur.

2. *The Elements of Classical Conditioning*. In classical conditioning, a neutral stimulus is paired with a stimulus that elicits a reflex or other response until the neutral stimulus alone elicits a similar response.
a. Unconditioned Stimulus (UCS)—stimulus of natural reflex

b. Unconditioned Response (UCR)—natural reflex

c. Conditioned Stimulus (CS)—neutral stimulus that is paired with the UCS

d. Conditioned Response (CR)—response to conditioned stimulus

B. Establishing a Conditioned Response

The process through which a CS begins to produce a CR is called acquisition. The ease and strength of acquisition is dependent on what the CS and UCS are and how they are paired.

1. *The Relevance and Intensity of Stimuli*. The CS must be a signal biologically relevant to the organism. A stronger UCS will produce a stronger CR.

2. *The Pairing of Stimuli*. The number of CS and UCS pairings and the order of their presentation will alter the strength of the CR.
a. Simultaneous Conditioning: The CS and UCS begin and end at the same time.

b. Trace Conditioning: The CS begins and ends before the UCS is presented.

c. Backward Conditioning: The CS is presented after the UCS ends.

d. Delayed Conditioning: The CS is presented, then followed by the UCS. Both stimuli end at the same time, producing the strongest CR.

3. *Predictive Value*. If only one CS is consistently paired with a UCS, a strong CR will be produced.

C. What is Learned in Classical Conditioning?

In classical conditioning, an organism learns whether the UCS can be predicted by the CS.

D. Conditioned Responses Over Time

1. *Stimulus Generalization and Discrimination*.
   a. Stimulus Generalization. Stimuli that are similar to but not identical to the CS will also elicit that CR.

   b. Stimulus Discrimination occurs when an organism learns to differentiate between stimuli that are similar, but not identical, to the CS.

2. *Extinction*. When the CS is repeatedly presented without the UCS, the strength of the CR will decrease. Reconditioning will cause the reappearance of the CR. Spontaneous recovery may also occur.

E. Classical Conditioning of Human Behavior

1. *Phobias and Anxiety*. Humans can learn situation-specific fears through classical conditioning.

2. *Hypertension*. Humans who associate some environmental cue (CS) with stress (UCS) may experience hypertension as a CR.

3. *Promoting Health and Treating Illness*. Classical conditioning and techniques based upon its principles, such as systematic desensitization, can be used to reduce human suffering.

III. INSTRUMENTAL CONDITIONING
(pp. 256–269)

In instrumental conditioning, responses are learned that help produce some rewarding or desired effect.

A. From the Puzzle Box to the Skinner Box

1. *The Law of Effect*. If a response made in the presence of a particular stimulus is followed by a reward, that response is more likely to be made the next time the stimulus is encountered.

2. *Operant Conditioning*. The process of learning responses that help produce some rewarding or desired effect is called operant conditioning, used synonymously with instrumental conditioning.

B. Basic Components of Instrumental Conditioning

1. *Operants and Reinforcers*. Two types of reinforcers exist: positive reinforcers and negative reinforcers.

2. *Discriminative Stimuli and Stimulus Control*. Discriminative stimuli signal to an organism that reinforcement is available if a certain response is made. This response is said to be under stimulus control.

C. Forming and Strengthening Operants

1. *Shaping*. Creation of new responses never before displayed can be accomplished through shaping, or reinforcing approximations of the desired behavior.

2. *Delay and Size of Reinforcement*. Operant conditioning is strongest when the delay in receiving a reinforcer is short and when the reinforcer is large.

3. *Schedules of Reinforcement*.
   a. Continuous Reinforcement Schedule. Every correct response receives a reward.

   b. Partial or Intermittent Reinforcement Schedules.

   (1) *Fixed Ratio*. A reward is given after a fixed number of responses.

   (2) *Variable Ratio*. A reward is given after an average number of responses.

(3) *Fixed Interval.* The first response displayed after a fixed time interval is rewarded.

(4) *Variable Interval.* The first response displayed after a varying time interval is rewarded.

4. *Schedules and Extinction.* The partial reinforcement extinction effect demonstrates that the ease or difficulty of extinguishing an operant behavior depends on the schedule of reinforcement.

5. *Secondary Reinforcement.* If the positive value of a reward must be learned, it is considered a secondary reinforcer. Primary (unlearned) reinforcers, such as food and water, are basic to survival.

D. Negative Reinforcement

With the use of negative reinforcement, an organism learns to terminate (escape conditioning) or avoid (avoidance conditioning) an aversive stimulus.

E. Punishment

Operant responses decrease when followed by an aversive stimulus (punishment) or removal of a pleasant stimulus.

F. Applications of Instrumental Conditioning

These include programmed instruction, decreasing undesirable behaviors, and increasing desirable behaviors.

IV. SOCIAL LEARNING (pp. 269–271)

A. Vicarious Conditioning

Reinforcements that are indirectly experienced through observation influence the observer's behavior.

B. Observational Learning

This occurs when an observer learns new behaviors as a result of watching others' behaviors.

1. *Determinants of Observational Learning.*
   a. Attention: people must pay attention to what is happening around them.

   b. Retention: what a person sees must be remembered.

   c. Reproduction: a person must be capable of performing the act that was observed.

   d. Motivation: people will perform the act only if there is some reason for doing so.

V. COGNITIVE PROCESSES IN LEARNING (pp. 271–275)

Learning can occur through cognitive process in addition to the process of associating two stimuli or of associating a response and its consequences.

A. Insight

The cognitive process of insight involves perceiving the global organization of a problem.

B. Latent Learning and Cognitive Maps

Learning that is not immediately evident in an organism's behavior is latent learning. Cognitive maps, which are mental representations of the environment, are a form of latent learning.

KEY TERMS

1. **Learning** is any relatively permanent change in behavior (response) of the organism that results from past experience. (p. 242)

REMEMBER: Throughout the chapter, the word response is used. It is equivalent to a behavior or mental process. If you become confused by the use of this word, simply substitute the words *mental process* or *behavior* and the sentence's meaning should become clear.

2. A **reflex** is an automatic reaction to stimuli. (p. 246)

Example: Close your eyes and imagine that you are biting into a big juicy wedge of lemon. Most likely you will begin to salivate. Your response, salivation, is involuntary or reflexive.

3. A **neutral stimulus** does not *initially* elicit a response. (p. 246)

Example: In 1850, the sight of a swastika probably would not have caused anyone discomfort. Then it was a *neutral stimulus*. However, since its association with the Nazis in World War II, most people find it repulsive.

4. **Classical conditioning** is a procedure in which a neutral stimulus is paired with a stimulus that elicits a reflex or other response until the neutral stimulus alone elicits a similar response. (p. 247)

Example: Cat owners who feed their cats canned food and use an electric can opener know that just the sound of the opener will cause the cat to come running into the kitchen and salivate. The sound of the opener (an originally neutral stimulus) is paired with food (a stimulus that elicits a reflex or other response) until the sound alone elicits the response. This occurs because the sound of the electric opener *predicts* the presence of food.

5. **Unconditioned stimulus (UCS)** is, in classical conditioning, the stimulus that elicits a response without conditioning or learning having to take place. (p. 247)

Example: In the cat example in key term 4, food is the unconditioned stimulus; it naturally causes the cat to salivate.

REMEMBER: Unconditioned means unlearned. The cats do not have to learn about food every time in order to respond to food.

6. An **unconditioned response (UCR)** is, in classical conditioning, the automatic or reflexive response to the unconditioned stimulus. (p. 247)

Example: In the cat example in key term 4, *classical conditioning*, salivation is an unconditioned response. This behavior or response is reflexive or unlearned and occurs in the presence of the unconditioned stimulus (food).

REMEMBER: Unconditioned means unlearned.

7. The **conditioned stimulus (CS)** (neutral stimulus) is, in classical conditioning, the stimulus which, only *after* repeated pairings with the unconditioned stimulus, causes a conditioned response that is similar to the unconditioned response. (p. 247)

Example: In the cat example in key term 4, *classical conditioning*, the sound of the can opener is the conditioned stimulus, because it initially elicited no response from the cat (as a neutral stimulus). Only when the sound of the opener was paired with the presentation of food did the sound predict the presence of food (UCS) and cause the cat to run to the kitchen and salivate.

REMEMBER: Conditioned means learned. The conditioned stimulus is originally neutral; the organism must learn that it predicts the presence of the UCS.

8. **Conditioned responses (CR)** are learned responses elicited by the conditioned stimulus. (p. 247)

Example: In the cat example in key term 4, *classical conditioning*, the cat's response of running to the kitchen and salivating when it hears the can opener is the conditioned response.

REMEMBER: Conditioned means learned. This response is learned.

9. **Simultaneous conditioning** is a type of classical conditioning in which the conditioned and unconditioned stimuli are presented and terminated at the same time. (p. 248)

REMEMBER: The word *simultaneous* means to occur at the same time. The CS and the UCS occur at the same time.

10. **Trace conditioning** is a type of classical conditioning in which the conditioned stimulus ends before the unconditioned stimulus is presented. (p. 248)

REMEMBER: The word *trace* means a mark, sign, or trail that is left. In order for the conditioned stimulus to *leave* a trace, it must begin and end before the presentation of the unconditioned stimulus.

11. **Backward conditioning** is a type of classical conditioning in which the unconditioned stimulus begins and ends before the conditioned stimulus is presented. (p. 248)

REMEMBER: The usual order of events in classical conditioning is to present the CS prior to the UCS. *Backward conditioning* means just what it says; the order of the CS and UCS are *backward*. The CS follows the UCS.

12. **Delayed conditioning** is a type of classical conditioning in which the conditioned stimulus is presented before the unconditioned stimulus and both stimuli are terminated at the same time. This procedure produces the strongest CR. (p. 248)

REMEMBER: The word *delay* means to put off until a future time. The unconditioned stimulus is *delayed*. Its presence is put off until the conditioned stimulus has been on for a given amount of time.

13. **Taste-aversion learning** occurs when, through the process of classical conditioning, an organism learns to avoid drinking or eating something because the taste (CS) has become associated with the effects of food or liquid containing discomfort-producing ingredients (UCS). (pp. 249–250)

Example: Eric has a *learned taste aversion* to whiskey. The last time he drank whiskey he had food poisoning and did not know it. The extreme nausea (UCR) that he experienced from the food poisoning (UCS) became associated with the taste of whiskey (CS). Now, Eric avoids drinking whiskey; he becomes queasy (CR) just from the smell of it.

14. **Stimulus generalization,** in classical conditioning, occurs when an organism displays a conditioned response to a stimulus that is similar but not identical to the conditioned stimulus. In operant conditioning, several different but similar stimuli can inform an organism that, should a particular response be made, a reinforcer or punishment will be presented. (p. 253)

Example: George was very curious as a child. He had never seen a spider (CS) before the time he picked up a big reddish-brown one to investigate closely. Eventually, the spider bit him (UCS), causing him to become ill (UCR) for several days. George is now an adult and avoids (CR) all spiders, not just reddish-brown ones. He is reacting to stimuli that are similar but not necessarily identical to the original conditioned stimulus (reddish-brown spiders).

15. **Stimulus discrimination** occurs when an organism learns that stimuli similar but not identical to the conditioned stimuli do not predict the occurrence of the unconditioned stimulus. See key term 23, discriminative stimuli, for more information about discrimination in operant conditioning. (p. 253)

Example: Ralph the dog receives an injection (UCS) at the veterinarian's every four months. Ralph usually loves to ride in the car. However, whenever his owner drives Ralph to the veterinarian's (CS), Ralph whimpers (CR) for most of the ride. Ralph has learned to discriminate between the route to the veterinarian's and the route to other places.

16. **Extinction,** in classical conditioning, occurs when the conditioned stimulus, after being presented without the unconditioned stimulus, loses its predictive value. Eventually, the conditioned stimulus no longer elicits the conditioned response. In operant conditioning, a response is extinguished when it is no longer reinforced. (p. 253)

Example: The story, "The Boy Who Cried Wolf," is an example of extinction in classical conditioning. Shepherds learned that hearing someone cry "Wolf!" (CS) meant that a wolf (UCS) had appeared and they would run (CR). When one little boy repeatedly cried "Wolf!" for no reason, the other shepherds stopped responding (CR) to his cry (CS) because it no longer predicted the presence of danger.

REMEMBER: To become *extinct* means to no longer exist. In the above example, the CR (running) no longer exists when the cry of "Wolf" (CS) is heard.

17. **Reconditioning,** in classical conditioning, refers to the re-pairing of the CS and the UCS after extinction has taken place. During reconditioning, an organism learns more quickly than it did the first time that the CS predicts the UCS. (p. 254)

REMEMBER: Conditioning involves the association of two stimuli such that one (CS) begins to predict the occurrence of the other (UCS). *Reconditioning* is simply repeating this process.

18. **Spontaneous recovery** is the reappearance of the conditioned response when the UCS is presented after extinction in the absence of reconditioning. (p. 254)

Example: Pavlov's dogs were conditioned to salivate (CR) in response to the sound of a bell. After extinction (hearing the bell without receiving food) the dogs no longer responded. If, after a long time following extinction, the dogs heard the sound of the bell again, they would most likely salivate. The conditioned response has *spontaneously "recovered."*

19. **The law of effect.** If a response made in the presence of a particular stimulus is followed by a reward, that same response is more likely to occur the next time the stimulus is encountered. Responses that are not rewarded are less and less likely to be performed again. (pp. 257–258)

REMEMBER: The *law of effect* means the law of *being effective.* If an organism learns that a behavior produces a desired effect, such as good grades or money, the organism will repeat the behavior. If the behavior is ineffective (it doesn't produce anything or it produces bad effects, such as a scolding), it will not be repeated.

20. **Instrumental conditioning/operant conditioning** is a procedure during which an organism learns that certain responses are instrumental in producing desired effects in the environment. (pp. 256, 258)

Example: Most students have learned that studying (response) results in receiving good grades (desirable effects).

21. **Positive reinforcers,** in operant conditioning, are similar to rewards. If presented following a behavior, they increase the likelihood of that behavior's future occurrence. (p. 259)

Example: If Rover gets a bone (a positive reinforcer) every time he rolls over, he will probably roll over frequently.

22. **Negative reinforcers,** in operant conditioning, are unpleasant stimuli, which, if removed following a behavior or response, will increase the likelihood of that behavior's future occurrence. (p. 259)

Example: Hunger pains are unpleasant stimuli. Eating causes them to go away. People learn the habit of eating when they experience hunger pains, because the pains (negative reinforcers) disappear.

23. **Discriminative stimuli,** in operant conditioning, are signals to an organism that, should a particular response be made, reinforcement is available. Such a response is said to be under *stimulus control,* because the response is usually made only when the discriminative stimulus, but not others, is present. (p. 260)

Example: Alice knows that her business partner is in a good mood if she is smiling, is not wearing her suit jacket, and has the window blinds opened. These *discriminative stimuli* inform Alice that she can approach her partner with a new idea (Alice's particular response) and expect her partner to be supportive (reinforcement). Alice's behavior is under stimulus control because Alice will not approach her partner unless the discriminative stimuli are present.

24. **Stimulus control.** See *discriminative stimuli,* key term 23. (p. 260)

25. **Shaping** is an operant conditioning process in which successive approximations of a behavior are reinforced until the entire desired behavior pattern appears. (p. 261)

Example: Trainers at Sea World want to teach a whale to jump through a hoop. Since wild whales do not normally perform this behavior, the trainers must shape it. They might begin by rewarding the whale for jumping out of the water. Then they will reward the whale for jumping toward a hoop and eventually for touching it. Each of these behaviors is a successive approximation of jumping through a hoop. Eventually, the entire behavior pattern will be learned and rewarded.

26. **Continuous reinforcement schedules** involve reinforcing a desired response every time it occurs. This is one type of fixed ratio schedule. See also key term 30, *fixed interval schedules.* (p. 261)

Example: Denise is a housekeeper. When she gets paid every time she cleans a house, she is experiencing *continuous reinforcement.*

27. **Partial** or **intermittent reinforcement schedules** are used when a desired response is reinforced only some of the time. (p. 261)

REMEMBER: Any reinforcement schedule other than a continuous one is an example of this.

28. **Fixed ratio schedules** provide reinforcement after a fixed number of responses. (p. 262)

Example: Phil, a real estate broker, receives a bonus for every ten houses he sells.

REMEMBER: The word *fixed* in a schedule always means set. The word *ratio* in a schedule always means behavior. A *fixed ratio schedule* indicates that a reward is given after a set number of behaviors.

29. **Variable ratio schedules** call for reinforcement after a variable number of responses. (p. 262)

Example: Sharon's parents will reward her with a gift of her choice when she gets one to three good report cards.

REMEMBER: The word *variable* means changing. The word *ratio* always means behavior. A reward is presented after a varying number of behaviors—in other words, after some variable number of responses has occurred.

30. **Fixed interval schedules** call for reinforcement for the first response that occurs after some fixed time has passed since the last reward. (p. 262)

Example: Lynne, a graduate teaching assistant, gets paid once a month.

REMEMBER: The word *fixed* in a schedule means set. The word *interval* in a schedule means a time period. An organism is rewarded for the first behavior after a set time period, or *fixed interval.*

31. **Variable interval schedules** reinforce the first response after some period of time, but the amount of time varies. (p. 262)

Example: Students who study a little every day in order to be prepared for surprise quizzes given at various times throughout the semester are on a *variable interval schedule.*

REMEMBER: The word *variable* in a schedule means changing. The word *interval* means time period. An organism is rewarded at changing periods of time.

32. Partial reinforcement extinction effect occurs when a partial reinforcement schedule has been used in the operant conditioning process. The more difficult it is for the organism to predict the occurrence of a reinforcement, the harder the response is to extinguish. (p. 263)

WHY: To extinguish an operant behavior, reinforcement is no longer given following a response. On a partial reinforcement schedule, an organism will have to perform a response more than once or wait for a period of time before realizing that responses are no longer being rewarded. An animal on a continuous reinforcement schedule could know after only one response that reinforcement has been withdrawn.

33. Primary reinforcers are those rewards which promote the survival of an organism. (p. 264)

Example: Food and water are basic to survival.

34. Secondary reinforcers are those rewards which have acquired meaning by their association with primary reinforcers. (p. 264)

Example: Before people used money in exchange for goods, they worked to produce or exchange life's basic necessities, such as food. Money, because it allows us to buy food and has therefore been associated with food, is a *secondary reinforcer.*

35. Escape conditioning occurs when an organism learns that a particular response will terminate an aversive stimulus. (p. 264)

Example: Lydia has recently set up a computer at home and now does most of her work there. Her cat, Spooky, has begun to sit next to the terminal and cry until Lydia gets up to feed him. Lydia has learned that her response of feeding the cat will remove the distracting sound of its cries.

36. Avoidance conditioning occurs when an organism responds to a signal in a way that prevents exposure to an aversive stimulus. (p. 265)

Example: Leslie has learned that accepting most men's invitations for dates allows her to avoid the awkwardness of explaining that she is not interested in them.

37. Punishment involves the presentation of an aversive stimulus, which decreases the frequency of the immediately preceding response. (p. 265)

Example: For people who want to break their nail-biting habit, there is a fingernail polish with a bad taste. When the people wearing this polish bite their nails, they are *punished* with an aversive stimulus (the taste of the polish). This is done to decrease the behavior (nail biting) immediately preceding the taste.

38. Vicarious conditioning occurs when an organism learns the relationship between a response and its consequences (either reinforcement or punishment) by watching others. (p. 269)

Example: Tara is the youngest of six children. By watching her brothers and sisters, she has learned which behaviors her parents will reward and which behaviors they will punish.

39. Observational learning occurs when people learn by watching others' responses. Learning takes place even if others' responses are not rewarded. (p. 269)

Example: Suppose you found a being from another planet on your doorstep. Charlie, the alien, is intelligent and looks just like a human being. That night, Charlie watches you brush your teeth. Then he picks up the tooth brush and imitates your behavior. This is not because he knows you get great checkups at the dentist. He is merely learning a behavior by watching you do it.

40. **Insight** is the sudden grasp of new relationships that are necessary to solve a problem and that were not learned in the past. (p. 273)

41. **Cognitive maps** are mental representations of the environment. (p. 275)

Example: When he was at college, Dale lost his sight in a car accident. When he got out of the hospital, he still knew how to get around the campus because he had a mental representation (or cognitive map) of the campus.

42. **Latent learning** refers to learning that is not demonstrated at the time that it occurs. (p. 275)

Example: You have discovered that you enjoy your psychology class. However, you do not demonstrate the knowledge that you learned during the first lecture until the first test several weeks later.

LEARNING OBJECTIVES

1. Know the definition of learning. (p. 242)

2. Define the elements of classical conditioning: conditioned stimulus, unconditioned stimulus, unconditioned response, and the conditioned response. Create an example of classical conditioning that illustrates the relationship between these variables. (p. 247)

3. Define acquisition. Explain why the stimuli's relevance, intensity, order of presentation, and number of pairings affect the speed and strength of acquisition. (pp. 247–249)

4. Define the four types of conditioning procedures: simultaneous, trace, delayed, and backward. Know which type of conditioning produces the strongest type of conditioned response. (p. 248)

5. Define taste-aversion learning. Explain why it is a special case of classical conditioning. (pp. 249–250)

6. Know what is learned in classical conditioning. (pp. 251–252)

7. Discuss the role of classical conditioning in drug abuse problems. (pp. 252–253)

8. Define and give an example of stimulus generalization and stimulus discrimination. (p. 253)

9. Describe the processes of extinction, reconditioning and spontaneous recovery in classical conditioning. (pp. 253–254)

10. Discuss the role of classical conditioning in human and animal behavior. (pp. 254–256)

11. Define instrumental or operant conditioning. Explain how it differs from classical conditioning. (pp. 256–258)

12. Define the law of effect. Discuss its role in instrumental conditioning. (pp. 257–258)

13. Define positive and negative reinforcement. (pp. 259, 264)

14. Define discriminative stimulus and stimulus control. Give an example of stimulus control. (p. 260)

15. Define shaping. Know when it is used in instrumental conditioning. (p. 261)

16. Describe the relationship between reinforcement schedules and the intensity of operant responses. Discuss the changes in extinction under different reinforcement schedules. (pp. 261–263)

17. Discuss the differences between primary and secondary reinforcers. (pp. 263–264)

18. Define escape conditioning and avoidance conditioning. Discuss their similarities and differences. (pp. 264–265)

19. Define punishment and describe its role in operant conditioning. (pp. 265–267)

20. Define learned helplessness. (pp. 268–269)

21. Define vicarious conditioning and observational learning. Discuss their similarities and differences. (pp. 269–270)

22. Define insight. Discuss the differences in *what* is learned in classical conditioning, instrumental conditioning and insight. (pp. 272–273)

23. Define and give an example of a cognitive map and latent learning. (pp. 273–275)

CONCEPTS AND EXERCISES

No. 1 Learning in Advertising

Completing this exercise should help you to achieve the following learning objectives.

(2) *Define the elements of classical conditioning: conditioned stimulus, unconditioned stimulus, unconditioned response, and conditioned response. Create an example of classical conditioning that illustrates the relationship between these variables. (p. 247)*

(6) *Know what is learned in classical conditioning. (pp. 251–252)*

(9) *Describe the processes of extinction, reconditioning and spontaneous recovery in classical conditioning. (pp. 253–254)*

(11) *Define instrumental or operant conditioning. Explain how it differs from classical conditioning. (pp. 256–258)*

(13) *Define both positive and negative reinforcement. (p. 259)*

(19) *Define punishment and describe its role in operant conditioning. (pp. 265–267)*

Advertising is all around you: television, magazines, radio, billboards, pencils, the back of cabs, matchbooks, just about anywhere you look. The people who create these ads often use learning principles to persuade you to buy their products. In the following exercise, you are the ads' creator. It is your job to tell your boss the learning principle behind each of the following ad descriptions. Choose from the list on page 131 (at the end of the exercise). Answers may be used more than once.

1. Television spot, 30 seconds. Scene: The counter at Speedy Dryclean. An anxious-looking woman enters carrying a yellow dress with chocolate stains on it.

Customer: I need to have this dress cleaned by noon.

Counter clerk: Don't worry; it'll be ready at noon.

Customer: I hope so. I really have to have the dress by noon.

Counter clerk: We'll have it by noon. No problem.

Shift of scene: Customer is at home, smiling as she talks on the phone.

Customer: Hi. I dropped a dress off there earlier—to be ready at noon. Can I pick it up now?

Pause: Customer's smile abruptly turns to a frown.

Narrator: Why take chances? Speedy Dryclean guarantees that your clothes will be ready on time.

a. This is an example of _____ conditioning.

b. The dress failing to be ready illustrates the use of _____ for the behavioral response of using a drycleaning service other than Speedy.

2. Television spot, 30 seconds. Scene: Mother checking on sleeping child. Mother speaking very quietly.

Mother: Jennifer went to the doctor today to get the stitches out of her knee. Before we went to the Stone Clinic, just mentioning the word "doctor" made her cry for fear of getting a shot. But the doctors and nurses at the Stone Clinic understand a child's needs; they're gentle, soothing, kind, and thoughtful. That makes Jennifer happy. I know that the Stone Clinic staff are experts in their fields, and, as a mother (mother looks lovingly at Jennifer) that makes me very happy. (Mother leans over, smooths Jennifer's hair, kisses her on the forehead, and tiptoes out of room.)

    a. This is an example of _____ conditioning.

    b. The doctors are a(n) _____ .

    c. Jennifer's old fear of doctors is a(n) _____ .

    d. What conditioning process caused Jennifer to lose her fear of doctors? _____

Instrumental

Positive reinforcement

Negative reinforcement

Punishment

Classical

Conditioned stimulus

Conditioned response

Unconditioned stimulus

Unconditioned response

Extinction

No. 2 Teaching an Alien

    Completing this exercise should help you to achieve the following learning objectives.

(5) *Define taste-aversion learning. Explain why it is a special case of classical conditioning. (pp. 249–250)*

(11) *Define instrumental or operant conditioning. Explain how it differs from classical conditioning. (pp. 256–258)*

(13) *Define positive and negative reinforcement. (pp. 259, 264)*

(14) *Define discriminative stimulus and stimulus control. Give an example of stimulus control. (p. 260)*

(17) *Discuss the differences between primary and secondary reinforcers. (pp. 263–264)*

(18) *Define escape conditioning and avoidance conditioning. Discuss their similarities and differences. (pp. 264–265)*

(19) *Define punishment and describe its role in operant conditioning. (pp. 265–267)*

(21) *Define vicarious conditioning and observational learning. Discuss their similarities and differences. (pp. 269–270)*

(23) *Define and give an example of a cognitive map and latent learning. (pp. 273–275)*

    To discover the prevalence of learning in our everyday lives, read the following story of Sam and Gufla, an alien. You will find many of the basic learning principles embedded in the plot. Afterwards, answer the questions using the list of terms at the end of the exercise. Answers may be used more than once.

    One day, while playing in the park, Sam met someone he thought was a boy his own age. Thinking the boy was human, Sam began a conversation. Even though the stranger spoke perfect English, Sam soon realized that he was from another planet and had landed here by accident. Eight-year-old Sam was more curious than afraid and invited the alien home for dinner.

    The trip home was eventful. Sam, worried about being late, decided to take a shortcut that one of his pals had told him about earlier. As they entered a backyard, a snarling German shepherd charged them. Sam quickly figured out that the dog's chain could not reach to the fence. He and the alien, whom he had named Gufla, ran along the fence until they were out of the yard. After slowing down and catching his breath, Sam realized that he would have to tell Gufla a few things about his family and how to behave so his mother would not suspect anything. Most importantly, Sam knew that he could not share his discovery with his sister, who would tell his mother. Gufla asked Sam what eating felt like. How would he recognize food? Sam replied that anything that smells good is edible. Gufla promptly picked a rose from a garden they were passing and ate it. Sam laughed, but Gufla was holding his stomach because the rose, which had fertilizer on it, made him feel ill. Gufla vowed never to go near a rose again.

Sam told Gufla that anytime Sam nodded his head, Gufla could eat whatever his fork was touching. Anytime he shook his head, Gufla was not to eat whatever his fork was touching. Sam tried to explain that food, not napkins or salt and pepper shakers, tastes good, which is a pleasant feeling. By the time they reached Sam's driveway, Sam realized that there was not enough time to teach Gufla all the behaviors he would need to know, so Sam told Gufla to imitate Sam's behavior whenever he felt confused. Sam said that, since it was Friday night, his mother might let them stay up and watch the late-night horror movie, a special treat, if all went well.

1. Sam's mother has probably successfully used _____ to decrease his tardiness.

2. (a & b). Sam is using a _____ to follow a shortcut home. This is also a case of _____ since Sam has never taken this shortcut before, even though he knew about it before that day.

3. Sam decides not to tell his sister about his find. This illustrates _____. Sam does not want his sister to tell his mother about Gufla.

4. Gufla became ill after eating the rose, probably because it had fertilizer on it. This is an example of learning a _____.

5 (a, b, & c). Gufla knows that the direction in which Sam moves his head is a _____, because this will let him know if what he puts in his mouth

(the behavior) will taste good or bad. Good food in this case is a _____ _____.

6. Gufla will watch and imitate what Sam does even though he won't really understand why he is doing it or if it will bring him any sort of pleasure. This is an example of _____.

7 (a & b). Sam and Gufla may be allowed to watch a late-night movie if they behave well at dinner. This illustrates the use of a _____ _____.

Primary

Secondary

Avoidance conditioning

Escape conditioning

Punishment

Positive reinforcer

Taste-aversion

Discriminative stimulus

Observational learning

Cognitive map

Latent learning

ANSWERS TO EXERCISES AND CONCEPTS

No. 1 Learning in Advertising

1a. Instrumental (p. 256). The customer is learning a relationship between a behavior (using a dry cleaners other than Speedy) and its consequence (clothes that aren't cleaned on time).

1b. Punishment (p. 265). The dress's failure to be ready will cause the customer problems and is, therefore, aversive.

2a. Classical (p. 247). Jennifer has learned that one stimulus (the doctor) predicts another (activities that cause pain).

2b. Conditioned stimulus (p. 247). Jennifer was not always afraid of doctors; originally, they were a neutral stimulus. When neutral stimuli begin to predict the presence of another stimulus, such as an injection, they become conditioned stimuli.

2c. Conditioned response (p. 247). Since Jennifer had to learn to be afraid of doctors, this is a conditioned (or learned) response.

2d. Extinction (p. 253). The association between the CS (doctors) and the UCS (activities that cause pain) has been eliminated, or at least greatly diminished. The CR (fear of doctors) has also been eliminated.

No. 2 Teaching an Alien

1. Punishment (p. 265). Sam has decreased his behavior of being late for dinner. Punishment decreases the occurrence of the behavior it follows. When Sam was late, he was probably punished.

2a. Cognitive map (p. 273). 2b. Latent learning (p. 273). Sam learned a shortcut by representing the information in his mind in the form of a map. We know that he learned the shortcut before he demonstrated his knowledge of it.

3. Avoidance conditioning (p. 265). Sam has learned to avoid having his sister inform his mother of his doings by simply not telling her what he does.

4. Taste-aversion (p. 249). Gufla has learned that roses (CS) predict the presence of fertilizer (UCS). Fertilizer causes stomachaches (CR). Gufla will stay away from (CR) all roses (CS) in the future.

5a. Discriminative stimulus (p. 260). 5b. Primary (p. 264) 5c. Positive reinforcer (p. 259). The direction in which Sam nods his head will be a discriminative stimulus, or signal, that will let Gufla know when to make a response (eating whatever his fork touches) in order to receive the reinforcement of eating food. Food is a pleasant stimulus and basic to survival. Therefore, it is a primary positive reinforcer.

6. Observational learning (p. 269). Gufla will attend to what Sam is doing, retain the information, and reproduce it because Sam has told him to. He is not performing each specific behavior to obtain a reward.

7a. Secondary (p. 264). 7b. Positive Reinforcer (p. 259). Watching a movie, although not basic to survival, is a pleasant stimulus. Therefore, this is an example of secondary positive reinforcement.

MULTIPLE CHOICE QUESTIONS

Facts and Definitions

1. A neutral stimulus
    a. is one that does not elicit a reflexive response.
    b. is synonymous with the unconditioned stimulus.
    c. causes an unconditioned response.
    d. predicts the presence of the unconditioned response.

2. Which of the following types of conditioning produces the strongest conditioned response?
    a. Trace conditioning
    b. Delayed conditioning
    c. Simultaneous conditioning
    d. Backward conditioning

3. When using simultaneous conditioning,

   a. the conditioned stimulus is presented after terminating the unconditioned stimulus.
   b. the unconditioned stimulus follows the conditioned stimulus and they are terminated simultaneously.
   c. the conditioned stimulus is turned on and off prior to presenting the unconditioned stimulus.
   d. the conditioned and unconditioned stimuli are presented and terminated together.

4. The optimal interval between the onset of the conditioned stimulus and the unconditioned stimulus is

   a. .5 to 1 second.
   b. 1 to 2 minutes.
   c. 2 to 5 minutes.
   d. 30 seconds to 1 minute.

5. In classical conditioning, an organism learns

   a. an association between the unconditioned stimulus and the conditioned response.
   b. that the conditioned stimulus is a substitute for the unconditioned stimulus.
   c. that the conditioned stimulus predicts the occurrence of the unconditioned stimulus.
   d. an association between the unconditioned response and the conditioned response.

6. Stimulus generalization involves responding to stimuli that

   a. had always occurred in the presence of the unconditioned stimulus.
   b. produce a reflexive response similar to the unconditioned response.
   c. are similar but not identical to the conditioned stimulus.
   d. are similar to the unconditioned stimulus but do not produce an unconditioned response.

7. Reconditioning refers to

   a. the appearance of a conditioned response following extinction.
   b. the elimination of the association between the conditioned and unconditioned stimulus.
   c. the occurrence of spontaneous recovery.
   d. the repairing of the conditioned and unconditioned stimulus after extinction.

8. Spontaneous recovery follows

   a. reconditioning.
   b. extinction.
   c. stimulus control.
   d. stimulus degradation.

9. In instrumental conditioning, negative reinforcers are

   a. pleasant stimuli presented following a response.
   b. unpleasant stimuli that are removed following a response.
   c. methods of decreasing a response.
   d. rewards considered basic to survival, such as food and drink.

10. In operant conditioning, discriminative stimuli

   a. automatically trigger a conditioned response.
   b. indicate the presence of reinforcement if a response is made.
   c. are successive approximations of a desired response.
   d. are similar but not identical to the conditioned stimulus.

11. Shaping is used when the conditioned response

   a. is physically difficult to perform.
   b. is to be decreased.
   c. has never been displayed before.
   d. is reflexive.

12. In operant conditioning, a reinforcer is presented to an organism on a fixed ratio schedule after

   a. a fixed amount of time.
   b. a fixed number of responses.
   c. an average number of responses.
   d. an average amount of time.

13. Which reinforcement schedule produces the highest response rate?

    a. Fixed ratio
    b. Fixed interval
    c. Variable ratio
    d. Variable interval

14. Which schedule produces the fastest extinction rate?

    a. Fixed ratio
    b. Fixed interval
    c. Variable ratio
    d. Variable interval

15. Punishment is

    a. the presentation of an aversive stimulus.
    b. the removal of a pleasant stimulus.
    c. used to decrease the occurrence of an undesired response.
    d. all of the above.

MULTIPLE CHOICE QUESTIONS

Application of Concepts

1. Johnny has learned that every time he cleans his room, his mother makes his favorite dessert. This is an example of

    a. classical conditioning.
    b. using a negative reinforcer.
    c. instrumental conditioning.
    d. learning to associate stimuli.

2. Brenda's first experience at the dentist was a traumatic one. During that first dental visit, the dentist used no Novocain before he began to drill her teeth. Now, just sitting in the waiting room and hearing the whirring sound of the drill makes Brenda nauseated. This is an example of what kind of conditioning?

    a. Classical conditioning
    b. Using a negative reinforcer

    c. Instrumental conditioning
    d. Using a positive reinforcer

Use the following situation to answer questions 3., 4., & 5.

When Tom rode the Ferris wheel at the amusement park for the first time, he became very dizzy. Now, when Tom sees an advertisement for amusement parks, he feels nauseated.

3. The unconditioned stimulus is

    a. the Ferris wheel ride.
    b. the feeling of dizziness.
    c. nausea.
    d. the sight of an amusement park.

4. The conditioned response is

    a. dizziness.
    b. the Ferris wheel ride.
    c. the sight of an amusement park.
    d. nausea.

5. The conditioned stimulus is

    a. dizziness.
    b. the Ferris wheel ride.
    c. seeing an amusement park.
    d. nausea.

6. Ten minutes before a movie starts, the theatre is filled with people who are talking or laughing. As soon as the lights go off everyone becomes quiet. A few people, who continue to laugh out loud and prevent the audience from hearing the show, are booed and hissed until they are quiet. Turning off the lights serves as a _____ in this example of operant conditioning.

    a. positive reinforcer
    b. negative reinforcer
    c. punishment
    d. discriminative stimulus

7. After Ernie, the lab rat, is exposed to repeated pairings of a dark blue light and electrical shock, he

becomes very nervous whenever a turquoise light is flashed in his cage. This phenomenon is called

   a. stimulus generalization.
   b. stimulus discrimination.
   c. stimulus degradation.
   d. stimulus control.

8. Every morning Floyd the cat knocks everything off his owner's bedside table, which makes a loud noise. Sometimes Floyd's owner gives in and gets up to feed him, and sometimes she rolls over and goes back to sleep. Which reinforcement schedule is producing Floyd's persistent behavior?

   a. Fixed ratio
   b. Variable ratio
   c. Fixed interval
   d. Variable interval

9. Kent does not like to take drugs of any kind. When he goes to the dentist, he tries not to ask for Novocain. However, sometimes he cannot handle the pain of drilling and he lets the doctor give him a shot. This illustrates the use of a

   a. positive reinforcer.
   b. negative reinforcer.
   c. punishment.
   d. All of the above.

10. A small boy is playing with a ball in the backyard. After several minutes, the boy is startled by a loud thunderclap. As the thunder subsides, the child throws down the ball and runs into the house. Several weeks later, the child is fearful of playing ball in the backyard. Which conditioning procedure is responsible for this fear?

   a. Delayed conditioning
   b. Trace conditioning
   c. Simultaneous conditioning
   d. Backward conditioning

11. On September 1, Jefferson High School's fire alarm sounded, and students ran from the building to escape the flames. For the next few weeks, the school experienced a rash of false alarms, and people began to ignore the sound. On December 15, a fire alarm sounded and students ran from the building in panic. What phenomenon was responsible for the student's renewed fear?

   a. Reconditioning
   b. Spontaneous recovery
   c. Stimulus control
   d. Stimulus generalization

12. As a sailor in World War II, Miguel developed a conditioned response to sirens that warned of approaching enemy aircraft. Yesterday he went to see a movie about World War II. When a ship's siren sounded in the film, the hair on the back of Miguel's neck stood on end. This is an example of

   a. reconditioning.
   b. escape conditioning.
   c. a very strong conditioned response.
   d. spontaneous recovery.

13. Anne is angry at her boss and would like to tell him exactly how she feels about him. But the last time Anne did something similar, she was fired. Now she is afraid of losing her job as well as her temper. What kind of learning does this represent?

   a. Escape
   b. Classical conditioning
   c. Avoidance
   d. Discriminative

14. Advertisements for breath mints frequently involve a chance meeting of strangers who end up falling in love because they had great breath when they met. Advertisers are hoping that people who watch the commercial will learn _____ that using breath mints will improve their love lives.

   a. vicariously
   b. by observation
   c. by classical conditioning
   d. by stimulus control

15. Gertrude's grandfather came to visit her recently for the first time. In the middle of the night he got up to use the bathroom. Half asleep, he took a

wrong turn and walked into a wall. This is an example of

    a. using an incorrect cognitive map.
    b. reverse insight.
    c. latent learning.
    d. vicarious learning.

ANSWERS TO MULTIPLE CHOICE QUESTIONS

Facts and Definitions

1. *a* is the answer. A neutral stimulus does not elicit a reflexive response (an orienting reflex is the only exception). A neutral stimulus becomes a conditioned stimulus (CS) and elicits a conditioned response (CR) only when it is paired with an unconditioned stimulus (UCS). (p. 246)

    b. An unconditioned stimulus elicits a reflexive response or an unlearned response that happens automatically. Therefore, a neutral stimulus is not synonymous with the unconditioned stimulus.

    c. A neutral stimulus does not elicit any response except an orienting reflex.

    d. A neutral stimulus does not elicit any response except an orienting reflex. A neutral stimulus becomes a conditioned stimulus and elicits a conditioned response only when it is paired with an unconditioned stimulus.

2. *b* is the answer. Delayed conditioning produces the strongest conditioned response. (p. 248)

    a., c., & d. Of the other three conditioning types, backward conditioning is the least effective.

3. *d* is the answer. In this type of conditioning, the conditioned stimulus and the unconditioned stimulus are presented simultaneously. (p. 248)

    a. This is backward conditioning.

    b. This is delayed conditioning.

    c. This is trace conditioning.

4. *a* is the answer. It is usually best to allow an interval of .5 to 1 second to elapse between the conditioned stimulus and the unconditioned stimulus. (p. 249)

    b., c., & d. The other options are much too long. Typically intervals longer than several seconds will fail to produce a conditioned response.

5. *c* is the answer. The conditioned stimulus predicts the occurrence of the unconditioned stimulus. (p. 251)

    a. There is no relationship between the UCS and CR.

    b. If the CS were merely a substitute for the UCS, the conditioned response would always be identical to the unconditioned response (UCR). This is not the case.

    d. No relationship between the CR and the UCR is learned.

6. *c* is the answer. An organism will generalize and respond to stimuli that are similar to the conditioned stimulus. (p. 253)

    a. Stimuli similar to the UCS that already elicit a CR need not have ever been presented before.

    b. In stimulus generalization the conditioned response is elicited by the CS or stimuli that resemble it. This response is always learned; it is never reflexive.

    d. Generalization refers to responses made to stimuli that are similar to the CS, not to the UCS.

7. *d* is the answer. Reconditioning is a repetition of the conditioning process. This occurs after extinction; if extinction had not already occurred, there would be no need for reconditioning. (p. 254)

    a. & c. The occurrence of a conditioned response after extinction is called spontaneous recovery.

    b. The process of extinction removes the association between the CS and the UCS so that the CS no longer predicts the presence of the UCS.

8. *b* is the answer. For a conditioned response to recover, it must first have been extinguished. (p. 254)

a. Reconditioning once again re-pairs the conditioned stimulus and the unconditioned stimulus. The conditioned response is relearned. Spontaneous recovery is just that, spontaneous. No relearning is necessary.

c. Stimulus control is associated with instrumental or operant conditioning.

d. There is no learning phenomenon called stimulus degradation.

9. *b* is the answer. In instrumental conditioning, reinforcers always produce a positive effect and work to increase a behavior. A negative reinforcer is a negative stimulus that is removed after the organism displays a desired response. (p. 259)

a. Positive reinforcers are pleasant stimuli that are presented after an organism displays a desired response.

c. Punishment and extinction are used to decrease the occurrence of a response.

d. Rewards that are basic to survival are primary reinforcements.

10. *b* is the answer. Discriminative stimuli allow the organism to discriminate between situations that will produce a consequence—a reinforcer or punishment—and those situations that will not. (p. 260)

a. Discriminative stimuli let an animal know when to make a response, they do not cause a response. Conditioned stimuli elicit or cause a conditioned response. There are no conditioned stimuli in operant conditioning.

c. Shaping involves rewarding successive approximations of a behavior (behaviors that come closer and closer to the desired response).

d. There is no conditioned stimulus in operant conditioning.

11. *c* is the answer. A behavior must occur before it can be reinforced. If an organism has never performed the desired behavior, behaviors that are successive approximations of the desired response are reinforced until the whole behavior appears. For an example of successive approximation, see the example of teaching your dog to "shake" on page 261 in your text.

a. Behaviors that are shaped are not always difficult to perform. It is not physically difficult for a dog to roll over, but if he has never done so, his behavior must be shaped.

b. Shaping is the creation of a new behavior, not decreasing an existing behavior.

d. Shaping allows an animal to learn new behavior. Reflexive behaviors are not new.

12. *b* is the answer. (p. 262)

a. This is called a fixed interval schedule.

c. This is called a variable ratio schedule.

d. This is called a variable interval schedule.

13. *a* is the answer. When the organism can predict how many responses are necessary for a reward, it will vigorously respond in expectation. (p. 263)

b. On a fixed interval schedule an organism will respond in order to receive a reinforcement, then wait until the next interval has passed before responding again.

c. A variable ratio schedule produces a high response rate but not as high as that produced by a fixed ratio schedule.

d. A variable interval schedule produces a slow, steady rate of response.

14. *a* is the answer. A fixed ratio schedule of reinforcement produces the fastest rate of extinction because the organism realizes very quickly that reinforcements have ceased to be presented. A continuous schedule of reinforcement, which is a type of fixed ratio schedule, produces the fastest rate of extinction possible. (p. 263)

b. Fixed intervals also produce a fast rate of extinction, but the organism must wait until the fixed interval elapses before it responds and finds no reinforcement.

c. & d. Organisms on a variable schedule of reinforcement cannot predict when the reinforcement will appear. They therefore take longer to realize that the reinforcement is missing once the extinction process has begun.

15. *d* is the answer. *a., b.,* & *c.* are all true. Punishment is not pleasant for the organism. It is accomplished by presenting an aversive stimulus (getting fired) or taking away a positive stimulus (the privilege of going out on the weekend). Punishment is used to decrease the occurrence of the behavior that precedes it. (p. 265)

ANSWERS TO MULTIPLE CHOICE QUESTIONS

Application of Concepts

1. *c* is the answer. Instrumental conditioning involves learning that responses involve consequences. When Johnny cleans his room (the response) his mom makes his favorite dessert (the consequence). (p. 256)

a. & d. Classical conditioning involves making an association between stimuli such that one (CS) comes to predict the presence of the other (UCS). This example involves learning that a behavior (cleaning the room) will bring about a reinforcer (dessert). This is called instrumental conditioning.

b. A negative reinforcer is an unpleasant stimulus that is removed following a desired response. In this case a positive reinforcer (a pleasant stimulus: dessert) is being presented following a desired behavior (cleaning the room).

2. *a* is the answer. The conditioned stimulus is the sound of the drill. The unconditioned stimulus is using the drill on the teeth. The unconditioned response is the pain that the drill causes. The conditioned response is nausea which is elicited by the sound of the drill. (p. 247)

b. & d. Reinforcers, both positive and negative, are used in instrumental conditioning.

c. Instrumental conditioning involves learning an association between a behavior and its consequences. Brenda is learning an association between two stimuli: the sound of the drill and the feeling of the drill on her teeth.

3a., 4d., 5c. This is an example of classical conditioning. The conditioned stimulus is the sight of the amusement park. The unconditioned stimulus is the ride on the Ferris wheel. The unconditioned response is feeling dizzy. The conditioned response is feeling nauseated. (p. 247)

6. *d* is the answer. A discriminative stimulus tells the people in the theater that if they are quiet (the response) they will be rewarded by seeing a movie (the reinforcement). Those who do not pay attention to the lights (those who are not under the control of the light stimulus) are punished by being booed and hissed at. (p. 253)

a. The lights are not turned off to reward the audience for its behavior.

b. The turned-off lights are not an unpleasant stimulus that is removed when a desired behavior is displayed.

c. Turning off the lights does cause a decrease in the behavior that precedes it, but turned-off lights are not aversive, so they cannot be considered punishment.

7. *a* is the answer. Ernie has been classically conditioned to a dark blue light. When he reacts to a turquoise light, he is generalizing his response to a different but similar stimulus. (p. 253)

b. If Ernie had learned to discriminate between stimuli then he would not react to any stimulus but the one that originally predicted the electric shock.

c. There is no stimulus degradation in this example.

d. Stimulus control occurs with the use of instrumental conditioning.

8. *b* is the answer. Floyd is being rewarded for the response of waking his owner, making this a ratio schedule. Floyd does not have to knock things over a set number of times before he is rewarded; the number of responses necessary before his owner gets up and feeds him varies, making this a variable schedule. The entire schedule is called a variable ratio schedule. (p. 262)

a. & c. This is a variable schedule, not a fixed one, because the amount of time or number of responses necessary to receive a reward is not fixed; it varies.

d. This is not an interval schedule because no time period must elapse before a response is rewarded.

9. *b* is the answer. The negative reinforcer is the removal of drilling pain by the Novocain. The behavior (asking for a drug to deaden the pain) will increase because the negative reinforcer has removed a potentially aversive stimulus (drilling pain). (p. 259)

a. A positive reinforcer is a pleasant stimulus that is added to the environment following a desired response. In this example, an unpleasant stimulus, pain, is being removed; a pleasant one is not being added.

c. If Kent were being punished, his behavior would be followed by an aversive stimulus or removal of a pleasant one. Being relieved of pain is the removal of an unpleasant stimulus.

d. b is the answer.

10. *a* is the answer. Playing with a ball in the backyard is the conditioned stimulus because the boy has learned that it predicts the occurrence of an unconditioned stimulus, the thunderstorm. The CS is present prior to the unconditioned stimulus, and both are terminated simultaneously since the boy throws down the ball and runs inside just as the thunder subsides. This order of events is called delayed conditioning. (p. 248)

b. For trace conditioning to occur, the boy would have to stop playing with the ball (CS) before the thunder starts.

c. For simultaneous conditioning to occur, playing with the ball (CS) and the thunder (UCS) would have to begin and end together.

d. For backward conditioning to occur, the thunder (UCS) would have to occur before the boy played with the ball (CS).

11. *b* is the answer. Spontaneous recovery is the recurrence of a conditioned response following extinction in the absence of reconditioning. (p. 254)

a. Reconditioning is the re-pairing of the CS and the UCS after extinction. The fire alarm (CS) would have to be paired with fire (UCS) again for reconditioning to occur.

c. Operant conditioned responses are under stimulus control. This is an example of classical conditioning.

d. If stimulus generalization had occurred, the students would have run out of the building in response to an alarm (CS) that was similar but not identical to the original fire alarm. The students heard the same fire alarm in December and September.

12. *c* is the answer. This is a very strong conditioned response, since after many years Miguel still is fearful when he hears the siren. (p. 254)

a. Reconditioning occurs after extinction. No mention of extinction is made in the question. For extinction to occur, the CS (siren) would have to be presented in the absence of the UCS (the enemy).

b. Escape conditioning involves learning to respond in order to end an aversive stimulus. Miguel did not attempt to escape or stop the noise of the siren at any time.

d. Spontaneous recovery occurs after extinction. Miguel never went through extinction. For extinction to occur, the CS (siren) would have to be presented in the absence of the UCS (enemy).

13. *c* is the answer. Anne is not going to tell her boss how she feels about him because she wants to *avoid* being fired. (p. 264)

a. Escape conditioning involves learning to respond in order to get away from an already-present aversive stimulus. Anne does not decide to not tell her boss what she is feeling in order to escape anything. She is trying to avoid the *possibility* of an aversive stimulus (getting fired) in the future.

b. This is an example of instrumental conditioning. Anne avoids making a behavioral response, because she has learned that the consequence of that response is getting fired. She has not learned that one stimulus (CS) predicts the occurrence of another (UCS).

d. Discriminative stimuli let an organism know when to respond in order to avoid punishment or receive reinforcement. There are no stimuli in the environment that let Anne know *when* not to tell her boss she is angry. She simply knows that she should not yell at her boss. A discriminative stimulus in this question would have been some clue that her boss was in a good mood and, therefore, more receptive to hearing what she had to say.

14. *a* is the answer. People learn by watching the commercials that using breath mints is rewarded or reinforced by meeting an attractive stranger with whom they will live happily ever after. This is called vicarious conditioning. (p. 269)

b. Observation learning does involve learning by watching the behavior of others. But the people being observed do not have to receive a reward or punishment for the person watching them to learn. Advertisers want people to use breath mints because using them supposedly provides a reward, and this reward is demonstrated in the ad itself.

c. This is an example of instrumental conditioning, not classical conditioning.

d. There is no stimulus mentioned in the question that lets a person know when to use breath mints. You may have thought that the presence of a stranger of the opposite sex was a discriminative stimulus, but this is not the case. The stranger is the reward or reinforcement in this example.

15. *a* is the answer. Gertrude's grandfather used a cognitive map of his house when he sleepily tried to find his way to the bathroom. (p. 275)

b. There is no such thing as reverse insight.

c. Latent learning occurs when an organism learns something but does not overtly demonstrate this new knowledge until later.

d. To learn a response vicariously, an organism must watch someone else display that response and be rewarded or punished for it.

Chapter 8

Memory

OUTLINE

I. THE SCOPE OF THE MEMORY SYSTEM (pp. 280–287)

A. Three Types of Memory

1. *Episodic memory.* Any memory of a specific event that happened while you were present is an episodic memory.

2. *Semantic memory.* This type of memory contains generalized knowledge of the world.

3. *Procedural memory.* This type of memory represents how to do various things.

B. Basic Memory Processes

1. *Encoding.* The process of putting information into memory is called encoding.
   a. Acoustic codes represent information as sequences of sounds.

   b. Semantic codes represent the meaning of information.

c. Visual codes represent information in the form of mental images.

2. *Storage.* Holding information in memory over time is called storage.

3. *Retrieval.* Pulling information out of memory after it has been stored is called retrieval.

C. Three Stages of Memory

1. *Sensory memory.* This stage of memory contains information from all of the senses in sensory registers for a fraction of a second.

2. *Short-term memory.* This stage of memory receives the information that was perceived in sensory memory, and if further processing occurs, it will disappear in twenty to thirty seconds.

3. *Long-term memory.* This stage of memory receives information processed through short-term memory. Information in long-term memory can remain there indefinitely.

II. SENSORY MEMORY (pp. 287–290)

The sensory registers hold information in short-term memory just long enough for it to be processed and recognized (perceived).

A. Capacity of the Sensory Registers

People can acquire a very large amount of information in one visual fixation. However, the information cannot be retained in the sensory registers for more than about 1 second.

B. Properties of Sensory Memory

1. *Icons.* Visual representations that last for only about 1 second in sensory memory, unless the stimulus is very strong.

2. *Echoes.* Representations of sound in sensory memory that often last for several seconds.

Selective attention determines which information in sensory memory will be perceived and transferred to short-term memory.

III. SHORT-TERM MEMORY (working memory) (pp. 290–298)

A. Encoding

Information is represented primarily by an acoustic code.

B. Storage

The immediate memory span is the number of items you can recall perfectly after one presentation of a stimulus. It is usually five to nine chunks of information.

1. *Duration.* Unless rehearsed, information stays in short-term memory for only about twenty seconds.

2. *Causes of Forgetting.* Information may decay. In addition, retroactive and proactive interference may disrupt the process of learning and remembering.

3. *What is stored?* Information is often represented in memory as a collection of attributes or features.

C. Retrieval

Information in short-term memory appears to be retrieved by an exhaustive serial search, not a parallel search.

IV. LONG-TERM MEMORY (pp. 298–307)

A. Distinguishing Between Short-term and Long-term Memory

1. *Serial Position Curves.* Serial position curves show both a primacy effect and a recency effect when memory is tested immediately after ex-

posure to test stimuli. However, the recency effect is eliminated if there is a delay before recall.

2. *Biological Research.* Anterograde and retrograde amnesia, caused by brain injury or drug use, create an inability to transfer information between short-term memory and long-term memory. The amnesia may be caused by a disruption in physiological trace consolidations.

B. Encoding

1. *The Early Investigations of Ebbinghaus.*

2. *Rehearsal.* There are two types of rehearsal: maintenance and elaborative.

3. *Semantic Coding.* Most information in long-term memory is stored by meaning. Although people can encode images into long-term memory, few individuals have eidetic imagery or photographic memories.

C. Storage

1. *The Course of Forgetting.* Ebbinghaus's demonstration of savings showed that the time required to relearn material is less than the original learning time.

2. *Causes of Forgetting.* Interference seems to be the key factor in forgetting information stored in long-term memory.

D. Retrieval

1. *Retrieval Cues.* According to the encoding specificity principle, these cues are more efficient when they are ideas that were originally encoded when the information was learned.

2. *Context and State Dependence.* People remember more material when their psychological state or physical location are similar to what they were when the material was originally learned.

3. *The Retrieval of Incomplete Knowledge.* We often retrieve features and attributes of the

things we wish to remember. Hence, we may not remember, for example, the name of a place, but we could remember many of its physical features.

V. CONSTRUCTING MEMORY (pp. 308–310)

Existing generalized information in long-term memory affects our perceptions of incoming information and serves to fill gaps left by incomplete retrieval.

VI. IMPROVING YOUR MEMORY (pp. 310–317)

A. Metamemory

Metamemory is the knowledge you have about memory, which should include the strengths and weaknesses of your memory, knowledge of different types of memory and knowing which strategies are most effective for learning new information.

B. Mnemonics

Mnemonics are strategies for remembering information.

1. *Classical Mnemonics*. The peg-word system and the method of loci are very efficient mnemonics that provide a context for organizing incoming information.

2. *Remembering Textbook Material*. Create a method for organizing the information. Do *not* just keep rereading material you do not understand. Use the SQ3R method.

3. *Lecture Notes*. Write summaries of the main points. Review your notes as soon as possible after the lecture and fill in the gaps.

KEY TERMS

1. **Episodic memory** is any memory of a specific event that happened while you were present. (p. 282)

Example: The memory of your first pony ride, or a surprise birthday party that you held for a friend, or your first day of college are all episodic memories.

REMEMBER: Episodic memories are *episodes* that involved you.

2. **Semantic memories** are those concerning factual knowledge. These memories are not associated with a specific event the way episodic memories are. (p. 282)

Example: Knowing that the freezing point is 32 degrees Fahrenheit, or that red lights mean stop, or that the capital of the United States is Washington, D.C. are all examples of semantic memories. You probably cannot remember the specific time or episode during which you learned these facts.

3. **Procedural memories** are "how to" methods or processes that usually involve some motor movement. (p. 283)

Example: Knowing how to waltz, do a somersault, tie a tie, or drive a car are all procedural memories.

4. **Encoding** is the process of coding information so that it can be placed in sensory, short-term, or long-term memory. There are three types of codes: visual, acoustic, and semantic. (p. 284)

5. **Acoustic codes** are representations of the sounds we hear. (p. 284)

Example: Think of your favorite song and hum it to yourself. The memory of how the melody sounds is in an acoustic code in long-term memory.

6. **Semantic codes** represent the meaning of an experience or factual information. (p. 284)

Example: If you visit Israel, you may notice that the children can sing the top rock songs from the United States but they do not know what the words mean. This is because they are using an acoustic code to remember the song and sing it, but they do not have a semantic code for the meaning of the words.

7. **Visual codes** represent our experiences in images. (p. 284)

Example: If you think of a Christmas tree or the car you would buy if you had enough money, you will most likely see images of these things in your mind. That is because you have visual codes for them.

8. **Storage** is the process of maintaining or keeping a memory. Memories of your kindergarten class or your second grade teacher, or the first house you lived in are old memories. They have been stored for quite some time. (p. 284)

9. **Retrieval** is the process of transferring memories from storage to consciousness. (p. 285)

Example: Whenever you remember anything, you are retrieving that memory from storage. Some memories are retrieved so quickly that you are unaware of the process. Answer the following questions. How old are you? How many people have been president of the United States? Both questions require you to retrieve information, but the retrieval process is much easier for the first question than for the second.

10. **Sensory memory** holds sensory information (primarily icons and echoes) for a fraction of a second in sensory registers. If the information is attended to and recognized, perception takes place, and the information can enter short-term memory. (p. 287)

11. **Sensory registers** hold incoming sensory information until it is processed, recognized and remem-bered. There is a sensory register for each sense. (p. 287)

12. **Icons** are mental representations of visual information and last for about 1 second in sensory registers. (p. 288)

13. **Iconic memory** is the sensory register that retains mental representations of visual images (icons). (p. 289)

14. **Echoes** are mental representations of auditory information (sound) in sensory registers. Echoes often last for three to four seconds. (p. 289)

Example: Sit in a very quiet place for several minutes. Then turn the radio on at a high volume and abruptly turn it off. You should be able to hear the echo of the music that was on the radio.

15. **Echoic memory** is the sensory register that retains mental representations of sounds (echoes). (p. 289)

16. **Short-term (working) memory** receives information that was perceived in sensory memory. Information in short-term memory is conscious but quite fragile and will be lost within seconds if not further processed. (p. 290)

17. **An immediate memory span** is the largest number of items or chunks of information that you can recall perfectly from short-term memory after one presentation of the stimuli. Most people have an immediate memory span of five to nine items. (p. 291)

Example: Use your telephone book to help you test your own immediate memory span. Read the first two names at the top of the page, look away, and then try to recall them. Then read the next three names, look away, and try to recall them. Continue this process, using a longer name list each time, until you cannot repeat the entire list of names. The number of names that you can repeat perfectly is your immediate memory span.

18. **A chunk** is a meaningful grouping of information that you place in short-term memory. The immediate memory span of short-term memory is probably between five and nine chunks of information. Each chunk contains bits of information grouped into a single unit. (p. 291)

Example: Bridget was a waitress at a local eating establishment when she was a college freshman. During her first night, it took all five to nine chunks in short-term memory to remember one order for one person. For example, a drink before dinner, a drink with dinner, a main dish, type of salad dressing, type of potato, and whether the customer wanted cream, sugar, or both with coffee made up five to nine chunks of information. After two years of waitressing, Bridget could easily hold in memory four to eight people's complete food and drink orders. Each person's order had become one chunk of information.

REMEMBER: It is important to realize that chunks can be anything—letters, numbers, words, names, or locations, to list a few. The more information you can condense or group into one chunk, the more information you can hold in short-term memory.

19. **Rehearsing** information is repeating it to yourself in order to indefinitely maintain the information in memory. See key term 30, *maintenance rehearsal,* and key term 31, *elaborative rehearsal,* for more information. (p. 293)

20. The **Brown-Peterson procedure** is a research method that prevents rehearsal. A person is presented with a group of three letters and then counts backward by threes from an arbitrarily selected number until a signal is given. The counting prevents the person from rehearsing the information. (p. 293)

21. **Retroactive interference** occurs when information in memory is displaced by new information. (p. 294)

REMEMBER: Retro means back. New information goes back and interferes with old information.

22. **Proactive interference** occurs when old information in long-term memory interferes with remembering new information. (p. 294)

Example: If you have ever learned something incorrectly and then tried to correct it, you may have experienced proactive interference. Young children who take music lessons once per week experience this. They learn an incorrect note and at their lesson the next week, their teacher points out the mistake. However, it is very difficult to learn to play the correct note because the old memory of the mistaken note interferes with the new memory of the correct note.

REMEMBER: Pro means forward. Old information goes forward and interferes with new information.

23. **Release from proactive interference** occurs when the attributes and features of old information are so different from those of new information, that proactive interference does not take place. (p. 294)

24. A **parallel search** is one possible method of scanning information in short-term memory. All of the information to be searched is examined all at once. (p. 295)

25. A **serial search** is another possible method of scanning information in short-term memory. Information in short-term memory is examined one piece at a time. (p. 295)

Example: Imagine you were given the following list of words: dog, cat, sheep, cow, horse, penguin, lion, eagle, and giraffe. Then you are asked if the word penguin is in the list. In an exhaustive serial search, you would scan the entire list of words, from "dog" to "giraffe," before answering.

REMEMBER: Research has shown that people scan all the material in short-term memory item by item, even if they are searching for something in the middle of a list. This is called an exhaustive serial search.

26. The **primacy effect** occurs when we remember words at the beginning of a list better than those in the middle of the list. (p. 296)

Example: See the example for key term 27, recency effect.

REMEMBER: Primacy means to be first. The primacy effect is to remember the first words in a list better than others.

27. The **recency effect** occurs when we remember the last few words in a list better than others in the list. The list's final items are in short-term memory at the time of recall. (p. 296)

Example: Leslie is a teacher. On the first day of class she starts in the front of the room and has each student say his or her name. After hearing all of her students' names once, she tries to recall them out loud one by one. She usually remembers the names of students in the first two rows (primacy effect), and the names of the students in the last two rows (recency effect), but she has difficulty recalling the names of students in the middle two rows.

REMEMBER: Recency means that which occurred most recently. The last items of a list were presented most recently.

28. **Anterograde amnesia** is a loss of memory for events that occur after a brain injury. Memory for experiences prior to the trauma remains intact. (p. 298)

REMEMBER: Anterograde amnesia is a loss of memory for the *future* or *in front of* some point in time.

29. **Retrograde amnesia** is a memory loss for events prior to a brain injury. Memories encoded days or years before the injury or trauma can be lost. Usually, most memories gradually return. (p. 298)

REMEMBER: Retro means backward. The memory loss goes back in time.

30. **Maintenance rehearsal,** repeating the information over and over, keeps or *maintains* information in short-term memory. (p. 300)

Example: Elmer has just arrived in New York to visit his cousin Alfred. He realizes that he has lost Alfred's phone number and calls directory assistance. The operator tells him the number and Elmer repeats it over and over to himself while he inserts coins for the call.

31. **Elaborative rehearsal** involves thinking about how new material is linked or related in some way to information already stored in long-term memory. It is an effective method of encoding information into long-term memory. (p. 300)

Example: Sandy is a world champion shopper. She has a mental image of all the major cities she has shopped in and imagines the locations of all her favorite stores on each street. When Sandy wants to store information about a new store, she uses her mental image and places the new store on its street. She thinks about the new store in relationship to the stores surrounding it. Sandy is not just repeating the address of the new store, but has related it to the addresses of all the other stores that she knows.

REMEMBER: New information is elaborated with information already in long-term memory. The new address is elaborated by relating its location to all of the old addresses of stores already in long-term memory.

32. The **level-of-processing model** holds that differences in how well something is remembered reflect the degree or depth to which incoming information is mentally processed. (p. 301)

Example: Elaborative rehearsal requires a great deal of processing and is effective for encoding into long-term memory. Maintenance rehearsal does not require much processing and is effective for encoding information into short-term memory. Information in long-term memory is remembered longer than information in short-term memory.

33. **Eidetic imagery** or **photographic memory** is the perfect recall of images, or pictures, from long-term memory. Nearly 5 percent of all children have this ability, but it deteriorates by the time they reach adulthood. (p. 303)

Example: Fritz can remember the words and pictures of a cartoon in perfect detail.

34. **Decay theory** suggests that if people do not use information in long-term memory, it gradually fades until it is lost completely. (p. 304)

35. **Interference theory** suggests that forgetting information in long-term memory is caused by the influence of other learning. (p. 304)

36. **Retrieval cues** help us to recognize information in long-term memory. In other words, they help us to "jog" our memories. (p. 306)

Example: On a multiple-choice exam, the answer appears somewhere on the page. Some of the words in the correct answer should "jog" your memory and allow you to answer the question correctly.

37. **The encoding specificity principle** concerns the similarity between the way information is encoded and the retrieval cues. If the similarity is great, remembering the information is easy. (p. 306)

38. **Context dependence.** When you learn new material, information about the place (your context) in which you learn is also encoded into long-term memory. Therefore, when you are trying to remember information, being in the same place that you were when you originally learned it improves retrieval. The environment acts as a retrieval cue. (p. 306)

Example: Many students study their psychology in the same rooms in which they will take their exams. Context dependence will become clear to you if you imagine two very different locations for learning and remembering. You learn in a classroom and in the place you choose to do your homework. After learning some new material, go to an equally quiet but different place; for example, the shower, your car, or even your closet, and test yourself. You will probably not remember as much of the material as you would if you were in your classroom or study spot.

39. **State dependence.** You will remember more material if your psychological state at the time of learning is similar to what it is when you are trying to remember. Your psychological state, be it drug-induced or a mood, acts as a retrieval cue. (pp. 306–307)

Example: On Thursday, Lydia went out for drinks at 5:00 P.M. with her friends. When she came home, she studied for a psychology quiz. The next afternoon, she did not do well on the quiz. Later, she went out for drinks with some students from her psychology class. After a few drinks, Lydia was in the same state as when she studied for the quiz and, to her amazement, she remembered some of the material that had escaped her during the quiz.

40. **Metamemory** is knowledge you have about how your memory works. It involves knowing your memory's strengths and weaknesses, the memory strategies you use for different memory tasks, and which strategies are most effective. (p. 310)

Example: Five-year-old Meryl was given a list of twenty-five words to memorize. She repeated them over and over to herself. When asked to recite the list, she could remember only nine words. Meryl used a very poor strategy for the task of remembering twenty-five words (she should have tried to elaborate the information in some way). Meryl was unaware of her memory's strengths and weaknesses. Therefore, her metamemory was very poor.

41. **Mnemonics** are encoding methods that will increase the efficiency of your memory. For examples of the most powerful techniques see key terms 42 and 43, the peg word system and the method of loci. (p. 311)

42. The **peg word system** is a mnemonic. First, you must memorize a list of words to serve as memory pegs. (One popular method links these pegs to numbers.) Second, for each item to be remembered create a visual image (the more bizarre the image, the better) between it and the previously learned peg word. This makes the list easier to remember. (p. 311–312)

Example: Your task is to memorize the following list: carrots, children, cat, thermostat, paycheck. Step 1: Memorize a list of "peg" words: one is a bun, two is a shoe, three is a tree, four is a door, and five is a hive. Step 2: Create an association between the words from the list and the "peg" words; remember that a visual image works best.

Peg	List Words
bun	carrot sandwich
shoe	children living in a shoe
tree	cat in a tree
door	a huge thermostat along the length of a door.
hive	bees in a hive lined up to receive their paychecks from the queen bee.

43. The **method of loci** is a mnemonic. First, pick a familiar location, such as your house, apartment, or dorm room. Second, place each object on the list to be memorized in a specific spot within the chosen location. To remember the list, mentally walk through the chosen location and pick up the items. (p. 312)

Example: Your task is to memorize the following grocery list: toothpaste, cat food, light bulbs, steak, head of lettuce. The location for this example is a house. Create a visual image between each item on the list and a place in the house. For example, imagine toothpaste all over the front doorknob. Second, imagine that the cats that live in the house have two plates of food in front of them; one contains steak and the other contains cat food. Third, as you reach to turn on the light, you find a light bulb instead of a switch attached to the wall. Finally, there is a head of lettuce on your bed. When you get to the store, mentally walk through your front door and find the toothpaste, pick up the plates with cat food and steak on them, turn the lights on by flipping the light-bulb switch, and move the head of lettuce off the pillow as you lie down to take a nap.

44. The **SQR3 method** is a strategy for remembering textbook material. Five activities are involved: surveying, questioning, reading, reciting, and reviewing. See page 315 in your text for a detailed explanation of this method. We strongly recommend this technique. Using it faithfully allows you to save time and learn and remember more of what you read. (p. 315)

LEARNING OBJECTIVES

1. Define and give an example of semantic, procedural, and episodic memories. (pp. 280–283)

2. Define and give an example of encoding, acoustic codes, semantic codes, and visual codes. (p. 284)

3. Define storage and retrieval. Discuss the importance of encoding, storage, and retrieval in memory processes. (pp. 284–285)

4. Describe the role of long-term memory in the encoding process. (pp. 285–287)

5. Define sensory registers and describe their role in sensory memory. Discuss the limitations on the amount of information and the length of time material stays in sensory memory. (pp. 287–288)

6. Define icon and echo. Know the role they play in sensory memory. (pp. 288–290)

7. Know the process that determines which information is transferred to short-term memory from sensory memory. (p. 290)

8. Describe the encoding of information into short-term memory. (p. 290)

9. Define immediate memory span and chunking. Discuss the role of long-term memory in the chunking process. Know how to improve your chunking abilities. (pp. 291–293)

10. Describe the importance of rehearsal in maintaining information in short-term memory. Discuss the possible explanations for why we forget or lose information from short-term memory. Define proactive and retroactive interference. (p. 293)

11. Know how information is stored in short-term memory. (pp. 294–295)

12. Define parallel search, serial search, and exhaustive serial search. Know the type of search used to retrieve information from short-term memory. (pp. 295–296)

13. Discuss the evidence from studies using the serial position curve that supports the existence of short- and long-term memory. Define the primacy effect and the recency effect. (pp. 296–298)

14. Discuss the evidence obtained from biological research that supports the existence of short- and long-term memory. Define anterograde and retrograde amnesia. (pp. 298–299)

15. Define maintenance and elaborative rehearsal. Discuss their role in encoding into short- and long-term memory. (p. 300)

16. Define semantic encoding and its importance in long-term memory. (pp. 301–302)

17. Define eidetic imagery. (p. 303)

18. Define savings. Compare and contrast the decay and interference theories regarding forgetting information stored in long-term memory. (pp. 303–305)

19. Define retrieval cue and know why its use can increase the efficiency of memory. Define the encoding specificity principle. (pp. 305–306)

20. Define context and state dependence. (pp. 306–307)

21. Describe the process of reconstruction in memory. (pp. 308–309)

22. Define metamemory and mnemonics and know why they improve memory. Give an example of the peg word system and the method of loci. (pp. 310–313)

23. Describe the SQ3R method and know its use. Describe the best method of taking notes in a lecture. (pp. 314–317)

CONCEPTS AND EXERCISES

No. 1 Memory Clues

Completing this exercise should help you to achieve the following learning objectives.

(1) *Define and give an example of semantic, procedural, and episodic memories. (pp. 280–283)*

(2) *Define and give an example of encoding, acoustic codes, semantic codes, and visual codes. (p. 284)*

(9) *Define immediate memory span and chunking. Discuss the role of long-term memory in the chunking process. Know how to improve your chunking abilities. (pp. 291–293)*

(10) *Describe the importance of rehearsal in maintaining information in short-term memory. Discuss*

the possible explanations for why we forget or lose information from short-term memory. Define proactive and retroactive interference. (p. 293)

(19) *Define retrieval cue and know why its use can increase the efficiency of memory. (pp. 305–306)*

(20) *Define context and state dependence. (pp. 306–307)*

There has been a robbery at a local bank. For questioning, the police have placed the witnesses in the locations they occupied during the robbery. Indicate what type of memory, code, or process is responsible for each statement. Draw your answers from the list following the exercise. Answers may be used more than once or not at all.

1. Police: We are questioning you here at the bank because we think it will improve your recall of the robbery. _____

What was the suspect wearing?

2. Teller 1: I know he had a coat on, but I don't remember the color. _____

3. Teller 2: I remember. It was green. _____

Police: To Teller 3: Where were you when the robbery took place?

4. Teller 3: I was standing in the manager's office when the man approached me and told me to unlock the door to the safe. _____

Police: Did you have to look up the combination to the safe?

5. Teller 3: No, sir. The manager had just given me the new combination for the day 10 seconds before the man approached me. I just grouped the numbers into a date so I'd remember them for the few minutes it would take me to walk from the office to the safe. Just as I'd finished thinking about the combination, the gunman was there ordering me to unlock the safe. _____

Police: Did the man speak with a lisp?

6. Teller 2: Yes, he did. I remember hearing him slur his *S*s. _____

Police: To Teller 1: Please demonstrate the steps you follow in order to sound the alarm.

7. Teller 1: I have to step on this foot pedal like this. _____

Police: Why did it take you so long to sound the alarm?

8. Teller 1: Well, sir, I've just started working at this bank. The alarm at my old job sounded at the push of a button. I guess I panicked a bit. I was looking for the button for a few seconds before I realized that here I have to push a foot pedal. _____

Police: Thank you, everyone. That will be all for now.

procedural memory

acoustic code

context dependence

chunking

semantic code

visual code

episodic memory

proactive interference

retroactive interference

No. 2 Testing Memory

Completing this exercise should help you to achieve the following learning objectives.

(5) *Define sensory registers and describe their role in sensory memory. Discuss the limitations on the amount of information and the length of time material stays in sensory memory. (pp. 287–288)*

(8) *Describe the encoding of information into short-term memory. (p. 290)*

(9) *Define immediate memory span and chunking. Discuss the role of long-term memory in the chunking process. Know how to improve your chunking abilities. (pp. 291–293)*

(20) *Define context and state dependence. (pp. 306–307)*

For his research, Dr. Walgren is conducting memory tests. Below are descriptions of the tests that he is using and the memory processes for which they test. Match the procedure with the appropriate memory process. Select your answers from the list following the exercise.

1. Children are presented with a picture of three rows of four items each for 1 second. Then a tone sounds. If the tone is high, the children must report what is in the top row. If the tone is low, they report what is in the bottom row. If the tone is neither low nor high, they are to report the middle row. _____

2. Subjects are presented with lists of words or letters and are asked to immediately recall as many words as possible. The recall errors they make are analyzed. Experimenters want to know if subjects substitute words that sound similar to or mean the same thing as correct responses. _____

3. Subjects are presented with lists of words and asked to immediately recall as many words as possible. _____

4. Subjects are given injections of adrenaline, a stimulant, and asked to learn a word list. Later, half of the subjects receive adrenaline injections and the other half do not. Subjects are then asked to recall as many words as possible. The differences between the two groups' scores are noted. _____

span of apprehension

encoding into short-term memory

immediate memory span

state dependence

No. 3 Learning How to Study

Completing this exercise should help you to achieve the following learning objectives.

(15) *Define maintenance and elaborative rehearsal. Discuss their role in encoding into short- and long-term memory. (p. 300)*

(19) *Define retrieval cue and know why its use can increase the efficiency of memory. Define the encoding specificity principle. (pp. 305–306)*

(22) *Define metamemory and mnemonics and know why they improve memory. Give an example of the peg word system and the method of loci. (pp. 310–313)*

(23) *Describe the SQ3R method and know its use. Describe the best method of taking notes in a lecture. (pp. 314–317)*

Below are descriptions of study methods that need improvement. Use the information you have learned in this chapter to fill in the blanks following the descriptions.

1. Theo is taking classes in history, philosophy, math, and music. He does not realize that he should probably use a different strategy to learn the information in each class. Theo's _____ is very poor.

2. Rodney is taking a vocabulary improvement class. He is learning to recognize the roots of words and their meanings. He tries to memorize the material by repeating it to himself over and over again. Instead of doing this, he should probably try using _____.

3. Ginny is a college freshman. She is taking a course in biology, a subject she never had in high school. When she takes notes, she desperately tries to write down every word the instructor says. Instead, she should _____ the information.

4. Carin hates to read. She wants to get it over with quickly, so she reads large amounts of material at a time. Then she complains that she

can never remember what she has just read. She should try using the _____ method.

ANSWERS TO CONCEPTS AND EXERCISES

No. 1 Memory Clues

1. *Context dependence.* The context, in this case the bank, will act as a retrieval cue and help the tellers remember as much as possible about the robbery. (p. 306)

2. *Semantic code.* Teller 1 remembers the fact that the robber had a coat on but does not have a visual code containing the color of the coat. (pp. 301–302)

3. *Visual code.* Teller 2 does have a visual code of the robber, which includes the color of the robber's coat. (p. 284)

4. *Episodic memory.* Teller 3 is remembering an event (or episode) in which he was a participant. (p. 282)

5. *Chunking.* Teller 3 has used chunking to remember the combination to the safe. He has grouped the numbers into one meaningful unit of information: a date. (p. 291)

6. *Acoustic code.* Teller 2 has an acoustic code for the sound of the robber's voice. (p. 284)

7. *Procedural memory.* Teller 1 has a procedural memory for how to sound the alarm. (p. 283)

8. *Proactive interference.* The old information, how to sound the alarm in the bank that Teller 1 used to work at, is interfering with his ability to remember how to sound the alarm at his present job. (p. 294)

No. 2 Testing Memory

1. *Span of apprehension.* The experimenter is trying to find out how much information is being stored in sensory memory. (p. 287)

2. *Encoding into short-term memory.* Experiments like this have shown that people tend to encode information into short-term memory acoustically. (p. 300)

3. *Immediate memory span.* The number of items that one can recall in perfect order after one presentation of a stimulus is called immediate memory span. (p. 291)

4. *State dependence.* The two groups of subjects are in different psychological states when they are asked to try to remember the information. Differences in their scores will demonstrate state dependent memory. (p. 306)

No. 3 Learning How to Study

1. *Metamemory.* Theo does not know very much about his own memory and how it works. Knowing what strategies to use for different types of memory tasks is a part of metamemory. For example, mnemonics might be a good strategy for learning dates and places for Theo's history class, whereas the information in his philosophy class should be encoded semantically or by meaning. (p. 310)

2. *Mnemonics.* Classical mnemonics are good tools for memorizing long lists of words as Rodney has to do. The peg word system or the method of loci will help to elaborate the material. Maintenance rehearsal is a good method for keeping information in short-term memory. However, it will not help Rodney place the information in long-term memory. (p. 311)

3. *Summarize.* Ginny should think about the lecture when she hears it in order to build a framework or overall organization for the material. She should only write down summaries of basic ideas. (pp. 316–317)

4. *SQ3R method.* The SQ3R method is a series of five steps that will increase the amount of information Carin remembers from her reading as-

signments. Detailed explanations of each step are listed on page 315 in your text.

MULTIPLE CHOICE QUESTIONS

Facts and Definitions

1. The memory for how to do something is called
   a. episodic memory.
   b. semantic memory.
   c. procedural memory.
   d. short-term memory.

2. An icon is a mental representation of a
   a. sound.
   b. visual image.
   c. semantic code.
   d. None of the above.

3. Perception determines what information is transferred to
   a. sensory memory.
   b. short-term memory.
   c. long-term memory.
   d. sensory registers.

4. In short-term memory, one chunk equals
   a. one letter or number.
   b. five to nine letters or numbers.
   c. five to nine units of information.
   d. one unit of information.

5. Chunking is a method of storage in _____ memory.
   a. sensory
   b. short-term
   c. episodic
   d. procedural

6. Unrehearsed information stays in short-term memory for about
   a. 1 second.
   b. 3 seconds.
   c. 20 seconds.
   d. forever.

7. Information in short-term memory is mentally represented
   a. in groups of features or attributes.
   b. acoustically.
   c. in single units.
   d. in parallel groups.

8. An immediate memory span is the number of items
   a. one can recall in perfect order following one presentation of a stimulus.
   b. that can be held in the sensory registers.
   c. stored in long-term memory.
   d. that can be held in semantic codes.

9. In order to chunk efficiently, you will need to
   a. use your long-term memory.
   b. group many items into one chunk.
   c. transfer information quickly from short-term to long-term memory.
   d. All of the above.

10. Retroactive interference occurs when
   a. new information interferes with the ability to recall old information.
   b. old information interferes with learning new material.
   c. old information decays.
   d. new information decays.

11. Better recall of the first few words of a list from long-term memory is called the
   a. primacy effect.
   b. recency effect.
   c. fatigue effect.
   d. parallel position effect.

12. Which of the following would be most effective for encoding information into long-term memory?

    a. Chunking
    b. Maintenance rehearsal
    c. Elaborative rehearsal
    d. Serial rehearsal

13. Multiple choice questions are easier than essay questions to answer because they contain

    a. less interference.
    b. more retrieval cues.
    c. more semantic memory.
    d. fewer eidetic images.

14. Context dependence means that information is easier to remember when

    a. it is organized, for example, in an outline.
    b. people are in the same place as they were when they learned the material.
    c. people are in the same psychological state of mind as they were when they learned the material.
    d. a mnemonic is used.

15. Mentally placing objects in specific geographic locations in order to remember them more efficiently is called

    a. the method of loci system.
    b. the peg word system.
    c. using a retrieval cue.
    d. context dependence.

MULTIPLE CHOICE QUESTIONS

Application of Concepts

1. A murder investigation is going on at the resort where you are vacationing. The police are asking you for your alibi. What kind of memory is this?

    a. Episodic
    b. Procedural
    c. Semantic
    d. Short-term

2. Remembering the phone number 217-1967 as your birthday of February 17, 1967 is an example of

    a. chunking.
    b. the Brown-Peterson procedure.
    c. a parallel search.
    d. the method of loci.

3. Colleen frequently loses her keys. To find them, she always has to sit and remember where she had them last. This is an example of

    a. semantic memory.
    b. procedural memory.
    c. episodic memory.
    d. acoustic coding.

4. Rachel was still studying ten minutes before her test. As she entered the classroom, she kept repeating the last sentence she had read: "Henry VIII had six wives." This is an example of

    a. elaborative rehearsal.
    b. maintenance rehearsal.
    c. using mnemonics.
    d. retrieval.

5. Which of the following sentences would require the most chunks in short-term memory?

    a. John has many friends.
    b. Ich liebe dich.
    c. Je ne sais pas.
    d. – · – – – · – · – · – (Morse Code)

6. Last week Belinda had to memorize a poem to recite in front of the class. When she rehearsed at home, her mom told her that she had memorized an incorrect word and told her what to say instead. However, Belinda had memorized the incorrect version so well that she had difficulty learning the correct word. This is an example of

    a. retroactive interference.
    b. proactive interference.

c. retrograde amnesia.

d. decay.

7. Ramona's mother has given her a grocery list and she is off to the store. As she enters the parking lot, she realizes that she forgot to bring the list with her. However, she can recall the first ten items on the list and decides to just buy those. Her recollection of the first ten items on the list is an example of

    a. the recency effect.

    b. the primacy effect.

    c. interference.

    d. retroactive amnesia.

8. When Robin moved to a new state, her new teacher told her that the class was learning the names of all the presidents. Robin was horrified. She had painstakingly memorized all those names the year before and could not remember very many of them. To her surprise, however, learning them the second time took much less time than it had the first time. This is an example of

    a. using mnemonics.

    b. release from proactive interference.

    c. savings.

    d. metamemory.

9. Alberta is a night owl. She loves to stay up late and study. However, she has so many classes this semester that she is forced to study calculus in the morning when she is sluggish and a bit sleepy. Alberta's calculus teacher has given the class a take-home test. Alberta should take the test

    a. in the evening.

    b. in the afternoon.

    c. in the morning.

    d. whenever she feels like it.

10. If you were to lose the ability to retrieve any information from long-term memory, you would not be able to

    a. chunk information.

    b. recognize information in sensory memory.

c. use the method of loci.

d. All of the above.

11. Kristi has memorized a list of names by imagining each person in a specific spot in her dorm room. One person is in the closet, another is under the bed, one is hanging upside-down from the ceiling, and so on. She is using the

    a. peg word system.

    b. the encoding specificity principle.

    c. method of loci.

    d. eidetic imagery.

12. Sherman is walking through his old school with his second grade teacher, Mrs. Spence. When they reach Sherman's old classroom, he is surprised to find so many things missing even though Mrs. Spence told him that nothing had changed. He remembers a map on the wall, the alphabet above the chalkboard, and a globe on Mrs. Spence's desk. What process could account for the discrepancy between Sherman's memory and what was actually in the classroom?

    a. Reconstructive memory

    b. Eidetic imagery

    c. Proactive interference

    d. Retrograde amnesia

13. Jose is frustrated. He had a very important exam in chemistry this morning and could not remember the answer to one of the questions. On the way home, however, the answer came to him. His inability to answer the question during the test was probably due to

    a. retrieval failure.

    b. partial knowledge retrieval.

    c. improper encoding.

    d. decay.

14. Janet is bewildered. She has just spent an hour making up a list of items to pack for her year of school abroad. She got up to take a look in her closet, came back to the desk, and now cannot find the list. With a sigh, she decides to just start pack-

ing. If she forgets anything it will probably be items from _____ of the list.

    a. the beginning
    b. the middle
    c. the end
    d. None of the above.

15. Ted is a tutor for children in grade six. He is trying to help a child remember the name of the president during the Civil War. He tells the child that this man wore a tall black hat, enjoyed reading by the fireplace, and was very tall. These clues will function as

    a. retrieval cues.
    b. peg words.
    c. echoes.
    d. acoustic codes.

ANSWERS TO MULTIPLE CHOICE QUESTIONS

Facts and Definitions

1. *c* is the answer. Remembering how to do something is procedural memory. (p. 283)

    a. Episodic memories are those of events that occurred while you were present, such as the memory of your first day at school.

    b. Semantic memories are of generalized knowledge, such as remembering the tribal names of the Plains Indians.

    d. Short-term memories can be procedural, semantic, or episodic.

2. *b* is the answer. An icon is a visual image. (p. 288)

    a. An echo is a mental representation of a sound.

    c. A semantic code is mental representation of meaning.

    d. *b* is the answer.

3. *b* is the answer. Perception determines which information in sensory memory will be transferred to short-term memory. (p. 290)

    a. Selective attention, not perception, determines which information in sensory memory will be processed.

    c. Scientists are not sure what causes consolidation or transformation into long-term memory.

    d. When your senses pick up information, it is automatically transferred to the sensory registers in sensory memory.

4. *d* is the answer. One chunk is equal to one unit of information. That unit of information may be in the form of many letters, such as a word; or many words, such as a sentence; or many numbers, such as 1987 (a year). (p. 291)

    a. A chunk is one unit of information. The chunk may be one letter, or it may be several letters that make up one word. In that case, a word is a unit of information.

    b. & *c.* Most people can hold five to nine chunks of information in short-term memory. One chunk may be a letter, several letters, several words, or even several sentences.

5. *b* is the answer. We store chunks of information in short-term memory. (p. 291)

    a. Information in sensory memory is stored in sensory registers.

    c. Episodic memories are an example of <u>what</u> may be stored in short- or long-term memory. However, we do not store information *in* episodic memory.

    d. Procedural memories are an example of <u>what</u> may be stored in short or long-term memory. However, we do not store information *in* procedural memory.

6. *c* is the answer. Unrehearsed information stays in short-term memory for about 20 seconds. (p. 293)

    a. Information in the visual sensory registers is maintained for about 1 second.

b. Information in the auditory sensory registers is maintained for about 3 seconds.

d. Information may stay in long-term memory until death or it may decay.

7. *a* is the answer. Studies on the release from proactive interference have shown that we mentally represent information in groups of features or attributes. (p. 294)

b. Information is *encoded* acoustically into short-term memory.

c. Information is stored in single units called chunks, but the information is mentally represented in groups of features or attributes.

d. There is no such thing as a parallel group.

8. *a* is the answer. An immediate memory span or the capacity of short-term memory is the amount of information one can remember after one presentation of a stimulus. (p. 291)

b. An unlimited amount of information can be stored in sensory memory, but only for a short time. This is called the span of apprehension.

c. There is no span or limit on the amount of information that can be stored in long-term memory.

d. Items in memory can take the form of a semantic code, but items are not stored *in* semantic code.

9. *d* is the answer. In order to chunk information efficiently, you must be able to put as many items as possible into one chunk, use long-term memory to recognize information in short-term memory, and be able to transfer information quickly from short-term to long-term memory. (pp. 292–293)

10. *a* is the answer. The presence of new information displaces old information in short-term memory. (p. 295)

b. Proactive interference occurs when old information disrupts the learning of new information.

c. & d. Decay is the gradual disappearance of memories.

11. *a* is the answer. Better recall of the first few words of a list from long-term memory is called the primacy effect. (p. 296)

b. Better recall of the last few words of a list from short-term memory is called the recency effect.

c. There is no such thing as the fatigue effect.

d. There is no such thing as the parallel position effect.

12. *c* is the answer. Elaborative rehearsal, which is relating the new information to be remembered to information in long-term memory, is an effective way to encode information into long-term memory. (p. 300)

a. Chunking is an effective method for storing information in short-term memory.

b. Maintenance rehearsal is an effective method for retaining information in short-term memory.

d. There is no such thing as serial rehearsal.

13. *b* is the answer. The answer to a multiple choice question is listed on the page. It will act as a retrieval cue by helping you recognize information stored in long-term memory. (p. 306)

a. Answering multiple choice questions actually creates less interference. The study described on page 306 of your text showed that retrieval cues (the answer to the multiple choice question listed on the page) decreased the effect of interference.

c. & d. Neither multiple choice questions nor essay questions *contain* semantic memory or eidetic images. A good answer to an essay question would require more extensive semantic memory than would a multiple choice answer. Most adults do not have eidetic images.

14. *b* is the answer. It is easier to remember material when you are in the place where you originally learned it. The surrounding environment acts as a retrieval cue. (p. 306)

a. Organizing material in an outline is one way to remember it more easily later on, but context dependence doesn't refer to this.

c. State dependence occurs when people find it easier to recall material when they are in the same psychological state of mind as they were when they learned the information. A psychological state acts as a retrieval cue.

d. Using mnemonics can improve your memory, but this is not the same thing as context dependence.

15. *a* is the answer. The method of loci involves mentally placing objects in various spots in a familiar location (loci). (p. 312)

b. The peg word system is also a mnemonic. However, this system requires that you learn a list of peg words, and create images to associate the peg words with the words to be remembered.

c. Using a retrieval cue helps you to recognize or retrieve material from long-term memory. Using mnemonics is a method of encoding by organizing information in a certain way.

d. Context dependence occurs when the environment (context) acts as a retrieval cue.

ANSWERS TO MULTIPLE CHOICE QUESTIONS

Application of Concepts

1. *a* is the answer. Where you were at the time of the murder would be a memory of an episode at which you were present. This is episodic memory. (p. 282)

b. Procedural memories involve how to do something or how to carry out a procedure.

c. Semantic memories involve general knowledge.

d. Short-term memory is where episodic, procedural, and semantic memories can be stored for a short amount of time, but it is not a specific type of memory.

2. *a* is the answer. Chunking is the ability to group information into a meaningful unit that can be stored in short-term memory. (p. 291)

b. The Brown-Peterson research method was used to determine how long unrehearsed information remains in short-term memory.

c. A parallel search involves scanning the items in short-term memory all at once. Research has shown that people use a serial search, not a parallel search.

d. The method of loci is a mnemonic.

3. *c* is the answer. Colleen has to remember where she was when she last had her keys. This is episodic memory; she will be present in the memory. (p. 282)

a. Semantic memories are of general knowledge. Since Colleen is trying to remember an incident or episode that involves her presence, this cannot be the answer.

b. Procedural memories are of how to do something. Colleen is trying to remember an episode, not a procedure.

d. Colleen is trying to remember where she left her keys, not a sound.

4. *b* is the answer. Maintenance rehearsal is a method of keeping information in short-term memory. Rachel is trying to keep in short-term memory the most recently read information. (p. 300)

a. Elaborative rehearsal occurs when new information is related to old information in long-term memory. If Rachel tried to integrate the number of wives that Henry VIII had with other information about him, she would have been using elaborative rehearsal.

c. Mnemonics are strategies for creating a new context for material in order to recall it later. Rachel was not doing anything other than repeating the information. She did not use mental imagery, the method of loci, or the peg word system.

d. Rachel was trying to keep the information in storage, not trying to retrieve it.

5. *d* is the answer. Morse code uses a different "alphabet" than English does. A person who does not

know Morse code would not have any information in long-term memory that would help put more than one symbol into one chunk. Therefore, this statement (the one-word sentence "No.") would require the greatest number of chunks in short-term memory. (p. 291)

a. The entire sentence could be one chunk for a native English speaker.

b. & c. Both French and German use the same alphabet as English. Therefore, each word would be a chunk because information stored in long-term memory would help recognize the letters as words. However, each dot or dash of a Morse code letter would be one unit of new information, causing that statement to require a greater number of chunks.

6. *b* is the answer. Proactive interference occurs when remembering new information is disrupted by the presence of old information. The old, incorrect version of the poem that Belinda had memorized kept getting in the way of her learning the correct word. (p. 294)

a. For retroactive interference to be the correct answer, learning the new word in the poem should have interfered with Belinda's ability to remember the old, incorrect version of the poem. Retroactive interference refers to new information disrupting the recall of old information.

c. Retrograde amnesia is the loss of memory for events prior to a brain injury. Belinda's brain has not been injured.

d. Decay is the gradual disappearance of a memory. Belinda would have had to learn the new word and then forget it for this to be the right answer.

7. *b* is the answer. Remembering the beginning of a list but forgetting the middle is called the primacy effect. (p. 296)

a. If the question said that Ramona could remember the end of the list, recency effect would have been the correct response.

c. Encoding specificity refers to similarity between information when it is encoded and retrieved. It does not refer to which material is remembered.

d. There is no such thing as retroactive amnesia. You may have been thinking of retrograde amnesia.

8. *c* is the answer. Ebbinghaus discovered that relearning took much less time than learning. Savings is the difference between learning and relearning time. (p. 303)

a. A mnemonic is a memory strategy that involves placing information in an organized context. In this question, Robin did not use any strategies or methods to relearn the names of the presidents.

b. Release from proactive interference occurs when new information differs greatly from old information so that the old information interferes less with learning the new information. Robin is trying to relearn exactly the same information. There is no new information with which the old information can interfere.

d. Metamemory refers to knowledge you have about your memory. This question does not discuss the characteristics of Robin's memory.

9. *c* is the answer. According to state dependence Alberta should try and remember her calculus when she is in the same psychological state of mind as when she originally learned it. Her state of mind will act as a retrieval cue. (pp. 306–307)

a., b., & d. At any other time of the day, Alberta would not be in the same psychological state as she was when she learned the material.

10. *d* is the answer. In order to chunk, you must use the information in long-term memory to help you group items into one chunk in short-term memory. The ability to recognize something in sensory memory involves retrieving a similar pattern of information or material from long-term memory. In order to use the method of loci, you must retrieve knowledge about a specific location or loci stored in long-term memory. (pp. 292, 286, & 312)

11. *c* is the answer. Kristi is using the method of loci to mentally place people in various spots in her dorm room. When she needs to remember these people, she will mentally look for them in her dorm room. (p. 312)

a. The peg word system involves creating an image association between peg words and the items on a list to be memorized. Kristi is using mental images of locations in her dorm room, not a list of words.

b. The encoding specificity principle refers to the similarity between information when it is learned and when it is retrieved. This is not a mnemonic.

d. Kristi is using imagery. However, eidetic imagery is the ability to perfectly recall a visual stimulus. This is not a mnemonic.

12. *a* is the answer. There may be a gap in Sherman's memory of his second grade classroom due to decay or interference. He filled in this gap with information from long-term memory concerning what he thinks belongs in a second grade classroom: the globe, the map, and the alphabet above the blackboard. (p. 308)

b. If Sherman had eidetic imagery, he would have remembered everything about his second grade classroom in perfect detail.

c. Proactive interference occurs when old information prevents a person from remembering new information. Sherman is not trying to remember new information, but very old information.

d. Retrograde amnesia is a memory loss for events that occurred prior to a brain injury. Sherman has not experienced any type of brain injury.

13. *a* is the answer. Jose had the answer in long-term memory but could not retrieve it during the test. (p. 305)

b. Jose did not remember anything during the test and remembered everything later. If he had

remembered some of the features of the answer during the test, this would have been the answer.

c. Jose had problems retrieving the material, whereas encoding is the process of learning or placing the information in long-term memory. This would have been the answer if the question had mentioned a difference in how the material was encoded and retrieved. Jose would then have had problems with encoding specificity.

d. If the memory had decayed, Jose would have been unable to remember the answer to the chemistry problem on the way home.

14. *b* is the answer. Because of the primacy and recency effects, she will probably remember those items at the beginning and end of the list better than those in the middle. (p. 298)

a. The information at the beginning of the list has had a chance to enter long-term memory. She probably will not forget these items.

c. The information at the end of the list is in short-term memory. She probably will not forget these items.

d. *b* is the answer. Janet will most likely forget information in the middle of the list.

15. *a* is the answer. Ted has listed features that should help his student recognize the correct information stored in long-term memory: the name Abraham Lincoln. (p. 306)

b. Peg words are part of a mnemonic that involves making associations between the peg word and the item to be remembered. Ted's clues do not contain any peg words.

c. Ted's clues will enter his student's sensory memory as an echo, but the clues function as retrieval cues.

d. Ted's clues will enter his student's short-term memory as an acoustic code, but the clues function as retrieval cues.

Chapter 9

Thought and Language

OUTLINE

I. FROM STIMULUS TO ACTION: AN OVERVIEW (pp. 322–328)

A. The Human Information-Processing System

An information-processing system has four stages: receiving information, perceiving and recognizing information, deciding what to do with information, and responding to information.

B. High-Speed Decision Making

1. *Reaction Times*. Several factors influence reaction time in quick decisions: stimulus intensity, ease of discrimination between stimuli, decision complexity, stimulus-response compatibility, expectations that the stimulus will appear, and necessity of a fast or accurate response.

2. *Evoked Brain Potentials*. Information about mental chronometry is provided by evoked brain potentials, which show the amount of time it takes for sensory processing and perception to occur.

C. Cognitive Processes

Thinking is the manipulation of mental representations.

II. THINKING (pp. 328–336)

A. Concepts

Concepts are classes or categories of objects, events, people, or ideas with common properties or features.

1. *Artificial and Natural Concepts*. Artificial concepts can be defined by a set of characteristics that all members have and no non-members have. Natural concepts are concepts whose members must have at least some of the characteristics which define the concept. Prototypes are objects or events that best represent a natural concept.

2. *Learning Concepts*. People can learn concepts by hypothesis testing or by expanding prototypes. Affirmation, conjunctive, and disjunctive rules define artificial concepts.

B. Mental Representations of Concepts

These may include lists of features, visual images, or schemas which are combined to form propositions and mental models.

1. *Propositions*. The smallest units of knowledge that can stand as separate assertions are called propositions.

2. *Mental Models*. Large clusters of propositions that represent people's understanding of how things work are called mental models.

C. Images and Cognitive Maps

1. *Operations on Images*. We can scan our visual images, sometimes for detail, and rotate objects in our minds.

2. *Maps and Spatial Cognition*. With experience we create cognitive maps, which are mental representations of our environment. Although useful, cognitive maps are often distorted by the rectangular bias.

D. Reasoning and Heuristics

Reasoning is the process by which we generate arguments, evaluate them, and reach conclusions. The procedures that yield a valid conclusion are known as logic. At the core of the study of logic is the evaluation of syllogisms, which are based on premises.

1. *Beliefs, Wishes, and Logic*. We tend to draw conclusions based on our beliefs as well as on logical reasoning.

2. *Heuristics and Biases*. We tend to use heuristics or mental short cuts rather than algorithms, which always yield a correct solution. There are several commonly used heuristics: the anchoring, representativeness, and availability heuristics.

III. PROBLEM SOLVING (pp. 336–344)

A. Problems in Problem Solving

1. *Multiple Hypotheses*. Testing the incorrect hypothesis first when more than one hypothesis exists can delay problem solving.

2. *Mental Sets*. Viewing a new problem from the perspective used for old problems can prevent the discovery of simpler solutions. Functional fixedness, the inability to use objects in new ways, can also impede problem solving.

3. *The Confirmation Bias*. Once a hypothesis is chosen, we tend to interpret available information as confirming it.

4. *Ignoring Negative Evidence*. We do not use the lack of evidence as often as we should when testing a hypothesis.

5. *Ignoring Base-Rate Information*. When testing hypotheses we tend to ignore probabilities of occurrence (base-rate) and focus on what is representative.

B. Improving Problem-Solving Skills

1. *Avoiding the Pitfalls*.
   a. Avoid errors in syllogistic reasoning.

   b. Avoid confirmation bias and the overuse of heuristics.

   c. Develop the technique of incubation.

   d. Develop the heuristic of decomposition.

2. *Imitating the Expert*. Experts efficiently use old information to organize new material into smaller, more meaningful units. However, experts need to beware of mental sets, functional fixedness, and confirmation biases.

3. *Teaching the Novice*. There are no shortcuts to becoming an expert. A solid base of extensive information is necessary for problem solving.

IV. RISKY DECISION MAKING (pp. 344–350)

A. Rational Decision Making

Multiattribute utility theory is a decision-making technique to use when the number of alternatives is great and their outcomes are certain. When uncertainty exists, the probability and utility of outcomes can be weighed.

B. Perceptions of Value

The perceived value of an alternative depends on its risk and the amount of gain (utility) it produces. When one alternative is a gain which is certain and another alternative is a larger gain, but risky, the certain alternative is chosen even though it may have a smaller expected utility. When choosing between a risky loss and a certain loss of the same expected utility, people usually choose the risky alternative.

C. Perceptions of Probability

People assess the probability of a decision incorrectly due to both the tendency to incorrectly estimate the probability of rare or frequent events, and having too much confidence in their own predictions.

V. LANGUAGE (pp. 350–362)

A. The Elements of Language

Each language is comprised of words and grammar.

1. *From Sounds to Sentences*. Words are made of morphemes which in turn consist of phonemes. Rules of syntax determine the ways words are combined to form sentences. Semantics is a set of rules that govern the meanings of words and sentences.

2. *Surface Structure and Deep Structure*. The surface structure of a sentence (the string of words) may have more than one meaning or deep structure.

B. Communicating Through Language

1. *Perceiving Words*. The use of speech spectrographs has shown that the gaps we hear between spoken words are not real but are perceived because of top-down processing.

2. *Understanding Sentences*. Syntax, memories, and our knowledge of the world help us to com-prehend and remember verbal and written communication.

3. *Understanding Conversations*. Context, which includes the situation and personal histories, helps us interpret the meaning of language and communications.

C. Stages in Language Development

Children first use one-word expressions, which then develop into two-word telegraphic statements. These are followed by three-word sentences which use subject-verb-object sequences. Word endings begin to appear but at first are used incorrectly. Finally, adjectives and auxiliary verbs are added. By age five, children have acquired most of the syntax of their native language.

D. How is Language Learned?

1. *Conditioning and Imitation*. Conditioning and imitation do not fully explain the development of language in children. However, when adults provide correct revisions of a child's conversation, the learning process is enhanced.

2. *Nature and Nurture*. Chomsky has suggested that children possess an innate language acquisition device that helps them learn the complexities of language (nature). There appears to be a critical period for language development (nurture).

E. How Important is Language?

1. *Is Human Language Unique?* No other species combines symbols in a way identical to the language of human beings.

2. *Does Language Determine Perception?* Experiments suggest that language does not always determine perception. We perceive subtle differences in objects and label them when necessary for survival.

3. Is Language Ability Necessary for Thought? Some cognitive abilities may not require language. However, language can enrich our thought and our ability to think.

KEY TERMS

1. **Information-processing systems** receive information, represent information through symbols, and manipulate those symbols. (p. 323)

REMEMBER: Psychologists consider people similar to information-processing systems in the way they take in information, pass it through several stages, and finally act on it.

2. A **reaction time** is the amount of elapsed time between the presentation of a physical stimulus and an overt reaction to that stimulus. (p. 324)

Example: Susan and several of her friends were standing in her office looking for her keys. Suddenly, Dave called out "Hey!" and threw her keys at her. The reaction time was the time it took Susan to look up and get ready to catch the keys after hearing Dave call out.

3. **Mental chronometry** is the timing of mental events. (p. 324)

Example: Psychologists view people as information processing systems. They are interested in the time necessary for a person to go through each stage of an information processing system.

REMEMBER: Chrono refers to time. *Meter* means to measure. Mental chronometry is the *measure* of the *time* mental events take.

4. **Evoked brain potentials** are small temporary changes in voltage that occur in the brain in response to stimuli. An average evoked potential is the average of several responses to the same stimulus. Psychologists can study information processing and can look for abnormal functioning in the brain by examining evoked potentials. (p. 326)

REMEMBER: Evoke means to cause or to produce. Stimuli *evoke* or produce small changes in the brain. Psychologists have instruments that allow them to record these changes for study.

5. **Thinking** can be thought of as part of an information-processing system. It involves the transformations or changes in information that have been encoded and stored in short- and long-term memory. (p. 328)

Example: A hunter is stalking a deer. He must observe the tracks of various forest animals and decide which was left by the deer. He must observe the weather and wind conditions and decide which direction will allow him to approach the deer without letting the deer know he is there. He must decide where and when to fire his gun and at what part of the deer's body.

6. **Artificial concepts** are concepts that are clearly defined by a set of rules or properties so that each member of the concept meets all of the rules or has all of the defining properties and no nonmember does. (p. 328–329)

Example: A square is an artificial concept. All members of the concept are shapes with four equal sides and four right-angle corners. Nothing that is not a square shares these properties.

7. **Natural concepts** are defined by a *general* set of features, not all of which must be present for an object to be considered a member of the concept. (p. 329)

Example: The concept of vegetable is a natural concept. There are no rules or lists of features that describe every single vegetable. Many vegetables are difficult to recognize as such because this concept is so "fuzzy." Tomatoes are not vegetables, but most people think they are. Rhubarb is a vegetable, but most people think it is not.

8. A **prototype** is the best example of a natural concept. (p. 329)

Example: Try this trick on your friends. Have them sit down with a pencil and paper. Tell them to write down all of the numbers that you will say and the answers to three questions that you will ask. Recite about 15 numbers of at least 3 digits each and then ask them to write down the name of a tool, a color and a flower. About 60 to 80 percent of them will write down "hammer," "red," and "rose" because these are common prototypes of the concepts for tool, color, and flower. Prototypes come to mind most easily when people try to think of a concept.

9. The **affirmation rule** defines an artificial concept. An object, event, or idea must have one defining feature or characteristic to be included in the concept. (p. 331)

Example: All legal drivers have a driver's license. Only one feature, the driver's license, must be present for a person to be a legal driver.

10. The **conjunctive rule** defines an artificial concept. It is based on two or more attributes and requires that all of them be present in each member of the concept. (p. 331)

Example: In order to be defined as a square, a shape must have four equal sides and four right-angle corners. *All* of these features must be present before the shape can be a member of the concept *square.*

REMEMBER: The conjunctive rule can be thought of as the <u>and</u> rule. This feature <u>and</u> this feature <u>and</u> this feature must be present before the object can be considered part of the concept.

11. The **disjunctive rule** defines an artificial concept. It holds that members of a concept must have one feature or another. (p. 331)

Example: The concept of a strike in baseball includes swinging at a pitch and missing <u>or</u> not swinging at a pitch that is in the strike zone.

REMEMBER: The disjunctive rule can be thought of as the <u>or</u> rule. One feature <u>or</u> another must be present, but all of them do not have to be present.

12. A **proposition** is the smallest unit of knowledge that can stand alone. Propositions are relationships between concepts or between a concept and a property of the concept. Propositions can be true or false. (p. 332)

Example: Carla (concept) likes to buy flowers (concept) is a proposition that shows a relationship between two concepts. *Dogs bark* is a proposition that shows a relationship between a concept (dog) and a property of that concept (bark).

13. **Mental models** are representations of our understanding of how things work. They guide our interaction with those things. (p. 332)

Example: There is a toy that is a board with different types of latches, fasteners, and buttons on it. As children play with it, they form a mental model of how these things work. Then when they see a button, perhaps a doorbell, they will have an understanding of how it works.

14. A **cognitive map** is a mental representation of one's environment. Our cognitive maps are subject to rectangular bias which is the tendency to impose a north-south-east-west orientation. (p. 333)

Example: Most people have a cognitive map of their neighborhood. Close your eyes and think of the path you would take to the closest grocery store or your favorite hang-out.

15. A **syllogism,** a component of the reasoning process, is an argument made up of two propositions, called premises, and a conclusion based on those premises. Syllogisms may be correct or incorrect. (p. 333)

Example: An incorrect syllogism: All cats are mammals (premise). All people are mammals (premise). Therefore, all cats are people (conclusion).

16. An **algorithm** is a systematic procedure that always produces a solution to a problem. In an algorithm, a specific sequence of thought or set of rules is followed to solve the problem. Algorithms can be very time-consuming. (p. 335)

Example: To solve this math problem, 3,999,999 × 1,111,111, using an algorithm, you would multiply it out:
3,999,999
× 1,111,111
4,444,442,888,889

This takes a long time. If you round the numbers to 4,000,000 × 1,000,000 the problem becomes much simpler. You multiply 4 × 1 and add the appropriate number of zeros (4,000,000,000,000). This is using a heuristic, and produces a less accurate solution than the algorithm.

17. A **heuristic** is a mental short cut or rule of thumb used to solve a problem. (p. 335)

Example: See key term 16, algorithm, for an example of a heuristic.

18. The **anchoring heuristic** is a biased method of estimating an event's probability by adjusting a preliminary estimate in light of new information. The preliminary value biases the final estimate. (p. 335)

Example: Jeannene just moved to the city. Her parents lived in that city ten years ago and were familiar with the area that she wants to move into. Ten years ago it was a very bad neighborhood. Since that time, many changes have taken place, and her area has one of the lowest crime rates in the city. Jeannene's parents think that the crime rate may have improved a little, but they just cannot believe that the area is all that safe, despite the lower crime rate.

19. The **representativeness heuristic** involves judging that an example belongs to a certain class of items by first focusing on the similarities between the example and the class, and then determining whether the particular example has essential features of the class. However, many times people do not consider the frequency of occurrence of the class (the base-rate frequency) and focus instead on what is representative or typical of the available evidence. (p. 335)

Example: After examining a patient, Dr. White recognizes symptoms characteristic of a disease that has a base-rate frequency of 1 in 22 million people. Instead of looking for a more frequently occurring explanation of the symptoms, the doctor decides that the patient has this very rare disease. She makes this decision based on the similarity of the set of symptoms (example) to those of the rare disease (a larger class of events or items).

20. The **availability heuristic** involves judging the probability of an event by how easily examples of the event come to mind. This leads to biased judgments when the probability of the mentally available events do not equal the actual probability of their occurrence. (p. 336)

Example: A friend of yours has just moved to New York City. You could not understand why he moved there, since the crime rate is so high. You hear from a mutual acquaintance that your friend is in the hospital. You assume that he was probably mugged because this is the most available information in your mind about New York City.

21. **Functional fixedness** occurs when a person fails to use a familiar object in a novel way in order to solve a problem. (p. 337)

Example: Lisa does not have functional fixedness; she is very creative in her use of the objects in her environment. One day she dropped a fork down the drain of the kitchen sink. She took a small refrigerator magnet and tied it to a chopstick. She then put the chopstick down the drain, let the fork attach itself to the magnet, and carefully pulled it out of the sink. If Lisa had viewed the magnet as being capable only of holding material against the refrigerator, and the chopstick as being useful only for eating Chinese food, she would have experienced functional fixedness.

22. **Incubation,** a method of improving problem solving, means gathering much more information about the problem, setting it aside for a while, and turning to some other mental activity. Later, the problem can be approached from a fresh perspective. (p. 340)

Example: Timothy designs new household products. For example, his newest project is to build a comfortable chair that can be converted into a table. He thinks about the ultimate functions of the item, all the parts he may need, and some of the problems he may encounter in the design. He then thinks about other things. Usually the solution comes to him later, sometimes quite suddenly.

23. **Decomposition** is a method of problem solving. A large problem is broken down into smaller subproblems by working backward from the final goal. (p. 340)

Example: Cassandra was about to write a novel. When she thought about the entire project, she became overwhelmed and had difficulty starting it. She decided to break the book into chapters, to break each chapter into three or four sections, and to write an outline for each section. Every day Cassandra completed one section. This way she was able to finish the book a little at a time.

REMEMBER: Decompose means to separate into parts. The process of decomposition is breaking a problem into separate parts.

24. **Multiattribute utility theory** is a decision-making technique that helps overcome the frailties of short-term memory. The procedure assumes that all the outcomes of the possible alternatives are certain. See Table 9.2 in your text for an example. (p. 345)

25. **Gambler's fallacy** is a biased perception of probability. People believe that a series of one kind of event in a random process is more likely to be followed by a different event than the same event again. (p. 349)

Example: A friend asks you to bet on ten flips of a penny. The first nine flips are all heads. If you decide that it is time for a tail just because there have been so many heads, your perceptions are being influenced by the gambler's fallacy. The tenth flip of the penny is completely independent of all the other flips. The probability of heads or tails is still fifty-fifty no matter how many heads or tails have appeared before.

26. **Language** is comprised of 2 elements: symbols, such as words, and a grammar. A grammar is a set of rules for combining the symbols, or words, into sentences. (p. 351)

Example: The German and English languages use the same symbols (Roman characters), but each has a different set of rules for combining those symbols. The Russian language has different symbols (Cyrillic characters) as well as different rules of grammar.

27. A **phoneme** is the smallest unit that affects the meaning of speech. (p. 351)

Example: Phonemes are sounds that make a difference in the meaning of a word. By changing the beginning phoneme the meaning of the following words is changed: beat, meet, seat.

REMEMBER: Phono means sound. Phonemes are sounds that change the meaning of a word.

28. A **morpheme** is the smallest unit of language that has meaning. (p. 352)

Example: Any prefix or suffix has meaning. The suffix *s* means plural, as in the words bat*s* or flower*s*. The prefix *un* means not, as in *un*happy or *un*rest. *S* and *un* are morphemes.

29. **Syntax** is the set of rules that dictate how words are combined to make phrases and sentences. (p. 352)

> *REMEMBER: Syn* means together (as in sychronized). Syntax is the set of rules that determine the *order* of words when they are put *together.*

30. **Semantics** is the set of rules that governs the meaning of words and sentences. (p. 352)

31. The **surface structure** of a sentence is the order in which the words are arranged. (p. 353)

> *Example:* See key term 32, *deep structure*, for an example.

32. The **deep structure** of a sentence is an abstract representation of the relationships expressed in a sentence or, in other words, its various meanings. (p. 353)

> *Example: The eating of the animal was grotesque.* The surface structure of this sentence is the order of the words. The sentence has several meanings or deep structures. The way the animal is eating could be grotesque, or the way people are eating an animal could be grotesque.

33. A **spectrograph** is a visual representation of the frequencies of speech sounds. A spectograph shows the gaps between sounds. (p. 354)

> *REMEMBER: Spec* refers to looking and *graph* means writing. A spectrograph is *writing* that represents speech so that one can *look* at it.

34. A **language acquisition device** is, according to Chomsky, a mechanism that gives children an innate ability to process speech and to understand both the fundamental relationships among words and the regularities of speech. (p. 359)

> *Example:* A language acquisition device allows children to gather ideas about the rules of language without even being aware of doing so.

They can then use these ideas to understand and construct utterances in their native language.

LEARNING OBJECTIVES

1. Define information-processing system. Discuss the relationship between information-processing systems and decision making in humans. (p. 323)
2. Define reaction time. Discuss the role of reaction time in studies of cognition. Describe the factors that influence reaction time. (pp. 324–326)
3. Define evoked brain potential and average evoked brain potential. Discuss the use of evoked brain potential in the study of mental chronometry and brain injuries. (pp. 326–327)
4. Define thinking. (p. 328)
5. Define artificial and natural concepts. Define prototype. Give an example of each. (pp. 328–329)
6. Describe the processes involved in learning both types of concepts. Define the affirmation rule, the conjunctive rule, and the disjunctive rule and give an example of each. (pp. 329–331)
7. Discuss the mental representation of concepts. Know the relationship between concepts, mental models, and propositions. (pp. 331–332)
8. Describe the manipulation of mental images. Define cognitive maps. Discuss the use of cognitive maps and the biases which distort them. (pp. 332–333)
9. Define logic and syllogisms. Describe the relationship between syllogisms and premises. Discuss the influence of syllogisms on thinking. (pp. 333–335)
10. Define heuristics and algorithms. Define the anchoring heuristic, the representativeness heuristic, and the availability heuristic. Give an example of each. (pp. 335–336)

11. Describe the four characteristics of problem solving. Explain why multiple hypotheses, mental sets, functional fixedness, confirmation bias, and ignoring negative evidence and base-rate information can hinder problem solving. Give an example of each hindering factor. (pp. 336–339)

12. Discuss the possible methods for improving problem solving. Define incubation and decomposition. Know the dangers of being an expert when solving problems. (pp. 339–341)

13. Define multiattribute utility theory. Give an example of the type of decision problem this theory can help solve. Describe the various approaches to making risky decisions. Define gambler's fallacy and give an example. (pp. 345–349)

14. Be able to list the components that make up language. Define phoneme and morpheme. Give an example of the phonemes and morphemes in any given word. (pp. 351–352)

15. Define syntax and semantics. Explain the ways syntax and semantics help us comprehend language. (p. 352)

16. Define surface structure and deep structure. Be able to describe the surface and deep structure of any given sentence. (pp. 352–353)

17. Define the spectrograph and its role in helping psychologists understand the perception of the spoken word. Describe the elements of sentence structure that increase comprehension and retention of communications. (pp. 354–355)

18. Discuss the role of context in the comprehension of spoken and written language. (pp. 355–356)

19. Describe language development in children. (pp. 356–357)

20. Discuss the role of conditioning and imitation in language development. Define motherese. Discuss the roles of nature and nurture in language development. (pp. 358–359)

21. Discuss the role of language in perception. (pp. 359–362)

CONCEPTS AND EXERCISES

No. 1 Learning Concepts

Completing this exercise should help you to achieve the following learning objectives.

(5) *Define artificial and natural concepts. Define prototype. Give an example of each. (pp. 328–329)*

(6) *Describe the processes involved in learning both types of concept. Define the affirmation rule, the conjunctive rule, and the disjunctive rule and give an example of each. (pp. 329–331)*

(7) *Discuss the mental representation of concepts. Know the relationship between concepts, mental models, and propositions. (pp. 331–332)*

Below are descriptions of several concepts. Name the concept and identify the rule that defines it.

1. This concept contains either a monster, a vampire, a psychopath, a murderer, a villain, aliens, or the psychological deterioration of one of the characters.

   What is the concept?

   What defines this concept?

2. This concept contains a red octagonal object with white writing on it.

   What is the name of the concept?

   What defines this concept?

3. This concept contains objects which are found in houses, apartments, condominiums, and sometimes garages. People use these objects for many reasons. One of the best examples of this concept is a chair.

   What is the name of the concept?

   What defines this concept?

No. 2 Approaches to Problem Solving

Completing this exercise should help you to achieve the following learning objectives.

(8) *Describe the manipulation of mental images. Define cognitive maps. Discuss the use of cognitive maps and the biases which distort them. (pp. 332–333)*

(10) *Define heuristics and algorithms. Define the anchoring heuristic, the representativeness heuristic, and the availability heuristic. Give an example of each. (pp. 335–336)*

(11) *Describe the four basic characteristics of problem solving. Explain why multiple hypotheses, mental sets, functional fixedness, confirmation bias, and ignoring negative evidence and base-rate information can hinder problem solving. Give an example of each hindering factor. (pp. 336–339)*

(12) *Discuss the possible methods for improving problem solving. Define incubation and decomposition. Know the dangers of being an expert when solving problems. (pp. 339–341)*

Below are several problems. Read the description of each problem and answer the questions following it.

1. Viola's parents have just moved to a suburb outside of Chicago. She is home for a visit for the first time since they have moved. To her embarassment, she is always getting lost. The streets seem to be arranged in a triangular pattern instead of a square one.

   What is Viola trying to develop?

   What bias is causing her problems?

2. Trixy and her brother Peter are home by themselves, and the lights have all gone off. Both children are terrified of the dark. Trixy remembers that her dad told her once about a fuse box. She hypothesizes that this is the problem. But Trixy and her brother do not want to enter the dark basement.

   How can they decide whether going to the basement is necessary?

What have they avoided if they do this?

The fact that the whole house is dark should be a clue to Trixy and Peter. What kind of evidence about their hypothesis are they ignoring?

3. Al is lost somewhere in Paris. He wants to get to a museum that a friend told him to visit, but he has no idea where he is. He stops someone on the street and asks for directions. The Parisian says that he can give Al either a tricky short cut or a very long set of directions that will be easy to follow. Al decides to take the long way since it will guarantee his arrival at the museum, even though it will take a bit longer.

   The Parisian has offered Al a choice between a (an) _____ and a (an) _____.

   Which of the above did Al choose?

4. Carl, a foreman at a paper mill, is upset because something is wrong with the paper's color as it comes off the machine. He and the people that work with him have thought about all the previous color problems they have encountered, but they cannot find a solution. Carl decides to bring in a person who has just started to work in the paper room and ask him what he thinks.

   Carl has realized that he is an expert and may have a _____ that is preventing him from solving the problem.

No. 3 Structures of Language

Completing this exercise should help you to achieve the following learning objectives.

(14) *Be able to list the components that make up language. Define phoneme and morpheme. Give an example of the phonemes and morphemes in any given word. (pp. 351–352)*

(16) *Define surface structure and deep structure. Be able to describe the surface and deep structure of any given sentence. (pp. 352–353)*

(18) *Discuss the role of context in the comprehension of spoken and written language. (pp. 355–356)*

Below are several sentences. Identify the structures of language as indicated. HINT: When looking for morphemes, use a dictionary to look for the prefixes, suffixes, and roots of words.

1. The husband's dinner was terrible.

   Underline all of the morphemes. Identify at least two deep structures.

2. My friend painted me in his back yard.

   Underline all of the morphemes. Identify at least two deep structures.

3. The concert was totally awesome.

   What role does context play in the comprehension of this sentence?

ANSWERS TO CONCEPTS AND EXERCISES

No. 1 Learning Concepts

Do not be overly concerned if you cannot name the concept. Your definition of the concept in each question may be different from ours. However, you should be able to answer the questions about how the concepts are defined.

1. This concept is *scary movies*. It is defined by the *disjunctive rule*. A movie must have at least one of the many possible features of the concept in order to be a scary movie. (p. 331)

2. The name of this concept is a *stop sign*. The *conjunctive rule* defines it. (p. 331)

3. This concept is *furniture*. It is a natural concept, and the prototype of a chair helps define it. (p. 329)

No. 2 Approaches to Problem Solving

1. Viola is trying to develop a *cognitive map*. She is being affected by rectangular bias. The main roads are in the shape of a triangle, but the *rectangular bias* causes her to attempt to put them into a north-south-east-west square. (p. 333)

2. Trixy has hypothesized that the fuse box is the cause of the sudden loss of lights in her house. In order to avoid *confirmation bias,* she and Peter could look out the window to see if other houses are without lights. If that is the case, then the problem is not the fuse box but rather a major power failure in the neighborhood. When the problem is a blown fuse, only part of the house is dark. This is the symptom that Trixy and Peter are overlooking. They are *ignoring negative evidence.* (p. 339)

3. The Parisian has offered Al a choice between a heuristic (the short cut) or an algorithm (the sure but longer way to get to the museum). Al chose the algorithm. (p. 335)

4. Carl has realized that being an expert has caused him to have a *mental set.* Therefore, he is bringing in someone who doesn't have old answers that will get in the way of thinking of new answers. (p. 337)

No. 3 Structures of Language

1. A. Morphemes: The husband's dinner was terrible. (p. 352)

   s after an apostrophe means possessive.

   Dinner is one meaningful unit.

   Was is one meaningful unit.

   Terrible is one meaningful unit.

   B. There are at least two possible deep structures. The husband had a dinner party at which the guests had a poor meal. Or the meal that the husband was eating was prepared poorly. (p. 353)

2. A. Morphemes: My friend painted me in his back yard.

   My is one meaningful unit.

Friend is one meaningful unit.

Paint is one meaningful unit.

ed is one meaningful unit.

Me is one meaningful unit.

In is one meaningful unit.

His is one meaningful unit.

Back is one meaningful unit.

Yard is one meaningful unit. (p. 352)

B. Surface structure: My friend painted me in his back yard.

Deep structure: My friend created a painting depicting me in his back yard, or my friend and I were in his back yard where he was painting my portrait, or my friend and I were in his back yard where he was putting paint on me. (p. 353)

3. Context is important in trying to understand any type of communication. To understand the sentence, "The concert was totally awesome," the listener must have personal knowledge of the slang words *totally awesome*. (p. 355)

MULTIPLE CHOICE QUESTIONS

Facts and Definitions

1. Reaction time is the
   a. time it takes to perceive a stimulus.
   b. time it takes to react to a stimulus after it has been perceived.
   c. time it takes to react to a stimulus after it has been presented.
   d. timing of mental events.

2. The specific evoked potential called the N100
   a. shows that initial sensory processing is taking place.
   b. indicates the novelty of a stimulus.
   c. indicates the speed of response selection.
   d. indicates the perception of a stimulus.

3. Natural and artificial concepts differ in that a natural concept is
   a. defined by the affirmation rule, and an artificial concept is not.
   b. defined by the conjunctive rule, and an artificial concept is defined by prototypes.
   c. sometimes defined by a prototype, and an artificial concept is defined by rules.
   d. more easily used than an artificial concept.

4. The objects, events, or ideas in a concept defined by the conjunctive rule
   a. have one feature in common.
   b. have two or more common features that must be present.
   c. must have one of several possible features.
   d. must be similar to a prototype.

5. Propositions
   a. are the basic components of words.
   b. show the relationships among concepts.
   c. are always true.
   d. show the relationship among mental models.

6. Imposing a north-south-east-west orientation on cognitive maps is called
   a. rectangular bias.
   b. reconstructive memory.
   c. directional bias.
   d. None of the above.

7. An algorithm
   a. is a short cut to the solution of a problem.
   b. will sometimes yield a correct answer to a problem.
   c. will always yield a correct answer to a problem.
   d. is subject to bias from the availability heuristic.

8. The representativeness heuristic
   a. causes us to ignore base-rate information.
   b. causes us to give improper weight to contradictory evidence when making a decision.

c. causes us to focus on solutions that are easily brought to mind.

d. causes us to consider only those hypotheses with which we are the most familiar.

9. Functional fixedness occurs when

a. a person uses old solutions to solve new problems.

b. a person only looks for information which will confirm a hypothesis.

c. a person ignores negative evidence.

d. a person cannot think of novel uses for familiar objects in order to solve a problem.

10. Decomposition is a method which can improve problem solving. It involves

a. putting the problem aside for awhile and then thinking about a possible solution.

b. gathering as much information as possible about the problem before trying to solve it.

c. breaking down a problem into smaller sub-problems.

d. using old solutions to produce ideas for new solutions.

11. The decision-making technique based on multi-attribute theory is useful when

a. evaluating a choice that involves so many alternatives and attributes that short-term memory is overloaded.

b. a decision must be made under time pressure.

c. a correct answer is essential.

d. evaluating a syllogism.

12. Gambler's fallacy occurs when people

a. overestimate the probability of very rare events.

b. overestimate the probability of very common events.

c. are overconfident about their predictions.

d. believe that if they have failed several times, their next attempt will probably be a success.

13. Which of the following is correct?

a. Phonemes make up morphemes, which make up words.

b. Morphemes make up phonemes, which make up words.

c. Words make up morphemes, which make up sentences.

d. Words make up phonemes, which make up morphemes.

14. The deep structure of a sentence is

a. the sequence of words in the sentence.

b. the meaning of the sentence.

c. the syntax of the sentence.

d. a reflection of the complexity of the sentence.

15. Context can alter the interpretation of a sentence. Which of the following would not be considered a part of context?

a. A person's knowledge of the world based on experience

b. The situation in which the communication is taking place

c. The inflection of a person's voice when communicating

d. All of the above contribute to the context of a situation

MULTIPLE CHOICE QUESTIONS

Application of Concepts

1. Cliff has just stopped his car at a red light, when the light changes to green. Which of the following will affect his reaction time?

a. Cliff is driving a stick shift for the first time.

b. Cliff did not expect the light to change to green so quickly.

c. This intersection has five intersecting roads. Cliff can turn onto one of these roads or go straight.

d. All of the above.

2.   (Refer to question 1 on page 175) If we could look at Cliff's evoked potentials when the light changed to green what would we see?

    a. A large positive N100 followed by a negative P300

    b. A positive P300 followed by a large negative N100

    c. A negative N100 followed by a large positive P300

    d. A negative N100 and a large positive P300 occurring simultaneously

3.   Charlie is six years old. At the zoo with his father, he points to a large panther and says, "Look, Dad, that animal looks just like our kitty at home. It has fur and a tail and it walks on all fours and it has whiskers and pointy ears. But it's too big to be a cat." What rule of concept formation is Charlie using to define his concept of cat?

    a. The conjunctive rule

    b. The disjunctive rule

    c. The affirmation rule

    d. The one-feature rule

4.   Which of the following choices defines the concept of a student using the affirmation rule?

    a. A student carries a backpack and takes classes.

    b. A student either attends a university, attends a junior college, or is taking a correspondence course.

    c. A student is anyone who is enrolled in a course.

    d. A student is anyone who resembles the characters in a movie about college students.

5.   Four items are listed below. Try to figure out the name of the natural concept to which they belong, and then choose the prototypical example.

    a. A fist

    b. A brick

    c. A gun

    d. Sharp fingernails

6.   Which of the following alternatives is an example of a proposition?

    a. *th*

    b. *Flowers*

    c. *ed*

    d. *Cats eat flowers.*

7.   Clinton is really frustrated. His uncle has been beating him at checkers all night. He is going to play another game, but this time he is going to base his strategy on an algorithm, not a heuristic. What problem will this cause?

    a. Clinton still may not win the game.

    b. Clinton and his uncle will be playing the same game of checkers for a very long time.

    c. Clinton is ignoring base-rate information.

    d. The representativeness heuristic will bias Clinton's choice of strategy.

8.   Cindy is 100 percent positive of her ability to find an advertising job in New York City. When she gets to New York, she reads in the paper that jobs are very, very scarce due to the great number of recent corporate mergers. Despite this, she is still very sure that with her qualifications she will land a job. Which heuristic is responsible for her reasoning?

    a. The anchoring heuristic

    b. The availability heuristic

    c. The representativeness heuristic

    d. The base-rate information heuristic

Use the following scenario for question 9 and question 10.

Many companies are reporting an inability to staff their foreign offices in Europe. Employees previously interested in overseas work are frightened of the terrorist activity they keep hearing about in the news. They are sure that something disastrous will happen to their families if they move to Europe.

9. Which heuristic are the employees using to assess the incidence of terrorist activities?

    a. The availability heuristic
    b. The representativeness heuristic
    c. The anchoring heuristic
    d. None of the above.

10. What should the companies do to increase the willingness of their employees to work overseas?

    a. Have their public relations departments make frequent reports to the major news networks about the positive experiences their employees have had abroad.
    b. Publish reports on the number of fatalities due to terrorism to show how small a threat it is.
    c. Reduce the minimum length of stay in a foreign country from two years to six months, so employees can have a trial period.
    d. None of the above will work.

11. Emmeline works as a lab technician in a neurobiological laboratory. She has just received an announcement that must be posted in the lab immediately. She rummages through her desk drawers but cannot find any thumbtacks. Instead, she uses the ends of hypodermic needles to attach the announcement to the bulletin board. What pitfall in problem solving has she just avoided?

    a. Functional fixedness
    b. Confirmation bias
    c. Ignoring negative evidence
    d. Faulty hypothesis testing

12. Winnie, a teacher, has been told that the test scores of one of her new students, Fred, suggest that he is very bright. The principal has asked her to keep an eye on Fred and let him know what she thinks of Fred's intelligence. All through the first six weeks of the semester she finds examples that seem to show that Fred is indeed very bright. However, during the seventh week she finds out that the records have been mixed up. Fred's actual test scores show him as being strictly average. What explains Winnie's observations?

    a. Confirmation bias
    b. Functional fixedness
    c. Mental set
    d. Decomposition

13. Many advertising campaigns designed for foreign countries have failed because the words in the ads had the wrong meanings in other languages. For example, *Nova,* the name of a car, means "does not go" in Spanish. The advertisers did not consider the _____ of the Spanish language when creating the ad.

    a. syntax
    b. language acquisition device
    c. semantics
    d. surface structure

14. Which of the following sentences would be the easiest to memorize?

A grickly aftla hicktored the bubla.

Oftla grick hickt bubla.

    a. The first sentence.
    b. The second sentence.
    c. Both will be equally easy to memorize.
    d. Cannot be determined.

15. In the Tarzan movies, a couple and their baby were shipwrecked. The baby survived and was raised by apes until a doctor found him twenty years later. The doctor took the wild man out of the jungle, taught him how to speak French and English, and introduced him to society. Although the wild man's accents were not perfect, he managed to live in England for some time before choosing to go back to the jungle. Why is this movie unrealistic?

    a. A language acquisition device needs to be learned.

b. A critical period exists for language acquisition.

c. The wild man should have been able to learn proper French and English accents.

d. None of the above.

ANSWERS TO MULTIPLE CHOICE QUESTIONS

Facts and Definitions

1. *c* is the answer. Reaction time is the time elapsed between the stimulus presentation and an overt response. (p. 324)

a. Perceiving a stimulus is only part of the activity that takes place between the presentation of a stimulus and the overt response to that stimulus.

b. The overt reaction to a stimulus is only part of the activity that takes place between the presentation of a stimulus and the overt response to that stimulus.

d. Mental chronometry is the timing of mental events. Making an overt response, which is one of the activities measured by reaction time, is not solely a mental event.

2. *a* is the answer. The N100 shows the initial sensory processing in the primary sensory cortex. (p. 326)

b. & d. The size of the P300 gives an indication of the novelty of a stimulus and shows the time that a stimulus is perceived.

c. The P300 signals when perception of a stimulus is completed and gives an indication of the novelty of a stimulus.

3. *c* is the answer. A prototype is the best example of a natural concept. Many children learn which objects, events, or ideas belong to a concept by comparing them to a prototype. (p. 329)

a. & b. Artificial concepts are defined by one of several rules (the affirmation, conjunctive or dis-

junctive rules). Natural concepts are defined by general sets of characteristics and prototypes.

d. Learning a natural concept is more difficult than learning an artificial concept. Artificial concepts are defined by rules. Each new object encountered can simply be evaluated in terms of those rules. Natural concepts are "fuzzy" because there are no clear distinctive rules to help a person decide if an object belongs in a concept or not.

4. *b* is the answer. The conjunctive rule specifies that all the features of a concept must be present before an object can be considered a part of that concept. (p. 331)

a. The affirmation rule defines an artificial concept in which all the elements share one common feature. That is why this rule is also called the one-feature rule.

c. The disjunctive rule specifies that one of many possible features must be present before an object can be considered part of a certain concept.

d. A prototype is the best example of a natural concept. Natural concepts are not defined by rules.

5. *b* is the answer. Propositions show the relationship between concepts or the relationship between a property or characteristic and a concept. (p. 332)

a. Propositions are made up of words. You may be thinking of phonemes and morphemes.

c. Propositions can be true or false.

d. Mental models are made up of propositions, not the other way around. Propositions show the relationship between concepts or the relationship between a property or characteristic and a concept.

6. *a* is the answer. Rectangular bias is the tendency to make our cognitive maps fit a north-south-east-west orientation. To remember this, think of a rectangle with the top as north, the bottom as south, and the right and left sides as east and west, respectively. (p. 333)

b. Reconstructive memory is the process of filling the gaps in our memories with information that has been stored in long-term memory.

c. There is no such thing as directional bias with regard to cognitive maps.

d. a is the answer.

7. *c* is the answer. The algorithm is a method of problem solving that will always yield a correct answer. We could use algorithms all the time to solve problems, but they would take a very long time to work through. (p. 335)

a. & b. Heuristics are short cuts or rules of thumb that we use to solve problems. They do not always yield a correct answer.

d. Algorithms always produce a correct answer and are therefore not subject to bias.

8. *a* is the answer. The representativeness heuristic leads us to look at an example and compare it to a larger class of items. We focus on the similar appearances of the example and the larger class of items, ignoring information on how often the larger class of items occurs (base-rate frequency). (pp. 335–336)

b. The anchoring heuristic causes us to give improper weight to contradictory evidence in making a decision.

c. & d. The availability heuristic causes us to focus on the solutions that are most easily brought to mind. These are usually the hypotheses that have occurred most frequently in the past.

9. *d* is the answer. Many objects designed for a particular purpose can be used to solve other types of problems. However, when people can think of an object as serving only its intended purpose, they are victims of functional fixedness. (p. 337)

a. A mental set causes people to use old solutions to solve new problems instead of looking for simpler solutions.

b. Confirmation bias occurs when people only look at information which will confirm a hypothesis.

c. Ignoring negative evidence means that people do not consider the lack of symptoms when testing a hypothesis.

10. *c* is the answer. Decomposition is breaking down a large problem or project into smaller parts by working backward from the final goal. (p. 340)

a. & b. Putting the problem aside for a while and then thinking about a possible solution is called incubation. Incubation produces the best results when as much information as possible is gathered before putting the problem aside.

d. The use of old solutions to create new solutions is a possible problem-solving method. However, it is not the decomposition technique.

11. *a* is the answer. Short-term memory can store from five to nine items. If you were to evaluate three choices, each of which had six important attributes, you would have to be able to hold at least eighteen items in short-term memory. You would also have to be able to compare each possible combination of choices in order to reach a final decision. The multiattribute technique allows you to do this more easily. (p. 345)

b. & c. You may have been thinking of algorithms and heuristics. An algorithm always yields a correct answer, but may take quite a bit of time. A heuristic is a short cut that may not yield a correct answer.

d. Most people use a combination of reasoning and real-world knowledge to evaluate a syllogism. The use of the multiattribute technique does not lend itself to the evaluation of a syllogism.

12. *d* is the answer. Random events are independent of each other. For example, the result of the flip of a coin, whether for the first, second, third, or hundredth time, is independent of the results of the previous flips. Each time the coin is flipped, there is a fifty-fifty chance of seeing heads. Gambler's fallacy occurs when someone thinks that because many heads have turned up, tails are soon due to appear. (p. 349)

a., b., & c. Incorrectly estimating the probability of events is a bias in perception of probability, but neither this nor overconfidence in one's own predictions is gambler's fallacy.

13. *a* is the answer. Phonemes (sounds that affect the meaning of a word) make up morphemes (the smallest units of meaning in a language), which make up words. (pp. 351–352)

b., *c.*, & *d.* Only *a* is correct.

14. *b* is the answer. Deep structure is the underlying meaning of a string of words. (p. 353)

a. Surface structure is the sequence of the words.

c. The syntax of the sentence is the set of rules that govern the way the words are strung together.

d. Deep structure refers to the meaning of a sentence, not its complexity.

15. *d* is the answer. All of the alternatives are contextual information that will influence the interpretation of a sentence. (p. 355)

ANSWERS TO MULTIPLE CHOICE QUESTIONS

Application of Concepts

1. *d* is the answer. Cliff will need more time to respond to the green light (the stimulus) since he is driving a stick shift for the first time, which requires a different starting procedure from that of an automatic. Also, the light turned green sooner than he expected, and unexpected stimuli lengthen reaction time. Finally, an increase in the complexity of the decision will lengthen reaction time. Cliff has more than the usual number of streets to choose from when the light turns green. (pp. 324–325)

2. *c* is the answer. A negative N100 potential, which indicates sensory processing in the cortex, is followed by a large positive P300, showing the perception and evaluation of a surprising stimulus. (pp. 326–327)

a. An N100 potential is negative and a P300 potential is positive.

b. & *d.* An N100 precedes a P300 because sensation precedes perception.

3. *a* is the answer. The conjunctive rule specifies that every feature defining the concept must be present before an object can be considered a member of that concept. Charlie has decided that the black panther cannot be a cat because it does not meet *all* the criteria of his concept of a cat. One of the features of Charlie's concept of cat is small size. (p. 331)

b. The disjunctive rule says that one or more but not all of the features that define a category must be present for membership. Charlie is insisting that all the features be present in the panther, including its size, before he will call it a cat.

c. & *d.* The affirmation or one-feature rule says that only one feature is necessary to define a concept. Charlie's concept of cat has many feature including fur, a tail, and pointy ears, as well as size.

4. *c* is the answer. One feature must be present before an object is considered part of a concept according to the affirmation rule. Alternative *c* says that anyone who is *enrolled in a class* is part of the concept of *student.* The concept has only one feature, which is enrollment. (p. 331)

a. The conjunctive rule says that two or more features must be present for membership. Carrying a backpack and taking classes must be present before a person can be considered a student.

b. The disjunctive rule says that one feature or another must be present. There are two or more features that define the concept, but not all of them must be present.

d. The characters in a movie about college students are prototypes. Defining the concept *student* in this way does not use any rule.

5. *c* is the answer. The concept is *weapons,* and a gun is the best example of a weapon. (p. 329)

6. *d* is the answer. *Cats eat flowers* is a proposition because it relates two concepts, cats and flowers. (p. 332)

    a. th is a phoneme.

    b. Flowers is just a concept.

    c. ed is a morpheme.

7. *b* is the answer. An algorithm will always produce the correct answer, which in this case is winning the game. However, Clinton and his uncle will be playing for a very long time. Clinton will have to evaluate the consequences of every possible move he can make each time it is his turn. (p. 335)

    a. Algorithms always produce a correct answer.

    c. & d. People usually ignore base-rate information when using a representativeness heuristic. Clinton is using an algorithm, not a heuristic.

8. *a* is the answer. Cindy started out being 100 percent sure that she would get a job. After reading the paper, she should have realized that her chances are very slim. Instead she is still very sure; she is anchored in her hypothesis that she will get a job. (p. 335)

    b. People use the availability heuristic when they judge the probability of an event by how easily examples of that event come to mind. If Cindy had thought of all of her many friends who had gotten jobs in the city, this would have been the correct answer.

    c. If Cindy were using the representativeness heuristic, she would focus on the representative information (the paper) instead of her original estimate.

    d. There is no such thing as the base rate heuristic. You may be thinking of the representativeness heuristic. Ignoring base-rate frequencies results in the use of this heuristic.

9. *a* is the answer. Employees are judging the probability of terrorism based on the information which is most available to them. This bias is due to the availability heuristic. (p. 336)

    b. The employees are not trying to determine whether an example is part of a class of objects as one would do when using the representativeness heuristic.

    c. The employees are not adjusting their hypothesis to match new information. They have made a decision about the degree of terrorist activity based on the information available to them.

    d. Only *a* is the answer.

10. *a* is the answer. If employees are relying on the most easily available information in order to decide how safe it is abroad, the companies should make positive information more available than the negative reports on terrorist activities. (p. 336)

    b. By publishing the numbers of fatalities, they will simply be making the information of terrorist activities "more available" to the minds of their employees.

    c. The problem is the employees' incorrect estimate of the probability of terrorism. Reducing the minimum length of stay in another country will do nothing to change the employees' incorrect estimates.

    d. Only *a* is the answer.

11. *a* is the answer. If Emmeline had thought of the hypodermics as being useful only for giving injections, she would have experienced functional fixedness. Instead she used them for something other than their traditional function and solved her problem. (p. 337)

    b. & d. Confirmation bias occurs because people always try to confirm their hypotheses instead of refute them. Emmeline is not testing a hypothesis, so neither of these alternatives is correct.

    c. People ignore negative evidence when looking for explanations of some event. Emmeline is not looking for an explanation, but rather a way to solve a problem.

12. *a* is the answer. Winnie has a hypothesis that Fred is very smart. She only takes into considera-

tion evidence which supports her hypothesis and ignores evidence that Fred is only average. (p. 338)

b. Winnie is testing a hypothesis, not trying to find a solution involving the use of an object.

c. A mental set means using the solutions to old problems to try to solve new ones. Winnie is not using old solutions to test her hypothesis about Fred's intelligence.

d. Decomposition is a way to simplify problem solving by breaking a problem into smaller subproblems.

13. *c* is the answer. Semantics is the set of rules governing the meanings of words and sentences. The words *no va* have a particular meaning in Spanish, but this particular combination of letters has no meaning in English. (p. 352)

a. Syntax is a set of rules governing the way words are put together.

b. Chomsky proposed a language acquisition device, or LAD, that is an innate ability to understand the regularities of speech and the fundamental relationships between words.

d. The surface structure is the sequence in which words are strung together.

14. *a* is the answer. The words *a* and *the* as well as the *ly* and *ed* suffixes make it easier for us to chunk the nonsense syllables in short-term memory. (pp. 354–355)

b. There are no words or suffixes which help us chunk information in the second sentence. It is more difficult to remember, even though it is shorter than the first sentence.

c. & *d*. Only *a* is the answer.

15. *b* is the answer. A critical period does exist for language development. The wild man was found when he was in his twenties and was past the critical period for language development. Therefore, he should not have been able to learn any language. (p. 359)

a. The language acquisition device Chomsky proposed is innate.

c. When people learn a second language after the age of twelve to fifteen, they usually cannot speak with a flawless accent.

d. Only *b* is the answer.

Chapter 10

Mental Abilities

OUTLINE

I. INTRODUCTION (pp. 366–368)

This chapter discusses differences in people's mental ability, their capacity to perform the higher mental processes of reasoning, understanding, and problem solving.

II. IQ TESTS (pp. 368–380)

Psychologists do not agree on how to define intelligence.

A. A Brief History

1. *The Stanford-Binet Test.* Binet's original test included a series of age-graded tasks that demonstrated differences among children in reasoning, judgment, and problem solving abilities. Children who answered questions above their age level were considered intellectually advanced. Louis Terman of Stanford University revised Binet's test to include ques-

tions for adults and developed the intelligence quotient or IQ.

2. *Early Testing in America.* Despite their cultural bias, IQ tests were given to help decide which immigrants could stay in the country and to place soldiers in appropriate assignments.

3. *The Wechsler Scales.* In 1949, David Wechsler developed a new test. There were two major subscales: a verbal scale measuring verbal abilities and a performance scale measuring spatial abilities.

B. IQ Tests Today

Revised versions of the Stanford-Binet and Wechsler's tests, the Wechsler Adult Intelligence Scale and the Wechsler Intelligence Scale for Children, are used today. Group testing, also used today, measures a narrower range of behaviors.

1. *Scoring IQ Tests.* The average score obtained by people at each age level is assigned an IQ score of 100. Each individual's score is compared to the average for his or her age level in order to compute an IQ. Therefore an IQ score is a relative measurement.

2. *Culture-Fair Tests.* A culture-fair test, designed to be free of cultural bias, uses more vocabulary-free performance scales.

C. Some Principles of Psychological Testing

Tests have three advantages over other means of evaluation: they are standardized, quantifiable (which allows the calculation of norms), efficient, and economical.

1. *Reliability.* If a test is *reliable,* a person will receive about the same score when tested on different occasions. There are three methods of checking the reliability of a test: test-retest, alternate form, and split-half reliability.

2. *Validity.* A valid test measures what it is designed to measure. There are four measures of

validity: content validity, construct validity, criterion validity, and predictive validity.

D. Evaluating IQ Tests

1. *Reliability and Stability of IQ Scores.* When IQ tests are administered to the same people several years apart, test-retest reliability may be low. Such findings indicate that intellectual capabilities change with development.

2. *What Do IQ Scores Predict?* IQ tests predict academic success moderately well.

3. *Are IQ Tests Biased?* IQ tests are not perfect predictors of academic success because many other factors, aside from intelligence, contribute to academic achievement. Also, motivation can positively or negatively affect test-performance, and tests may be culturally biased.

III. INTERPRETING AND USING IQ SCORES (pp. 380–388)

A. Heredity and the Environment

The influences of heredity and the environment interact to produce intelligence.

1. *Correlational Studies.* Twin studies suggest that heredity influences the development of IQ. However, the environment also exerts a strong influence on IQ.

2. *Environmental Intervention.* Previously underprivileged children placed in homes that provide an enriching intellectual environment have shown moderate but consistent increases in IQ. Also, children placed in enrichment programs show improved health, academic achievements, and intellectual skills.

3. *The Interplay of Heredity and Environment.* Genetics can produce a reaction range or potential for intelligence. A child may move up or down within this range depending on the environment.

B. Group Differences

Examining the differences between group means on IQ tests does not provide information about specific individuals in those groups. The range of IQ scores for members of different races and socioeconomic groups is very large. Hence, the groups have a great deal of overlap.

1. *Socioeconomic Differences.* A child's ability is influenced by genetic factors and perhaps by effects of the parents' occupation and education on the home environment. Also, higher income families may encourage a higher level of motivation to succeed.

2. *Racial Differences.* Jensen argued that the difference in mean IQ scores between black and white Americans was due more to heredity than to environment. However, the genetic differences between blacks and whites are very small compared to the range of genetic differences within each group. Research indicates that differences in IQ between blacks and whites may be due to differences in parental education, nutrition, health care, and schools. Also, black children may not be as motivated as others to succeed during testing.

C. IQ Scores in the Classroom

IQ scores may influence teachers' expectations about the abilities of their students. In turn, these expectancies may influence students' academic performance.

IV. INTELLIGENCE AND THE DIVERSITY OF MENTAL ABILITIES (pp. 388–398)

A. The Psychometric Approach: General and Specific Intelligence

The psychometric approach tries to describe the structure of intelligence by examining the correlations between scores on various tests.

1. *Spearman's g.* The _g-factor_ is general intelligence. The _s-factors_ represent the specific skills and knowledge needed to answer the questions on a particular test.

2. *Other Views.* Thurstone used factor analysis, a statistical technique, to find several independent primary mental abilities, including numerical ability, reasoning, verbal fluency, spatial visualization, perceptual ability, memory, and verbal comprehension. Cattell argued that a g-factor exists and it consists of fluid intelligence and crystallized intelligence.

3. *Conclusions.* Most psychologists agree that there is a g-factor. They do not agree on just what the g-factor is.

B. The Information-Processing Approach

Psychologists have tried to understand intelligence by examining the mental processes involved in intelligent behavior.

1. *Components and Metacomponents.* Components are the information-processing capacities of perceiving stimuli, holding information in working (short-term) memory, performing transformations on that information, and retrieving information from memory. Metacomponents are the processes involved in organizing and setting up a problem. There is a correlation between metacomponent processing and reasoning ability.

2. *The Role of Attention.* Research suggests that those with greater intellectual ability have more attentional resources available when performing a task.

3. *Conclusions.* Attention or any other single entity is not the g-factor that accounts for intelligence. However, particular information-processing abilities are elements of many intellectual tasks.

C. The Symbols-Systems Approach.

This approach focuses on how people learn and use various symbol systems, such as language, mathematics, and music.

D. Creativity

Creativity is often assessed by tests of divergent thinking, which measure the ability to generate many different but plausible responses to a problem.

1. *Creativity and IQ.* There is not a very high correlation between IQ scores and creativity. IQ tests measure convergent thinking, whereas creativity is characterized by divergent thinking.

2. *Creativity and Personality.* Research indicates that personality disorders are no more likely to occur in the creative than in the noncreative person. However, creative people do tend to share some personality traits: they are more independent, rely more on intuitive thinking, have a higher degree of self-acceptance, and have more energy.

E. Cognitive Style

Cognitive complexity is the ability to anticipate future events and to alter a chosen course of action based on unexpected happenings, a set of abilities related to flexibility of thought. Cognitively complex people can think multidimensionally. Cognitive complexity is one dimension of cognitive style. Other dimensions are impulsive versus reflective styles and field-dependent versus field-independent styles.

KEY TERMS

1. **Intelligence** is those attributes that center around reasoning skills, knowledge of one's culture, the ability to arrive at innovative solutions to problems, and the ability to deal effectively with one's en-

vironment. Note, however, that psychologists do not agree on an exact definition of intelligence. (pp. 368–369)

2. The **Stanford-Binet test** was a revised version of Binet's original test of mental abilities. Each set of age-graded questions could be answered correctly by a substantial majority of the children in that age group. Children were above average if they could correctly answer questions above their age grade. The score received, called mental age, was divided by chronological age and then multiplied by 100, resulting in an IQ. (pp. 369–371)

Example: Mark's IQ has been tested. Although he is only twelve, he answered questions designed for children up to fourteen years old. The following steps are used to determine his IQ.

a. Mark's mental age is fourteen.

b. Mark's chronological age is twelve.

c. 14/12 = 1.16

d. 1.16 × 100 = 116.

e. Mark's IQ is 116.

3. The **Wechsler scales,** developed in 1949, consist of performance and verbal scales. The performance scales have little or no verbal content. The Wechsler scales include the Wechsler Preschool and Primary Scale of Intelligence and two revised versions of the Wechsler tests, the Wechsler Adult Intelligence Scale—Revised and the Wechsler Intelligence Scale for Children—Revised. (p. 372)

4. The **verbal scales** in the Wechsler tests measure verbal skills. To do well on these tasks, a person must be familiar with the English language and American culture. (p. 372)

Example: Among the several types of questions included in the verbal scale are vocabulary questions and mathematical word problems. If a math problem involves money, test takers must be familiar with American currency to answer correctly.

5. The **performance scales** in the Wechsler test measure spatial ability and the ability to manipulate materials, using tasks such as block assembly, mazes, and picture completion. (p. 372)

Example: One of the tasks on the performance scale is putting blocks together to match a given design. Another task requires a person to look at a picture and decide what is missing.

6. **Intelligence Quotient** reflects relative standing on a test within a population of the same age group. IQ values reflect how far each score deviates from the age-group average. (p. 373)

7. A **culture-fair test** is constructed so that the test taker does not need extensive knowledge of the ideas or language of any specific culture to do well. (p. 374)

Example: See Figure 10.3 in your text. Pattern recognition tests are common attempts at culture-fair tests. No prior knowledge of the pattern is necessary for the test taker to choose the correct response.

8. A **test** is a systematic procedure for observing behavior in a standard situation. A test describes behavior with the help of a numerical scale or a category system. (p. 374)

Example: To give a test in a standard situation, the directions, setting, and scoring methods used are the same regardless of the people involved. An example of a *numerical scale* would be the calculation of an IQ.

9. **Reliability** means that the results of a test will be consistent or stable over repeated test occasions. Unreliability indicates that variable factors, unrelated to the test's material, in the test taker or in the test environment may be affecting the results. (p. 375)

10. **Test-retest reliability** is assessed by giving the same test twice. If the two scores are similar, the test is reliable. Problems occur when taking the test the first time lets the test taker know the correct answers. The test taker may also learn the answers to the questions between test situations. (p. 375)

Example: José has taken a test containing spatial tasks. Some of the problems were easy, but there were a few that he could not answer. After taking the test, he went home and thought until he solved them. The next time he took the test, he knew all the answers. His score on the second test was much higher than his score on the first test. Therefore, it is impossible to assess the test's reliability based on José's scores.

11. **Alternate forms** of a test can be used to check reliability by comparing one person's scores on each form of the test. (p. 375)

Example: Mildred is a history professor who has four classes of fifty students each. She knows that some of the students in her earlier classes will give their copies of the test to students in the later classes, giving them an unfair advantage. She decides to create alternate forms of the same test. The questions on each test are different, but cover the same material, are at the same level of difficulty, and are written in the same way.

12. **Split-half reliability** assesses reliability using one test that is divided into two comparable halves when it is scored. The test is not divided between a first half and a second half because test takers' fatigue may cause a test taker to do less well on the second half than he or she did on the first half. (p. 375)

Example: A test can be split in any number of ways. All of the even numbers can be placed in one half and all of the odd numbers can be placed in the other half. Another method might be to take questions 1 through 5, 11 through 15,

and 20 through 25 for one half and 6 through 10, 16 through 20, and 26 through 30 for the other.

13. A **valid test** measures exactly what it is designed to measure. (p. 375)

Example: Defining a list of words is a valid test of vocabulary but may not be a valid test of intelligence.

14. **Content validity** is the degree of relevance of the questions on the test. Does the content of the questions on a test relate to the ability, talent, or skill that the test is designed to measure? (pp. 375–376)

Example: If you wanted to test people's musical ability, you would not give them a test that measured their sense of balance. But you might ask them to reproduce a series of tones or rhythms, play an instrument for you, and analyze a musical score. The first test is not valid because balance is not relevant to or correlated with musical talent. The second test has content validity.

15. **Construct validity** is the extent to which scores on a test behave in accordance with a theory about the underlying construct of interest. (p. 376)

Example: You are giving a test for creativity. Theoretically, creative people are supposed to be divergent thinkers. Scores from your test should correlate quite highly with scores on a test of divergent thinking.

16. **Criterion validity** is the extent to which the scores on a test correlate with another direct and independent measure of what the test is supposed to assess. (p. 376)

Example: You have developed a neurological test of reflex speed. To check the validity of your test, you develop several artificial situations that require quick reflexes. For example, you may simulate a computerized race car situation and see how fast someone can avoid danger as the driver. The race car situation is an independent measure or criterion. People who score very high on the neurological test of reflex speed should also do well in the simulated race car situation.

17. **Predictive validity** is similar to criterion validity. In this case the criterion is some measure of future performance that the test is supposed to predict. (p. 376)

Example: You have designed a test to predict how well someone in medical school will perform as a doctor. In order to check the test's predictive validity you will have to follow the progress of the test takers when they become doctors. Those who score well on your test should become excellent doctors.

18. The **psychometric approach** is a method of analyzing test scores in order to describe the structure of intelligence. Psychologists have examined correlations of test scores in order to find the skills and talents that define intelligence. (p. 388)

REMEMBER: Psych refers to "mental". *Metric* means to measure. Those who use the psychometric approach study *measures* (test scores) of *mental functions* (in this case, intelligence).

19. The **g-factor** is a representation of general mental ability or intelligence. **S-factors** are specific abilities needed for a particular test, such as reading comprehension or spatial reasoning skills. (pp. 388–389)

REMEMBER: The *g* in *g*-factor stands for *general* intelligence; the *s* in *s*-factor stands for *specific* skills.

20. **Factor analysis** is a statistical technique Thurstone used to study intelligence. He found that test scores that were highly correlated seemed to represent several *primary mental abilities,* such as numerical ability, reasoning, verbal fluency, spatial visualization, perceptual ability, memory, and verbal

comprehension. Thurstone said that these abilities, not a *g*-factor, represented intelligence. (p. 389)

REMEMBER: Factor analysis is a statistical tool used in many social sciences to study many different phenomena. In order to remember its role in Thurstone's theory, think of factors as primary mental abilities.

21. **Fluid intelligence** is the basic power of reasoning and problem solving. It produces deduction, induction, reasoning, and understanding the relationships between different ideas. (p. 389)

Example: To be a good detective you must be able to look at all of the available clues and deduce "who done it." The powers of deduction and reasoning represent fluid intelligence. (Read the example of crystallized intelligence to understand the difference between the two types.)

22. **Crystallized intelligence** involves specific knowledge gained as a result of applying fluid intelligence. It produces verbal comprehension and skill at manipulating numbers. (p. 389)

Example: Detectives who have been working for a long time have gained specific knowledge about how to read clues and people. An experienced detective may be able to examine the scene of a crime and notice clues that tell him when the crime took place. This specific knowledge (crystallized intelligence) gained from previous experience (previous applications of fluid intelligence) will increase his overall chances of solving the crime.

23. The **information-processing approach** studies intelligence by examining the mental processes that underlie intelligent behavior. (p. 390)

Example: A psychologist using this approach to study intelligence would ask the following types of questions: What influence does effective chunking ability have on intelligent behavior? Does being able to rapidly access information in long-term memory increase ability to behave intelligently? Chunking and accessing long-term memory are ways of processing information.

24. **Components** are the information-processing capacities of perceiving stimuli, holding information in working memory, comparing values, retrieving information from memory, and calculating sums and differences. (p. 390)

Example: See example for key term 23, information-processing approach.

25. **Metacomponents** are the processes involved in organizing and setting up a problem. More specifically, metacomponents are the processes that determine how people decide which components to use in solving a problem. (pp. 390–391)

Example: Mathematical word problems involve metacomponents and components. Deciding which mathematical concepts are being tested and deciding how to set up the words in the problem in mathematical terms both use metacomponents. Doing the addition, multiplication, division, and subtraction necessary to find the solution is the process of using components.

26. The **symbols-systems approach** studies intelligence by looking at different systems of symbol usage. Language, music, and mathematics are areas that require the use of symbols. Gardner proposed that these symbolic systems are different "intelligences." Biology provides the capacity unique to each of these intelligences and our culture provides a symbolic system that mobilizes that capacity. (p. 394)

Example: In a Western society, verbal fluency is a symbol system that is highly valued and developed. In many pre-industrial societies, using symbols involved in tracking animals or in navigating is highly valued and developed.

27. **Creativity** is the ability to generate unusual but viable or workable solutions to a problem. (p. 395)

28. **Divergent thinking,** characteristic of creative people, is the ability to think along many alternative paths to generate many different solutions to a problem. (p. 395)

Example: Consider the following question: What can you use a newspaper for? Answers that relate to gaining information or news represent convergent thinking. Answers that are examples of divergent thinking include: using newspapers to create a papier mâché object, to light a fire, or to pad a package; to cover oneself for warmth, to provide insulation from noise, or to stuff shoes so that they keep their shape; to make a higher seat for a short child; to make a toy for a cat, to make an airplane, to wrap a box, or to train a puppy; to humidify the air (by draping wet newspapers over a radiator), to make a ransom note (by cutting out letters from a newspaper), and to soak up water (by putting newspaper in wet shoes).

29. **Convergent thinking** is the ability to apply the rules of logic and what one knows about the world to reduce the number of possible solutions to a problem. (p. 395)

Example: See example for key term 28, divergent thinking.

30. **Cognitive complexity** is a set of abilities related to flexibility of thought (the ability to anticipate future events and to incorporate unexpected occurrences into one's plans or behavior) and the ability to view a problem from several different perspectives. (pp. 397–398)

31. A **cognitive style** is the manner or style of performing cognitive tasks. This includes cognitive complexity, impulsive versus reflective styles and field-dependent versus field-independent styles. (p. 398)

Example: Field-dependent people tend to perceive individual objects in a way that is greatly influenced by the surrounding environment.

LEARNING OBJECTIVES

1. Discuss the history of intelligence test construction. Be able to explain the scoring methods used in the Binet and Stanford-Binet intelligence tests. (pp. 369–371)

2. Discuss the use and abuse of intelligence testing in the United States in the early 1900s. (pp. 371–372)

3. Describe Wechsler's intelligence test. Explain why it is different from tests that were used previously. (p. 372)

4. Describe the process of IQ test scoring used today. (p. 373)

5. Define culture-fair tests. Form an opinion on whether it is possible to design a test that is completely free of cultural bias. (pp. 373–374)

6. Discuss the major advantages of using tests over other methods of evaluation, such as interviews. (pp. 374–375)

7. Define reliability. Describe the process of assessing reliability using test-retest, alternate forms, and split-half testing. Give an example of each. (p. 375)

8. Define validity. Define content, construct, criterion and predictive validity. (pp. 375–376)

9. Discuss the answers to the following questions: What do IQ scores predict? Are IQ tests biased? (pp. 378–380)

10. Discuss the possible interpretations of evidence from correlational twin studies on the role of heredity in the development of intelligence. (pp. 380–381)

11. Discuss the possible interpretations of evidence from studies on environmental intervention on the role of the environment in the development of intelligence. (pp. 381–384)

12. Describe the interaction of heredity and the environment in the development of intelligence. (pp. 384–385)

13. Correctly interpret differences in group intelligence scores. Discuss the variables that may account for these differences. (pp. 385–386)

14. Discuss the consequences of using an IQ as a label, not only in the classroom, but in any situation. (pp. 386–388)

15. Describe the psychometric approach to studying intelligence. Define g-factor, s-factor, primary mental abilities, fluid intelligence, and crystallized intelligence. Give an example of each. (pp. 388–390)

16. Describe the information-processing approach to studying intelligence. Define components and metacomponents. Describe the role of attention in intelligent behavior. (pp. 390–392)

17. Describe the symbols-systems approach to studying intelligence. (pp. 394–395)

18. Discuss the relationship between creativity and intelligence. Discuss the relationship between creativity and personality. Define convergent and divergent thinking. (pp. 395–396)

19. Define cognitive complexity. Define cognitive style. Be able to give examples other than cognitive complexity that define cognitive style. (pp. 397–398)

CONCEPTS AND EXERCISES

No. 1 Defining Intelligence

Completing this exercise should help you to achieve the following learning objectives.

(14) *Discuss the consequences of using an IQ as a label, not only in the classroom but in any situation. (pp. 386–388)*

(15) *Describe the psychometric approach to studying intelligence. Define g-factor, s-factor, primary mental abilities, fluid intelligence, and crystallized intelligence. Give an example of each. (pp. 388–390)*

(16) *Describe the information-processing approach to studying intelligence. Define components and metacomponents. Describe the role of attention in intelligent behavior. (pp. 390–392)*

(17) *Describe the symbols-systems approach to studying intelligence. (pp. 394–395)*

(18) *Discuss the relationship between creativity and intelligence. Discuss the relationship between creativity and personality. Define convergent and divergent thinking. (pp. 395–396)*

Following is a conversation between several professors who want to begin a new university. They are arguing about what admission requirements would ensure that only the brightest students attend their school. You should be able to tell which approach each professor would use to study intelligence and who generated the original ideas behind those approaches.(Choose your answers from the list following the conversations.)

Pete: I think we should have several tests: one for language, one for musical abilities including dancing, one for analytical skills, and a self-knowledge test.

1. Pete would follow the _____ approach as suggested by _____.

Pam: How many engineers do you know who can do the polka? I think we should give them a general intelligence test and look at the correlations among the various subscales to see how high their *g*-factors are.

2. Pam would follow the _____ approach as suggested by _____.

Steve: The *g*-factor theory doesn't explain all the available data. Besides, we could end up admitting someone with a high *g*-factor who doesn't have many of the primary mental abilities like reasoning, spatial visualization, perceptual ability, memory, and verbal comprehension.

3. Steve would follow the _____ approach as suggested by _____.

Ellen: *G*-factor, schmee-factor, and who cares about primary mental abilities? Let's get down to what counts. I want to know if someone can get info from short-term into long-term memory and get the stuff back out again. It's simple. Can the kids approach a problem correctly, and do they have the component skills to then solve the problem?

4. Ellen would follow the _____ approach as suggested by _____.

Leigh: We really need to find people who can think creatively. I know a ton of dull but brilliant people. Let's ask them to produce a film on what would happen if all higher-level education was banned by the government and decide on the basis of that.

5. Leigh wants to test for _____.

Sternberg

divergent thinking

Gardner

psychometric

Spearman

Thurstone

information-processing

symbols-systems

No. 2 The Testing Business

Completing this exercise should help you to achieve the following learning objectives.

(5) *Define culture-fair tests. Form an opinion on whether it is possible to design a test that is completely free of cultural bias. (pp. 373–374)*

(6) *Discuss the major advantages of using tests over other methods of evaluation, such as interviews. (pp. 374–375)*

(7) *Define reliability. Describe the process of assessing reliability using test-retest, alternate forms, and split-half testing. Give an example of each. (p. 375)*

(8) *Define validity. Define content, construct, criterion and predictive validity. (pp. 375–376)*

Mr. Dorgan has recently begun a testing service. Following are some descriptions of his activities. Fill in the blank with the correct term by either choosing from the list at the end of the exercise or by recalling the appropriate information from your reading.

1. Mr. Dorgan has just received information on a new test on the market. He has ordered a sample copy of the test and plans to give it to the same group of people twice. Mr. Dorgan is using the _____ method to check for reliability.

2. Mr. Dorgan is going through the day's mail and is delighted to learn that one of his former clients is doing well in engineering at school. She had come to him for help in deciding what major would best match her skills. Since she is doing well, Mr. Dorgan believes that the _____ that he gave her has _____.

3. Mr. Dorgan has just received a new achievement test. He knows that it has already been successfully tested for reliability. Since the test is reliable, does Mr. Dorgan have to test it for validity?

4. Mr. Dorgan wants to attract newcomers from foreign countries as clients. To do this, he will have to develop _____ tests.

5. Mr. Dorgan has just issued a memo to all his employees. It says that all tests are to be administered in exactly the same way, given in the same room, and scored in exactly the same way. Mr. Dorgan wants to ensure that all of his tests are _____.

6. Mr. Dorgan has just received a new test of mathematical ability. He is confused because there are no math problems on the test. What kind of validity is Mr. Dorgan worried about?

standardized

culture-fair

aptitude test

achievement test

predictive validity

construct validity

content validity

reliability

test-retest

alternate forms

split-half

ANSWERS TO CONCEPTS AND EXERCISES

No. 1 Defining Intelligence

1. Pete would follow the *symbols-systems* approach as suggested by *Gardner*.

2. Pam would follow the *psychometric approach* as suggested by *Spearman*.

3. Steve would follow the *psychometric approach* as suggested by *Thurstone*.

4. Ellen would follow the *information-processing approach* as suggested by *Sternberg*.

5. Leigh wants to test for *divergent thinking*.

No. 2 The Testing Business

1. Mr. Dorgan is using the *test-retest method* for checking reliability.

2. Mr. Dorgan believes that the *aptitude test* that he gave his client has *predictive validity*.

3. When a test is valid it "measures what it is designed to measure." When a test is unreliable, the temperature of the room, the test giver, and many other factors can affect the test results. An unreliable test may be measuring the effects of temperature on test-taking skills instead of what it is designed to measure. This makes it invalid. Similarly, a test may be reliable but invalid because it does not test the correct abilities.

4. Mr. Dorgan must develop *culture-fair* tests so that unfamiliarity with the English language or Western culture will not bias the results.

5. For a test to be *standardized* it must be administered, scored, and interpreted in exactly the same way for every person taking the test.

6. Mr. Dorgan is worried about *content validity* (whether the questions on the test are related to the skills the test is supposed to assess).

MULTIPLE CHOICE QUESTIONS

Facts and Definitions

1. The original IQ test, created by Binet, was designed to
   a. assess intelligence in children.
   b. determine which children would benefit from special education.
   c. determine which immigrants should be allowed into the country.
   d. determine the intelligence of army recruits.

2. Questions in the Binet and the original Stanford-Binet tests were age-graded. This means that questions for a particular age group could be answered by
   a. most of the children in that age group.
   b. children below that age but not by children above that age.
   c. adults but not children.
   d. children of a particular age but not by adults.

3. Terman would calculate an intelligence quotient by
   a. dividing mental age by chronological age.
   b. dividing chronological age by mental age.
   c. dividing mental age by chronological age and multiplying the result by 100.
   d. dividing chronological age by mental age and multiplying the result by 100.

4. Wechsler's test of intelligence differs from the original Stanford-Binet test in that
   a. Wechsler's test has two subscales: verbal and performance.
   b. Wechsler's test is more culturally biased.
   c. Wechsler's test requires greater familiarity with the English language.
   d. Wechsler's test is a group test.

5. Which of the following would you *not* find on the performance scale of an intelligence test?
   a. Block design
   b. Maze solving
   c. Picture completion
   d. Mathematical word problems

6. Today, IQ scores are relative scores. This means that your IQ will tell you
   a. your *g*-factor.
   b. how many primary mental abilities you possess.
   c. how intelligent you are in comparison to other people your age.
   d. how creative you are.

7. A test is reliable if it
   a. measures what it is supposed to measure.
   b. predicts a person's success in some field.
   c. yields consistent and stable results.
   d. None of the above.

8. Field-dependence versus field-independence, cognitive complexity, and impulsive versus reflective are

   a. dimensions of cognitive style.
   b. symbol systems.
   c. s-factors.
   d. primary mental abilities.

9. What factors explain the inability of an IQ test to perfectly predict academic performance?

   a. Academic success is not wholly determined by intelligence.
   b. IQ tests may be culturally biased.
   c. IQ tests may measure factors other than intelligence that do not influence academic success.
   d. All of the above could explain the imperfect correlation between IQ and academic performance.

10. When interpreting the differences between group scores of intelligence, _____ should be considered.

   a. socioeconomic status
   b. the range of scores within each group
   c. the test takers' level of motivation
   d. All of the above should be considered.

11. According to Cattell, fluid intelligence

   a. is the basic power of reasoning and problem solving.
   b. is one dimension of cognitive style.
   c. involves specific knowledge gained from experience.
   d. None of the above.

12. Studying scores on intelligence tests in order to understand the structure of intelligence is using

   a. the psychometric approach.
   b. the information-processing approach.
   c. the symbols-systems approach.
   d. the divergent-convergent approach.

13. Convergent thinking is

   a. typical of creative people.
   b. characterized by thinking of many alternative solutions to a problem.
   c. measured by intelligence tests.
   d. All of the above.

14. _____ refer to the specific abilities required to solve a problem; _____ refer to the abilities necessary to set up a problem.

   a. Divergent thoughts, convergent thoughts
   b. Convergent thoughts, divergent thoughts
   c. Components, metacomponents
   d. Metacomponents, components

15. Which of the following is true about how the interaction between heredity and environment affects intelligence?

   a. Genetics determine a range of potential intelligence and the environment pushes an individual up or down in that range.
   b. The environment sets a range of potential intelligence and genetics pushes an individual up or down in that range.
   c. The environment has very little impact on a person's intelligence.
   d. Genetics has very little impact on a person's intelligence.

MULTIPLE CHOICE QUESTIONS

Application of Concepts

1. Ed, an economically disadvantaged man from a rural area, joined the army in 1915. He was forced to take an intelligence test. One of the tasks on the test was to fill in the gaps in a picture. Ed took

   a. the Alpha Test.
   b. the Beta Test.
   c. the Wechsler Adult Intelligence Scale.
   d. Binet's test.

2. If the gradual increase in intelligence tapers off during the mid-twenties, _____ method of calculating an IQ would make older people look very unintelligent.

    a. Binet's
    b. Spearman's
    c. Terman's
    d. Wechsler's

3. Which of the following could jeopardize the standardization of a test?

    a. Individual variations in how the instructions are read to test takers.
    b. Changes in the way the test is scored.
    c. Variations in the environment in which the test is taken.
    d. All of the above.

4. Consuela is giving a test that she has devised to the same group of people twice. She is testing for

    a. reliability.
    b. validity.
    c. achievement.
    d. aptitude.

5. Randy's students are very upset with him. He told them that he was going to give a quiz on the principles of learning, but instead asked about the principles of memory on the quiz. The students told him that his quiz had no

    a. construct validity.
    b. predictive validity.
    c. content validity.
    d. criterion validity.

6. Comparing someone's job success with test scores received prior to employment results in an assessment of

    a. construct validity.
    b. content validity.
    c. predictive validity.
    d. split-half validity.

7. Rachel has written a test for her psychology class. She is not sure of the test's reliability, so she compares the scores on just the odd questions to the scores on just the even questions. Which method is she using to test for reliability?

    a. Test-retest
    b. Alternate forms
    c. Split-half
    d. Criterion forms

8. Following are questions from an intelligence test for adults. The instructions, test environment, and scoring are the same for all test takers.

    1. What color is the sun?

    2. How many fingers are on each hand?

    3. How many biological mothers do you have?

    4. The weather in summer is usually _____.

What is wrong with this test?

    a. This test has no reliability.
    b. This test has no validity.
    c. This test is not standardized.
    d. What is wrong cannot be determined from the information given.

9. Sam and Jerry are both twelve years old. They have been given identical boxes and are told to open them. Sam finds the latch and pushes it up, down, and then sideways. Even though he cannot get the latch to open, he persists in his efforts. Jerry realizes that the latch is not going to open the box, so he looks at it from many different angles, trying to find another way to open it. Sam is thinking _____ and Jerry is thinking _____.

    a. convergently, divergently
    b. divergently, convergently
    c. convergently, convergently
    d. divergently, divergently

10. Derek is a ten-year-old from an inner-city culture. He is taking an IQ test that requires him to match patterns. Derek is most probably

a. mentally retarded.

b. taking a culture-fair test.

c. taking a culture-free test.

d. taking a mathematical achievement test.

11. If scientists ever capture an alien, they will want to check its creativity. Which of the following will be the best way to do that?

a. See how fast it learns to speak English.

b. Administer the verbal scale of the WAIS-R.

c. Administer the performance scale of the WAIS-R.

d. Administer a test of divergent thinking.

12. Which of the following is true with respect to reliability and validity?

a. A reliable test is always valid.

b. A valid test must have a substantial level of reliability.

c. There is no relationship between reliability and validity.

d. Reliability and validity are the products of standardization procedures.

13. Anna wants to be an engineer. What kind of test should she take to see if she has the intellectual capabilities to become an engineer?

a. An achievement test

b. An IQ test

c. An aptitude test

d. None of the above.

14. The Shulman family has five children: Eric and Elsa are fraternal twins, Jessica and Jennifer are nine-year-old identical twins, and Frederick is six years old. The highest correlation should be between the IQ scores of

a. Eric and Frederick, because they are the only male siblings.

b. Eric and Elsa, because they are twins.

c. All of them should be equally correlated, because they are all siblings.

d. None of the above.

15. Your assignment is to read an article written by Arthur Jensen. Unfortunately, you have four articles with no authors' names written on them. Knowing what you do about Jensen, which article is he most likely to have written?

a. "Improving Your Baby's IQ in Utero"

b. "Working with the Intelligence God Gave You"

c. "Nutritional Hints for Feeding an Intellectual Child"

d. "Motor Skill Games to Improve Your Child's IQ"

ANSWERS TO MULTIPLE CHOICE QUESTIONS

Facts and Definitions

1. *b* is the answer. Binet's original test was designed to identify those children who would benefit from or need special instruction. He did not try to create an intelligence test. (p. 369)

a. Binet did not try to create an intelligence test. He only wanted to identify those children who would benefit from special instruction.

c. & d. Psychologists in the United States revised Binet's test and used it to assess the intellectual capacity of immigrants and army recruits.

2. *a* is the answer. Questions in the seven-year-old group could be answered correctly by most seven-year-olds, could not be answered by most six-year-olds, and could be answered correctly by most children older than seven. (p. 370)

b. Questions answered correctly by most seven-year-olds should not be answered correctly by most children under seven. If this were the case, then the questions could not discriminate between the age groups.

c. & d. Binet's original test was designed for children, not adults.

3. *c* is the answer. The first intelligence quotient, developed by Terman, was calculated by dividing mental age by chronological age and multiplying the result by 100. (p. 371)

4. *a* is the answer. Wechsler's test contained two subscales, a verbal scale and a performance scale. (p. 372)

b. Wechsler developed the performance scale, which included items such as block design and spatial reasoning tasks, in order to avoid bias caused by lack of familiarity with the English language or Western culture.

c. Performance scale items do not test language ability or cultural familiarity.

d. Wechsler's test was designed for individual administration, not group testing.

5. *d* is the answer. Although math skills in general do not require a great deal of language ability, mathematical word problems do. You must be able to read, interpret, and set up the problem using language skills as well as mathematical reasoning in order to arrive at the solution. (p. 372)

a., b., & c. Block design, mazes, and picture completion are all problems that do not require verbal skills.

6. *c* is the answer. An IQ score tells you how smart you are *relative* to other people your age. If your IQ is 100, then you are average with respect to others your age. A higher IQ means you scored higher than others your age. (p. 373)

a. Spearman suggested that intelligence is a general mental ability. However, your *g*-factor is not relative to the *g*-factors of others.

b. Thurstone suggested that intelligence is comprised of primary mental abilities. An IQ score may tell you about these abilities, but more important, the score tells about them relative to other people.

d. An IQ score will not tell you how creative you are. IQ scores are not highly correlated with creativity.

7. *c* is the answer. Reliable tests yield consistent and stable scores over time. (p. 375)

a. When a test is valid, it measures what it is designed to measure.

b. When a test can predict someone's success in a particular field it has predictive validity.

d. c is the answer.

8. *a* is the answer. Cognitive style is the manner of performing cognitive tasks. Cognitive complexity, field dependence-independence, and impulsive versus reflective styles are various dimensions of cognitive style. (p. 398)

b. Symbol systems include language, mathematics, and music. Each symbol system is used in conjunction with one of Gardner's specific intelligences.

c. S-factors, according to Spearman, are specific skills needed for success at various tasks on intelligence tests.

d. Thurstone, using the psychometric approach to study intelligence, found what he called primary mental abilities. These include numerical ability, reasoning, verbal fluency, spatial visualization, perceptual ability, memory, and verbal comprehension.

9. *d* is the answer. Cultural bias, other factors affecting academic success, and the fact that IQ tests may measure factors other than intelligence (such as motivation) all contribute to the imperfect correlation between IQ scores and academic success. (p. 379)

10. *d* is the answer. Group scores can be affected by socioeconomic differences. Motivation of individual test-takers can affect scores. And if there is a difference in group means, the distributions of group scores may overlap. (pp. 385–386)

11. *a* is the answer. Cattell argued that there are two types of *g*-factor: fluid intelligence and crystallized intelligence. Fluid intelligence is the basic power of reasoning and problem solving. It produces induc-

tion, deduction, reasoning, and understanding of relationships between different ideas. (p. 389)

b. Cognitive style is the manner or style of performing cognitive tasks. Cognitive complexity, field-dependence versus independence and impulsive versus reflective styles are all dimensions of cognitive style.

c. Crystallized intelligence involves the specific knowledge gained from past experiences as a result of applying fluid intelligence.

d. a is the answer.

12. *a* is the answer. Psychologists who seek to understand the structure of intelligence by examining the correlations between scores on IQ tests are following the psychometric approach. (p. 388)

b. The information-processing approach studies the mental processes underlying intelligent behavior, such as the speed of information transfer from short-term to long-term memory.

c. The symbols-systems approach examines the use of symbols in many different domains such as language, math, and music.

d. There is no such thing as the divergent-convergent approach to studying intelligence.

13. *c* is the answer. Convergent thinking is the ability to apply rules of logic and general knowledge of the world in order to solve problems. IQ tests measure convergent thinking. (p. 395)

a. Divergent thinking is characteristic of creative people.

b. Divergent thinking is characterized by thinking of many alternative solutions to a problem.

d. Only *c* is the answer.

14. *c* is the answer. Components are the specific skills necessary to complete a problem and metacomponents are processes involved in setting up the problem. (pp. 390–391)

a. & b. Divergent and convergent thinking refer to *methods* of thinking, not different processes.

d. Metacomponents are processes involved in setting up a problem; components are the specific skills necessary to complete the problem.

15. *a* is the answer. Genetics does seem to set a range of potential for intelligence. The quality of the environment can cause people to fall short of or come close to their fullest potential. (p. 384)

b. The environment does not set the range. Genetics set the range of potential, and the environment fine-tunes a person's intelligence within that range.

c. & d. Neither of these statements is true. Both genetics and the environment have a large impact on the development of intelligence.

ANSWERS TO MULTIPLE CHOICE QUESTIONS

Application of Concepts

1. *b* is the answer. Ed took a Beta Test, which was created by psychologists to determine the intelligence of army recruits. The Beta Test consisted of picture completion tasks instead of verbal problems. (p. 371)

a. The Alpha Test was also constructed by psychologists to determine the intelligence of army recruits. However, it required literacy in English.

c. Wechsler's intelligence tests were not developed until 1949.

d. Binet's test was not designed to test intelligence but to indicate which French children would benefit from special instruction.

2. *c* is the answer. Terman developed the first IQ quotient. If the increase in mental abilities levels off during the mid-twenties, then as people get older their IQs will decrease. Example: Kirk is twenty-five; his mental age is twenty-five. His IQ is 100.

But when he is seventy-five, his IQ will be 25/75 multiplied by 100, which is only 33. (p. 371)

a. Binet did not use IQ scores.

b. Spearman did not create a scoring method. He used IQ test scores to study the structure of intelligence.

d. Wechsler's IQ scores are relative scores comparing you to others of your age.

3. *d* is the answer. Variations in administration, scoring, or the test-taking environment could jeopardize the standardization of a test. (p. 374)

4. *a* is the answer. A reliable test is one that gives stable and consistent answers. If a test is given twice and yields consistent results it is considered reliable. (p. 375)

b. Giving the same test twice is a test of reliability, not validity. To check validity, you must make sure that the content of the questions relates to the skills or knowledge being tested, or that the test scores are correlated with scores on other tests relating to the same constructs or criteria.

c. An achievement test assesses the knowledge someone has gained through past experience. Your tests in psychology assess how much you have learned or achieved by taking the course.

d. A score on an aptitude test indicates how well someone will perform in some academic or professional area.

5. *c* is the answer. The questions on the quiz did not assess the knowledge they were supposed to test. (p. 376)

a. When test scores correlate highly with the theoretical basis of the trait or construct of interest, then the test has high construct validity.

b. Using a test to predict ability to successfully carry out some later endeavor, such as a job or major in school, requires the test to have predictive validity.

d. The correlation of a test score with some other measure of the ability tested is the test's criterion validity.

6. *c* is the answer. A test score should predict the future performance of the test taker on the job. This is predictive validity. (p. 376)

a. When test scores correlate highly with the theoretical basis of the trait or construct of interest, then the test has high construct validity.

b. If a test measures what it is supposed to measure it has high content validity.

d. There is no such thing as split-half validity. You may have been thinking of split-half reliability.

7. *c* is the answer. Comparing the scores on one half of a test to scores on the other half is the split-half method of testing reliability. (p. 375)

a. The test-retest method requires the same people to take the same test twice. Their scores on the first test should be very similar to those on the second test.

b. The alternate forms method requires giving two different but equivalent forms of the test to the same people.

d. There is no such thing as the criterion forms method.

8. *b* is the answer. Most people could answer these questions. Therefore, this test will not tell you how people differ in intelligence. (p. 375)

a. This test is very reliable. You would give exactly the same answers every time you took it.

c. This test is standardized; it is administered and scored in exactly the same way every time for everyone.

d. b is the answer. Therefore, this test will not measure individual differences in intelligence.

9. *a* is the answer. Sam is thinking convergently, but Jerry, by imagining all the possible ways to open the box, is thinking divergently. (p. 395)

10. *b* is the answer. Derek is taking a test that does not rely heavily on education and verbal abilities. This test is attempting to measure intelligence instead of the effect of cultural advantages, such as an education. (p. 374)

a. Many children take IQ tests, not just mentally retarded children.

c. There is no such thing as a culture-free test.

d. Derek is being asked to match patterns, not do mathematical tasks. Secondly, an achievement test measures what you have learned already; Derek is taking an IQ test, which attempts to measure intelligence, not knowledge.

11. *d* is the answer. Tests of divergent thinking measure creativity. (p. 395)

a. The ability to learn a new language is not correlated with creativity.

b. & c. IQ scores do not correlate highly with creativity.

12. *b* is the answer. If a test is valid it must be reliable. If a test produces scores that vary from one test occasion to another, there is no way that the test would correlate highly enough with a criterion to establish validity. Suppose that you want to use body weight to predict heart disease. If the scale for measuring weight is unreliable, radically different weights could be associated with the same degree of heart disease. You would never be able to predict heart attacks from weight, and your test would lack validity. (pp. 375–376)

a. Suppose you take an engineering aptitude test that asks you to count to ten out loud. If you took this test every day for three weeks, you would receive perfect scores. However, even though this test is reliable, it is not valid. Your engineering aptitude cannot be measured from your scores.

c. There is a relationship between reliability and validity. A valid test must have a substantial level of reliability.

d. If a test is valid it measures what it is supposed to measure. This is not dependent on standardization procedures. Standardization does not guarantee validity.

13. *c* is the answer. Anna wants to know how well she will do in the field of engineering in the future. An aptitude test measures someone's potential for doing well in a particular field. (p. 376)

a. An achievement test will tell Anna how well she has learned material that she has already been exposed to. This is not what she wants to know.

b. An IQ test may reveal Anna's global potential but it will not tell her which particular talents and skills she should capitalize on in a career choice.

d. c is the answer.

14. *d* is the answer. The highest correlation should be between the IQs of the identical twins. (p. 381)

a. The correlation between the IQs of male siblings is not higher than the correlation between the IQs of identical twins.

b. Eric and Elsa are not identical twins; their IQs would probably not be as highly correlated as the IQs of the identical twins.

c. Correlations between the IQs of all the siblings in a family are not as high as between identical twins.

15. *b* is the answer. Jensen believed that genetics is primarily responsible for intelligence. All of the other titles assume that intelligence can be affected by environmental influences. (p. 385)

a. Jensen believed that much of intelligence is determined by heredity. He would not have written this article, because it is about improving IQ by influencing the baby's environment or by learning.

c. & d. Jensen believed that much of intelligence is inherited. These two titles assume that intelligence can be affected by environmental influences, such as nutrition and motor skill training.

Chapter 11

Motivation

OUTLINE

I. BASIC CONCEPTS OF MOTIVATION (pp. 404–415)

Motivation can be defined as the influences that account for the initiation, direction, intensity, and persistence of behavior.

A. Finding Unity in Diversity and Change

A motive, acting as an intervening variable, may provide a single reason for the occurrence of many different behaviors and may explain fluctuations in behavior over time.

B. Sources of Motivation

Four factors can serve as sources of motivation: biological, cognitive, emotional, and social factors.

C. Instinct Theory

Instincts were once thought to be a major factor in motivation. Instinct theory, however, may provide a description rather than an explanation of behavior.

There is no scientific way to disprove the existence of instincts. In addition, instinct theory failed to accommodate the role of learning in human behavior. Therefore, instincts play some role in motivated behavior, but other factors are also involved.

D. Drive Theory

Primary and secondary drives reduce biological needs or arousal arising from an imbalance in homeostasis. But, drive theory cannot explain all behavior. For example, drive theory cannot explain why humans sometimes seek to increase arousal.

E. Arousal Theory

According to arousal theory, people are motivated to maintain their optimal level of arousal, increasing arousal when it is too low and decreasing it when it is too high. An individual's optimal level of arousal is influenced by biological factors.

F. Incentive Theory

According to incentive theory, behavior is goal-directed; we behave in ways that allow us to attain desirable stimuli and avoid negative ones.

G. Opponent-Process Theory

According to opponent-process theory, any reaction to a stimulus is automatically followed by an opposite reaction called the opponent process. After repeated exposure to the same stimulus, the initial reaction weakens and the opponent process becomes stronger. We are motivated to seek a pleasurable opponent process or to avoid a negative one by quickly repeating exposure to the initial stimulus.

H. Maslow's Hierarchy

Maslow proposed that there are five levels of motives arranged in a hierarchy: physiological, safety, belongingness and love, esteem, and self-actualization. We must satisfy needs or motives low on the hierarchy before we are motivated to satisfy needs at the next level.

II. BIOLOGICAL MOTIVES (pp. 415–428)

A. Hunger

1. *The Role of Stomach Cues*. The stomach may partially control the hunger motive but experiments show that other factors are involved.

2. *The Role of Taste Cues*. Taste influences the amount of food eaten. More will be eaten when a variety of tastes are offered, but taste alone doesn't fully control eating.

3. *The Role of the Brain*. The lateral and ventromedial hypothalamus play a crucial role in the initiation of hunger and the regulation of eating. The hypothalamus may be involved in the homeostatic maintenance of a set-point.

4. *Signals for Hunger*. The brain monitors blood content for the presence of glucose and other substances. Cholecystokinin may be a substance that controls the cessation of eating. Factors other than the brain, involving learning and social cues, are also important in the regulation of hunger and eating.

B. Thirst

Having a dry sensation in one's mouth is not an important regulator of thirst. Osmoreceptor cells in the hypothalamus and volumetric cells in the heart and kidneys can detect low levels of water in the body and signal the need to drink.

C. Sex

1. *Describing Sexual Behavior*. Kinsey and his colleagues collected much information in the 1950s through surveys. Masters and Johnson have described the sexual response cycle through laboratory research.

2. *The Biological Basis of Sexual Motivation*. The hypothalamus controls the release of luteinizing hormone (LH) from the pituitary gland. LH controls the release of masculinizing (androgens) and feminizing (estrogens and progestins) hormones from the ovaries and testes. Sex hormones have both organizational and activational effects.

3. *Social and Psychological Influences on Sexual Motivation*. Attitudes formed by past experiences, social influences, and the physical characteristics of a potential partner can increase or decrease sexual motivation. Many people fantasize to increase sexual arousal.

4. *Sexual Orientation*. Homosexuality has three possible aspects: engaging in sexual activity with a partner of one's own sex, being attracted to or aroused by members of the same sex, or having a self-acknowledged sexual preference for members of one's own sex. People who engage in sexual activity with partners of both sexes are called bisexual.

5. *Sexual Problems*. These problems, or sexual dysfunctions, include a low level of desire, impotence or erectile dysfunction, premature ejaculation, and infrequent or nonexistent orgasm. Possible causes include the effects of medicine, fatigue, general stress, recreational drugs, alcohol, and abnormal hormone levels.

III. SAFETY MOTIVES (pp. 428–430)

Children have a need for physical and emotional support from a caregiver. This need is not, as shown by the Harlow experiments, due strictly to nutritional factors. Failure to satisfy these safety motives can have significant social and emotional consequences.

IV. MOTIVES FOR BELONGINGNESS AND LOVE (pp. 430–432)

A. Parenting

Biological factors, instinctive responses to signals from young children, and responses learned from one's own parents may all contribute to learning how to become a parent. In many species, parents will forfeit their own lives in order to protect their young.

B. Affiliation

Interaction with other people provides a source of social comparison, support, and comfort, and helps us meet esteem needs.

V. MOTIVATION FOR ESTEEM (pp. 432–438)

The desire for approval, admiration, and other types of positive evaluation from ourselves and others motivates much of human behavior.

A. Achievement Motivation

1. *Characteristics of Achievement Motivation.* People with a high need to achieve set challenging but realistic goals for themselves that have clear-cut outcomes. They actively pursue present and future successes and are willing to take risks in that pursuit. They persist after repeated failures, plan for the future, and take pride in their successes.

2. *Development of Achievement Motivation.* The need for achievement is learned, to some extent, from parents and other cultural agents.

3. *Sex Differences in Achievement Motivation.* Men and women who are equally motivated by achievement often behave differently. Women tend to display fewer behaviors that are typical of those striving for achievement. This may be due to the type of criticism and reinforcement that they receive in the classroom.

B. Jobs and Motivation

1. *Job Satisfaction and Dissatisfaction.* Job satisfaction is related to the intrinsic aspects of the job that provide esteem to workers. Dissatisfaction arises from extrinsic factors such as inadequate salary or poor supervision.

2. *Designing Jobs that Motivate.* Workers should be encouraged to participate in decisions, given problems to solve, taught many skills, and given lots of individual responsibility. In short, a greater sense of control over one's job leads to an increase in satisfaction and productivity.

3. *The Importance of Goals.* Allowing employees to set goals that are specific, concrete, and personally meaningful increases motivation.

KEY TERMS

1. **Motivation** is defined as the influences that account for the initiation, direction, intensity, and persistence of behavior. (p. 404)

> *Example:* What causes us to initiate the movements necessary to get up from the couch and get something to drink? What causes us to persist in our work, sometimes to the point of staying up all night? Why do some people exert intense effort and others no effort at all? These are the kinds of questions asked by people studying motivation.

2. A **motive** is a reason or purpose for behavior. One motive can often account for many behaviors. (p. 406)

> *Example:* A woman drives a Jaguar, wears expensive sports clothes, and joins a country club. Her motive is to appear to belong to a specific group of people who are quite wealthy.

3. An **intervening variable** cannot be directly observed, but helps explain the relationship between a

stimulus and a response. A motive is an example of an intervening variable. (p. 406)

> *Example:* You cannot observe hunger, and yet it helps explain the behavioral response of eating in the presence of food stimuli.

4. **Instinct theory** attempted to explain behavior on the basis of instincts. An *instinct* is an innate automatic predisposition to respond in a particular way when confronted with a specific stimulus. An organism does not decide to respond; the response occurs automatically. Instinct theory stated that much of human behavior was instinctual. (p. 408)

> *Example:* According to instinct theory, a person acts aggressively because of an aggressive instinct.

5. **Drive theory** states that biological needs created by imbalances in homeostasis produce drives. Drives are psychological states of arousal that compel us to take action to restore our homeostatic balance. When balance is restored, the drive is reduced. (p. 409)

> *Example:* See examples for key terms 6 and 7, *primary drives* and *homeostasis*.

6. **Primary drives** are drives that arise from biological needs. (p. 409)

> *Example:* You have primary drives for obtaining food, water, and warmth. These are basic biological needs.

7. **Homeostasis** is the tendency in an organism to maintain its physiological systems at a stable, steady level, or in equilibrium. This is done by constantly adjusting to changes in internal or external stimuli. (p. 409)

> *Example:* Suppose that you had to walk outside in bitter cold weather. Your body would sense this change in an external stimulus (the cold) and would begin taking action to maintain your temperature. Shivering, an adjustment that generates body heat, would help keep your temperature from dropping.

8. **Secondary drives** are learned through operant or classical conditioning. We learn drives that prompt us to obtain objects that are associated with the reduction of a primary drive. (p. 410)

9. **Arousal theory** states that people are motivated to behave in ways which maintain an optimal level of arousal. The level of arousal considered optimal varies from person to person. There is a negative effect on performance when arousal level is anything other than optimal. (p. 411)

> *Example:* George is sitting in his office after a twelve-hour day, unhappy and bored. His level of arousal is too low. He decides to take a vacation in a country he has never visited. Toward the end of his vacation, he begins to look forward to getting back to work. Now George's level of arousal is too high. He wants to go back to a well-known environment where his arousal level will decrease.

10. **Incentive theory** states that human behavior is goal directed. Our goals are to obtain positive stimuli and avoid negative stimuli. Positive stimuli or incentives vary from person to person and can change over time. (p. 412)

> *Example:* When Joanna and David were first married, they saved money to buy a house (incentive). Now their mortgage is paid, and buying a house is no longer an incentive that guides their behavior. Instead, they save money to take vacations in Europe.

11. The **opponent-process theory** is based on two assumptions. First, any reaction to a stimulus is followed by an opposite reaction, the opponent process. Second, over time, the opponent process becomes stronger while the initial reaction becomes weaker. (pp. 412–413)

> *Example:* Joan's father came up behind her and scared her, causing her to scream. When she realized who it was, she relaxed and laughed. Now it is a game with them. Joan enjoys the

relief she feels when she discovers that it is her father who startled her, not a stranger.

12. The **lateral area of the hypothalamus,** when stimulated, causes an animal to eat large quantities of food. Destroying fibers in the lateral area of the hypothalamus causes an animal to stop eating almost entirely. (p. 416)

REMEMBER: Use a mnemonic to help remember the results of stimulating the various parts of the hypothalamus. Let the *L* in lateral stand for *Lots* of food. When the lateral area of the hypothalamus is stimulated, a rat will eat lots of food.

13. The **ventromedial nucleus of the hypothalamus,** when stimulated, causes an animal to stop eating. (p. 416)

REMEMBER: Use a mnemonic to help remember the results of stimulating this part of the hypothalamus. Let the *VMN* in ventromedial nucleus stand for *Voice many nos.* When the ventromedial nucleus of the hypothalamus is stimulated, the animal voices many nos in response to food.

14. The **set-point** concept suggests that a homeostatic mechanism in the brain establishes a level based on body weight or some related metabolic signal. Normal animals eat until their set point is reached. (p. 417)

Example: When you are below your set point for weight, your body desires food. Diets that suggest a very low calorie intake, which causes a quick drop in weight, are not effective. Once weight drops below the set point, the desire for food becomes greater and a person will eat until weight returns to the set point. The result is weight loss followed by a sometimes even greater weight gain.

15. **Cholecystokinin** is a chemical that is released from the gut and from neurons in the hypothalamus

as you are eating. It may be a signal to stop eating. (p. 417)

16. **Osmoreceptor cells** in the hypothalamus, by monitoring levels of salt, can detect the amount of water in cells and then cause feelings of thirst. (p. 421)

REMEMBER: Osmo*receptor* cells *receive* information about the level of water within our cells.

17. **Volumetric receptors** are located in the heart and kidneys. They monitor the volume and pressure of blood and other fluids outside the cells. When the volume or pressure drops below a certain point, these receptors stimulate the kidneys to release a hormone called angiotensin. When angiotensin reaches the brain, it stimulates a feeling of thirst. (p. 421)

REMEMBER: Volumetric receptors receive information about the *volume* of fluid in the body.

18. **Heterosexual behavior** is sexual activity between people of opposite sexes. (p. 422)

19. The **sexual response cycle** is the pattern of arousal during and after sexual activity. (p. 422)

20. **Erogenous zones** are areas of the body that produce sexual arousal when stimulated. There is great variety in what people find stimulating. At different times the same stimulation can be arousing or annoying. (p. 422)

21. **Luteinizing hormone** is released from the pituitary gland into the bloodstream. It controls the release of hormones from the gonads (ovaries in females and testes in males). (p. 422)

22. **Androgens** are masculinizing hormones of which the principal one is testosterone. Androgens are found in both males and females and play a role in sexual motivation. (p. 423)

23. **Estrogens and progestins** are feminizing hormones, which include estradiol and progesterone.

These hormones are found in both males and females. (p. 423)

24. **Sexual dysfunctions** are problems which can involve sexual motivation, arousal, or orgasmic response. *Erectile dysfunction,* the inability to gain or maintain an erection, is the most common arousal problem in men. *Infrequent orgasm* or *lack of orgasm* is the most common arousal problem in women. *Premature ejaculation* is ejaculating sooner than a man or his partner would like. (p. 427)

25. **Need achievement,** postulated by Murray, is reflected in the degree to which people establish specific goals, care about meeting those goals, and experience feelings of satisfaction doing so. According to Maslow's hierarchy of needs, achieving provides us with a sense of esteem. The intensity of the need for achievement varies from person to person. The development of this need is affected by parents, culture, and experiences in school. (p. 433)

LEARNING OBJECTIVES

1. Define motivation. Discuss the types of behavior that motivation may help to explain. Define intervening variables and explain their role in understanding motivation. (pp. 404–407)

2. Describe the sources of motivation. (p. 408)

3. Define instinct. Discuss the attempts of instinct theorists to explain behavior. Explain why they failed to do so. (pp. 408–409)

4. Define drive. Discuss the attempts of drive theorists to explain behavior. Explain why they failed to account for all types of behavior. Define homeostasis, primary drive, and secondary drive. Discuss their role in motivation. (pp. 409–411)

5. Define arousal. Discuss the role of an optimal level of arousal in motivation. Describe the effect on behavior of anything other than an optimal level of arousal. (pp. 411–412)

6. Define incentive. Discuss how incentive theory attempts to explain behavior. (p. 412)

7. Describe the opponent-process theory of motivation. Give an example of the kinds of behavior it attempts to explain. (pp. 412–413)

8. Describe Maslow's hierarchy of needs. Give examples of each kind of need on the hierarchy. (pp. 413–415)

9. Discuss the role of stomach cues, taste cues, and the brain in controlling hunger and eating. Understand the role of the lateral and ventromedial hypothalamus in hunger and eating. Define set point. (pp. 415–418)

10. Describe the interaction of the hypothalamus with intracellular and extracellular mechanisms in the regulation of thirst. Define osmoreceptors and volumetric receptors. Describe the kinds of information they receive. (pp. 420–421)

11. Describe some of the sources of human sexual motivation. Define sexual response cycle and erogenous zones. (p. 422)

12. Describe the role of the hypothalamus in the release of sexual hormones. Describe the organizational and activational effects of the sexual hormones in males and females. (pp. 423–424)

13. Discuss the social and psychological influences on sexual motivation. Define heterosexual and homosexual behavior. (pp. 424–427)

14. Define sexual dysfunctions, erectile dysfunction, and premature ejaculation. Discuss some of the probable causes for these problems. (pp. 427–428)

15. Describe the need for safety. Discuss the ways in which this need is fulfilled and the consequences if it is not. (pp. 428–430)

16. Discuss the ways in which parenting and affiliation can satisfy the need for belonging and love. (pp. 430–432)

17. Define achievement motivation. Describe the characteristics of achievement motivation and

the factors that can affect it. Explain the possible reasons for the differences in behavior of males and females who are equally motivated to achieve. (pp. 432–436)

18. Describe the extrinsic and intrinsic factors that affect job satisfaction and dissatisfaction. Give an example of a job that has been designed to increase motivation. (pp. 436–437)

19. Discuss the importance of goals in job satisfaction. Describe the kinds of goals that increase job satisfaction. (pp. 437–438)

CONCEPTS AND EXERCISES

No. 1 Theories of Motivation

Completing this exercise should help you to achieve the following learning objectives.

(3) *Define instinct. Discuss the attempts of instinct theorists to explain behavior. Explain why they failed to do so. (pp. 408–409)*

(4) *Define drive. Discuss the attempts of drive theorists to explain behavior. Explain why they failed to account for all types of behavior. Define homeostasis, primary drive, and secondary drive. Discuss their role in motivation. (pp. 409–411)*

(5) *Define arousal. Discuss the role of optimal levels of arousal in motivation. Describe the effect on behavior of anything other than an optimal level of arousal. (pp. 411–412)*

(6) *Define incentive. Discuss the attempt of incentive theorists to explain behavior. (p. 412)*

(7) *Describe the opponent-process theory of motivation. Give an example of the kinds of behavior it attempts to explain. (pp. 412–413)*

(8) *Describe Maslow's hierarchy of needs. Give examples of each kind of need on the hierarchy. (pp. 413–415)*

Below is a list of several different behaviors. Which theory of motivation would best explain the motivation underlying each behavior?

1. Vivien has been working in a laboratory for six months. She has learned all of the techniques necessary for the job and is now very bored. She wants to go to work for a different lab or apply to graduate school.

2. Diane spent the entire day working on the family farm. She and some friends went into town after work to have a beer. She realized several hours later that although she was no longer thirsty, she was still drinking beer.

3. David is terrified of heights but repeatedly jumps off the high dive at the swimming pool. The lifeguards no longer pay any attention to him as he screams until he reaches the water. They know he will surface with a big smile on his face.

4. Karl and Sarah got married in the middle of the Depression of the 1930s. They have spent most of their lives working very hard and investing their money. Their children would like them to take some time off or retire and enjoy the fruits of their labor, but Karl and Sarah insist on working to make more money.

5. Brian, six years old, went Christmas shopping with his mother and got lost. Soon his crying turned to sobs of panic. Within minutes, several adults knelt down, comforted him, and said they would help him find his mother.

No. 2 Recognizing Achievement Motivation

Completing this exercise should help you to achieve the following learning objectives.

(17) *Define achievement motivation. Describe the characteristics of achievement motivation. Discuss the factors that can affect achievement motivation. Explain the possible reasons for the differences in the behavior of males and females who are equally motivated. (pp. 432–436)*

(18) *Describe the extrinsic and intrinsic factors that affect job satisfaction and dissatisfaction. Give an*

example of a job that has been designed to increase motivation. (pp. 436–437)

(19) *Discuss the importance of goals in job satisfaction. Describe the kinds of goals that increase job satisfaction. (pp. 437–438)*

John Drake is an interviewer for a large advertising agency in Chicago. It is his job to weed out all job applicants who do not have a high level of achievement motivation. Below are a list of the questions he asked and the answers of three job candidates. As his assistant, you have been asked to give your opinion. Whom should John hire?

Question 1: What are your goals in the advertising field?

Mike Conners: I don't really have any goals in the field except to get a job. I don't see how I can have goals until I work in the field for at least a year or two.

Pam Brown: Eventually I would like to run my own agency. For that reason, I would like to gain expertise in every area of marketing, including advertising.

Mary Fuller: I just want to see if I like the field first.

Question 2: What have you failed at, and how have you handled that failure?

Mike Conners: I developed an advertising campaign for the radio station that I worked for, and it was a flop. We asked people in the streets if they remembered hearing it, and nobody did. I decided to dump the campaign altogether and wait until the new budget came through before I started thinking about what new campaigns we could create.

Pam Brown: I always wanted to be a neurobiologist. However, it slowly dawned on me that I might not have the intellectual capability to be a star in the field. I kept thinking that if I just worked harder, I would eventually make it. Finally, after several years, I decided that I had other skills that neurobiology hadn't tapped, and that I would try to find a field I could excel in and enjoy.

Mary Fuller: I have never really failed at anything. I'd be devastated if I did. It's very difficult for me to think of failing.

Question 3: How did you decide to get into advertising?

Mike Conners: I had a friend who was interested in advertising. I thought it would be interesting, so I applied. I liked it so I stayed.

Pam Brown: As I said before, I eventually decided that neurobiology was not for me. I made a list of all my personal and academic strengths. I also made lists of all the things that I like to do and all the jobs that I could possibly do. I looked at all three lists and tried to come up with several common threads. These were interior design, industrial design, and advertising. I read about all three fields and decided to pursue advertising.

Mary Fuller: I just sort of fell into it. I did well so I stayed in it. It is sort of the old story, "everything works out for the best."

Question 4: How did your parents react when you told them you were going to get your master's degree in advertising?

Mike Conners: My parents do not care what I do as long as I am happy doing it. Once they made sure that I liked advertising, they didn't say too much.

Pam Brown: I remember my father telling me when I was just a little kid that I could do anything that I wanted to do if I really put my mind to it. That's exactly what he said when I told him I had dropped neurobiology and gone into advertising.

Mary Fuller: They were very happy for me. My mom and dad have both had some experience in the field. My mom helps me on projects a lot, and my father advised me on what to look for in a graduate program.

ANSWERS TO CONCEPTS AND EXERCISES

No. 1 Theories of Motivation

1. *Arousal Theory* (p. 411). Boredom put Vivien below her optimal level of arousal. Her attempts to reach her new goals will raise her arousal to its optimal level.

2. *Incentive Theory* (p. 412). Diane has been drinking beer for positive incentives, which are its taste and the way she feels, not because she is thirsty.

3. *Opponent-Process Theory* (p. 412). When David first jumped off the high dive, his initial reaction was fear followed by the thrill of landing safely in the water. As time passed, the thrill has increased (opponent process) and the fear has decreased.

4. *Drive Theory* (p. 409). Karl and Sarah have learned a secondary drive of making money. They probably learned during the Depression that a lack of money prevented them from eating as much as they wanted. Therefore, they learned that making money, a secondary drive, was essential to reducing the primary drive of hunger.

5. *Instinct Theory* (p. 408). Some parenting behaviors, such as automatic reactions to a child displaying distress signals, may be unlearned. Therefore these behaviors can be considered similar to an instinct.

No. 2 Recognizing Achievement Motivation

John should hire Pam Brown. She consistently shows the characteristics of a high achiever.

Question 1: What are your goals in the advertising field?

Most people with a high need for achievement have goals that are difficult and challenging but not impossible. They also actively plan for the future. (p. 433)

Mike Conners has no definite goals.

Pam Brown wants to run her own agency.

Mary Fuller has no goals.

Question 2: What have you failed at, and how have you handled that failure?

People with a high need for achievement persist in the face of failure. Also, if they feel they have done their best, they are not bothered by failure. (p. 433)

Mike Conners did not persist in the face of failure, but rather dumped his campaign.

Pam Brown persisted at neurobiology before she went on to a new field.

Mary Fuller said that she does not handle failure very well.

Question 3: How did you decide to get into advertising?

People with a high need for achievement plan for the future. They prepare themselves by gathering information, investigating alternatives, generating goal-oriented plans, and so on. (p. 433)

Mike Conners got into advertising by accident.

Pam Brown actively sought out information and decided to pursue advertising.

Mary Fuller believed that "everything works out for the best." She does not actively plan for the future.

Question 4: How did your parents react when you told them you were going to get your master's degree in advertising?

The parents of children with high achievement motivation encourage the child to attempt difficult tasks, especially new ones; offer praise and other rewards for success; encourage the child to find ways to succeed, instead of complaining about failure; and prompt the child to go on to the next, somewhat more difficult challenge. The parents of children with low achievement motivation have a tendency to interfere with the child's tasks, sometimes completing them for the child. Also, the children are sometimes encouraged to give up. (p. 434)

Mike Conners's parents were happy for him but he did not mention encouragement specifically.

Pam Brown's parents, especially her father, told her that she could accomplish any goal if she put her mind to it.

Although Mary Fuller's parents were very happy for her, they tended to interfere with the completion of her tasks.

MULTIPLE CHOICE QUESTIONS

Facts and Definitions

1. Motivation is considered an intervening variable because
   a. it is a stimulus that causes a response.
   b. motives or needs are causes of behavior.
   c. it helps explain the relationship between stimuli and responses.
   d. motives or needs are responses to external stimuli.

2. Which of the following can be a source of motivation?
   a. Hunger and thirst
   b. Panic and anger
   c. Parents and peers
   d. All of the above.

3. Instinct theory is no longer a predominant theory of motivation. Why?
   a. Instincts often described behavior but did not explain it.
   b. Humans never display automatic responses to stimuli.
   c. Instinct theorists said that learning could explain most of human behavior.
   d. Too many instincts were proven to exist.

4. Homeostasis is a key concept in which theory of motivation?
   a. Instinct theory
   b. Arousal theory
   c. Incentive theory
   d. Drive theory

5. Drive theory cannot explain which of the following behaviors?
   a. Eating when hungry
   b. Drinking when thirsty
   c. Putting on warm clothes when cold
   d. Exploring a new environment

6. Goal-directed behavior is a key concept in which theory of motivation?
   a. Drive theory
   b. Incentive theory
   c. Arousal theory
   d. Instinct theory

7. Which of the following orders of Maslow's hierarchy of needs is correct?
   a. Safety, physiological, belongingness, self-actualization, esteem.
   b. Belongingness, esteem, physiological, safety, self-actualization

c. Physiological, belongingness, safety, esteem, self-actualization

d. Physiological, safety, belongingness, esteem, self-actualization

8. Which of the following has been a criticism of Maslow's hierarchy of needs?

a. There are too many needs.

b. Some basic human needs are missing from the hierarchy.

c. Sometimes higher needs are fulfilled before lower ones.

d. Safety needs should be lower on the hierarchy than physiological needs.

9. When stimulated, the lateral hypothalamus

a. initiates eating behavior.

b. has the same effect as the removal of the ventromedial hypothalamus.

c. stops eating behavior.

d. both *a* and *b*.

10. Cholecystokinin is involved in the regulation of

a. eating.

b. thirst.

c. sex.

d. arousal.

11. Anorexia nervosa is characterized by

a. eating more calories than necessary for body maintenance.

b. self-starvation and weight loss.

c. overeating and self-induced vomiting.

d. None of the above.

12. _____ are located in the _____ and detect the _____.

a. Osmoreceptor cells; liver; pressure and volume of fluid

b. Volumetric receptors; liver; presence of water

c. Osmoreceptor cells; stomach; presence of water

d. Volumetric receptors; heart and kidneys; pressure and volume of fluids

13. Which of the following is *not* true?

a. There are organizational differences in male and female brains.

b. Sexual behavior patterns are established by androgens during development.

c. Androgens are found in males but not in females.

d. Estrogen levels in females are high during the middle of the menstrual cycle.

14. Which of the following is a possible cause of erectile dysfunction?

a. Fatigue

b. Hormonal problems

c. Diabetes

d. All of the above.

15. People with a high need for achievement

a. do not worry about the future but rather live for the here and now.

b. are preoccupied with their own successes.

c. establish relatively easy goals so they can always achieve them.

d. are extremely bothered by failure.

MULTIPLE CHOICE QUESTIONS

Application of Concepts

1. According to Maslow, if you were shipwrecked on a desert isle, which of the following would you most likely do first?

a. Look for dinner and fresh water.

b. Look for inhabitants.

c. Establish a form of self-government.

d. Build a place to live.

2. Stewart desperately wants a job in the computer field. He has just finished an interview during which

he was aggressive about his thoughts and ideas. An incentive theorist would say

    a. Stewart has a strong aggressive instinct.
    b. Stewart thinks that being aggressive will land him the job.
    c. Stewart has a very high optimal level of arousal.
    d. Stewart is worried about having enough money to live on.

3.   Drew thinks that the concept of learning is vital to understanding motivation. Which of the following theories of motivation would he be least likely to agree with?

    a. Opponent-process theory
    b. Drive theory
    c. Instinct theory
    d. Incentive theory

4.   Herman loves a certain candy and will eat boxes of it at a time. Which of the following theories could explain his behavior?

    a. Instinct theory
    b. Drive theory
    c. Incentive theory
    d. None of the above.

5.   Liza has been working at home during the summer. However, she is finding it difficult to work due to the heat and has decided to buy an air conditioner. This is an example of a

    a. secondary drive.
    b. learned drive.
    c. primary drive.
    d. tertiary drive.

6.   Josephine is obese. She and several of her friends with similar problems want to hold a dinner party but do not want to overeat. Which of the following entrees would be best?

    a. Crab legs in the shell
    b. Broiled fish
    c. Cajun chicken
    d. Enchiladas

7.   Jerry, who has a high need for achievement, has just enrolled in a physiology course. Which goal would he likely set for the semester?

    a. He will study hard enough to get a 98 percent or higher on every test.
    b. He will not care if he gets a C because the course does not count toward his grade point.
    c. He will learn as much from this course as he can since it will help in his upcoming pre-med courses.
    d. None of the above.

8.   Julie, who has a high need for achievement, is trying to decide where to work. Which job should she take?

    a. Company 1: High pay, little responsibility, great boss.
    b. Company 2: Low pay, lots of responsibility, mediocre boss.
    c. Company 3: Medium pay, lots of responsibility, chances for advancement, demanding boss.
    d. Company 4: Very high pay, easy work, not much chance for advancement, great boss.

9.   Kate has a high need for achievement. Which of the following would most likely best describe her parents?

    a. They encouraged her to try new challenges and rewarded her successes.
    b. They always got involved with her work and even helped her finish assignments.
    c. When the going got tough, Kate's parents told her to quit torturing herself and give up.
    d. They did not praise Kate very much because they did not want her to become satisfied and quit trying new things.

10. Connie is in the hospital to have her tonsils removed and is afraid of the pain. She is told that she can stay in any room she wishes. Which of the following should she pick?

a. A room to herself

b. A room with one other person in for a routine physical

c. A room with other people who will also be having their tonsils removed

d. A room with many other people in for routine physicals

11. Eugene is a homosexual. Which factor(s) played a part in the development of his sexual orientation?

a. He has a high level of circulating androgens.

b. He has a low level of circulating androgens and a high level of circulating estrogens.

c. He did not have a close relationship with his father and had a close relationship with his mother.

d. The interaction of family, sociosexual, and biological factors led to his orientation.

12. Stephen is working a late night shift in the emergency room. His next patient is a girl who is very dehydrated. Upon examination, Stephen finds that the girl's weight is normal, but she has nutritional imbalances and intestinal damage. Stephen's patient is probably suffering from

a. anorexia nervosa.

b. bulimia.

c. obesity.

d. None of the above.

13. Lisa, a waitress, feels like screaming. One of her customers ordered steak and shrimp. When she brought it to him, he said that he had ordered steak and lobster. If she tells him he is wrong, she could lose a big tip. If she takes the food back to the cook, he might get angry and make mistakes with her orders all night long, which would also ruin her tips. This is an example of what kind of motivational conflict?

a. Approach-approach

b. Approach-avoidance

c. Avoidance-avoidance

d. Multiple approach-avoidance

14. Jill wants to buy a new stereo, but she knows the cost might cause her financial hardship. What kind of motivational conflict is this?

a. Approach-approach

b. Approach-avoidance

c. Avoidance-avoidance

d. Multiple approach-avoidance

15. Paula is lonely. She chose a school that is far away from home, and all of her friends are at different universities. She really misses being able to tell her best friend about her day. According to Maslow, Paula is not able to fulfill which need at this point in her life?

a. Physiological

b. Safety

c. Belonging

d. Esteem

ANSWERS TO MULTIPLE CHOICE QUESTIONS

Facts and Definitions

1. *c* is the answer. Intervening variables help us understand why a given stimulus caused a given response. For example, hunger helps explain why someone would order a pizza after hearing an advertisement. The ad is the stimulus and ordering the pizza is the response. The motive of hunger also explains why the person did not display some other response, such as ignoring the ad. (p. 406)

   a., b., & d. Motivation, motives, and needs are neither stimuli nor responses, but can affect the responses made to stimuli.

2. *d* is the answer. Hunger, thirst, emotions such as panic and anger, and people such as parents and peers can all be sources of motivation. (p. 408)

3. *a* is the answer. Saying that someone is acting aggressively because he or she has an aggressive in-

stinct is a description instead of an explanation of behavior. (p. 409)

b. Humans do display some automatic responses to stimuli. These are called reflexes. For example, the doctor hits your knee and your leg moves, or an object comes flying toward you and your eyes close.

c. Instinct theorists said that learning played a very small role, if any, in behavior. Instincts are not learned; they are automatic, innate, responses to specific stimuli.

d. Instinct theory was attacked because too many instincts were suggested to exist and there is no scientific way to disprove their existence.

4. *d* is the answer. Homeostasis is the process of maintaining an equilibrium in our physiological systems. Drives prompt us to behave in a way that maintains this balance or equilibrium. (p. 409)

a. Instinct theorists said that our behavior occurs in response to specific stimuli rather than in order to maintain a balance in our systems.

b. Arousal theorists said that we behave in order to maintain an optimal level of arousal rather than to maintain a balance in our systems.

c. Incentive theorists said that we behave in ways that will allow us to reach our goals of obtaining positive incentives and avoiding negative incentives.

5. *d* is the answer. Drives cause us to do things that will reduce needs such as hunger and thirst. Exploring a new environment doesn't reduce any known drive. (p. 411)

a., b., & c. Eating when hungry, drinking when thirsty, and making yourself warm are all behaviors that reduce drives.

6. *b* is the answer. Incentive theorists would say that our behavior is goal-directed. We behave in ways that allow us to reach our goals of obtaining positive rewards or incentives. (p. 412)

a. Drive theory says that we behave in ways that reduce drives rather than in ways that reach goals or obtain incentives.

c. Arousal theory says that we behave in ways that maintain an optimal level of arousal, not to reach goals or incentives.

d. Incentive theorists would say that our behavior is goal-directed. An instinct theorist would say that our behavior is a set of automatic and fixed responses displayed in the presence of specific stimuli.

7. *d* is the answer. (p. 413)

a., b., & c. The order of needs in Maslow's hierarchy is as follows: physiological, safety, belongingness and love, esteem, and, finally, self-actualization.

8. *c* is the answer. In some cases higher needs are fulfilled before lower ones. For example, many people fast in observance of religious holidays, which fulfills a need above physiological needs. (p. 414)

a. & b. Most researchers agree that most basic human needs are represented on the list.

d. No researcher has ever argued that safety needs should come before physiological needs on Maslow's hierarchy.

9. *d* is the answer. A rat will begin to eat large amounts of food when either its lateral hypothalamus is stimulated or its ventromedial hypothalamus is removed. (p. 416)

c. A rat will cease to eat when the lateral hypothalamus is removed or when the ventromedial hypothalamus is stimulated.

10. *a* is the answer. Cholecystokinin (CCK) is a chemical which is released from the gut and from neurons in the hypothalamus during a meal. It is involved in the cessation of eating. (p. 417)

b. Cholecystokinin is not involved in the regulation of thirst.

c. Cholecystokinin is not involved in the regulation of sex.

d. Cholecystokinin is not involved in the regulation of arousal.

11. *b* is the answer. Anorexics starve themselves and lose weight, in some cases to the point of death. (p. 419)

a. Obesity is characterized by eating more calories than necessary for body maintenance.

c. Bulimia is characterized by overeating and then inducing vomiting.

d. b is the answer.

12. *d* is the answer. Volumetric cells are located in the heart and kidneys and monitor the pressure and volume of body fluids. (p. 421)

a. Osmoreceptors are located in the hypothalamus and detect the presence of water in cells.

b. Volumetric cells are located in the heart and kidneys and monitor the pressure and volume of body fluids.

c. Osmorcceptors are located in the hypothalamus and detect the presence of water in cells.

13. *c* is the answer. Both males and females have androgens. Males simply have more androgens than females. (p. 423)

a. There are organizational differences in male and female brains.

b. Sexual behavior patterns are established by androgens during development.

d. Estrogen levels in females are high during the middle of the menstrual cycle.

14. *d* is the answer. Erectile dysfunction can be caused by fatigue, hormonal problems, or diabetes. Other possible causes include anxiety, excessive use of alcohol or other drugs, kidney disease, hypertension, and some prescription drugs. (p. 427)

15. *b* is the answer. People with a high need for achievement are often preoccupied with their own level of ability and successes. (p. 433)

a. People with a high need for achievement do worry about the future. They tend to plan their futures very carefully.

c. People with a high need for achievement set difficult and challenging but realistic goals for themselves. If they were to succeed at very easy goals, their feelings of achievement would be low.

d. People with a high need for achievement are not bothered by failure. They simply keep trying.

ANSWERS TO MULTIPLE CHOICE QUESTIONS

Application of Concepts

1. *a* is the answer. Physiological needs include food, water, oxygen, activity, and sleep. These are lowest on the hierarchy and, according to Maslow, are satisfied first. (p. 413)

b. Looking for natives might satisfy belongingness needs but would probably be done after food and water were found.

c. Establishing a form of self-government might satisfy belonging or esteem needs but would probably be done after food and water were found.

d. Shelter is a safety need and would be satisfied after physiological needs.

2. *b* is the answer. An incentive theorist would say that Stewart was behaving in a way that he thought would bring him closer to a goal or positive incentive. (p. 412)

a. An instinct theorist would say that Stewart has an aggressive instinct.

c. An arousal theorist would say that Stewart has a very high level of optimal arousal.

d. A drive theorist would say that Stewart wants the job so that he will have enough money to buy food.

3. *c* is the answer. Instincts arc *unlearned,* automatic, innate responses to specific stimuli. (p. 408)

a. According to arousal theory you will behave in ways that maintain your optimal level of arousal. Some of the activities that increase or decrease your level of arousal are probably learned.

b. According to drive theory we learn secondary drives.

d. According to incentive theory we will behave in ways that allow us to reach certain goals. Some of the behaviors that allow us to reach certain goals are learned. For example, you learn how to study in order to reach your goal of getting good grades.

4. *c* is the answer. The taste of the candy is an incentive. Herman will eat it so that he can reach his goal of tasting it. (p. 412)

a. An instinct theorist might say that there is an instinct to eat this candy, but the existence of such an instinct is highly unlikely.

b. If Herman were eating just to satisfy his hunger, then this would be the answer. However, Herman's hunger should be satiated without having to eat boxes of candy.

d. c is the answer.

5. *c* is the answer. Feeling too hot is an unlearned need which will cause psychological arousal or a drive to motivate behavior to find some way of cooling off. (p. 409)

a. & b. Secondary drives are learned needs. If the question had said that Liza needed an extra job so that she could always have enough money to satisfy *any* primary drives, this would have been the correct alternative.

d. There is no such thing as a tertiary drive.

6. *a* is the answer. Obese people are not willing to expend much energy in order to obtain food. Eating crab would necessitate digging the meat out of the shell. This would make it more difficult to obtain the food than any of the other alternatives. Also, crab doesn't have a pronounced taste. Obese people prefer food that is very tasty. (p. 418)

b. Broiled fish can be rather bland, but it is not as difficult to obtain the fish as digging meat out of a shell is. Therefore *a* is a better answer.

c. Cajun chicken is very spicy. Obese people like to eat very tasty food and a lot of food would probably be eaten.

d. Enchiladas are very spicy. Obese people like to eat very tasty food and a lot of food would probably be eaten.

7. *c* is the answer. Jerry has a high need for achievement, which means he will set difficult and challenging but realistic goals for himself. Jerry would like to learn. This is a difficult but realistic goal. (p. 433)

a. Getting a 98% or above on every test is not only a difficult challenge but is also unrealistic. People with a high need for achievement do not set unrealistic goals.

b. People with a high need for achievement are preoccupied with their own abilities and successes and set difficult goals for themselves. Getting a C is not a difficult goal.

d. c is the answer.

8. *c* is the answer. It is important that Julie take the job that will yield the most satisfaction, which is found in jobs that provide opportunity for advancement and individual responsibility. She should also take the job with the fewest dissatisfying characteristics, which include low pay and a mediocre boss. (p. 436)

a. Company 1 has very few dissatisfying characteristics but no satisfying characteristics either.

b. Company 2 offers a large amount of responsibility but several dissatisfying characteristics, such as low pay and a mediocre boss.

d. Company 4 has very few dissatisfying characteristics but no satisfying characteristics. The job carries no responsibility and does not provide any chances for advancement.

9. *a* is the answer. Children whose parents encourage them to try new things and reward them for

their successes develop a high need for achievement. (p. 434)

b. Children with parents that interfere in their work would not develop a high need for achievement.

c. Children with parents who let them give up would not develop a high need for achievement.

d. Praise for a job well done and encouragement to try new challenges helps to develop a high need for achievement.

10. *c* is the answer. Research data shows that people affiliate when they need support. Also, people will choose to be with others who are experiencing the same problem. (p. 432)

a. People affiliate when they are anxious and need support.

b. & d. Connie would rather be alone when anxious than be with someone who is not anxious. Being in the hospital for a routine physical would not produce as much anxiety as surgery would.

11. *d* is the answer. There is some evidence that family relationships and biological factors play a role in a person's sexual orientation. However, family, sociosexual, and biological factors are usually combined. (p. 427)

a. & b. Homosexuals' levels of circulating hormones have not been found to be different from heterosexuals'.

c. Although there is some evidence that negative relationships with the same-sex parent are correlated with homosexuality, it is usually the interaction of family, sociosexual, and biological factors that affect a person's sexual orientation.

12. *b* is the answer. Bulimics usually maintain a normal weight. However, due to frequent vomiting, they experience dehydration, nutritional imbalances, and intestinal damage. (p. 420)

a. Anorexics do have nutritional imbalances but do not maintain a normal weight. They starve themselves, causing a severe drop in weight.

c. Obese people are much heavier than they should be. They are at a higher risk for diabetes, heart attack, and high blood pressure, but not nutritional imbalances.

d. b is the answer.

13. *c* is the answer. Lisa is facing a situation in which she has two negative choices; the cook will probably be angry, and the customer will probably be irritated. This is characteristic of an avoidance-avoidance situation. (p. 438)

a. An approach-approach situation is a choice between two equally positive choices.

b. An approach-avoidance situation is a choice which has both a positive and a negative aspect.

d. A multiple approach-avoidance decision is a choice between two situations, each of which has a positive and a negative aspect.

14. *b* is the answer. Buying the stereo will provide entertainment (positive aspect) but will also involve financial hardship (negative aspect). This is characteristic of an approach-avoidance situation. (p. 439)

a. An approach-approach situation is a choice between two equally positive choices.

c. An avoidance-avoidance situation is a choice between two equally negative choices.

d. A multiple approach-avoidance decision is a choice between two situations, each of which has a positive and a negative aspect.

15. *c* is the answer. Paula's need for belongingness and love (on Maslow's hierarchy) is not being fulfilled. (p. 432)

a. We have physiological needs for things that are basic to survival such as food and water.

b. Children's safety needs refer to physical and emotional support from a primary caregiver.

d. Our needs for esteem are met when we gain approval, admiration, and other types of positive evaluation from ourselves or others. Paula can give these to herself and does not necessarily need to have these needs fulfilled by others.

Chapter 12

Emotion

OUTLINE

I. WHAT IS EMOTION? (pp. 442–446)

A. A Definition

1. Emotions are experiences, not overt behaviors or specific thoughts.

2. Emotions are passions, not actions, because you can decide to act, but passions happen whether you want them to or not.

3. Emotions are partially dependent on your cognitive appraisal or interpretation of a situation.

4. Emotions are accompanied by learned and reflexive responses.

An emotion is felt as happening to the self; is generated by the cognitive appraisal of a situation; and is accompanied by both learned and reflexive physical responses.

B. Classification of Emotion

Many different classifications of emotions have been created. It is difficult to determine which, if any, is correct.

II. WHERE IS EMOTION? (pp. 446–460)

A. Emotions and the Autonomic Nervous System (ANS)

1. *The ANS is a Modulator*. Information is sent from the central nervous system to a ganglion of the ANS and then to a target organ. Signals from the ANS modify the ongoing activity of the organs and glands in the body.

2. *The sympathetic and parasympathetic nervous systems*. The ANS is made up of two branches, the sympathetic and parasympathetic nervous systems, both of which communicate with all the organs and glands in the body. Because of different neurotransmitters used at the target organs, the two branches have opposite effects. The parasympathetic system initiates activity related to the nourishment and growth of the body. The sympathetic system prepares the body for vigorous activity and stimulates the adrenal medulla to cause the fight-or-flight syndrome, which prepares the body for action in the face of a threat.

3. *The ANS and Consciousness*. The ANS and consciousness are indirectly linked. Although you are unconscious of ANS activity, you can be conscious of the *effects* of ANS activity.

B. Self-Observation: The James-Lange Theory

According to this theory, people experience emotions based on observations of their own physical behavior and peripheral responses.

1. *Evaluating the James-Lange Theory*. If the James-Lange theory is correct, there should be a unique peripheral physiological response for

every emotion, and people who cannot feel their peripheral responses should not experience emotion.

2. *The Facial-Feedback Hypothesis*. If James was correct, information about the movements of your face (smiling, for example) should lead to changes in emotion (for instance, happiness).

C. Direct Central Experience: The Cannon-Bard Theory

According to this theory emotion starts in the thalamus and is then passed simultaneously to the cerebral cortex, where it becomes conscious, and to the autonomic nervous system. Recent evidence suggests that the locus coeruleus releases noradrenaline, which modifies activity in brain cells and the peripheral autonomic nervous system. A direct experience of emotion results from modulation of the activity of brain cells.

D. Attribution of Arousal: The Schachter Theory

According to the Schachter theory, emotions are produced by both feedback from peripheral responses and a cognitive appraisal, or attribution, of what caused those responses.

1. *Evaluating the Schachter Theory*. First, if Schachter is correct, elimination of physiological responses should reduce the experience of emotion. Second, if you attribute physiological arousal to a nonemotional cause, your experience of emotion should be reduced. Finally, if you experience artificially produced arousal, you should experience emotion and attribute it to some situation.

2. *The Transfer of Excitation*. When arousal from one experience carries over to an independent emotional situation, it is transferred excitation. People sometimes attribute prior arousal to the situation at hand, thereby intensifying their present emotion.

E. Conclusions

Emotion has both a physiological and a cognitive component. It is not yet known which component is primarily responsible for emotion.

III. EXPRESSING AND RECOGNIZING EMOTIONS (pp. 460–465)

Facial movement and expressions play the primary role in communicating human emotions.

A. Facial Movements and Emotions

1. *Innate and Learned Expressions*. Many facial expressions of emotions appear to be innate. However, we learn how to express other emotions through operant shaping or by following social rules.

2. *The Brain and Facial Expressions*. The pyramidal motor system controls voluntary facial movement and the extrapyramidal motor system controls involuntary facial movement. Although the right hemisphere is primary in the overall expression of emotion, the left hemisphere is involved in expressing positive emotion.

B. Perceiving Emotions

The right hemisphere is predominantly active in the perception and recognition of emotion in others, as well as in the expression of emotion.

IV. FUNCTIONS AND EFFECTS OF EMOTION (pp. 465–469)

A. The Functions of Emotional Expression

Darwin argued that facial expressions are genetically determined and that those we see today have been effective communicators in the past. Zajonc has suggested that facial expressions of emotion have important physiological functions. People look to the emotional expressions of other people to determine the safety of their environments. This is called the social referencing phenomenon.

B. The Effects of Experiencing Emotions

1. *Motivation and Emotions.* Experiencing too much or too little emotion can be detrimental to motivation.

2. *Emotions and Health.* Positive emotions may reduce pain or the level of stress-related hormones.

KEY TERMS

1. **Emotions** are involuntary experiences that are generated by cognitive appraisals of a situation and are accompanied by both learned and reflexive physical responses. (p. 445)

Example: Imagine that your boss unjustly says that your work is worthless. Rage wells up inside you because you have worked very hard. The involuntary experience of rage just happens; you do not make it happen. Your cognitive appraisal of the situation is also important. You have determined that your boss is not kidding, but very serious. When in a rage, you may feel your face flush and your heart rate increase (reflexive physical responses).

2. The **autonomic nervous system,** part of the peripheral nervous system, carries information from the brain to the organs and glands of the body. Emotions are associated with the activity of both the parasympathetic and sympathetic nervous systems, which are subdivisions of the autonomic nervous system. (p. 446)

Example: See example for key term 4, sympathetic nervous system.

3. The **parasympathetic nervous system,** a subdivision of the autonomic nervous system, is involved in activities relating to the growth and nourishment of the body. When emotions are ex-perienced this system may be activated; it is responsible for some of the reflexive physiological responses that accompany emotion. (p. 447)

4. The **sympathetic nervous system,** a subdivision of the autonomic nervous system, helps to prepare the body for vigorous activity. When emotions are experienced this system may be activated; it is responsible for the *fight-or-flight syndrome.* (p. 447)

Example: Imagine that you are in bed, just about to fall asleep. Suddenly, you realize that your dog has been barking for at least fifteen minutes. She never makes a sound unless someone is there. If visitors were outside they would have rung the doorbell already. You can feel terror creep through your body. Your mouth is dry, you shake, your heart beats very fast and hard, your palms start to sweat and many other changes that you are unaware of occur in your body. Your pupils dilate to let in more light and your blood sugar rises, while your digestive system shuts down temporarily. Your body begins these preparations so that you can either run from the threatening situation *(flight)* or *fight* whoever is making the dog bark. You have just experienced the *fight-or-flight syndrome.*

5. The **fight-or-flight syndrome** is initiated by the sympathetic nervous system. Many changes occur in your body that will allow you to escape quickly or fight whatever is threatening you. (pp. 447–448)

Example: See example for key term 4, sympathetic nervous system.

6. The **adrenal medulla** is the inner part of the adrenal gland. When stimulated by the sympathetic nervous system, it releases adrenaline into the system and activates all the target organs of the sympathetic nervous system. Adrenaline initiates the *fight-or-flight syndrome.* (p. 448)

7. The **James-Lange theory** states that you become conscious or aware of an emotion when your brain observes the physiological responses of your body

to a situation. Therefore each emotion should have a unique pattern of physiological responses. If you are unable to perceive these physiological responses, then no emotion should be felt. (p. 452)

Example: According to this theory, you know you are unhappy because your brain receives feedback from the muscles in your face that are active when you cry.

8. The **facial feedback hypothesis** states that involuntary movements of the face send information (feedback) to the brain about which emotion is being felt. (p. 453)

Example: You have probably heard the expression, "Smile and you will feel happy." Whoever originated this saying would have supported the facial feedback hypothesis, which says that if you smile, your brain registers the facial movements involved in smiling and your emotion should become positive or happy.

9. The **Cannon-Bard theory** states that the thalamus is responsible for interpreting a situation and deciding what emotion is experienced. The thalamus then sends sensory signals to the cerebral cortex, where the emotion becomes conscious. Simultaneously, the thalamus sends signals to the autonomic nervous system, which initiates the physiological responses that accompany emotion. Presently it is thought that the thalamus does not produce the experience of emotion. (p. 454)

Example: You must walk home after dark. You realize that someone is following you. Your brain interprets this situation through the thalamus, and sends signals to your autonomic nervous system to initiate the fight-or-flight syndrome so that you will be able to run away.

10. The **locus coeruleus** is a structure in the brain that may function as the autonomic system of the brain. The *locus coeruleus* releases noradrenaline, which modulates the activity of other brain cells, and sends signals to the peripheral autonomic nervous system. The cells of the *locus coeruleus* appear

to be involved in emotions and emotional disturbances. (p. 455)

11. **The Schachter theory** of emotion states that emotion is due to the perception of physiological responses <u>and</u> our cognitive appraisal or interpretation of their causes. These together are responsible for the experience of emotion. (p. 457)

Example: You would probably interpret (cognitive appraisal) an increase in heart rate and a breathless feeling (physiological responses) as pleasurable anticipation if you were waiting for your best friend's plane to arrive. However, if you were sitting outside the dentist's office, hearing the sound of a drill and people moaning, you might interpret your physiological reactions as terror.

12. **Attribution** is the process of identifying the cause of some event. In Schachter's theory of emotion, people may attribute physiological arousal to different emotions, depending on the information that is available about the situation. (p. 457)

Example: See example for key term 11, Schachter theory.

13. **Transferred excitation** occurs when arousal from one experience carries over to a different situation. People stay aroused longer than they think they do. If people have been aroused and then encounter a new situation, they may interpret their arousal as an emotional reaction to the new situation. (p. 459)

Example: You have run to class. Just outside the door of the classroom, one of the people working on your group project tells you that she could not finish her part of the paper that is due this period. Normally you would be angry, but your increased arousal from the run intensifies your emotion. You are not just angry; you are furious.

14. The **social-referencing phenomenon** demonstrates one of the functions of emotional expression.

We use other people's expressions of emotion to help us interpret ambiguous situations. (p. 466)

Example: You and your best friend are taking a class taught by a new professor. Your best friend has had this woman before for another class, but this is your first experience with her. During the class a heated discussion takes place and it looks to you as though the professor is very angry. You look to your friend (you *refer* to your friend) to see if she is upset, but she has a slight smile on her face. You decide that the professor is simply a passionate speaker and not really angry with the class.

LEARNING OBJECTIVES

1. Be able to give a definition of emotion. Give examples of each component of the definition. (pp. 442–445)

2. Explain the autonomic nervous system's role in emotion. Describe the pathways from the brain to the target organs for the sympathetic and parasympathetic branches of the autonomic nervous system. (pp. 446–447)

3. Describe the fight-or-flight syndrome. Explain the role of the sympathetic nervous system and the adrenal medulla in the initiation of the fight-or-flight syndrome. (pp. 447–449)

4. Describe the James-Lange theory. Give an example of how an emotion would occur according to this theory. (pp. 450–452)

5. Discuss the research evidence that either confirms or attempts to disprove the James-Lange theory. Describe the facial feedback hypothesis. (pp. 452–453)

6. Compare and contrast the Cannon-Bard theory of emotion and the James-Lange theory. Discuss the role of the locus coeruleus in the revised version of the Cannon-Bard theory. (pp. 453–456)

7. Describe Schachter's theory of emotion. Compare and contrast this theory with the James-Lange and Cannon-Bard theories. Define attribution. (pp. 456–457)

8. Discuss the research evidence that either confirms or appears to disprove Schachter's theory. (pp. 457–459)

9. Discuss transferred excitation and give an example of it. (pp. 459–460)

10. Discuss the role of facial movements in expressing human emotion. Discuss the role of learning and genetic factors in the expression of emotion. (pp. 460–462)

11. Describe the role of the brain in the expression and perception of emotion. (pp. 462–465)

12. Compare and contrast the theories about the function of emotion proposed by Darwin, Zajonc, and Campos. Define the social-referencing phenomenon. (pp. 465–467)

13. Describe the effects of experiencing emotion on health and motivation. (pp. 467–469)

CONCEPTS AND EXERCISES

No. 1 Frankenstein's Emotions

Completing this exercise should help you to achieve the following learning objectives.

(2) *Explain the autonomic nervous system's role in emotion. Describe the pathways from the brain to the target organs for the sympathetic and parasympathetic branches of the autonomic nervous system. (pp. 446–447)*

(3) *Describe the fight-or-flight syndrome. Explain the role of the sympathetic nervous system and the adrenal medulla in the initiation of the fight-or-flight syndrome. (pp. 447–449)*

(11) *Describe the role of the brain in the expression and perception of emotion. (pp. 462–465)*

Dr. Frankenstein is still trying to create the perfect human. He is now in the process of installing the necessary nervous system equipment for the perception, recognition, and expression of emotion.

As Frankenstein's assistant, your job is to tell him what part of the malfunctioning nervous system is responsible for the behaviors described. Choose from the list below. Remember, answers may be used more than once or not at all.

the right hemisphere

the left hemisphere

the pyramidal motor system

the extrapyramidal motor system

interhemispheric communication

the sympathetic nervous system

the parasympathetic nervous system

1. The creature is lifeless. You cannot initiate the fight-or-flight syndrome, no matter what stimulus you present. You have checked the cortical activity and everything is functioning, but there is no increase in the heart rate, decrease in salivation, or increase in pupil dilation. The adrenal medulla is intact but not being stimulated. What is causing the problem? _____

2. The creature is laughing at everything. You knew when he laughed at Dr. Frankenstein's bad jokes that something was seriously amiss. What could be causing the problem? _____

3. The creature complains that he cannot make himself smile or frown. What structure needs adjustment? _____

4. Usually the creature becomes very scared when Dr. Frankenstein is angry. But today the creature just hums silently to himself despite the angry looks on Dr. Frankenstein's face. What could be causing the problem? _____

5. You have the creature hooked up to machines that record sympathetic nervous system activity. You notice that his sympathetic nervous system

is very active. Concerned, you ask what the matter is, but the creature just shrugs his shoulders and says that everything is fine. What is not happening? _____

No. 2 Emotions at the Prom

Completing this exercise should help you to achieve the following learning objectives.

(4) *Describe the James-Lange theory. Give an example of how an emotion would occur according to this theory. (pp. 450–452)*

(5) *Discuss the research evidence that either confirms or attempts to disprove the James-Lange theory. Describe the facial feedback hypothesis. (pp. 452–453)*

(6) *Compare and contrast the Cannon-Bard theory of emotion and the James-Lange theory. Discuss the role of the locus coeruleus in the revised version of the Cannon-Bard theory. (pp. 453–456)*

(7) *Describe Schachter's theory of emotion. Compare and contrast this theory with the James-Lange and Cannon-Bard theories. Define attribution. (pp. 456–457)*

(8) *Discuss the research evidence that either confirms or appears to disprove Schachter's theory. (pp. 457–459)*

(9) *Discuss transferred excitation and give an example of it. (pp. 459–460)*

(12) *Compare and contrast the theories about the function of emotion proposed by Darwin, Zajonc, and Campos. Define the social-referencing phenomenon. (pp. 465–467)*

Following are some of the experiences of the Franklin High School students at their school dance. After each description, choose the phenomenon or theory of emotion that best matches the experience. Remember, each answer may be used more than once or not at all.

the James-Lange theory

Schachter's theory

the Cannon-Bard theory

the transfer of excitation

the social referencing phenomenon

1. Gene, who always worries about being "cool," walks into the dance and watches everyone's reactions to the band before he decides whether or not he likes the music. _____

2. Joya, after dancing with Ted, runs back to where her friends are standing. She realizes that she is a little breathless and has a quickened heartbeat and shaky knees. Delighted, she realizes that these are the cues her sister said would "tell" her that she was in love. _____

3. Helen arrived at the dance twenty minutes late. She ran all the way from the parking lot to the school. She spent several minutes talking with her friends in the bathroom, brushing her hair and putting on new lipstick. Just as she steps into the gym to survey the crowd, she trips and falls, ripping her dress. Absolutely furious, she yells at the boy who tries to help her up, "You idiot, look what you made me do!" What could explain her intense emotional reaction? _____

4. Cecelia is dancing with her boyfriend. She simultaneously realizes how much she loves him and notices how fast her heart is beating and the butterflies in her stomach. _____

ANSWERS TO CONCEPTS AND EXERCISES

No. 1 Frankenstein's Emotions

1. The evidence points to some kind of malfunction in the sympathetic nervous system. The brain is working, because the cortical (cortex) activity is normal. The adrenal medulla is normally stimulated by the sympathetic nervous system. (p. 447)

2. Uncontrolled laughter could be a result of damage to the extrapyramidal system, which controls involuntary facial movement, or damage to the right hemisphere. Damage to this hemisphere can cause pathological laughter. (pp. 462–463)

3. The pyramidal system is malfunctioning, because the creature reports that he has lost control over his *voluntary* facial movements. (p. 462)

4. Since the creature is not reacting to other people's emotional expressions, you conclude that he is having problems in detecting others' emotions. Therefore, his right hemisphere must be malfunctioning in some way. (p. 465)

5. You know that the creature should be experiencing some sort of emotion, since his sympathetic activity is so high. For some reason he is suppressing the verbal expression of that emotion. A decrease in interhemispheric communication can cause a reduction in verbal reports of emotion. (p. 465)

No. 2 Emotions at the Prom

1. Jean wants to make sure other people think the band is good before he gives his own opinion. Watching other people's reactions in order to gain clues about how to react is called the social referencing phenomenon. (p. 466)

2. The James-Lange theory could explain Joya's emotional reaction, since it is based solely on her physiological responses. She has decided that she is happy because she is experiencing all of the physiological responses that her sister has told her will occur when she falls in love. (p. 450)

3. Helen was probably still physiologically aroused from running into the school from the parking lot. She transferred this excitation to the anger she experienced when she ripped her dress. This intensified her emotional reaction. (p. 459)

4. Cecelia is simultaneously experiencing the conscious emotion of being in love and a heightened physiological arousal. According to the Cannon-Bard theory, the thalamus sends information to the cortex (where the emotion is consciously experienced) and signals to the peripheral nervous system (which reacts by increasing physiological arousal) at the same time. (p. 454)

MULTIPLE CHOICE QUESTIONS

Facts and Definitions

1. Which of the following would *not* be part of an emotional experience?

   a. An increase in heartbeat
   b. Cognitive appraisal of a situation
   c. Pupil dilation
   d. All of the above are part of an emotional experience.

2. The _____ is responsible for the *peripheral* initiation of the fight-or-flight syndrome.

   a. sympathetic nervous system
   b. parasympathetic nervous system
   c. adrenal cortex
   d. locus coeruleus

3. Activation of the sympathetic nervous system would cause all of the following except

   a. pupil dilation.
   b. an increase in heartbeat.
   c. a rise in blood sugar.
   d. an increase in digestive activity.

4. Which of the following is true of polygraph testing?

   a. The guilty are very often found innocent.
   b. The innocent are very often found guilty.
   c. Most people can "outsmart" a polygraph test.
   d. The evidence suggests that polygraph tests produce fairly accurate results.

5. The facial feedback hypothesis is similar to which theory of emotion?

   a. James-Lange
   b. Cannon-Bard
   c. Schachter
   d. Autonomic

6. According to the Cannon-Bard theory of emotion, the _____ is the core or base of the emotional experience.

   a. adrenal medulla
   b. adrenal cortex
   c. hypothalamus
   d. thalamus

7. Schachter's theory is unique because it addresses

   a. the influence on emotion of our interpretation of the environment.
   b. the physiological responses which occur during an emotional experience.
   c. the role of specific brain structures in emotion.
   d. the role of specific neurotransmitters in emotion.

8. Which theory requires the existence of unique physiological states for every emotion?

   a. James-Lange
   b. Cannon-Bard
   c. Schachter
   d. Darwin

9. People from many different cultures can recognize a smile as an indication of positive emotion. This suggests that the expression of emotion is

a. innate.
b. culturally determined.
c. learned.
d. lateralized.

10. The pyramidal motor system is involved in the expression of

a. voluntary facial movements.
b. involuntary facial movements.
c. positive emotions.
d. negative emotions.

11. Reduced or suppressed emotional expression may be due to

a. left-hemisphere domination of emotional expression.
b. right-hemisphere domination of emotional expression.
c. reduced interhemispheric communication.
d. damage to the pyramidal motor system.

12. Darwin did not say which of the following?

a. Emotional expressions are biologically determined.
b. The emotions we see expressed today were instrumental to survival in the past.
c. The expression of emotion causes changes in blood flow in the brain.
d. Emotional expressions help us understand how another person is feeling.

13. People have learned to improve performance by altering their interpretation of previously stressful situations, thus reducing their negative emotional arousal. This process is based on which theory of emotion?

a. Schachter
b. James-Lange
c. Cannon-Bard
d. Both *a* and *b*

14. Looking to others' emotional reactions to help determine what is happening in a social situation is called

a. cognitive appraisal.
b. social referencing.
c. transfer of excitation.
d. attribution.

15. Attribution is

a. the determination of what caused some event or our physiological arousal to occur.
b. the transfer of arousal from one situation to another.
c. the continual blaming of others for our emotional experiences.
d. part of the social referencing phenomenon.

MULTIPLE CHOICE QUESTIONS

Application of Concepts

1. Janet and Joan are experiencing identical patterns of physiological arousal: increased heart rate, sweaty palms, pupil dilation, and increased breathing rate. Janet feels happy and Joan is very scared. Which theory of emotion can explain the differences in their emotions?

a. James-Lange
b. Schachter
c. Darwin
d. None of the above.

2. Lori and Carol are discussing the best places in town for meeting gorgeous men. Which do you think would be on the top of their list?

a. A grocery store
b. A laundromat
c. A local dance bar
d. A restaurant

3. Matt is very interested in a girl he has met at the gym. When would be the best time to approach her to talk?

a. As she is warming up before her workout
b. During her workout
c. When she is towelling off after her workout
d. As she is lifting weights

4. Kurt, who is about to take a lie detector test, has sneakily put a tack in his shoe. After what kinds of questions should he jam the tack into his toe in order to show an increase in physiological response?

a. After specific questions about the crime
b. After general or "control" questions
c. After questions relevant to the crime
d. After questions about his age, education, and income

5. When people are scared to get married they are said to have cold feet. Fear really does cause bloodflow to decrease in the feet and hands. This supports the _____ theory of emotion.

a. James-Lange
b. Cannon-Bard
c. Schachter
d. None of the above.

6. Fear decreases bloodflow to the hands and feet. What is this associated with?

a. The fight-or-flight syndrome
b. The activity of the parasympathetic nervous system
c. The activity of the pyramidal motor system
d. The activity of the extrapyramidal motor system

7. Which of the following does not reduce the level of negative emotion that one experiences or expresses?

a. Reducing the level of physiological arousal
b. Relabeling situations in the environment as positive
c. Damage to the left hemisphere
d. Preventing information about physiological responses from reaching the brain

8. Joshua's parents have just called to let him know that they will financially contribute to his summer trip to Europe. He is ecstatic. After saying goodbye, he sits down to cram for his history final covering the Holocaust. How well will Joshua do on his final?

a. His good mood will help him study. He will get an *A*.
b. His good mood will interfere with retrieval during the exam.
c. His good mood will interfere with processing tragic information.
d. We cannot determine how well he will remember the material.

9. Gloria went to the doctor for her usual anti-allergy shots. The nurse mistakenly gave her a shot of epinephrine, which caused a great deal of physiological arousal. As Gloria sailed out of the office she decided that she was feeling shaky from drinking too much caffeinated coffee. Her lack of emotion despite physiological arousal can be explained by which theory of emotion?

a. Darwin
b. James-Lange
c. Schachter
d. Cannon-Bard

10. Karl, due to epileptic seizures, injured his eyes, rendering him unable to obtain right visual field information. His corpus callosum was cut, eliminating interhemispheric communication to prevent future severe seizures. What changes in emotional expression would you expect?

a. A suppression of verbal emotional expression
b. An increase in verbal emotional expression
c. There should be no change in the verbal expression of emotion.
d. An increase in verbal expression of positive emotion

11. A team of alien psychologists has landed in your backyard. They want to learn how to communi-

cate emotions to humans. You would probably spend most of your time teaching them

    a. body postures.

    b. facial movements.

    c. hand gestures.

    d. None of the above.

12. Kimberly has been in an accident; the right hemisphere of her brain has been damaged. She will experience which result?

    a. An inability to verbally express positive emotions

    b. Increased ability to verbally express negative emotions

    c. Decreased ability to recognize faces

    d. An increase in the speed with which she can recognize faces

13. Martha is going on her first trip to Japan. Since she had no time to read about Japanese cultural norms before leaving, she has decided to watch other people's faces for information about how she should behave. This is an example of

    a. the facial feedback hypothesis.

    b. Schachter's theory of emotion.

    c. the social-referencing phenomenon.

    d. the James-Lange theory of emotion.

14. Trudy is extremely emotionally aroused before her audition for a Broadway play. Her overly aroused state might

    a. cause her to perform very well.

    b. cause her to perform less well than if she were more moderately aroused.

    c. have no positive or negative effect on her performance.

    d. cause her performance to be either very good or very poor.

15. Which of the following events will be remembered in the greatest detail?

    a. Feeding your cats in the morning

    b. Winning an olympic gold medal

    c. Getting an *A* on your first-grade homework assignment

    d. All of the above will be remembered equally well.

ANSWERS TO MULTIPLE CHOICE QUESTIONS

Facts and Definitions

1. *d* is the answer. Physiological changes and cognitive appraisal or interpretation of one's environment are both part of an emotional experience. (p. 445)

2. *a* is the answer. The sympathetic branch of the autonomic nervous system prepares the body for action in a threatening situation. (p. 447)

    b. The parasympathetic branch of the autonomic nervous system is involved in growth and nourishment of the body. It is active during digestion.

    c. The adrenal medulla, not the adrenal cortex, releases the neurotransmitter norepinephrine, which is involved in the initiation of the fight-or-flight syndrome.

    d. The locus coeruleus releases norepinephrine in the brain. This may in turn stimulate the sympathetic nervous system to initiate the fight-or-flight syndrome. However, the question asks what peripheral, not what central, structure is involved in this syndrome.

3. *d* is the answer. The *parasympathetic* nervous system is involved in digestive activity. (p. 447)

    a., b., & c. Activation of the sympathetic nervous system will cause pupil dilation, an increase in heartbeat, and an increase in blood sugar.

4. *b* is the answer. Although people disagree on the accuracy of polygraph testing, polygraph tests often find innocent people guilty. (p. 450)

    a. Guilty people are usually found out. However, people who are innocent are often found guilty.

c. Most people cannot outsmart polygraph tests.

d. There is great controversy over the accuracy of polygraph tests. In extreme cases, research has shown results to be incorrect up to 50 percent of the time.

5. *a* is the answer. The James-Lange theory states that we experience emotion after receiving feedback from physiological responses. The facial feedback hypothesis is similar to this theory. Feedback from the facial muscles involved in smiling, frowning, and other facial expressions provides information about what emotion is being felt. (p. 453)

b. The Cannon-Bard theory states that feedback from the body does not generate emotion.

c. Cognitive appraisal, according to Schachter, is very important in labeling emotions. A single pattern of physiological response or facial expression can be labelled in many different ways. Therefore cognitive appraisal is what determines the emotion, not facial feedback.

d. There is no such thing as the autonomic theory of emotion.

6. *d* is the answer. According to the Cannon-Bard theory, emotion originates in the thalamus. The thalamus then sends information to the cortex, where the emotion becomes conscious. Signals are also sent from the thalamus to the autonomic nervous system. (p. 454)

a. & *b.* The adrenal medulla and the adrenal cortex are in the adrenal gland, which is part of the peripheral nervous system. According to Cannon-Bard, the thalamus, part of the central nervous system, is the core of emotion.

c. The hypothalamus is located just below the thalamus, but does not play a primary role in emotion according to the Cannon-Bard theory.

7. *a* is the answer. According to Schachter, our cognitive interpretations of the environment help determine which emotions we attribute arousal to. (p. 456)

b. All theories of emotion include the functioning of physiological peripheral responses.

c. The Cannon-Bard theory states that the thalamus is the core of emotion.

d. No theory addresses the *specific* role of neurotransmitters.

8. *a* is the answer. The James-Lange theory of emotion states that we experience emotion based on our physiological responses. If this is true, every emotion should be associated with a unique pattern of physiological arousal. (p. 452)

b. According to the Cannon-Bard theory, the thalamus is the core of emotion. Peripheral responses do not determine which emotion we are feeling.

c. According to Schachter's theory, the same pattern of physiological arousal can be attributed to different emotions based on our cognitive appraisal of the environment. Therefore, it is not necessary to have unique patterns of physiological arousal for every emotion.

d. Darwin discussed the functions that emotion serves in survival.

9. *a* is the answer. Something innate should not be affected to any great degree by cultural influence. People from many different cultures all relate smiles to positive emotions. (p. 461)

b. & *c.* Events that are culturally determined are usually different in every culture. If expression of happiness were culturally determined, every culture would interpret a smile in a different way. However, this is not the case. All cultures relate smiling to positive emotion.

d. There is no causal relationship between universal recognition of emotion and the particular structure of the nervous system responsible for emotional recognition.

10. *a* is the answer. The pyramidal motor system controls voluntary facial movements. (p. 462)

b. The extrapyramidal motor system controls involuntary facial movements.

c. The right hemisphere is involved in the expression of negative emotion.

d. The left hemisphere is involved in the expression of positive emotion.

11. *c* is the answer. When communication between the hemispheres is reduced, the left half of the brain cannot verbally report what the right has experienced. If the right side of the brain experiences emotion, the left will not receive this information. Therefore, the expression of emotion cannot be verbalized. (p. 465)

a. & b. The right hemisphere is more active than the left in the expression of emotion. The right hemisphere is more active during the expression of negative emotion and the left is more active during the expression of positive emotion. The *suppression* of emotional expression seems to be due to reduced communication between the hemispheres.

d. People with damage to the pyramidal motor system cannot make their faces express emotion. For example, people with this type of damage cannot *make* themselves smile, although they can smile as a result of positive emotion.

12. *c* is the answer. Waynbaum suggested that different emotions cause changes in blood flow to the brain. (p. 467)

a., b., & d. Darwin did say that emotional expressions are biologically determined, and that the emotions we see today were probably instrumental to survival in the past because they help a person understand how other people are feeling.

13. *a* is the answer. According to Schachter, our interpretation or cognitive appraisal of the environment determines an emotion. Changing a negative interpretation to a positive one should reduce the level of negative emotional arousal. (p. 457)

b. The James-Lange theory states that emotion is a result of interpreting our physiological responses. The question discusses changes in the interpretation of the environment, not changes in the interpretation of physiological responses.

c. According to the Cannon-Bard theory, physiological arousal accompanies emotion but does not determine whether or not an emotion will be experienced. In other words, cutting off the physiological arousal with drugs, for example, will not decrease the conscious experience of emotion.

d. a is the answer.

14. *b* is the answer. Other people's reactions often help reduce ambiguity in a situation. We look to them to understand what is going on in a situation. (p. 466)

a. We cognitively appraise our environment for causes of emotions, but specifically examining others' reactions is called social referencing.

c. When arousal from one experience carries over to another situation, it is transferred excitation.

d. Attribution is the process of finding the causes of some event, such as our own physiological arousal.

15. *a* is the answer. Attribution is the determination of what caused some event or our physiological arousal to occur. (p. 457)

b. This phenomenon is called transfer of excitation.

c. Although the process of attribution does allow us to label the cause of our arousal, we do not always attribute that arousal to other people.

d. Attribution is not part of the social referencing phenomenon.

ANSWERS TO MULTIPLE CHOICE QUESTIONS

Application of Concepts

1. *b* is the answer. According to Schachter, our cognitive appraisals of situations can cause us to label identical physiological responses in several different ways. (p. 457)

a. According to the James-Lange theory, every emotion is associated with a unique physiological response.

c. Darwin did not address the mechanism labeling emotions. He said that emotional expressions are inherited.

d. b is the answer.

2. *c* is the answer. Research has shown that, compared with people at rest, exercise-aroused people experience stronger feelings of attraction when they meet an attractive member of the opposite sex. When Lori and Carol get off the dance floor, they will transfer the excitation caused by dancing to the attractive men they see in the bar. (pp. 459–460)

a., b., & d. A grocery store, laundromat, and restaurant do not offer any activity that causes an increase in physiological arousal.

3. *c* is the answer. People remain physiologically aroused longer than they think they do. The girl at the gym will feel calm by the time she is towelling off, even though she is still somewhat aroused. If Matt approaches her at this point she will probably attribute any left over arousal to him instead of to exercising. (pp. 459–460)

a. The girl at the gym will experience very little physiological arousal while she is warming up. If she does experience any arousal, she will attribute it to exercising, not to Matt.

b. & d. Weight-lifting and aerobics will cause physiological arousal. However, the girl will probably attribute her arousal to these activities instead of to Matt.

4. *b* is the answer. Innocent people usually react more strongly to general or "control" questions, like "Have you ever tried to hurt someone?" Therefore, Kurt should jam the tack in his toe, in order to produce physiological arousal, after general questions. (p. 449–450)

a. & c. "Relevant" questions are those that specifically refer to the crime. Guilty people react more strongly to questions that specifically ask about the crime than to control questions.

d. Reactions to "relevant" and control questions are compared in order to determine guilt or innocence. Questions about age, education, and income are neither control nor "relevant" questions.

5. *a* is the answer. According to the James-Lange theory, there are unique changes in physiological arousal associated with each emotion. It has been found that bloodflow decreases in the hands and feet of a frightened person. This physiological response seems to be unique to fear. (p. 452)

b. According to the Cannon-Bard theory, physiological reaction does not play a role in the labeling of emotion.

c. According to Schachter, a physiological reaction can be labeled with different emotions depending on a cognitive appraisal of the situation. Therefore, a unique physiological reaction is not necessary for each emotion.

d. a is the answer.

6. *a* is the answer. When a person is fearful, increased activity in the sympathetic nervous system causes the fight-or-flight syndrome. (p. 447)

b. The parasympathetic system is active in periods of quiet and rest. Fear is not a quiet or restful emotion.

c. & d. The pyramidal and extrapyramidal motor systems control involuntary and voluntary facial movements.

7. *c* is the answer. Damage to the left hemisphere causes an increase in the expression of negative emotion. (p. 463)

a. & d. Reducing the level of physiological arousal and preventing physiological information from reaching the brain both result in a decrease in emotion overall, including negative emotion.

b. According to Schachter, our cognitive appraisal allows us to label an emotion. Therefore, relabeling the situation as positive should lead to a decrease in negative emotion and an increase in positive emotion.

8. *c* is the answer. The processing of information is much easier and more effective if the tone of the information is similar to the tone of our emotional state. (p. 468)

a. Joshua's good mood would assist him in processing information only if he were studying information as pleasant as his mood.

b. Retrieval is state-dependent. In other words, if we are in the same mood during retrieval as we were while we originally learned the material, we will remember much more efficiently. However, the time period of the question is concerned with processing (taking information in), not retrieval.

d. *c* is the answer.

9. *c* is the answer. According to Schachter, if we attribute arousal to a nonemotional cause (for example, caffeine), then the experience of emotion should be reduced. Gloria was not experiencing any emotion. She simply thought she had had too much coffee that morning. (p. 457)

a. Darwin did not propose a theory of how we experience emotion.

b. According to the James-Lange theory, Gloria should have interpreted her physiological arousal as due to an emotion.

d. According to the Cannon-Bard theory, Gloria should have cognitively experienced an emotion when she felt the physiological arousal. This cannot be the answer, since Gloria felt the arousal but no emotion.

10. *a* is the answer. Karl can no longer see his right environment. This means that visual information travels only to the right hemisphere. Since his corpus callosum has been cut, the information cannot travel to the left hemisphere, which is responsible for verbalizing emotion. Therefore, there should be a decrease in the verbalization of emotional expression. (p. 465)

b. Due to the severed corpus callosum, information cannot get to the left hemisphere where it would have been verbalized.

c. Verbal expression will decrease.

d. Positive or negative, there will be a *decrease* in the verbal expression of emotion.

11. *b* is the answer. In humans, facial expressions communicate emotion better than any other part of the body. (p. 461)

a. & *c*. In humans, facial expressions serve to communicate emotion better than body postures or hand gestures.

d. *b* is the answer.

12. *c* is the answer. The right hemisphere is better and faster at recognizing faces than the left hemisphere is. If the right hemisphere is damaged, a decrease in the ability to recognize faces is likely. (p. 465)

a. The right hemisphere expresses negative emotion. When it is damaged, more positive than negative emotion is expressed due to the activity of the still intact left hemisphere.

b. Although the left hemisphere is involved in verbal reports, the right hemisphere is more active in expressing negative emotion.

d. The right hemisphere is better and faster at recognizing faces than the left hemisphere is. If the right hemisphere is damaged, the recognition process might take much longer.

13. *c* is the answer. Social referencing occurs when we look to others for cues about how to behave in ambiguous situations. (p. 466)

a. Facial feedback occurs when the movement of our facial muscles influences our emotions.

b. Schachter's theory addresses the labeling of our own emotions, not other people's.

d. The James-Lange theory addresses the labeling of our own emotions, not other people's.

14. *b* is the answer. Too much or too little arousal causes problems in performance. Trudy will perform best at a moderate level of arousal. (p. 467)

    a. Trudy will perform best with a moderate level of arousal. Too much or too little emotion causes problems in performance.

    c. b is the answer. Trudy will not perform very well.

    d. Only *b* is the answer.

15. *b* is the answer. Memories of events that are particularly emotional are quite vivid. Winning an Olympic medal is certainly more emotional than feeding the cat or getting an *A* on a first-grade homework assignment. (p. 469)

    a. & c. These experiences are not as emotional as winning an Olympic gold medal and so will not be remembered in as much detail.

    d. b is the answer. Highly emotional events are remembered in much greater detail.

Chapter 13

Stiess and Coping

OUTLINE

I. WHAT IS STRESS? (pp. 472–474)

Stress is the process of adjusting to circumstances that disrupt, or threaten to disrupt, a person's equilibrium. Stress always involves a relationship between stressors and stress reactions.

II. STRESSORS (pp. 474–479)

A. Some Major Psychological Stressors

Anything, either positive or negative, that requires adaptation is considered a stressor. Circumstances that involve frustration, pressure, boredom, trauma, conflict, or change are stressors.

B. Measuring Stressors

Small daily hassles should be assessed in conjunction with major stressors when measuring a person's total level of stress.

III. STRESS RESPONSES (pp. 479–494)

A. Physical Stress Responses

1. *The General Adaptation Syndrome (GAS).* There are three stages in the GAS: the alarm reaction, the resistance stage, and the exhaustion stage. Illnesses due to stress are called diseases of adaptation.
2. *Beyond Selye's GAS Model.* The GAS model underemphasizes the role of psychological factors in the effect of stress. How much control a person feels over the stressor (a psychological factor) can change a stressor's effect.

B. Psychological Stress Responses

1. *Emotional Stress Responses.* Common emotional responses include anxiety, anger, and depression. Emotional responses come and go with the onset and termination of a stressor. Prolonged emotional reactions can lead to one of several psychological problems, such as generalized anxiety disorder.
2. *Cognitive Stress Reactions.* An inability to concentrate, think clearly, or remember things accurately are common cognitive reactions to stress. Catastrophizing and defense mechanisms are common cognitive responses to stress.

C. Behavioral Stress Responses

Although moderate amounts of stress-induced arousal improve performance, overarousal usually disrupts behavioral skills and physical coordination. Escape in the form of suicide, drugs, or physical withdrawal from the situation are all behavioral stress responses.

D. Interactions Between People and Stressors

1. *Predictability.* Predictable stressors cause fewer stress responses.

2. *Control.* Stressors have less impact if people can control, or at least think they can control, the stressors' onset, duration, or level of intensity.

3. *How Stressors are Interpreted.* Interpreting stressors as a challenge can reduce the level of stress response. Those with an internal locus of control manage stress better than those with an external locus of control.

4. *Social Support.* A social support network, friends and family who lend support during stress, can greatly reduce the impact of stressors. Too much support, however, can inhibit a person's attempt to cope with stress.

5. *Coping Skills.* Having coping skills, and knowing when and how to use them, can reduce stress responses.

E. Stress and Illness

Physical and psychological stress and stress responses can lead to illness. People who display Type A behavior are at increased risk for coronary heart disease. Hostility, anger, cynicism, and selfishness are especially harmful aspects of the Type A pattern. Being able to predict and control stress, thinking positively about stress, having a social support network, expressing emotions and thoughts, and exercising coping skills can reduce the likelihood of stress-related medical problems.

IV. COPING WITH STRESS (pp. 494–500)

A. A Plan for Coping

Coping with stress can be achieved by identifying the sources of stress and one's stress responses. One may then select a goal of either removing the stressors or changing one's responses to them.

B. Methods of Coping

1. *Cognitive Coping Strategies.* Cognitive restructuring—changing the way a person thinks about stressors—can help make stressors less threatening or disruptive.

2. *Behavioral Coping Strategies.* Changing behaviors as a result of time management or analysis of possible new behaviors can reduce the impact of stressors.

3. *Physiological Coping Strategies.* People often use drugs to change their physiological reaction to stress. However, prolonged drug use can create new stressors. Progressive relaxation training, biofeedback, exercise, and meditation are more adaptive ways to reduce physiological arousal.

C. Some Stress-Coping Programs

1. *Changing Type A Behavior.* Activities such as reviewing the ineffectiveness of Type A behavior, learning methods of anticipating and avoiding stress, and improving cognitive coping reduce the effects of stress.

2. *Facing Illness and Surgery.* Many hospitals inform patients about procedures, explain how they will feel afterward, and teach cognitive coping strategies and relaxation skills.

3. *Dealing with Trauma.* Counselors can provide information and support and can guide trauma victims to counseling sessions. These sessions provide the victim with an opportunity to express feelings and learn cognitive and behavioral strategies for coping with stress.

4. *Coping with Major Changes: Widowhood and Divorce.* Programs that offer social support, coping strategies, and information have helped reduce the impact of divorce or widowhood.

KEY TERMS

1. **Stress** is the process of adjusting to circumstances that disrupt, or threaten to disrupt, a person's equilibrium. (p. 472)

Example: Marcus is five years old. He has just started day care and has been exposed to many childhood diseases. He is under stress because his body must *adjust* to fighting off these diseases. His mother has just received a promotion accompanied by a large raise. Her job responsibilities have doubled. Her stress is that she must *adjust* to doing twice as much at work, while continuing to be a mother.

2. **Stressors** are events and situations to which people must *adjust*. Almost any event or situation that causes change is a stressor. Other common factors that are considered stressors include frustration, boredom, trauma, conflict, and pressure. Small daily hassles are also stressors. (p. 472)

Example: Sharon has just been offered a new job. After she graduates, she will move from a small town to a big city, have new responsibilities, and need to make new friends. Although these events are positive, they will involve big changes and, therefore, will be stressors.

3. **Stress reactions** are the physical, psychological, and behavioral responses people display when stressors appear. (p. 472)

Example: Linda gets a rash (physical reaction) every time she has to study for an important exam. Marsha gets nervous (psychological reaction) in the middle of an exam. If she cannot answer the first few questions immediately, she begins talking to herself, saying, "I am going to flunk this exam, which will make my grade point go down. I will never get into law school. I'll probably have to work at minimum wage for the rest of my life. I'll hate it and probably get fired for my bad attitude. Face it, I am going to be a bag lady." When Jean started her new job, she was under a great deal of pressure. To relax, she started drinking a glass of wine (behavioral reaction) each evening after work. Her drinking has escalated to more than a bottle of wine per night.

4. The **general adaptation syndrome (GAS)** is Hans Selye's name for a series of physical reactions to stress. There are three stages: the alarm reaction, the resistance stage, and the exhaustion stage. (p. 480)

Example: In order to satisfy his intellectual curiosity, Roger is taking a full load of classes, teaching undergraduates, writing a book, and doing research for a professor in his department. At the beginning of the semester, Roger can feel his heart race as he hurries to make an appointment here or there on campus (alarm). During midterm exams, he is in a constant state of arousal but does not really notice it. He is almost used to being so busy all day (resistance). By the end of the semester, he has a constant cold, feels tired, and has high blood pressure (exhaustion). His doctor has told him that he needs to take time to relax over term break. His body must have time to recuperate from trying to adjust to the extraordinary level of stress.

5. The **alarm reaction** is the first stage in the general adaptation syndrome. Physiological reactions, such as the fight-or-flight syndrome, appear as a result of new stressors. (p. 480)

Example: The sudden increase in heart rate and respiration that accompany a person's efforts to avoid a car accident are part of the alarm stage of the GAS.

6. The **resistance stage** is the second stage in the general adaptation syndrome. The outward signs of a stress reaction are no longer apparent, but the body is fighting very hard to adjust to the stressors. The adrenal glands, the thymus, the liver, and the kidneys release several substances that increase

blood pressure, fight inflammation, enhance muscle tension, increase blood sugar, and promote the physical changes needed to cope with stressors. (p. 480)

Example: People in the resistance stage may have severe tension in their back, neck, and other muscles, but they may not be aware of it.

7. The **exhaustion stage** is the third phase of the general adaptation syndrome. The body no longer has the ability to fight or meet the demands of a stressor. A very severe stressor can result in death. (p. 480)

Example: An acute infection or the breakdown of the functioning of the digestive tract or other organs can appear in the exhaustion stage.

8. **Diseases of adaptation** are illnesses promoted or caused by stressors. These can include colds and flu, arthritis, coronary disease, and high blood pressure. (p. 481)

Example: See examples for key terms 4 and 7, general adaptation syndrome and exhaustion stage.

REMEMBER: Diseases of adaptation are due to the body's efforts to *adapt* to stress.

9. **Generalized anxiety disorder** (or free-floating anxiety) is a clinical pattern in which a person is unable to explain his or her constant feelings of tension and anxiety. The disorder may result from constant emotional arousal. (p. 484)

10. **Catastrophizing,** a cognitive reaction to stress, occurs when negative events are dwelt on or over-emphasized. (p. 484)

Example: John is waiting to interview for a job. Any minute now the interviewer will enter the room. John says to himself, "I know I look awful. The 3 pounds I gained on vacation is hanging over the waistband of my pants. I'll probably say something really stupid. I'll never get a job. I'll have to move home and live, in

utter humiliation, with my parents. I'll never get married."

REMEMBER: Catastrophe means a disaster. *Catastrophizing* is creating a mental *disaster* by thinking about the negative side of events or situations.

11. **Defense mechanisms** are psychological responses that help protect a person from anxiety and other negative emotions that accompany stress. (p. 485)

Example: Denial is a defense mechanism in which the person denies that there is anything wrong. Josephine is in deep financial trouble. She delays paying her bills, saying she is too busy to do it. This procrastination allows her to avoid thinking about her lack of funds and the anxiety this would cause. However, defense mechanisms can make a problem worse. By ignoring her financial situation, Josephine will not take steps, such as temporarily taking another job, to remove the stressor.

REMEMBER: Defense mechanisms are *mechanisms* that provide a *defense* against anxiety produced by stressors.

12. A **social support network** is a group of friends or other social contacts who can be relied upon to help during stressful situations. (p. 491)

Example: Betty and Sarah are sisters and best friends. Whenever one of them has a problem, she knows the other one will lend an ear or help in any way she can.

13. **Type A behavior** is characterized by nonstop work, intense feelings of competitiveness, aggressiveness, impatience, a strong need to control one's environment, and an overemphasis on achieving instead of developing satisfying social relationships. (p. 492)

Example: Anthony displays Type A behavior. He is a workaholic, preferring to spend his evenings at the office instead of with his family. He is impatient with his employees and attempts to check all the work that leaves the office. His goal is to own and run the company he works for. Nothing else really matters.

14. **Cognitive restructuring** is a coping strategy. Cognitive stress reactions can often prevent a person from dealing with a stressor. Changing or restructuring thoughts can help either reduce the stress or decrease the stress reaction. (p. 496)

Example: Renada is a perfectionist. Whenever she has to give a presentation at work, she worries about every detail and every word she is going to say. This causes her to feel extremely anxious most of the time. Cognitive restructuring would entail changing her thoughts. Instead of expecting perfection at every presentation she might say to herself, "I am going to do the best that I can, and my best is usually more than satisfactory."

REMEMBER: Cognition means to think. Restructuring means to alter a form. Cognitive restructuring is *altering* the form of *thoughts* in order to remove a stressor or reduce a stress reaction.

15. **Progressive relaxation training,** a physiological method for dealing with stress, involves training a person to relax the muscles in the body that are under voluntary control, which leads to reductions in heart rate and blood pressure and creates mental and emotional calmness. (p. 498)

LEARNING OBJECTIVES

1. Define stress, stressors, and stress reactions. Explain why stress is defined as a process instead of a thing. (pp. 472–474)

2. Define frustration and describe it as a stressor. Give an example of frustration. (p. 476)

3. Define pressure. Give an example using pressure as a stressor. (p. 476)

4. Define boredom. Give an example using boredom as a stressor. (p. 476)

5. Define trauma. Give an example using trauma as a stressor. (p. 476)

6. Define conflict. Give an example using conflict as a stressor. (p. 476)

7. Define change. Explain why positive change can be a stressor. Give an example using change as a stressor. (pp. 476–477)

8. Discuss the importance of daily hassles in stress measurement. (pp. 478–479)

9. Define Selye's general adaptation syndrome. Name and describe the three stages in this syndrome. Discuss the major criticisms of Selye's model. (pp. 480–482)

10. Name and describe some common emotional stress reactions. Discuss the psychological consequences of prolonged emotional stress reactions. (pp. 483–484)

11. Define catastrophizing and defense mechanisms. Give an example of each as a stress reaction. (pp. 484–485)

12. Describe some categories of behavioral stress responses. Give an example of at least one of them. (pp. 485–487)

13. Explain why predictable stressors, a feeling of control, the interpretation of stressors, and social support networks can reduce the impact of stressors. (pp. 488–491)

14. Discuss the role of coping skills in combating stress. (p. 491)

15. Describe the relationship between stress and illness. Define Type A behavior. (pp. 492–493)

16. Describe the steps involved in assessing stress. Discuss the importance of setting goals when taking steps to reduce stress and stress reactions. (pp. 494–495)

17. Describe the cognitive coping methods listed in the text. Give an example of each. Define cognitive restructuring. (pp. 495–496)

18. Describe the behavioral coping methods listed in the text. Give an example of at least one method. (pp. 496–497)

19. Describe the possible problems of using drugs to alter stress or stress reactions. Define progressive relaxation training. Discuss the use of biofeedback in reducing stress and stress reactions. (pp. 497–498)

20. Describe some of the programs discussed in your text that attempt to help people reduce stress in various situations. (pp. 498–500)

CONCEPTS AND EXERCISES

No. 1 Recognizing Stressors

Completing this exercise should help you to achieve the following learning objectives.

(1) *Define stress, stressors, and stress reactions. Explain why stress is defined as a process instead of a thing. (pp. 472–474)*

(2) *Define frustration and describe it as a stressor. Give an example of frustration. (p. 476)*

(3) *Define pressure. Give an example of pressure as a stressor. (p. 476)*

(4) *Define boredom. Give an example of boredom as a stressor. (p. 476)*

(5) *Define trauma. Give an example of trauma as a stressor. (p. 476)*

(6) *Define conflict. Give an example of conflict as a stressor. (p. 476)*

(7) *Define change. Explain why positive change can be a stressor. Give an example of change as a stressor. (pp. 476–477)*

(8) *Discuss the importance of daily hassles in stress measurement. (pp. 478–479)*

Following are several descriptions of people's daily lives. Underline all the stressors that you can find.

1. Michelle and Ned have been married for ten years and have two children. This morning Michelle got a run in her nylons just as she was on the way out the door to take the children to school. She was going to go up and change but remembered that she had to come back to the house anyway to pick up the dog for his veterinary appointment. When she did get back home she started cleaning the house only to find that the vacuum was broken. Sighing, she decided to scrub the bathrooms instead. By the time Ned came home, she had a headache from the children screaming, the dog whimpering, having to face dirty floors yet again, and struggling with dinner for the family.

2. Sam is trying to finish writing a block grant for National Institute of Mental Health funding. The deadline for submitting the grant is in one week. He also must face a new crisis of some sort daily at work. His wife is starting to complain that he never spends time with her. Recently, he has started to have dizzy spells and can feel his heart pound.

3. Jenny is five years old. Today is the first day of first grade. Jenny is horrified because she has to sit next to the neighborhood bully. He is always ramming his tricycle into hers or grabbing her swing on the playground and pushing it too high into the air. She is spending the entire day imagining what he will do now that he sits next to her in class.

4. Jerry has just met his new roommate and cannot believe his bad luck. His roommate has told him that he goes to bed at 8:00 P.M., wants to study in the room every night until 7:45 P.M. and must have total silence, and has a bunch of great posters of Bambi to hang on the walls. Jerry wants to do well in school; he was first in his high school class and wants to keep his ranking in college. But he also is worried about his social life. He decides that instead of getting upset over his weird roommate, he will go to a bar and get drunk with some friends.

No. 2 Recognizing Stress Reactions

Completing this exercise should help you to achieve the following learning objectives.

(9) *Define Selye's general adaptation syndrome. Name and describe the three stages in this syndrome. Discuss the major criticisms of Selye's model. (pp. 480–482)*

(10) *Name and describe some common emotional stress reactions. Discuss the psychological consequences of prolonged emotional stress reactions. (pp. 483–484)*

(11) *Define catastrophizing and defense mechanisms. Give an example of each as a stress reaction. (pp. 484–485)*

(12) *Describe some categories of behavioral stress responses. Give an example of at least one of them. (pp. 485–487)*

Following are several descriptions of stress reactions. Choose the name of the reaction from the list.

burnout

behavioral stress reaction

intellectualization

catastrophizing

resistance stage of GAS

1. Sam's doctor has told him that he has an elevated level of corticosteroids. _____

2. Rose's mother tells her that she constantly makes a mountain out of a molehill. _____

3. Paula has decided to quit her job in the advertising business before she gets fired. She tells her colleagues that advertisers spend billions of dollars each year that do not contribute to the well-being of mankind. _____

4. Lois, recently divorced, has been working three jobs for the past year to support her children. She is tired, irritable, and depressed. Her bosses are concerned because the quality of her work has gradually decreased. _____

5. Nancy knows that her husband is drinking too much. His behavior bothers her so much that she has begun taking Valium daily. _____

ANSWERS TO CONCEPTS AND EXERCISES

No. 1 Recognizing Stressors

1. got a run in her nylons
   dog for his vet appointment
   the children screaming
   dog whimpering
   dirty floors
   struggling with dinner

2. deadline
   new crisis
   wife starting to complain

3. first day of first grade
   sit next to the neighborhood bully
   ramming his tricycle into hers
   grabbing her swing on the playground
   pushing it too high into the air
   imagining what he will do

4. new roommate
   he goes to bed at 8 PM
   wants to study in the room every night until 7:45 PM and
   must have total silence
   has a bunch of great posters of Bambi to hang on the walls
   wants to keep his ranking in college
   worried about his social life

No. 2 Recognizing Stress Reactions

1. Resistance stage
2. Catastrophizing
3. Intellectualization

4. Burnout

5. Behavioral stress reaction

MULTIPLE CHOICE QUESTIONS

Facts and Definitions

1. Stress reactions are
   a. physical.
   b. psychological.
   c. behavioral.
   d. All of the above.

2. Reactions to stress, such as the fight-or-flight syndrome, are part of the _____ of the GAS.
   a. resistance stage
   b. alarm reaction
   c. exhaustive stage
   d. adaptation stage

3. Which of the following could alter the impact of a stressor?
   a. The interpretation of stressors
   b. A person's social support network
   c. The perceived ability to control stressors
   d. All of the above.

4. Which of the following is true of stress measurement?
   a. Stressors always involve major life events.
   b. Major stressors have a greater impact than minor stressors.
   c. Sometimes consistent daily hassles cause severe stress reactions.
   d. None of the above.

5. Which of the following has been said of Selye's model?
   a. It underemphasizes the biological processes involved in stress responses.
   b. It adequately explains the contribution of psychological factors in reactions to stress.
   c. It overemphasizes the contribution of psychological factors in the determination of stress responses.
   d. It overemphasizes the biological processes involved in stress responses.

6. _____ is the field that examines the interaction of psychological and physiological processes that affect the body's ability to defend itself against disease.
   a. Neurology
   b. Psychobiology
   c. Immunology
   d. Psychoneuroimmunology

7. Cortisol, which is released from the adrenal cortex,
   a. destroys the T-cells in the immune system.
   b. increases the activity of the B-cells.
   c. decreases the responsiveness of the immune system.
   d. increases the activity of natural killer cells.

8. Generalized anxiety disorder occurs
   a. in the alarm reaction of the GAS.
   b. after prolonged emotional stress reactions.
   c. in response to identifiable stressors.
   d. when the activity of the immune system is very efficient.

9. Which of the following is a defense mechanism?
   a. Burnout
   b. Post-traumatic stress disorder
   c. Denial
   d. Catastrophizing

10. Suicide is
   a. an emotional reaction to stress.
   b. a behavioral reaction to stress.
   c. a cognitive reaction to stress.
   d. a physiological reaction to stress.

11. Psychosomatic disorders

    a. are brought on by psychological factors.

    b. are associated with increases in autonomic activity.

    c. include stomach ulcers, arthritis, and dermatitis.

    d. All of the above.

12. Type A behavior is characterized by

    a. patience.

    b. low levels of aggression.

    c. a high interest in achievement.

    d. very few emotional stress reactions.

13. A good stress-management program includes

    a. systematic stress assessment.

    b. goal-setting.

    c. effective plans for coping with stressors.

    d. All of the above.

14. Cognitive restructuring is

    a. an emotional reaction to stress.

    b. an attempt to change stress-producing thought patterns.

    c. a plan to restructure the use of one's time.

    d. a process of systematic relaxation.

15. Progressive relaxation training is a _____ coping method.

    a. cognitive

    b. behavioral

    c. physiological

    d. chemical

MULTIPLE CHOICE QUESTIONS

Application of Concepts

1. Which of the following would not be considered a stressor?

    a. Taking a three-week vacation

    b. Planning a wedding reception for 500 guests

    c. Being able to hear the neighbor's baby cry

    d. All of the above are stressors.

2. Which of the following would cause the least stress?

    a. Pop quizzes, scheduled by the teacher

    b. Quizzes scheduled by the students' unanimous vote

    c. Quizzes given every Friday

    d. One quiz per month at an unannounced time

3. Mr. Sepor is the head of personnel at his company. He knows that the employees have very stressful jobs. One Friday each month he invites several employees who do not know each other to go to a local bar together from lunch time until after dinner. Mr. Sepor has

    a. engaged his employees in cognitive restructuring.

    b. set up a social support network for his employees.

    c. provided his employees with a sense of control over their stress.

    d. None of the above.

4. Edward is learning a coping technique. His instructor has told him to alternate between tensing and relaxing his muscles. Which method is he learning?

    a. Biofeedback training

    b. A behavioral coping method

    c. Progressive relaxation training

    d. None of the above.

5. Sergeant Bustin has told his soldiers that stress will do them all a little good; it will even make them healthier. Why is he incorrect?

    a. Stress causes a decrease in the release of cortisol.

    b. The secretion of adrenaline is reduced when under stress.

    c. Stress causes an increase in cortisol release.

    d. Stress causes the immune system to function more efficiently.

6. Karen has just broken her mother's favorite vase. She says to herself, "Boy, is Mom going to be angry. She'll ground me for a month! I'll never get to meet that cute new guy at school, which means I won't get a date for the prom. People who don't go to the prom aren't cool—no guy is going to ask me out again. I'll never get married—I'll die an old maid." This is an example of

    a. cognitive restructuring.
    b. catastrophizing.
    c. trauma.
    d. None of the above.

7. Glenda feels like she has had a rotten day. She got a run in her stocking before she left the house, slammed her finger in the car door, forgot to buy cat litter at the grocery store, and just missed a phone call from her boyfriend. Based on this information, what would be her score on the Social Readjustment Rating Scale?

    a. low
    b. moderate
    c. high
    d. extremely high

8. Aaron is lost in New York City with no money at 2:00 A.M. His sympathetic nervous system has initiated the fight-or-flight syndrome. What stage of the General Adaptation Syndrome (GAS) is he in?

    a. Alarm
    b. Resistance
    c. Exhaustion
    d. The fight-or-flight syndrome is not part of the GAS.

9. An intelligent alien has been keeping a human well cared for but captive on another planet. The human is alone and has nothing to do. This is an illustration of what kind of situation commonly associated with stress?

    a. Trauma
    b. Boredom
    c. Pressure
    d. Conflict

10. Andy has decided to switch careers. He used to be a lawyer but has decided to become an actor. Andy cannot wait to begin his new career. This is an illustration of what kind of situation commonly associated with stress?

    a. Change
    b. Trauma
    c. Boredom
    d. Pressure

11. The strain of living in different cities made Bill and Kim's relationship slowly deteriorate. Bill finally broke their engagement. Kim will not accept the fact that they are no longer a couple. She still calls Bill, sends him letters, and is even looking for a condo for them to move into when he can move to her city. Kim is using which defense mechanism?

    a. Repression
    b. Denial
    c. Displacement
    d. Projection

12. Shane, a veteran, occasionally has flashbacks that are recollections of his experiences in Vietnam. This is a symptom of (the)

    a. generalized anxiety disorder.
    b. post-traumatic stress disorder.
    c. General Adaptation Syndrome.
    d. fight-or-flight syndrome

13. Which of the following people probably has an internal locus of control?

    a. Peter thinks he is going to get rich by playing the lottery.
    b. Mary thinks that studying will result in good grades.
    c. Sally thinks she will get good grades if her professor likes her.
    d. Allen thinks it is not important to vote in elections.

14. Melissa and Randy both have mountains of work on their desks. Melissa rolls up her sleeves in eager anticipation. She knows this project will earn

her a promotion. Randy cringes every time he walks into his office and surveys the mess. He can only think of how long it is going to take him to finish. Which of them will experience the most stress?

    a. Melissa, because she is worried about getting promoted.

    b. Randy, because he interprets the work as a stressor.

    c. Melissa, because women are more prone to stress than men.

    d. Randy and Melissa will both experience an equally large amount of stress.

15.   Stephen is taking sedatives in order to reduce his stress reactions. His family is trying to convince him to use another coping method. What might their reason be?

    a. Chemical coping methods only provide temporary relief from stress.

    b. Chemical coping methods can lead to addiction.

    c. Chemical coping methods will not help Stephen to feel that he has control over the stressors in his life.

    d. All of the above.

ANSWERS TO MULTIPLE CHOICE QUESTIONS

Facts and Definitions

1. *d* is the answer. Stress responses can be physical (illness), psychological (generalized anxiety disorder), and behavioral (reduced efficiency at work). (p. 472)

2. *b* is the answer. The fight-or-flight syndrome occurs during the first stage of the General Adaptation Syndrome (the alarm reaction). (p. 480)

    a. Resistance is the second stage of the General Adaptation Syndrome.

    c. Exhaustion is the third stage of the General Adaptation Syndrome.

    d. There is no such thing as the adaptation stage.

3. *d* is the answer. Interpretation of stressors, existence of a social support network, and perceived ability to control stressors can alter the impact of a stressor. (pp. 488–491)

4. *c* is the answer. Minor daily hassles can have a larger impact than one or two major stressors. (p. 478)

    a. Major life events, either positive or negative, are stressful, but small daily hassles are also stressful.

    b. Sometimes the cumulative effect of small but consistent stressors is larger than the effect of one or two major stressors.

    d. c is the answer.

5. *d* is the answer. Selye's model was criticized because it overemphasized the role of biological processes in determining a stress response. Selye did not emphasize the role of psychological factors in his model. (p. 481)

    a. Selye *overemphasized* the role of biological factors in the determination of stress responses.

    b. & c. Selye did not focus on the role of psychological factors in the determination of stress responses.

6. *d* is the answer. Psychoneuroimmunology is the study of the interaction of psychological and physiological processes that affect the body's ability to defend itself against disease. (p. 483)

    a. Neurology is the study of the nervous system.

    b. Psychobiology is the study of the biological factors that underlie mental processes and behavior.

    c. Immunology is the study of the physiological processes that affect the body's ability to defend itself against disease.

7. *c* is the answer. Cortisol, released from the adrenal cortex during stress, reduces the efficiency of the immune system. (p. 482)

a. Cortisol does not destroy T-cells.

b. & d. T-cells and natural killer cells are part of the body's immune system. Cortisol *reduces* the efficiency of the immune system.

8. *b* is the answer. When people are emotionally aroused for a long period of time, they may no longer be able to identify the stressor. This can cause generalized anxiety. (p. 484)

a. A generalized anxiety disorder occurs when emotional arousal has been prolonged. When arousal is prolonged, the resistance or exhaustion stages are present. The alarm reaction is the first stage of the General Adaptation Syndrome.

c. Anxiety is generalized when there is no specific identifiable source.

d. If the immune system is operating efficiently, the level of stress experienced should be relatively low. Increased stress reduces the efficiency of the immune system.

9. *c* is the answer. Defense mechanisms are psychological responses that help protect a person from anxiety and the other negative emotions accompanying stress. Denial is the refusal to admit that a stressor exists. (p. 485)

a. Burnout is a gradually intensifying pattern of physical, psychological, and behavioral dysfunctions in response to a continuous flow of stressors.

b. Post-traumatic stress disorder is a pattern of adverse and disruptive reactions following a traumatic event.

d. Overemphasizing the consequences of a negative event is catastrophizing, a cognitive stress reaction.

10. *b* is the answer. Suicide is a dramatic escape from stress, a behavioral reaction. (p. 486)

a. Emotional reactions to stress may include anger, frustration, and depression.

c. Cognitive reactions to stress may include catastrophizing and using defense mechanisms.

d. Physiological reactions to stress include illness due to reduced efficiency of the immunological system.

11. *d* is the answer. Psychosomatic disorders are brought on by psychological factors, such as frustration and conflict. They are associated with increases in autonomic activity and include arthritis, ulcers, and dermatitis. (p. 492)

12. *c* is the answer. People who exhibit Type A behavior arc highly competitive and very concerned with their achievements, often to the exclusion of personal relationships. (p. 492)

a. & b. Type A behavior is characterized by impatience and aggression.

d. People who exhibit Type A behavior usually experience relatively constant emotional stress responses.

13. *d* is the answer. An effective stress-management program includes a systematic stress assessment. You have to know what the problem is before you can solve it. Setting goals helps you decide whether to eliminate the stressor or attempt to reduce the impact of that stressor. Finally, an effective plan must be made in order to deal with the stressors you face. (p. 495)

14. *b* is the answer. Cognitive restructuring involves substituting constructive thought for stressful, destructive thoughts. (p. 496)

a. Emotional stress reactions include frustration, anger, and depression.

c. Time management is important in reducing the stress caused by a tight schedule. However, this coping method is behavioral, not cognitive.

d. Progressive relaxation is the physiological coping method in which people are taught to completely relax their bodies.

15. *c* is the answer. Progressive relaxation is a technique used to relax the muscles, leading to reduced heart rate and blood pressure. (p. 498)

a. Cognitive coping methods include cognitive restructuring.

b. Behavioral coping methods include time management improvements.

d. Chemical coping methods include taking sedatives.

ANSWERS TO MULTIPLE CHOICE QUESTIONS

Application of Concepts

1. *d* is the answer. Positive life events (marriage), any type of change (vacation), and consistent daily hassles (listening to a baby cry) are all stressors. (pp. 474–477)

2. *b* is the answer. When one can predict and control the presence of a stressor, the impact of that stressor is usually reduced. To students, being able to control and predict the occurrence of a quiz is much less stressful than any of the other alternatives. (pp. 488–489)

a. Pop quizzes are not predictable, and are therefore more stressful.

c. Even though quizzes given every Friday are predictable, the students have no control over their scheduling.

d. One unannounced quiz per month is neither predictable nor controllable.

3. *b* is the answer. By arranging for employees to get together and socialize, Mr. Sepor has created the potential for a social support network at work. (p. 491)

a. Cognitive restructuring involves substituting constructive thoughts for negative, debilitating thoughts.

c. Mr. Sepor has not been able to give his employees a sense of control over the stressful events at work. But he has provided his employees with the beginnings of a social support network.

d. *b* is the answer.

4. *c* is the answer. Progressive relaxation training is a physiological coping method in which people learn to completely relax their muscles, thus reducing heart rate and blood pressure. To learn this technique, people are told to alternately tense and relax their muscles in order to better recognize the feelings of relaxation. (p. 498)

a. Biofeedback training is also a physiological coping method. People are hooked up to machines that tell them about the physiological changes occurring in their bodies. Many people, once they recognize these changes, can learn to control them.

b. Behavioral coping methods might involve taking a time management course. Progressive relaxation training is a physiological coping method.

d. *c* is the answer.

5. *c* is the answer. Stress increases the amount of cortisol released from the adrenal cortex, thus reducing the efficiency of the immune system. (p. 482)

a. Stress *increases* the release of cortisol from the adrenal cortex.

b. The secretion of adrenaline increases under stress.

d. Stress can reduce the efficiency of the immune system.

6. *b* is the answer. Catastrophizing is an overemphasis of the negative consequences of an event. Although Karen has only broken a vase, she has inflated the negative consequences of that event until she thinks she will never get married. (p. 484)

a. Cognitive restructuring is a cognitive coping method. Positive, constructive thoughts are substituted for negative, destructive thoughts.

c. Trauma is a major and shocking physical or emotional experience. Breaking a vase is not.

d. *b* is the answer.

7. *a* is the answer. Glenda's day has been filled with small daily hassles. The Social Readjustment Rating Scale (SRRS) measures the stress due to *major* life events. Glenda's rating would be low. But remember that small daily hassles can be just as stressful in some cases as major life events. (pp. 476–477)

b., c., & d. The SRRS measures stress due to major life events. Glenda has not experienced a major life event, so she has a low score. However, she still has experienced stress.

8. *a* is the answer. The fight-or-flight syndrome is associated with the alarm reaction of the General Adaptation Syndrome. (p. 480)

b. & c. The resistance and exhaustion stages are the second and third stages of the General Adaptation Syndrome. They are not associated with the fight-or-flight syndrome.

d. The fight-or-flight syndrome is part of the alarm reaction of the General Adaptation Syndrome.

9. *b* is the answer. The human will be bored living on a planet with nothing to do, having every need catered to on a daily basis. Boredom or understimulation can be a stressor. (p. 476)

a. Trauma is a major, shocking physical or emotional event. Being totally cared for and having no challenges to face or overcome is not traumatic.

c. Pressurized situations are those which require a person to do too much in too little time.

d. Conflict involves disputes or disagreements. Being without a challenge is boring but does not involve conflict.

10. *a* is the answer. A career switch is a major life event filled with change. Even though he is happy, Andy will have to adjust to his new lifestyle. Changes require adjustment, which is stressful. (pp. 476–477)

b. Trauma is a major and shocking physical or emotional event.

c. Andy certainly will not be bored or understimulated as he changes careers.

d. Pressurized situations are those which require a person to do too much in too little time. Andy is not on a tight schedule.

11. *b* is the answer. By refusing to readjust her behavior and life plans, Kim is denying the break-up with Bill. (p. 485)

a. Repression is the exclusion of harmful or anxiety-producing thoughts from consciousness. See Table 3 in the text for an example.

c. Displacement is displaying emotions toward objects or people that have not caused them.

d. Projection is blaming others for one's own troubles or seeing one's own anxiety-producing thoughts or actions in others.

12. *b* is the answer. Post-traumatic stress disorder is a pattern of adverse and disruptive reactions following a traumatic event. In rare cases, flashbacks occur. (p. 487)

a. Generalized anxiety disorder occurs when a person experiences constant emotional arousal with no identifiable cause.

c. The General Adaptation Syndrome is a series of three stages of physiological adaptation to stress.

d. The fight-or-flight syndrome is caused by an increase in adrenaline in response to a stressor. It prepares the body to either fight or flee.

13. *b* is the answer. People with an internal locus of control think they can control what happens to them. Mary thinks that the quality of her grades depends on her own behavior, not luck or other external factors. (p. 490)

a. Peter thinks that he will get rich by playing the lottery. Peter has no control over whether or not he wins. He believes in luck.

c. Sally thinks good grades are not a result of her behavior but rather the result of her professor's whims. She does not have an internal locus of control.

d. People who do not vote in elections may not feel that their single vote can have any effect on (control) the outcome of the election. Allen does not have an internal locus of control.

14. *b* is the answer. The way that people interpret their stress affects the impact of their stressors. Randy is interpreting his work as a stressor instead of as an opportunity. Melissa, on the other hand, thinks of her work as a vehicle for furthering her career. (p. 489)

    a. Melissa sees her work load in a positive way, so she will not experience as much stress.

    c. Women are no more prone to stress than men are.

    d. Randy will experience more stress than Melissa.

15. *d* is the answer. Chemical methods of coping provide only temporary relief from stressors; they can be addictive; and they do not provide a sense of control over stressors. People attribute their enhanced sense of well-being to the drug instead of to their behavior. (p. 497)

Chapter 14

Personality

OUTLINE

I. INTRODUCTION (p. 504)

Personality is the pattern of psychological and behavioral characteristics that makes each of us an identifiable and unique individual.

II. STUDYING PERSONALITY (pp. 504–510)

A. Methods of Assessing Personality

All of the methods typically used to measure or assess personality use some combination of three basic tools: observation, interviews, and tests.

1. *Objective Tests*. The typical objective test is a paper and pencil test containing clear, specific questions, statements, or concepts to which a person is asked to give yes-no, true-false, or multiple choice answers. Scores are objective and can be compared mathematically.

2. *Projective Tests*. Tests consisting of unstructured stimuli, which can be perceived and responded to in many ways, are called projective tests. Responses to projective tests reflect many aspects of an individual's personality. These tests are relatively difficult to score and tend to have low validity.

3. *Using Personality Tests*. All tests of personality should be reliable and valid. A qualified person should explain the test's results to the individual who is being assessed.

B. Systematic Approaches to Personality

All approaches to personality contain certain basic components.

1. A set of basic assumptions that forms a personality theory.

2. Theory-guided decisions about where to look for evidence about personality.

3. Ways of measuring or assessing personality.

4. A set of special research methods designed to evaluate the personality theory.

III. THE PSYCHODYNAMIC APPROACH (pp. 510–518)

The psychodynamic approach, developed by Freud, emphasizes the interplay of unconscious mental processes in determining human thought, feelings, and behavior. The basis of this approach is psychic determinism, the idea that psychological factors play a major role in determining behavior and shaping personality. Psychoanalysis, which uses methods such as frce association and dream analysis, was designed to uncover the content of the unconscious.

A. The Structure of Personality

Personality is made of three structures: the id, ego, and superego. The id, which operates according to the pleasure principle, contains the libido or psychic energy. The ego, which evolves from the id and operates according to the reality principle, attempts to satisfy id impulses, while obeying society's rules.

As we internalize, or introject, society's rules, the superego forms to house the conscience and ego ideal.

B. Ego Defense Mechanisms

We use defense mechanisms to protect us from feeling guilt or anxiety about id impulses. Repression, projection, reaction formation, displacement, intellectualization, rationalization, denial, and sublimation are all defense mechanisms.

C. Stages in Personality Development

Freud believed that personality developed in psychosexual stages. Failure to resolve conflicts at any stage can cause fixation.

1. *The Oral Stage.* The first year or so of life is called the oral stage because the mouth is the center of pleasure then. Conflict arises if weaning takes place too early or too late.

2. *The Anal Stage.* Because the anus becomes the center of physical pleasure during the second year of life, Freud called this the anal stage. Conflict arises as children are toilet trained and must refrain from having bowel movements whenever they wish.

3. *The Phallic Stage.* The genitals are the center of pleasure from ages three to five, and Freud called this period the phallic stage. According to Freud's theory of the Oedipus complex, a boy's id impulses involve sexual desire for the mother and a wish to eliminate, or even kill, the father. Eventually, the boy becomes fearful of retaliation (castration anxiety). This fear becomes so strong that the ego represses the incestual impulses and the boy identifies with the father. After discovering that she does not have a penis, a girl begins to hate the mother and transfers her love to the father who has the sex organs she wants. To avoid the mother's disapproval she identifies with the mother.

4. *The Latency Period and the Genital Stage.* During the latency period, sexual impulses lie dormant and children focus on education. During adolescence, the genitals again become the focus of pleasure and the genital stage begins.

D. Variations on Freudian Personality Theories

1. *Carl Jung's Analytic Psychology.* Jung believed that people tend to resolve conflicts by blending real-world demands and basic drives, and called this growth-oriented tendency the transcendent function. Every person has a personal unconscious and a collective unconscious, a memory bank of the human race that contains images called archetypes. Personality is developed as people tend toward introversion or extraversion and toward reliance on specific psychological functions.

2. *Alfred Adler's Individual Psychology.* According to Adler, people strive for superiority in order to become fulfilled as persons (not to be better than others). The manner in which each person attempts to reach personal and social fulfillment, which Adler calls style of life, constitutes personality.

3. *Ego Psychology and the Neo-Freudians.* Some ego psychologists view the ego as a creative force and think that our attempts to meet social needs shape personality. Object relations theorists focus on the early relationships between infants and their primary caregivers.

E. Some Practical Applications

The psychodynamic approach led to the creation of psychoanalytic psychotherapy and psychodiagnosis through the use of interviews and projective tests. This approach has stimulated research on how the mind can influence health and has generated tips on child care.

F. Criticisms of the Psychodynamic Approach

Freud's theory is criticized for being sexist, and Freud himself is thought by some to have explained his patients' reports of sexual abuse as fantasies and wish fulfillment. His theory was based on his own patients, an unrepresentative sample, and the psychodynamic concepts of the id, ego, unconscious, and the like, which are difficult to measure scientifically.

IV. THE DISPOSITIONAL APPROACH
(pp. 519–526)

The dispositional approach has three basic assumptions:

1. Each person has stable, long-lasting dispositions to display certain behaviors, attitudes, and emotions.

2. These dispositions are general, in that they appear in diverse situations.

3. Each person has a different set or pattern of dispositions.

A. Personality Types

Physiognomy is the study of the relationship between body type and personality. Research has not shown the body-type approach to be a valid predictor of personality.

B. Personality Traits

Personality can be seen as the combination of varying strengths of many traits.

1. *Allport's Trait Theory*. Allport believed that there are usually about seven basic or central traits. Secondary traits are more specific to certain situations and control less behavior. In those people who have them, cardinal traits are so strong that that they govern everything the person does.

2. *The Factor-Analytic Methods of Eysenck*. Eysenck identified three basic personality factors: introversion-extraversion, psychoticism, and emotionality-stability. Eysenck proposed that the ease with which the nervous system can be aroused relates to positions on these personality dimensions.

C. Personality as Reflecting Needs

Henry A. Murray said that personality develops as people attempt to meet needs while adjusting to their life circumstances. He also believed that some of our personality traits are unconscious and can only be measured by projective tests.

D. Some Practical Applications

Assessment based on the dispositional approach has been used to diagnose mental disorders. The dispositional approach has also been used to predict job performance and to guide jury selection.

E. Criticisms of the Dispositional Approach

Dispositional theories are better at describing behavior than at explaining behavior. Secondly, dispositional theories do not create a unique description of every individual. Personality tests based on the dispositional theories often have low reliability and low validity.

V. THE BEHAVIORAL APPROACH (pp. 527–531)

The behavioral approach equates personality with behavior. Behavior, which is situation specific, is a result of learning, especially from interactions with other people. Personality is measured by observing behavior.

A. B. F. Skinner and the Functional Analysis of Behavior

Skinner employed the functional analysis of behavior to determine the relationship between behavior and the situation in which it occurs.

B. Cognitive-Behavioral Theories

Cognition, or thinking (the internal environment), has a significant effect on behavior.

1. *Rotter's Expectancy Theory*. Rotter suggested that behavior is determined by 1) what the person expects to happen following behavior and 2) the value the person places on the outcome. He developed a test that measures the degree to which people expect events to be controlled by their own internal efforts or by external forces over which they have no influence.

2. *Albert Bandura and Observational Learning*. Through observational learning people can 1) learn new behaviors, 2) learn to inhibit responses, 3) learn to disinhibit responses (doing something not previously attempted after seeing someone successfully do it), and 4) learn to facilitate or prompt responses that might not otherwise have occurred. Bandura focuses on reciprocal determinism and emphasizes the role of learned expectations for success, called self-efficacy.

3. *Mischel's Person-Situation Theory*. According to Mischel, person variables, as well as situation variables, are important in explaining behavior. The most important person variables are 1) competencies, 2) perceptions, 3) expectations, 4) subjective values, and 5) self-regulation and plans.

4. *Behavioral Personality Assessment*. Data on personality can be gathered in interviews and role-play situations, through self-monitoring, and by written tests.

C. Some Practical Applications

The prediction of behavior is based on past behavior and situational factors. Behavioral theorists have been successful at teaching people how to alter their personalities and at developing effective child-rearing practices.

D. Criticisms of the Behavioral Approach

As in other approaches, behavioral assessment procedures, such as interviews, may be biased or distorted. Also, it is very difficult to measure cognitive variables. Finally, some people think the narrow focus on behavior and the environment ignores the individual.

VI. THE PHENOMENOLOGICAL APPROACH (pp. 531–537)

Phenomenological or humanistic approaches define personality as the unique way each individual perceives and interprets the world. The primary human motivator is an innate drive toward growth that prompts people to fulfill their unique and natural potential.

A. The Personal Construct Theory of George Kelly

According to Kelly, each person has a set of expectations about reality called personal constructs. The nature of each person's unique set of constructs determines personality and guides behavior. When people cannot accurately anticipate the world, the result is discomfort or anxiety.

B. The Self Theory of Carl Rogers

Rogers emphasized the concept of self-actualization; people, if unhampered by experiences, will fully realize their potential.

1. *The Concept of Self*. The *self* is what people come to identify as *I* or *me*. According to Rogers, the development of self-concept

depends on self-evaluations and the positive regard shown by others. Incongruities between self-evaluations and others' evaluations cause anxiety and other problems. The self-actualizing tendency and others' evaluations shape personality.

2. *Conditions of Worth*. Whenever people, instead of their behaviors, are evaluated, conditions of worth are created. People come to believe they are worthy only under certain conditions; those in which rewarded behaviors are displayed.

3. *Methods of Assessment*. Rogers used unstructured interviews and a method called the Q-sort to measure personality.

C. Maslow's Humanistic Psychology

Maslow saw personality as the expression of the tendency toward growth and self-actualization. He thought that personality reflects perceptual orientation and the level of needs on which people focus their attention and energy. People can approach satisfying needs with a deficiency orientation or a growth orientation.

D. Some Practical Applications

The phenomenological approach has been instrumental in the development of many types of psychotherapy, short-term group experiences (such as encounter groups), child-rearing practices, and educational techniques.

E. Criticisms of the Phenomenological Approach

The belief that all humans are driven by a positive and innate growth potential may be naive and unrealistic. Most phenomenological assessment methods are better at describing behavior than explaining it, and their reliability and validity have been questioned. Finally, many phenomenological concepts are difficult to scientifically measure and define.

KEY TERMS

1. **Personality** is the blend of inherited and acquired tendencies that produces the patterns of psychological and behavioral characteristics that make each individual unique. (p. 504)

REMEMBER: Those who study *person*ality are interested in what makes each *person* unique.

2. An **objective test**, one type of personality test, is a paper-and-pencil test containing clear, specific questions, statements, or concepts that can be responded to with true-false, yes-no, or multiple-choice answers. (p. 508)

Example: The multiple-choice tests that you take in your classes are called objective tests because they can be graded objectively. Your score on a test can be compared mathematically with other students' scores.

REMEMBER: Objective tests are scored *objectively*, and one person's results can be compared mathematically with another's. Objective means that your results reflect your personality and not the scorer's bias.

3. **Projective tests** are composed of unstructured stimuli that can be perceived and responded to in many ways. People who use these kinds of tests assume that responses will reflect aspects of a person's personality. It is relatively difficult to transform these tests' responses into numerical scores. (p. 508)

Example: The Thematic Apperception Test is a projective test that involves showing people pictures and asking them to tell a story about each picture.

4. The **psychodynamic approach** to personality, developed by Freud, emphasizes the role of unconscious mental processes in determining thoughts, feelings, and behavior. (p. 510)

REMEMBER: Freud introduced the idea that psychological activity plays a major role in behavior, mental processes, and personality. *Psych* refers to mental and *dynamic* pertains to energy, motion, and forcefulness. Psychological factors have energy and play a forceful role in the determination of personality, behavior, and mental processes.

5. **Free association**, a Freudian psychoanalytic technique, involves asking people to say whatever comes to mind. Freud believed that the pattern of associations can reveal thoughts, feelings, and impulses that are normally unconscious. (pp. 510–511)

6. **Psychoanalysis** is the name for Freud's theory and psychotherapy techniques, which include free association and dream analysis. (p. 511)

> *REMEMBER:* Freud thought psychological factors played a major role in the development of personality. He used *psychoanalysis* to *analyze* the *psychological* factors in a person's personality.

7. The **id,** one of the structures of personality, contains the basic instincts, desires, and impulses with which people are born and operates on the pleasure principle. Eros is the instinct for pleasure and sex, and Thanatos is a death instinct, which can motivate aggressive and destructive behavior. The id seeks immediate gratification, regardless of society's rules or the rights and feelings of others. (p. 511)

> *Example:* See key term 10, ego.

8. **Libido** is unconscious psychic energy that is contained in the id. (p. 511)

9. The **pleasure principle** is the operating principle by which the wants and desires of the id push people to do whatever feels good. (p. 512)

> *REMEMBER:* The id operates on the pleasure principle, guiding us to do whatever gives us *pleasure*.

10. The **ego** evolves from the id and attempts to satisfy the id's demands without breaking society's

rules. The ego operates according to the reality principle. (p. 512)

> *Example:* Suppose the id instinct Thanatos creates a desire to cut up people with knives. The ego would consider society's rules and laws about this type of activity, which say cutting up other people is wrong. But a person can become a surgeon and cut up people on a daily basis. Being a physician and cutting up people does not violate society's rules and may symbolically satisfy the id's demands.

11. The **reality principle** is the operating principle of the ego because the ego must find compromises between irrational id impulses and the demands of the real world. (p. 512)

12. The **superego** is formed from introjected values and tells what people should do (the ego ideal) and what people should not do (the conscience). The superego can be thought of as operating on the morality principle. (p. 512)

> *Example:* Suppose you are a small child in a candy store. Your id is "screaming" for candy. The conscience (part of the superego) is saying "You know it is wrong to steal candy." The ego decides that the best way to handle this dilemma is for you to go home and ask your mother for your allowance. Then you can go back and buy the candy, satisfying both the id and the superego.

13. **Introjection** is the process of internalizing parental and social values into the personality as part of the superego. (p. 512)

14. **Defense mechanisms** are unconscious psychological and behavioral tactics that help protect a person from anxiety by preventing conscious awareness of unacceptable id impulses and other unconscious material. (p. 512)

> *Example:* See examples for key terms 15–22, repression, projection, reaction formation, dis-

placement, intellectualization, rationalization, denial, and sublimation.

15. **Repression,** a defense mechanism, unconsciously forces unacceptable thoughts and impulses out of awareness, so that a person is unaware of ever having the unacceptable thoughts or impulses. (pp. 512–513)

Example: Mike is tired of being a husband, father, and breadwinner. He would like to leave his family to fend for themselves. These thoughts, if conscious, would cause him severe anxiety. Mike has repressed these thoughts and desires and does not know they exist in his unconscious.

16. **Projection,** a defense mechanism, operates so that people see their own unacceptable thoughts, impulses, or behavior in others. (p. 513)

Example: Bob is attracted to a married teaching assistant. Instead of recognizing his own feelings, he tells his best friend that he thinks the teaching assistant is attracted to him.

17. **Reaction formation** is a defense mechanism in which behavior is exactly the opposite of one's true thoughts and feelings. (p. 513)

Example: John hates his sister, Marla, because she is their mother's favorite. To keep these thoughts from becoming conscious, John pours affection and care on his sister.

18. **Displacement** is a defense mechanism in which unacceptable impulses, like anger at a parent, are directed toward other, safer targets. (p. 513)

Example: Brenda gets so angry with her mother that she sometimes wants to explode in rage. Instead of venting her anger on her mother, she yells at her employees.

19. **Intellectualization** is a defense mechanism in which people talk or think in cold and abstract terms about the impulses that are bothering them. (p. 513)

Example: Frank is a young doctor with many patients suffering from terminal diseases. Their deaths disturb him terribly because he unconsciously feels at fault. In order to reduce his anxiety, he refers to his patients by their diseases rather than by their real names.

20. **Rationalization**, a defense mechanism, attempts to "explain away" unacceptable behavior and thoughts. (p. 513)

Example: Ben's girlfriend has left him for another man. Instead of thinking that something is wrong with him, Ben tells himself that his ex-girlfriend could not handle his superior intelligence.

21. **Denial,** the most primitive defense mechanism, distorts reality by leading one to act, think, and feel as if unacceptable impulses are not there. (p. 513)

Example: Jack has been told that his son is retarded. He refuses to accept this information and takes no action that will help the child adjust to his environment.

22. **Sublimation,** a defense mechanism, converts unacceptable impulses and desires into socially acceptable activity. (p. 513)

Example: People with strong, but unacceptable, sexual impulses might throw themselves into artistic or other creative pursuits.

23. The **psychosexual stages** of development are part of Freud's psychodynamic theory of personality. Each stage is distinguished by the part of the body from which a person derives sexual pleasure at a particular time. The five stages are, in their respective order: *oral, anal, phallic, latent,* and *genital.* Failure to resolve the problems that occur during any stage can lead to *fixation.* (p. 514)

24. **Fixation** occurs when the conflicts within a particular psychosexual stage are not adequately resolved. This results in an unconscious preoccupation with the pleasure area associated with that stage of development. (p. 514)

25. The **oral stage** occurs during the first year of life, when the child derives pleasure from the mouth. If a child is weaned too early or too late, problems that can lead to fixation may arise. (p. 514)

Example: George was weaned much too early, thus depriving him of pleasure during the oral stage of personality development. He is fixated at the oral stage. As an adult, he talks quite a bit, is a heavy smoker, and loves to eat.

26. The **anal stage** occurs during the second year of life when pleasure is derived from the anus. If toilet training is too demanding or is begun too early or too late, problems that can lead to fixation may arise. (p. 514)

Example: Phil was toilet trained at a very young age and is fixated at the anal stage. As an adult he is very neat, orderly, and extremely organized.

27. The **phallic stage** occurs from three to five years of age when pleasure is derived from the genital area. Boys desire their mothers and want to eliminate or kill their fathers (Oedipus complex). However, they fear that their fathers may castrate them in jealous retaliation (castration anxiety). Eventually, the boy comes to identify with his father and acquires male sex-role behaviors. (pp. 514–515)

28. The **Oedipus complex** is a constellation of impulses that occurs during the phallic stage. A boy's id impulses involve sexual desire for the mother and a desire to eliminate, even kill, the father, with whom the boy must compete for the mother's affection. (p. 515)

29. The **latency period** occurs after the phallic stage and lasts until puberty. During this time a child tends to concentrate on educational activities. Sexual impulses lie dormant during the latency period. (p. 515)

30. The **genital stage** occurs from puberty onward. The genitals are once again the the primary source of sexual pleasure. The satisfaction obtained during this stage is dependent upon the resolution of conflicts experienced in the earlier stages. (p. 515)

Example: See key terms 25 and 26, oral and anal stages.

31. The **collective unconscious,** proposed by Carl Jung, is the memory of all the images and ideas the human race accumulated as it evolved from lower forms of life. Some of these images are called archetypes. (p. 515)

32. **Archetypes** are images that reside in the collective unconscious. They consist of classic images or concepts, such as the idea of Mother or the Devil, the most basic instincts from our prehuman centuries. (p. 515)

33. **Style of life** constitutes personality, according to Adler, and is the ways in which each person goes about trying to reach personal and social fulfillment. (p. 516)

34. **Ego psychologists** base their theories on Freud's ideas, but see the ego not only as a mediator in conflicts among id, superego, and environment, but also as a creative, adaptive force in its own right. (p. 516)

35. **Psychosocial stages** were proposed by Erikson and represent his idea that the most important developments occur in relation to social crises rather than to sexuality. (p. 516)

36. **Object relations theories** focus on the very early relationships between infants and their love objects, usually the mother and other primary caregivers, as important influences on personality development. (p. 517)

37. **Psychotherapy** is the attempt to alleviate various forms of mental disorder through psychological means. (p. 517)

38. The **dispositional approach** views personality as a unique combination of dispositions or tendencies to think and behave in certain ways. The three basic assumptions of this approach are: 1) dispositions are stable and consistent over time; 2) the tendency or disposition to think and behave in certain ways is evident in diverse situations; and 3) each person has a unique combination of dispositions. (p. 519)

39. **Factor analysis** is a complex mathematical procedure that trait theorists used to identify groups of traits that are related to each other, but unrelated to other groups. (p. 521)

40. The **behavioral approach** views personality as synonymous with behavior; behavior *is* personality. People learn which behaviors are appropriate in each specific situation. Situation-specific behavior accounts for behavioral variability from situation to situation. (p. 527)

Example: See key term 41, situational specificity.

41. **Situational specificity** is a concept associated with the behavioral view of personality, whereby behaviors are specific to the situations in which they have been rewarded or punished. Behaviors do not have to be consistent from one situation to the next. (p. 527)

Example: Lynne is never late for an appointment with her boss. She knows that he does not like tardiness. However, Lynne is always just a little late for parties because she does not like being the first person to arrive. A behaviorist would point to the rewards and punishments present in each situation to explain Lynne's behavior.

42. The **functional analysis of behavior** was employed by Skinner to better understand behavior. This type of analysis enabled Skinner to identify observable behavior and its relationship to observable environmental consequences. (pp. 527–528)

Example: Brian, a seventeen-year-old, usually ends up denting or slightly damaging the family car whenever he drives it. Skinner would look for consistencies in the environment every time this behavior appeared. As it turns out, Brian only takes the car when his usually inattentive father has gone out of town on a business trip. When Brian's father returns, he always spends an hour or so talking with Brian about his behavior. Skinner might suggest that Brian's father's attention is so reinforcing that he will even ruin the car to get it.

43. **Reciprocal determinism** refers to Bandura's idea that people's overt behaviors, cognitions, and the environment constantly influence one another. (p. 529)

44. **Self-efficacy,** a term used by Bandura, is the expectation of success in a given situation. These cognitive expectations may play a major role in determining behavior in a given situation. (p. 529)

Example: Sandra has low self-efficacy in interviewing situations and expects to do very poorly. She can never think of answers to questions or creative solutions to the problems posed by the interviewer. Jessica, on the other hand, has high self-efficacy in interviewing situations. Because she expects to do well, she is confident and approachable. Interviewers enjoy talking with her because she is enthusiastic and energetic. The interviewers' responses further enhance Jessica's self-efficacy.

45. The **phenomenological approach** (also called the humanistic approach) to personality focuses on the individual's unique perception, interpretation, and experience of reality. Phenomenological theorists assume that humans have an innate drive to grow and to fulfill their own unique potentials. (pp. 531–532)

46. **Personal constructs** are our expectations of what will happen in the world. If our experiences validate or confirm our personal constructs, we will

be comfortable. If not, our ability to accurately anticipate the world is diminished, and the result is anxiety. (p. 532)

> *Example:* Carla has a personal construct that says "Those who work hard will be rewarded;" she expects that her efforts will always be rewarded. Recently, she was passed over for a promotion. The person competing against Carla for the job was not as diligent or as intelligent a worker, but was on friendlier terms with the boss. Carla is now very uncomfortable and anxious.

47. **Self-actualization** is an innate tendency toward one's potential which motivates all human behavior. This concept is important in many phenomenological personality theories. If growth toward self-actualization is not impeded, a person will tend to be happy and comfortable. (p. 533)

48. **Self concept** is the way one thinks about oneself. (p. 534)

49. **Conditions of worth** are the beliefs that a person's worth depends on displaying the "right" attitudes, behaviors, and values. They are created whenever people, instead of their behaviors, are evaluated. (p. 534)

50. A **deficiency orientation** occurs when people are preoccupied with meeting needs for what they do not have. In other words, people focus on what is missing from their lives instead of what they have. (p. 535)

> *Example:* Jacqueline is the chief executive officer of a major corporation. She has a beautiful house, a membership in the "right" country club, and a large salary. However, instead of being satisfied, Jacqueline is constantly worrying about what she does not have enough money to buy.

51. A **growth orientation** occurs when people focus on drawing satisfaction derived from what they have. (p. 535)

> *Example:* David is a developmental psychologist. He does not get paid as much as some people, but he loves his research. He also has a supportive family and a few very close friends. David concentrates most of his effort on work and on enjoying his family to the fullest. He does not worry about what he cannot have. Instead, he derives a great deal of pleasure, indeed joy, from what he does have.

LEARNING OBJECTIVES

1. Define personality. (p. 504)
2. Define and describe the general methods of personality assessment. (pp. 506–509)
3. Discuss the differences between objective and projective tests. (p. 508)
4. Know the characteristics of a good test. (pp. 508–509)
5. State the basic components of all personality theories. (pp. 509–510)
6. Describe Freud's psychodynamic approach to personality. Define psychoanalysis, free association, and dream analysis. (pp. 510–511)
7. Define and describe the nature and function of the id, ego, and superego. Define defense mechanism and give an example of each defense mechanism listed in your text. (pp. 511–513)
8. Name, define, and describe the psychosexual stages of development. (pp. 513–515)
9. Compare and contrast Jung's, Adler's, and the Neo-Freudian approaches to personality. (pp. 515–517)
10. Describe some applications and criticisms of the psychodynamic approach to personality. (pp. 517–518)
11. Describe the three basic assumptions of the dispositional approach to personality. (p. 519)
12. Describe the type approach (a version of the dispositional approach) to personality. Compare

and contrast Allport's, Eysenck's, and Murray's dispositional approach to personality. (pp. 520–523)

13. Describe some applications and criticisms of the dispositional approach to personality. (pp. 524–526)

14. Describe the basic assumption of the behavioral approach to personality. Define situation specificity. (p. 526)

15. Compare and contrast Skinner's views, cognitive behavioral theories, and Bandura's and Mischel's views of personality. (pp. 527–529)

16. Describe some applications and criticisms of the behavioral approach to personality. (pp. 530–531)

17. Describe the phenomenological approach to personality. (pp. 531–532)

18. Compare and contrast Kelly's personal construct theory, Rogers's self theory, and Maslow's humanistic psychology. (pp. 532–535)

19. Describe some applications and criticisms of the phenomenological or humanistic approach. (pp. 535–537)

CONCEPTS AND EXERCISES

No. 1 Explaining Behavior

Completing this exercise should help you to achieve the following learning objectives.

(6) *Describe Freud's psychodynamic approach to personality. Define psychoanalysis, free association, and dream analysis. (pp. 510–511)*

(8) *Name, define, and describe the psychosexual stages of development. (pp. 513–515)*

(12) *Describe the type approach (a version of the dispositional approach) to personality. Compare and contrast Allport's, Eysenck's, and Murray's dispositional approach to personality. (pp. 520–523)*

(14) *Describe the basic assumption of the behavioral approach to personality. Define situation specificity. (p. 526)*

(17) *Describe the phenomenological approach to personality. (pp. 531–532)*

(18) *Compare and contrast Kelly's personal construct theory, Roger's self theory, and Maslow's humanistic psychology. (pp. 532–535)*

Amy's office is extremely neat and organized. Her books are arranged alphabetically and there is not a stray paper on her desk. Her pencils, neatly arranged from shortest to longest, are so sharp that she could use them as weapons. Amy is a meticulous dresser. Her clothes are never wrinkled, spotted or torn. Match the following explanations of her behavior with the appropriate theorist or approach.

1. Amy has learned that being organized and well dressed will further her career. _____

2. Amy is fixated at the anal stage. _____

3. Being organized is one of the central traits of Amy's personality. _____

4. Amy has a personal construct that says "People who are neat and clean are good." _____

5. Amy may believe that she is worthwhile only if she displays neat and tidy behaviors. _____

Carl Rogers
Behavioral
Gordon Allport
Alfred Adler
Sigmund Freud
George Kelly

No. 2 Defense Mechanisms

Completing this exercise should help you to achieve the following learning objectives.

(6) *Describe Freud's psychodynamic approach to personality. Define psychoanalysis, free association, and dream analysis. (pp. 510–511)*

(7) *Define and describe the nature and function of the id, ego, and superego. Define defense mechanism and give an example of each defense mechanism listed in your text. (pp. 511–513)*

Leslie Anne is six years old. She hates her little sister, who is three years old. Ever since her sister was born, Leslie Anne has not received as much attention from her parents or grandparents. Whenever her family has company, Leslie Anne is no longer the center of attention. She wishes her sister would die. There are several ways that Leslie Anne could deal with these unacceptable thoughts and wishes. Fill in the blanks with the appropriate defense mechanism.

1. Leslie Anne treats her friend's younger siblings very badly. _____

2. Leslie Anne loves to help her mother take care of her sister. She likes to pretend that she is her sister's mother. _____

3. Leslie Anne tells her mother that her friends do not treat their younger brothers and sisters very nicely. _____

4. Leslie Anne is completely unaware that she has such negative feelings about her three-year-old sister. _____

No. 3 Treatment Goals

Completing this exercise should help you to achieve the following learning objectives.

(6) *Describe Freud's psychodynamic approach to personality. Define psychoanalysis, free association, and dream analysis. (pp. 510–511)*

(11) *Describe the three basic assumptions of the dispositional approach to personality. (p. 519)*

(12) *Describe the type approach (a version of the dispositional approach) to personality. Compare and contrast Allport's, Eysenck's, and Murray's dispositional approach to personality. (pp. 520–523)*

(13) *Describe some applications and criticisms of the dispositional approach to personality. (pp. 524–526)*

(14) *Describe the basic assumption of the behavioral approach to personality. Define situation specificity. (p. 526)*

(15) *Compare and contrast Skinner's views, the cognitive behavioral theories, Bandura's and Mischel's views of personality. (pp. 527–529)*

(16) *Describe some applications and criticisms of the behavioral approach to personality. (pp. 530–531)*

(17) *Describe the phenomenological approach to personality. (pp. 531–532)*

(18) *Compare and contrast Kelly's personal construct theory, Rogers's self theory, and Maslow's humanistic psychology. (pp. 532–535)*

Bobby is extremely anxious and unhappy. Match the following goals with the appropriate approach to personality.

1. Bobby should become aware of his unconscious conflicts and work to resolve them. _____

2. Bobby should become aware of his real feelings and beliefs instead of trying to fulfill the conditions of worth that his parents and others impose on him. _____

3. Bobby should learn to think positively and realize that he controls what happens to him. _____

4. Bobby should take some tests to assess his personality traits. If he then goes through some form of treatment, he can take the tests again to monitor his progress. _____

Phenomenological
Behavioral
Psychodynamic
Dispositional

ANSWERS TO CONCEPTS AND EXERCISES

No. 1 Explaining Behavior

1. *Behavioral.* A behaviorist would explain Amy's behavior by finding out what behaviors have been rewarded in the past. (p. 527)

2. *Sigmund Freud.* Freud believed that an unresolved crisis during the psychosexual development would lead to fixation. Adults who are fixated at the anal stage are extremely neat and tidy. (p. 514)

3. *Gordon Allport.* Allport was a dispositional theorist. He believed that people had about seven central traits. (p. 521)

4. *George Kelly.* Kelly was a phenomenological theorist. He believed that people have personal constructs or expectations about how the world works. (p. 532)

5. *Carl Rogers.* Rogers was a phenomenological theorist. He said that many people display behaviors because they believe these are the only ways to gain approval and, thus, positive self-evaluation. (p. 533)

No. 2 Defense Mechanisms

All answers can be found on pages 512 and 513 of your text.

1. *Displacement.* Instead of treating her sister (the source of her conflict) very badly, she vents her feelings toward an alternate target.

2. *Reaction Formation.* This defense mechanism guides our behavior in a direction opposite to our true feelings. Leslie Anne hates her little sister, but showers her with love and affection.

3. *Projection.* Leslie Anne sees her own unwanted impulses and thoughts in other people.

4. *Repression.* Leslie Anne has forced all her unwanted thoughts and feelings into her unconscious. They are prevented from becoming conscious and causing her anxiety.

No. 3 Treatment Goals

All answers can be found in Table 14.3 in your text.

1. *Psychodynamic.* Freud said that unconscious conflicts are the primary root of all mental disorders. In order to eliminate the anxiety these conflicts produce, patients should be made aware of them and work to resolve them.

2. *Phenomenological.* Carl Rogers said that unhappy people are out of touch with their true feelings. They are probably behaving according to others' values instead of according to their own feelings and values.

3. *Behavioral.* A cognitive-behavioral approach suggests that Bobby learn and practice more positive ways of thinking and behaving.

4. *Dispositional.* A dispositional theorist might suggest that Bobby take objective tests, such as the Minnesota Multiphasic Personality Inventory (MMPI), to describe his personality and identify any type of possible personality disorders.

MULTIPLE CHOICE QUESTIONS

Facts and Definitions

1. A projective test is usually
   a. reliable.
   b. valid.
   c. easy to score.
   d. None of the above.

2. The belief that behavior can be situation-specific is a main argument against which approach to personality?
   a. Psychodynamic

b. Behavioral

c. Phenomenological

d. Dispositional

3. Which of the following is not one of the basic components of a personality theory?

a. A method of assessing personality

b. A method of evaluating a personality theory

c. A set of basic assumptions about personality

d. All of the above.

4. The _____ approach to personality assumes that the unconscious plays a major role in determining behavior.

a. dispositional

b. behavioral

c. psychodynamic

d. phenomenological

5. The Oedipus complex is part of the _____ stage of psychosexual development.

a. oral

b. anal

c. phallic

d. genital

6. The ego operates according to the

a. pleasure principle.

b. reality principle.

c. morality principle.

d. ethical principle.

7. Seeing our unacceptable impulses, thoughts, and behaviors in other people is called

a. reaction formation.

b. projection.

c. intellectualization.

d. displacement.

8. Fixation occurs when

a. psychosexual conflicts are not resolved.

b. we use defense mechanisms to relieve anxiety.

c. the rewards in a given situation fix our behaviors.

d. our progress toward self-actualization is fixed at some stage.

9. Central traits

a. were suggested by a behaviorist to explain behavior.

b. organize and control behavior across many situations.

c. are more situation specific than are secondary traits.

d. are seen in growth-oriented individuals.

10. Which of the following is *not* a criticism of the dispositional theories of personality?

a. They describe behavior better than they explain it.

b. They create descriptions that may be too general.

c. Tests based on the dispositional theories may not be reliable.

d. They place too much emphasis on the unconscious.

11. The learning process is most central to which personality theory?

a. Psychodynamic

b. Dispositional

c. Behavioral

d. All of the above.

12. Rotter's concept of locus of control is part of which type of personality theory?

a. Dispositional

b. Behavioral

c. Cognitive-behavioral

d. Psychodynamic

13. Self-efficacy is

a. our collection of learned expectancies for success in given situations.

b. the efficiency with which we resolve unconscious conflicts.

c. our ability to recognize rewards for our behavior in a situation.

d. the similarity between the real and ideal self on a Q-sort test.

14. From a phenomenological point of view, which of the following would be the best measure of personality?

a. Behavioral observation
b. An objective test
c. Assessment of physiological activity
d. Personal interviews

15. A deficiency orientation occurs when

a. people make do with less than perfect conditions.
b. people focus on things they do not have.
c. people attempt to fulfill their potentials.
d. None of the above.

MULTIPLE CHOICE QUESTIONS

Application of Concepts

1. Joe is an internal according to Rotter's expectancy theory of personality. Therefore, you would expect Joe to

a. ignore physical symptoms of illness.
b. work on a factory assembly line.
c. take a self-paced course at school.
d. All of the above.

2. Mark has just looked through a series of pictures and described what he thinks are the stories underlying the scenes. Mark has just

a. taken an objective test.
b. taken the Minnesota Multiphasic Personality Inventory (MMPI).
c. taken a projective test.
d. been interviewed.

3. Harold has developed a personality theory. Harold thinks that the amount of hair on a person's body indicates how healthy one's personality is. He already has several clients in therapy aimed at increasing the amount of hair on their bodies. Harold's theory is missing which basic component?

a. A set of basic assumptions about personality
b. A specific place to look for evidence of personality
c. A method of measuring personality
d. A method to evaluate his theory

4. The following is a conversation going on in someone's head.

X: I am so mad that I could bash that person's skull in. I cannot believe he did that.

Y: You know you are not supposed to hurt other people.

Z: Why not tell him to behave in some other way so that this incident will not be repeated.

X is the _____, Y is the _____, and Z is the _____.

a. id, ego, superego
b. ego, id, superego
c. superego, id, ego
d. id, superego, ego

5. Amy loves to chew on her fingernails, smokes one package of cigarettes a day, loves to chew gum, and has always been a little heavy due to overeating. Amy is most likely fixated at which psychosexual stage of development?

a. oral
b. anal
c. phallic
d. latency

6. Lynne, a married woman, is incredibly attracted to her physician. Her _____ decides that the only way to see her doctor more often is to have more frequent physicals and have even the slightest symptom investigated immediately.

a. id
b. ego

c. superego

d. ego ideal

7. Oliver thinks that everyone in all his lecture courses is cheating. Oliver probably feels like cheating himself. This is an example of which defense mechanism?

a. Creativity

b. Reaction-formation

c. Intellectualization

d. Projection

8. Tom finds his wife stupid and sexually unattractive. Instead of telling his wife about his feelings, he is rude to his secretary, pointing out all her mistakes with cruel relish. He also makes derogatory remarks about her appearance. This is an example of which defense mechanism?

a. Rationalization

b. Displacement

c. Reaction-formation

d. Projection

9. At home, Rebecca's daughter is very polite. Rebecca is horrified when she finds out that her daughter is rude at school. She suggests that the teacher begin rewarding her daughter for being polite. Rebecca would take which approach to personality?

a. Psychodynamic

b. Behavioral

c. Phenomenological

d. All of the above.

10. According to Bandura, a child could _____ through observational learning.

a. learn to be truthful

b. learn how to con Dad into giving up the car

c. learn how to be assertive

d. All of the above.

11. Michael and Burke are having a heated argument over which theory of personality is correct. Michael says that Burke's theory reduces humans to machines and ignores their perceptions, values, and beliefs. Michael is probably a _____ theorist and Burke is a _____ theorist.

a. behavioral; psychodynamic

b. phenomenological; psychodynamic

c. dispositional; behavioral

d. phenomenological, behavioral

12. Toni describes her best friend as intelligent, caring, extroverted, and lots of fun to be with. Which type of theorist would use the same type of description that Toni docs?

a. Dispositional

b. Behavioral

c. Psychodynamic

d. Phenomenological

13. Cassandra has just bounded into the room with her latest artistic creation. She bubbles on and on about her friends at school and how much she likes her teacher. She is nine years old. Which psychosexual stage of development is she in?

a. Oral

b. Anal

c. Phallic

d. Latency

Use the following conversation to answer questions 14 and 15.

Joe: I don't think we should hire him. I saw him in a barroom brawl a few months ago. Why hire someone who is going to be aggressive in any given situation?

Kim: His MMPI scores indicate that he isn't prone to violence.

Richard: The results of his Q-sort indicate very little incongruity between his real and ideal self.

Erika: Joe, how do you know that he's always going to be aggressive? Maybe the guy was just under stress at the time. Maybe he knows from past experience that a good fist fight relieves tension.

14. Which two speakers agree with the dispositional approach to personality?

    a. Joe and Richard
    b. Erika and Kim
    c. Joe and Kim
    d. Richard and Erika

15. Which of the following approaches is *not* represented in the above conversation?

    a. Behavioral
    b. Psychodynamic
    c. Phenomenological
    d. Dispositional

ANSWERS TO MULTIPLE CHOICE QUESTIONS

Facts and Definitions

1. *d* is the answer. Projective tests involve presenting a subject with an unstructured and ambiguous stimulus. Personality is supposedly reflected in the subject's response. Because the tasks are unstructured, they tend to be relatively difficult to score, unreliable and tend to have low validity. (p. 508)

2. *d* is the answer. Dispositional theorists argue that behavior is a reflection of consistent and stable traits. They do not believe that environmental or situational factors determine behavior. (p. 519)
    a. Psychodynamic theorists have been criticized for adhering to Freud's emphasis on the unconscious and Freud's use of patients' reports as a basis for psychosexual development theory. Freud was also accused of being sexist.
    b. Behaviorists have been accused of using unreliable and invalid measures of personality. Also, they overemphasize overt behavior and the environmental factors of reward and punishment and ignore the individual's perceptions, feelings, and thoughts.
    c. Phenomenological concepts are difficult to measure, more descriptive than explanatory, and

naive, since they are so optimistic about the nature of man.

3. *d* is the answer. All of the above are components of a personality theory. (p. 509)

4. *c* is the answer. The psychodynamic approach assumes that personality is determined by unconscious mental processes. (p. 510)
    a. The dispositional approach assumes that personality is a stable combination of traits or type characteristics.
    b. The behavioral approach assumes that personality is essentially the same thing as behavior.
    d. The phenomenological approach assumes that personality is a product of each person's values, beliefs, and perceptions.

5. *c* is the answer. The Oedipus complex occurs during the phallic stage. According to Freud, boys desire their mothers and wish to kill their fathers. This is similar to the plot of the Greek tragedy *Oedipus Rex*. (p. 514)
    a. The oral stage occurs during the first year of life, when a child derives pleasure mainly from the mouth.
    b. The anal stage occurs during the second year of life, when a child derives sexual pleasure mainly from the anus.
    d. The genital stage lasts from puberty onward. The pleasure found in relationships during this stage is dependent upon the resolution of conflicts at earlier stages.

6. *b* is the answer. The ego, trying to satisfy the id while not breaking society's rules, operates according to the reality principle. (p. 512)
    a. The id operates on the pleasure principle.
    c. The superego operates on the morality principle.
    d. There is no such thing as the ethical principle in psychodynamic theory.

7. *b* is the answer. Seeing our unacceptable thoughts and impulses in others instead of in ourselves is called projection. (p. 513)

    a. Reaction formation is behaving in a manner that is the opposite of one's feelings.

    c. Intellectualization reduces anxiety by dealing with unpleasant thoughts in cold and abstract terms.

    d. Displacement occurs when unacceptable impulses are directed at alternate targets.

8. *a* is the answer. Fixation occurs when we do not resolve psychosexual conflicts during development. For example, those who are weaned too early engage in oral activities such as smoking, excessive talking, or overeating. (p. 514)

    b. Freud suggested that we use defense mechanisms to relieve anxiety, but this is not called fixation.

    c. Fixation has nothing to do with the rewards and punishments for our behavior in any given situation.

    d. Fixation has nothing to do with self-actualization.

9. *b* is the answer. According to Allport's dispositional theory, about seven central traits guide our behavior in many situations. (p. 521)

    a. Central traits were proposed by Allport, who is a dispositional theorist, not a behavioral theorist.

    c. Secondary traits are more situation specific than are central traits.

    d. According to Allport, who is a dispositional theorist, central traits are seen in everyone. Growth orientation is a phenomenological concept proposed by Maslow.

10. *d* is the answer. Dispositional theories do not emphasize the unconscious as much as psychodynamic theories do. (p. 518)

    a. Traits are much better at describing than explaining behavior.

    b. Many trait descriptions seem to fit a large number of people, thus reducing their value for describing a given person.

    c. Results of dispositional personality tests vary with the test taker's mood, the testing situation, and the like. Therefore, they may be unreliable.

11. *c* is the answer. The learning process is most central to the behavioral theory of personality. Behaviorists consider personality and behavior to be the same. Behavior is learned from experiences in many different situations. (p. 527)

    a. The psychodynamic approach focuses on the influence of unconscious mental processes on personality.

    b. The dispositional approach attributes much of personality to inherent characteristics; it does not emphasize learning as much as the behavioral approach.

    d. c is the answer.

12. *c* is the answer. Rotter's locus of control concept is part of a cognitive behavioral theory. Thinking (cognition) that one has control over what happens to one influences behavior. (p. 528)

    a. Locus of control is not associated with dispositional theories.

    b. Strict behavioral theorists do not consider thinking a major focus for understanding behavior. Instead, they emphasize the rewards and punishments in the environment that shape behavior.

    d. Psychodynamic theorists do not emphasize locus of control. They tend to focus on unconscious mental processes.

13. *a* is the answer. According to Bandura, our learned expectations for success can influence our behavior. (p. 529)

    b. Bandura is a cognitive behavioral theorist. Psychodynamic theorists, not cognitive behavioral theorists, focus on unconscious mental processes.

    c. Strict behaviorists focus on the rewards and punishments that shape behavior in any given situation. Expectations (recognizing future rewards) are thoughts.

    d. Rogers, a phenomenological theorist, used the Q-sort test to measure personality.

14. *d* is the answer. Those who take a phenomenological view of personality believe that everyone sees a reality that is unique. Therefore, interviews, during which people can explain their points of view, would be the best method of assessment. (p. 534)

a. A phenomenological theorist would say that one cannot interpret someone's behavior without knowing that person's interpretation or perception of reality. For example, consider the illustration of the party conversation on page 309 in your text. Each person had a different interpretation of the behavior. Therefore, in order to assess someone's behavior, we must see the world as they see it.

b. An objective test assumes that people have the same general interpretation of the questions on it. If this were not the case, the questions could not be used to compare one person to another. Phenomenological views assume that each person's view of anything, including a true-false or multiple choice question, would be unique.

c. Phenomenological theorists do not depend on physiological data in personality assessment; they are more interested in conscious experience.

15. *b* is the answer. A deficiency orientation, according to Maslow, occurs when individuals focus on what they do not have instead of on what they do have. (p. 535)

a. If people focus on or derive satisfaction from what they have, they have a *growth* orientation.

c. Phenomenological theorists assume that we all attempt to fulfill our potentials.

d. b is the answer.

ANSWERS TO MULTIPLE CHOICE QUESTIONS

Application of Concepts

1. *c* is the answer. Joe would be most likely to take a self-paced course, because he would prefer being in control of his work pace. (p. 528)

a. & b. Joe would probably not ignore physical symptoms of illness or work very well on an assembly line. Externals have been found to exhibit these types of behavior.

d. c is the answer.

2. *c* is the answer. Mark has just taken a projective test, specifically the Thematic Apperception Test. (p. 508)

a. & b. An objective test is a paper and pencil test. Answers are written, not explained by the respondent. The MMPI is an objective test.

d. Interviews usually revolve around either structured or unstructured questions, not ambiguous stimuli such as pictures and inkblots.

3. *d* is the answer. If Harold would evaluate his theory, he would probably find no correlation between the amount of hair on someone's body and that person's personality. (p. 509)

a. Harold does have a basic assumption: the amount of hair on the body is correlated with personality.

b. Harold does have a specific place to look for evidence of personality: hair follicles.

c. Harold does have a method of measuring personality. He measures the amount of hair on someone's body.

4. *d* is the answer. X wants to be aggressive. Y knows all the rules about what behaviors one should and should not display, and Z will try to obey the rules of society as well as satisfy the id and superego. (p. 512)

5. *a* is the answer. Amy is most likely fixated at the oral stage. The adult behavior of people fixated at this stage is characterized by excessive smoking, eating, drinking, or talking, all of which are oral activities. (p. 514)

b. The adult behavior of people fixated at the anal stage is characterized by excessive neatness and organization.

c. People fixated at the phallic stage will have sexual desires for people or objects other than the opposite sex.

d. People do not become fixated at the latency stage. There are no unconscious conflicts to resolve at this stage.

6. *b* is the answer. Lynne's ego has devised a solution that will let her spend more time with a man she is attracted to (thereby satisfying the id) without breaking the rules of society or doing something that the superego would disapprove of. (p. 512)

a. The id wants to have sex with the doctor and does not particularly care what rules are broken.

c. The superego would tell Lynne that she is married and cannot have sex with anyone but her husband.

d. The ego ideal is a subdivision of the super-ego.

7. *d* is the answer. Oliver is projecting his unwanted impulses onto other people. (p. 513)

a. Creativity is not a psychodynamic defense mechanism.

b. Reaction formation guides behavior in the direction opposite to that of the unwanted impulse. If Oliver made sure that he was extremely honest in all situations, this would be the correct answer.

c. If Oliver spent a great deal of time talking about cheating among college students, why they do it, how they do it, and what can be done to stop it, intellectualization would be the answer.

8. *b* is the answer. Instead of venting his frustration on his wife (the source of his feelings), Tom is taking it out on his secretary. He is displacing his feelings from the original source to an alternate source, his secretary. (p. 513)

a. Rationalization is an attempt to explain away behavior. If this were the case, Tom might have told himself that all marriages have their low spots.

c. Reaction formation guides behavior in the direction opposite that of the unwanted impulse. If this were the case, Tom would have showered his wife with attention and affection, telling her how intelligent and beautiful he thought she was.

d. Projection occurs when we see our unwanted impulses and desires in others. If this were the case Tom might start noticing that his friends treated their wives very badly.

9. *b* is the answer. Rebecca is probably a behaviorist. She believes that behavior is shaped by the presence of rewards and punishments in the environment. (p. 527)

a. A psychodynamic theorist would want to find out what the daughter's unconscious thoughts and feelings were before suggesting a corrective measure.

c. A phenomenological theorist would suggest that the daughter's *behavior,* not just the daughter, be rewarded. Also, a phenomenological theorist would probably want to know how the daughter perceives the situation at school.

d. b is the answer.

10. *d* is the answer. According to Bandura, we can (a) learn new behaviors, (b) learn to inhibit behaviors, and (c) learn how to prompt or facilitate behaviors. (p. 529)

11. *d* is the answer. Michael is a phenomenological theorist because he thinks that values, beliefs, and perceptions of reality influence personality. Burke is a behaviorist; behaviorists have been accused of viewing people as machines that can be programmed using rewards and punishments. (p. 531)

a. Behaviorists tend not to focus on people's values, beliefs, or perceptions of the world.

b. & c. Psychodynamic and dispositional theorists have not been accused of ignoring people's values or beliefs, nor do they view people as machines controlled by rewards and punishments.

12. *a* is the answer. A dispositional theorist would describe a person using traits. (p. 519)

b. A behavioral theorist would describe a person in terms of behaviors. (A cognitive behaviorist would also be interested in thought patterns.)

c. A psychodynamic theorist would discuss the underlying unconscious conflicts that are responsible for a person's behavior.

d. A phenomenological theorist would describe a person's perception of reality, values, and beliefs.

13. *d* is the answer. The latency period lasts from about age five until puberty. During this time a child focuses on education and social development. (p. 515)

a. The oral stage occurs during the first year or so of life.

b. The anal stage occurs during the second year or so of life.

c. The phallic stage occurs during approximately the third to fifth years of life.

14. *c* is the answer. Joe assumes that the man in question will always be aggressive. Dispositional theorists assume that people have several traits that will be present in many different situations. Kim is talking about the MMPI, a personality test developed by dispositional theorists. (pp. 519, 524)

a. Richard agrees with phenomenological theorists.

b. Erika agrees with behavioral theorists.

d. Richard agrees with phenomenological theorists while Erika agrees with behavioral theorists.

15. *b* is the answer. Richard represents phenomenological theory, Erika represents behavioral theory, and Kim and Joe represent dispositional theory. Psychodynamic views of personality are not represented by anyone. (pp. 519–537)

Chapter 15

Abnormal Behavior

OUTLINE

I. NORMALITY AND ABNORMALITY (pp. 545–555)

A. What Is Abnormality?

There are several approaches to defining normality, but none are perfect. No behavior is universally abnormal.

1. *The Statistical Approach*. Those behaviors displayed by the greatest number of people are considered normal. Behaviors that deviate from the average person's behavior are considered abnormal. The approach equates normality with conformity and abnormality with nonconformity.

2. *The Valuative Approach*. Behavior that is not valued is considered to be abnormal. Some common valuative criteria are intelligibility, consistency, control, and morality.

3. *The Practical Approach*. The content of behavior (whether behavior is bizarre, dysfunc-

tional, or harmful) and the context of behavior (where and when a behavior occurs) are considered when judging whether behavior is abnormal. Cultures and subcultures determine which behaviors are appropriate for a given situation.

B. Changing Beliefs About Abnormality

1. *Ancient Concepts*. Abnormal behavior was thought to be caused by the action of demons or gods (demonological model). In the fourth century, Hippocrates suggested that mental illness was caused by physical problems (medical model).

2. *Middle Ages*. Supernatural explanations of behavior disorders were prominent.

3. *Biological and Psychodynamic Models*. After the Middle Ages, medical or *biological models* were used to explain abnormal behavior. In the late 1800s, Freud developed the psychodynamic model, theorizing that abnormal behaviors were symptoms of underlying psychological conflicts.

4. *The Behavioral Model*. People learn many maladaptive abnormal behaviors in the same basic ways that they learn adaptive, normal behaviors.

5. *The Phenomenological Model*. Behavior disorders occur when psychological growth stops because of a failure to recognize and express one's own true feelings.

6. *An Integrated View: The Diathesis-Stress Model*. The combination of an individual's diathesis—physical predispositions that leave a person vulnerable to certain types or amounts of stress—and how much stress is present in the environment determine if abnormal behavior will appear.

C. Classification of Abnormal Behavior

The Diagnostic and Statistical Manual of Mental Disorders (DSM-III-R) describes each form of disorder and provides criteria for psychodiagnosis. DSM-III-R consists of a series of evaluations on five dimensions called axes. Every person is rated on each axis.

Axis I: a list of descriptive criteria of sixteen major mental disorders.

Axis II: developmental problems and personality disorders.

Axis III: physical conditions or disorders.

Axis IV: types and levels of stress.

Axis V: rating of highest functional level.

II. ANXIETY DISORDERS (pp. 555–559)

A. Phobia

A phobia is an anxiety disorder involving a strong, irrational fear of an object or situation that should not cause such a reaction. Simple phobias involve fear of physical objects, places or activities. Social phobias involve fear of being negatively evaluated by others or publicly embarrassed by doing something impulsive, outrageous, or humiliating.

B. Generalized Anxiety Disorder

The condition called generalized anxiety disorder involves milder but long-lasting feelings of anxiety, worry, dread, or apprehension that is not focused on any particular object or situation.

C. Panic Disorder

Periodic episodes of extreme terror (panic attacks) without warning or obvious cause are characteristic of people with panic disorder. Panic attacks can ultimately lead to agoraphobia, a strong fear of being alone or away from the security of home.

D. Obsessive-Compulsive Disorder

The persistent intrusion of thoughts or images or a compulsive need to perform certain behavior pat-terns are symptoms of obsessive-compulsive disorder. When the obsessive thinking or compulsive behaviors are interrupted, severe anxiety results.

E. Causes of Anxiety Disorders

Biological explanations of anxiety disorders include low levels of a particular neurotransmitter and an overreaction to lactic acid. Those who support the behavioral model view anxiety disorders as a learned reaction to past experiences.

III. SOMATOFORM DISORDERS (pp. 559–560)

Somatoform disorders are characterized by physical symptoms with no physical cause. In conversion disorder, a person appears to be, but is actually not, functionally impaired (for example, blind, deaf, or paralyzed). The physical symptoms often help to reduce stress and the person may seem unconcerned about them. Hypochondriasis involves strong fears of severe illness that are usually accompanied by complaints of many vague symptoms. Somatoform pain disorder is characterized by severe, often constant pain, with no apparent physical cause. Behavioral and psychodynamic theorists believe that somatoform disorders may appear because they relieve the individual from unpleasant responsibilities.

IV. DISSOCIATIVE DISORDERS (p. 560)

Dissociative disorders are characterized by a sudden, usually temporary, disruption in memory, consciousness, or identity. The most dramatic and least common dissociative disorder is multiple personality, which involves having more than one identity, each of which speaks, acts, and writes differently.

Psychodynamic theorists believe that dissociative disorders are methods of repressing (forgetting) unwanted impulses or memories. Behavioral theorists believe that dissociative disorders are examples of learned behavior patterns that have become so discrepant that a person may feel like and be perceived as a different person from time to time.

V. MOOD DISORDERS (pp. 561–566)

Mood disorders or affective disorders are characterized by persistent extreme mood swings that are inconsistent with environmental events.

A. Depressive Disorders

Major depression involves feelings of sadness, hopelessness, inadequacy, worthlessness, and guilt that persist for long periods. A more common pattern of depression is dysthymic disorder, which involves symptoms similar to those of major depression, but to a lesser degree and for a shorter time.

B. Bipolar Disorder

Once known as manic depression, bipolar disorder is characterized by alternating feelings of depression and mania. Delusions of grandeur may be present.

C. Causes of Mood Disorders

1. *Psychological Theories.* Some psychologists believe that the feelings of worthlessness, guilt, and self-blame so common in depression are emotions meant for others that have been turned inward. Behavioral theorists believe that people become depressed when they lose important reinforcements. The cognitive-behavioral view agrees with this idea, and adds that negative mental habits, such as always blaming oneself and learned helplessness, are causative factors in depression.

2. *Physiological Theories.* Altered levels of norepinephrine and serotonin (neurotransmitters), changes in the control of the stress-related hormone cortisol, changes in biological rhythms, and genetic influences are causative

factors in affective disorders. There is strong evidence that bipolar disorder may be inherited.

VI. SCHIZOPHRENIA (pp. 566–571)

A. Symptoms of Schizophrenia

1. *Disorders of Thought.* People with schizophrenia often display incoherent forms of thought; neologisms, word salad, and loose associations are common symptoms. The content of schizophrenics' thought is equally disturbed; common symptoms include ideas of reference and thought broadcasting, blocking, and insertion.

2. *Disorders of Perception and Attention.* Symptoms of schizophrenia include an inability to focus attention or concentrate. Changes in perception of body parts or other people may also occur. Many schizophrenics report hallucinations of voices.

3. *Disorders of Emotion and Movement.* Emotions are either absent or inappropriate for a given situation. Movements may range from constant agitation to almost total immobility.

4. *Other Schizophrenic Symptoms.* Lack of motivation and social skills, deteriorated personal hygiene, and an inability to function from day to day are other common characteristics of schizophrenia.

B. Types of Schizophrenia

1. *Disorganized Schizophrenia.* Delusions, hallucinations, poor communication, flat or inappropriate affect, and poor personal hygiene characterize disorganized schizophrenia.

2. *Catatonic Schizophrenia.* Disorder of movement is the most significant feature of catatonic schizophrenia.

3. *Paranoid Schizophrenia.* The most prominent features of paranoid schizophrenia are delusions of persecution or grandeur accompanied by

anxiety, anger, superiority, argumentativeness, or jealousy.

C. The Search for Causes

1. *Biological Factors.* Possible biological causes of schizophrenia include inherited predispositions; excess amounts of or oversensitivity to dopamine; loss, deterioration, or disorganization of certain brain cells; reduced blood flow in certain parts of the brain; and abnormal brain lateralization.

2. *Psychological Factors.* Psychodynamic theory suggests that schizophrenic symptoms are a reaction to anxiety caused by the threat of expressing or becoming aware of unacceptable unconscious impulses. Behaviorists believe that schizophrenic symptoms are learned methods of trying to cope with anxiety. They may also be the product of patterns of reinforcement and punishment in early life. The vulnerability model includes biological and psychological factors as possible causes of schizophrenia.

VII. PSYCHOACTIVE SUBSTANCE-USE DISORDERS (pp. 571–574)

This disorder is the result of the prolonged use of, or addiction to, psychoactive drugs which can cause physical or psychological harm to the users and, consequently, to others around them.

A. Alcoholism

Alcoholism is a pattern of continuous or intermittent drinking which may lead to addiction and almost always causes severe social, physical, and other problems.

1. *Causes of Alcoholism.* The behavioral approach suggests that people learn to use alcohol because it helps them cope with stressors and reduce stress reactions. Biological evidence suggests that alcoholism may be due to an inherited predisposition, especially in males.

B. Heroin and Cocaine Addiction

Heroin is a highly addictive illegal drug that produces a pleasurable reaction or "rush." Cocaine is a stimulant that produces a feeling of self-confidence, well-being, and optimism. Continued use of both drugs produces a wide range of psychological and physical problems. Addiction to heroin and similar drugs is largely a biological process.

VIII. SEXUAL DISORDERS (p. 574)

Sexual disorders include sexual dysfunctions (discussed in Chapter 11 on motivation) and paraphilias, in which a person's sexual interest is directed toward stimuli that are culturally or legally inappropriate.

IX. PERSONALITY DISORDERS (pp. 574–576)

Personality disorders, less severe than mental disorders, are lifestyles which begin in childhood or adolescence and create problems, usually for others.

A. Narcissistic Personality Disorder

The main characteristic of narcissistic personality disorder is an exaggerated sense of self-importance and abilities coupled with a deep feeling of self-doubt. These people need to be the center of attention at all times and have few real friends.

B. Antisocial Personality

People with antisocial personality disorder display a long-term, persistent pattern of impulsive, selfish, unscrupulous and even criminal behavior. These individuals are intelligent and charming, but do not feel guilty after causing harm or discomfort to others. Possible causes include a low level of emotional arousal, low sensitivity to physical punishment, and childhood problems.

X. ORGANIC MENTAL DISORDERS (pp. 576–577)

Organic mental disorders have symptoms such as delirium and dementia and have a clearly biological basis.

XI. MENTAL ILLNESS IN SOCIETY (pp. 577–581)

A. Does Mental Illness Exist?

Traditional professionals in psychiatry and psychology believe that mental illness is similar to physical illness. Szasz and other critics of the illness view argue that labelling those with behavior disorders as ill may place them in a passive, stigmatized, helpless role.

B. Behavior Disorder and Criminal Responsibility

A person can be found not guilty by reason of insanity if, at the time of the crime, mental illness prevented him or her from (1) understanding that the act was wrong or (2) resisting the impulse to do wrong. These laws were designed to protect the mentally ill, but critics question the idea of protection. Those who think that mental illness does not exist feel that these laws allow people to escape from responsibility for criminal acts.

KEY TERMS

1. **Psychopathology** involves patterns of thinking and behaving which are maladaptive, disruptive, or uncomfortable either for the person affected or for those with whom he or she associates. (p. 542)

> *REMEMBER: Psych* refers to mental or psychological and *pathos* refers to illness or sickness. Psychopathology means the study of mental illness or disorder.

2. The **statistical approach,** one method of defining abnormality, states that behaviors that commonly occur within a population are normal and those which rarely occur are abnormal. However, some behaviors that are valued and desirable are statistically rare. (pp. 546–547)

> *Example:* Very few people murder one person per day in cold blood. This behavior is unusual and abnormal. However, Gladys gives 30 percent of her income to charity. This behavior is quite uncommon but it is not abnormal.

3. The **valuative approach** considers any behavior that is not valued by society to be abnormal. However, determining who is society—or in other words, who is to decide which behaviors are valued—poses difficult problems. (p. 547)

> *Example:* Gladys gives 30 percent of her income to charity. This behavior is valued and considered normal. However, Gladys also likes to get drunk and race her sports car down the main street. This behavior, because it is not valued, would be considered abnormal.

4. The **practical approach** defines abnormality based on the content and context of behavior. To analyze the content of behavior, the following question may be asked: Is the behavior bizarre or weird, or dysfunctional? To analyze the context of behavior the following question may be asked: Is the behavior displayed at the wrong time or in an inappropriate situation? (p. 547)

> *Example:* Nick, an advertising executive, loves to take all of his clothes off in the summer, turn his radio up, sing at the top of his lungs, and dance to the music. This is hardly abnormal. However, if Nick decided to do his imitation of Bruce Springsteen in the middle of a client meeting, his behavior would be considered abnormal because it is displayed at an inappropriate time.

5. The **demonological model,** the earliest model of abnormal behavior, attributes behavioral disorders to the supernatural powers of demons or gods. (p. 548)

6. The **medical model,** also called the **biological model,** attributes abnormal behavior to the presence of biochemical, genetic or other physical problems. (p. 548)

Example: Joanna is depressed. Her doctor believes that the levels of neurotransmitters, especially norepinephrine and serotonin, are not balanced. She is taking an antidepressant to correct this physical problem.

7. The **psychodynamic model** attributes abnormal behavior to the presence of unresolved, mostly unconscious psychological conflicts between one's instinctual desires and the demands of the environment and society. (p. 549)

Example: A person may have an instinctual desire to kick dogs, but society or parents disapprove of this behavior. Being in contact with dogs will make the person conscious of this prohibited instinctual desire and cause anxiety. To avoid anxiety the person develops a phobia of dogs.

8. The **behavioral model** considers abnormal behaviors to be products of unfortunate learning experiences. (p. 550)

Example: Suppose someone who has had several good friends who have drowned has *learned* through experience that water is dangerous and may develop a phobia, refusing to go swimming or to take a bath. The phobia may become so severe that the person is afraid to drink water or stand in the rain. Another possibility is that other objects similar to water will evoke the same fear; any liquid may cause the person to become afraid.

9. The **phenomenological model** considers abnormal behavior the result of a person's failing to be in touch with or failing to express his or her true feelings. When this happens, a person's perception of the world changes and abnormal behaviors appear. (p. 550)

10. The **diathesis-stress model** attributes abnormal behavior to the interaction between a person's biological predisposition to react to stress and the actual amount of stress present in a person's life. It takes into account physical, psychological, and environmental factors. (p. 551)

Example: Frank has a biological predisposition to be susceptible to stress. Entering the combined medical and doctoral program put him under a lot of stress. He was very depressed by the end of his first semester. Jill tends to be less stress-sensitive and is handling the same program with much less trouble.

11. **Diathesis** is an inherited physical predisposition that leaves a person vulnerable to psychological problems. (p. 551)

12. **Neurosis** refers to conditions in which a person is uncomfortable (usually anxious) but can still function. The term is no longer used in DSM-III-R, although it was a major category in DSM-I and DSM-II. (p. 553)

13. **Psychosis** includes conditions involving loss of contact with reality or an inability to function day to day. The term is no longer used in DSM-III-R, although it was a major category in DSM-I and DSM-II. (p. 553)

14. An **anxiety disorder** is characterized by anxiety that causes a disruption in a person's life. Anxiety disorders include phobias, generalized anxiety disorders, and obsessive-compulsive disorders. (p. 555)

15. **Phobias** are strong irrational fears of an object or situation that should not cause such a reaction. (p. 556)

16. A **simple phobia** is the fear of physical things, such as heights, animals, or air travel. (p. 556)

Example: Claustrophobia is the fear of being in closed places.

17. A **social phobia** is the fear of being negatively evaluated by others or of doing something impulsive or outrageous that will result in public humiliation. (p. 556)

Example: Rosa is terrified of giving a speech in her science class. She is afraid that she will start screaming obscenities during her talk.

18. **Generalized anxiety disorder** involves relatively mild, but long-lasting anxiety that is not focused on any object or situation. (p. 556)

Example: Leslie has had a feeling of vague apprehension for about six weeks and always feels as though something bad is going to happen to her. She cannot sleep and is constantly tired and irritable.

19. **Panic disorder** consists of attacks of extreme fear and panic that occur with no warning and no obvious cause. (p. 556)

Example: Tom, a university professor, often experiences panic attacks. He can be in the middle of lecturing, driving his car, or browsing in a bookstore when he suddenly becomes terrified for no specific reason. He also experiences chest pain and dizziness during these episodes.

20. **Agoraphobia** is the fear of being alone or away from the security of home. (p. 556)

Example: Elizabeth is afraid to leave her house. She cannot go shopping or out for an evening. She cannot hold a job or visit her friends and family. She cannot take her children to the doctor or drive them where they need to go. Although she is less fearful when accompanied by her husband, she is still uncomfortable in any situation outside her home. Elizabeth suffers from agoraphobia.

21. **Obsessive-compulsive disorder** involves either an obsession with particular thoughts or images or a compulsion to perform certain behaviors. (p. 557)

Example: Jennifer cannot enter a room and feel comfortable unless she touches all of the walls first. If she is in a situation that prevents her from doing this, she becomes very anxious and highly agitated.

22. **Somatoform disorders** are characterized by the presence of physical symptoms of illness in the absence of a physical cause. They include conversion disorder, hypochondriasis, and somatoform pain disorder. (p. 559)

23. A **conversion disorder** is a condition in which a person appears to be, but actually is not, blind, deaf, paralyzed, insensitive to pain, or even pregnant. The physical disabilities often help to reduce stress and the individual may seem unconcerned about what appears to be a serious problem. (p. 559)

Example: Lisa is a volunteer nurse on a cancer ward. She has called the hospital and calmly told them that she cannot come to work because she cannot move her legs. There is nothing physically wrong, but the problem allows her to avoid dealing with patients who are in great pain and near death.

24. **Dissociative disorders** involve a sudden and usually temporary disruption in a person's memory, consciousness, or identity. (p. 560)

Example: Bill, lost in New York City, does not remember his name, home address, or where he works. He cannot remember anything that will give him a clue to his identity. Bill is suffering from a dissociative disorder.

REMEMBER: Dissociate means to break a connection or disunite. Bill, in the example, is disconnected from his past.

25. **Multiple personality** (the least common dissociative disorder) is a condition in which a person reports having more than one identity, each of

which speaks, acts, and writes in a very different way. (p. 560)

26. **Mood disorders** (affective disorders) are extreme changes in mood, lasting for extended periods of time, that are inconsistent with the happy or sad events in a person's life. They include major depression, dysthymia, mania, and bipolar disorders. (p. 561)

27. **Major depression** is an affective disorder typified by feelings of sadness, hopelessness, and an inability to enjoy oneself or take pleasure in anything. Simple tasks seem to require enormous effort and concentration is impaired. (p. 561)

Example: Shelly is depressed. She sits on the couch and watches television without enjoying the shows. She lacks the energy to clean the house or to care for the children. She cries frequently for no apparent reason other than that she feels life is hopeless and has no purpose.

28. **Delusions** are false beliefs. There are several types of delusions. (p. 561)

Example: Regina believes that she has been selected by the government to take over the moon once it is colonized. She anxiously checks the mail each day to see if her instructions have arrived from the president. Regina has delusions of grandeur.

29. **Dysthymic disorder** is a form of affective disorder that is similar to depression but is less severe and lasts for a shorter time. (p. 562)

30. **Bipolar disorder** (manic depression) is a form of affective disorder that involves extreme mood changes in which feelings of mania are followed by severe depression. (p. 564)

REMEMBER: Bi means two and *polar* refers to extremes. A bipolar disorder is an affective disorder in which mood alternates between two opposite feelings: elation (mania) and extreme sadness (depression).

31. **Mania** is an elated, very active emotional state. (p. 564)

Example: George is a carpenter. While in a manic state, he decided to build a copy of the Empire State Building in his backyard. He called his office and quit his job, ordered supplies, and asked his neighbors to help him. When the people down the street tried to tell George that he should check the city building codes before undertaking such an enormous task, he became belligerent. He stormed out of their house, accusing them of having no faith in the will, determination, and ability of American neighborhoods.

32. **Schizophrenia** is characterized by several types of abnormal behaviors or disorders. Abnormalities in thinking, perception and attention, affect, motor behavior, personal identity, motivation, and day-to-day functioning are common symptoms. There are three types of schizophrenia: disorganized, catatonic, and paranoid. (p. 566)

Example: Neologisms, an abnormality seen in schizophrenics' speaking and writing, are words that have meaning only to the person speaking them. For example, the word *teardom* in "I hereby teardom your happiness" is a neologism. There is no such word as teardom.

33. **Disorganized schizophrenia** includes symptoms of delusions and hallucinations, ritualistic movements, flat affect, and possible loss of bladder and bowel control. (p. 568)

34. **Catatonic schizophrenia** is usually diagnosed when movement disorders are present. An individual can alternate between stupor or total immobility and wild agitation. (p. 568)

35. **Paranoid schizophrenia** accounts for about 50 percent of all schizophrenia diagnoses. The most common symptoms include delusions of grandeur or persecution, which can be accompanied by jealousy and violence. (p. 568)

36. The **vulnerability model** suggests that people have differing degrees of susceptibility to schizophrenia that may be inherited or due to psychological factors related to a history of poor parenting or other past experiences. (p. 571)

37. **Psychoactive substance-use disorders** are characterized by long-term drug use that causes physical or psychological harm to the user or others. (p. 571)

Example: Nancy has been an alcoholic for twenty years. She began drinking socially when she moved to the suburbs. Eventually, she drank every day to the point of being drunk and finally lost her job. Her children have suffered because they do not have regular meals, cannot bring their friends home for fear of Nancy being drunk, and often hear their parents argue about their mother's drinking.

38. **Addiction** is a physical need for a substance. It is evident when a person needs more and more of a substance to achieve the desired effect. (p. 571)

Example: After much prodding from her friends, Jill decided to try alcohol and enjoyed the effects, so much that she began drinking whenever she could. Eventually, she found that the more alcohol she consumed, the more she needed to get the same pleasant effect. When alcohol is not available to her, Jill spends a great deal of time trying to find it. She is depressed, irritable, and has great difficulty concentrating. In fact, all she can think about now is how to get more alcohol.

39. **Paraphilia** is a sexual disorder in which a person's sexual interest is directed toward stimuli that are culturally or legally inappropriate. (p. 574)

Example: Recurrent sexual urges or fantasies which involve non-human objects (women's shoes or purses), children or other non-consenting partners, and the infliction of suffering or humiliation on oneself or one's sexual partner are behaviors related to paraphilia.

40. **Personality disorders** are lifelong behavior patterns that create problems, usually for others, and are not as severe as mental disorders. There are several types of personality disorders, including narcissistic and antisocial personality disorders. (p. 574)

41. **Narcissistic personality disorders** are diagnosed when people have an exaggerated sense of self-importance, have to be the center of attention, have severe feelings of self-doubt, and have very few true friends. (p. 575)

Example: Tom is inconsiderate of everyone, especially the people who work for him. He thinks nothing of borrowing money from them, stopping at their homes at all hours of the night, and demanding that they run their lives around his schedule. If one of his workers approaches him with a problem, Tom always ends up talking about himself instead of focusing on the person who has asked him for help. Tom's primary goal in life is to become famous, and he tells everyone how brilliant his ideas are. But deep down he has a very strong fear that he is not very good at his job.

42. **Antisocial personality disorder** involves a long-term persistent pattern of impulsive, selfish, unscrupulous, even criminal, behavior. People with antisocial personalities appear to have no morals and can be dangerous to the public, because they very rarely experience deep feelings for anyone. Typically, they are smooth talkers, intelligent, charming, good liars, and have no sense of responsibility. (p. 575)

43. **Organic mental disorders** are clearly caused by abnormal biological functioning. The symptoms include delirium and dementia. (p. 576)

44. **Delirium** is a clouded state of consciousness characterized by confusion and difficulties in concentration. (p. 576)

45. **Dementia** is a loss of intellectual functions. Alzheimer's disease creates severe dementia. (p. 576)

Example: Ross, a carpenter, has Alzheimer's, a disease which is incurable. His memory problems started with forgetting to run errands he had promised to do, forgetting to return phone calls to clients and friends, and leaving all the lights on in a room. Now he does not recognize his family and friends, or even the houses he built in the neighborhood, and he does not remember that he was a carpenter.

LEARNING OBJECTIVES

1. Define psychopathology. Explain why psychopathology is a social, as well as a personal, matter. (p. 542)

2. Describe the three basic approaches to defining abnormality. Know the advantages and disadvantages of each approach. Evaluate, within the framework of each approach, a behavior that you think is abnormal. (pp. 546–548)

3. Describe the role of culture in each approach to defining abnormality. (pp. 545–548)

4. Name the six theoretical models that describe the possible causes of abnormal behavior. Give possible causes, within the framework of each model, for a behavior that you think is abnormal. (pp. 548–551)

5. Describe the historical development of each model of abnormality. (pp. 548–551)

6. Define psychodiagnosis. Describe the process of psychodiagnosis using DSM-III-R. Know why DSM-III-R is different from earlier versions. Know how DSM-III-R has improved inter-rater reliability. (pp. 551–555)

7. Define anxiety disorder. Know what disorders are classified as anxiety disorders. (pp. 555–559)

8. Define phobia and give a brief description of simple phobia and social phobia. (pp. 555–556)

9. Define generalized anxiety disorder, panic disorders (including agoraphobia), and obsessive-compulsive disorders. (pp. 556–557)

10. State the causes, according to various theoretical models, of anxiety disorders. (pp. 557–559)

11. Define somatoform disorder. Give a brief description of conversion disorder, hypochondriasis, and somatoform pain disorder. (pp. 559–560)

12. State the causes, according to various theoretical models, of somatoform disorders. (p. 560)

13. Define dissociative disorder. Give a brief description of multiple personality disorder. (p. 560)

14. State the causes, according to various theoretical models, of dissociative disorders. (p. 560)

15. Define mood or affective disorders. Give a brief description of major depression, bipolar disorders, mania, and dysthymic disorder. (pp. 561–564)

16. State the psychological and physiological causes, according to various theoretical models, of affective disorders. Discuss the relationship between learned helplessness and depression. (pp. 564–566)

17. Define schizophrenia. Describe the different symptoms and disorders that are characteristic of schizophrenia. Define neologism and loose associations. Be able to distinguish between disorders of thought content and disorders of thought form. (pp. 566–568)

18. Know the names of the various types of schizophrenia, the percentage of the total schizophrenic population each type represents, and the distinguishing characteristics of each type. (pp. 568–569)

19. State the possible causes of schizophrenia, according to various theoretical models. (pp. 569–571)

20. Define psychoactive substance-use disorder and addiction. (pp. 571–572)

21. Know the physical effects of alcohol, cocaine and heroin. Know how common abuse of each is. Know the problems resulting from abuse of these drugs. (pp. 572–574)

22. Define sexual disorder, sexual dysfunction, and paraphilia. (p. 574)

23. Define personality disorder. Give a brief description of narcissistic and anti-social personality disorder. (pp. 574–576)

24. Define organic mental disorder. Contrast delirium and dementia. State the probable biological causes for these types of disorders. (pp. 576–577)

25. Discuss the advantages and disadvantages of labelling a person suffering from a behavior disorder as mentally ill. (pp. 577–579)

26. State the rights of the mentally ill. Describe the current laws concerning the use of mental illness as grounds for exemption from prosecution or punishment following criminal behavior. (pp. 580–581)

CONCEPTS AND EXERCISES

No. 1 Choosing a Jury

Completing this exercise should help you to achieve the following learning objectives.

(2) *Describe the three basic approaches to defining abnormality. Know the advantages and disadvantages of each approach. Evaluate, within the framework of each approach, a behavior that you think is abnormal. (pp. 546–548)*

(3) *Describe the role of culture in each approach to defining abnormality. (pp. 545–548)*

Connie, a fifty year old woman, has killed her husband. She has pleaded not guilty and will stand trial to determine sentencing. The prosecution and the defense lawyer are now in the process of select-ing jurors. Connie's lawyer will attempt to convince the jury that, although she has committed a crime, the longstanding physical and mental abuse that she and her children endured make her behavior understandable. She should, therefore, receive a lesser sentence.

Connie's lawyer will want jurors with a particular approach to defining abnormality. Each juror will be presented with the following list of behaviors and asked if he or she thinks that the behaviors are abnormal and why. If you were Connie's lawyer, which of the following two prospective jurors would you choose?

List of Behaviors:

1. getting drunk and singing at the top of your lungs

2. leading a hunger strike outside of the White House

3. having a very high IQ

4. owning 100 cats

Prospective Juror 1. I think there are times when the situation calls for a little celebration. I remember when my first grandkid was born. I whooped it up a little myself. As for a hunger strike, well, I think that some people, due to the circumstances in their lives, have been mistreated in this society. Someone should protest for them.

I know this fella who is powerful smart and he is a bit strange, but heck, if we didn't have people who were a little bit different, the world would be an awful boring place.

'Bout them cats. Hmmm. I had an aunt who had more cats than she did hairs on her head. She loved those varmints as if they were kids. She wasn't any stranger than the other folk that I knew. She just didn't have anybody living at home anymore and the cats gave her something to care for and love. Everybody needs something to love.

Prospective Juror 2. The law strictly forbids drinking where I live and, based on that, I think people should not do it. Furthermore, if people want to change the system they should do it through the proper channels. Holding a hunger strike is not the way to make a difference. People will only think you are a little touched if you sit on some steps and don't eat.

I don't like very smart people. All the brainy people I knew in school were either uppity or nerds, not like everybody else.

There are laws about the number of pets one is allowed to own and I think that the law should be upheld at all times.

Connie's lawyer should choose Prospective Juror number _____ .

No. 2 The Who's Who of Mental Disorders

Completing this exercise should help you to achieve the following learning objectives.

(7) *Define anxiety disorder. Know what disorders are classified as anxiety disorders. (pp. 555–559)*

(8) *Define phobia and give a brief description of simple phobia and social phobia. (pp. 555–556)*

(10) *State the causes, according to various theoretical models, of anxiety disorders. (pp. 557–559)*

(13) *Define dissociative disorder. Give a brief description of multiple personality disorder. (p. 560)*

(14) *State the causes, according to various theoretical models, of dissociative disorders. (p. 560)*

(15) *Define mood or affective disorders. Give a brief description of major depression, bipolar disorders, mania, and dysthymic disorder. (pp. 561–568)*

(16) *State the psychological and physiological causes, according to various theoretical models, of affective disorders. Discuss the relationship between learned helplessness and depression. (pp. 564–566)*

(17) *Define schizophrenia. Describe the different symptoms and disorders that are characteristic of*

schizophrenia. Define neologism and loose associations. Be able to distinguish between disorders of thought content and disorders of thought form. (pp. 566–568)

(18) *Know the names of the various types of schizophrenia, the percentage of the total schizophrenic population each type represents, and the distinguishing characteristics of each type. (pp. 568–569)*

(19) *State the possible causes of schizophrenia, according to various theoretical models. (pp. 569–571)*

Cheryl, a hospital receptionist, is in trouble. She has several patients sitting in the reception room and she has misplaced all of the morning files. She does not know which patient is supposed to see which doctor. She has written a list of everything she can remember in order to get each patient to the right doctor. See if you can help her with the rest of her list.

Doctor 1 always checks the level of dopamine in the patient's system to see if he is taking his medication.

Doctor 2 attempts to find out what memories or impulses the patient has repressed.

Doctor 3 talks to his patients for an hour or so. However, the discussion revolves around ways that a person can take control over life and not feel helpless.

Doctor 4 has been investigating the presence of affective disorders in the family history of her patient.

Doctor 5 is trying to discover what experience(s) has made his patient so afraid of saying the year 1952 in public.

Patient A has been standing alone in a corner for over an hour with one foot off the floor and her arms outstretched. Cheryl remembers that last week, this woman was agitated and became wildly excited while in the reception room.

Patient B is sitting next to the window and sobbing. Cheryl remembers that last week this man was trying to get the support of all the people in the office to help him run for president.

Patient C is trying to console patient B.

Patient D is sobbing silently to herself. Her hair and clothing are dirty. Cheryl knows this women lost her job after staying home and sleeping for two weeks.

Patient E is very well dressed. Cheryl chuckles to herself as she remembers her first few encounters with this man. Each week he would write a check to pay his bill, but his handwriting and name would change. She tried to accuse him of fraud.

Doctor 1 is probably seeing patient _____.

Doctor 2 is probably seeing patient _____.

Doctor 3 is probably seeing patient _____.

Doctor 4 is probably seeing patient _____.

Doctor 5 is probably seeing patient _____.

No. 3 The Causes of Abnormal Behavior

Completing this exercise should help you to achieve the following learning objectives.

(10) *State the causes, according to various theoretical models, of anxiety disorders. (pp. 557–559)*

(14) *State the causes, according to various theoretical models, of dissociative disorders. (p. 560)*

(16) *State the psychological and physiological causes, according to various theoretical models, of affective disorders. Discuss the relationship between learned helplessness and depression. (pp. 564–566)*

(19) *State the possible causes of schizophrenia, according to various theoretical models. (pp. 569–571)*

Reread the descriptions of the treatments used by each doctor in exercise 2. Which theoretical model does each doctor seem to favor?

Doctor 1 _____

Doctor 2 _____

Doctor 3 _____

Doctor 4 _____

Doctor 5 _____

ANSWERS TO CONCEPTS AND EXERCISES

No. 1 Choosing a Jury

Connie's lawyer would want jurors who define abnormal behavior from the practical approach. He wants jurors who think that her behavior is understandable given the context or situation of her home-life. Connie's lawyer should choose prospective juror 1. When evaluating the abnormality of each behavior listed, he considers the context as well as the content of the behavior. Prospective juror 2 is very concerned about the frequency of behaviors (the statistical approach) and the social value of behaviors based on the legal system (the valuative approach). (pp. 545–548)

No. 2 Who's Who of Mental Disorders

Doctor 1 is seeing a catatonic schizophrenic (Patient A). This type of schizophrenia is characterized by abnormal movement ranging from stupor to wild excitement. According to the dopamine hypothesis, a high level of dopamine is a causative factor in schizophrenia. (p. 568)

Doctor 2 is seeing a patient who has multiple personality, a dissociative disorder (Patient E). The doctor is trying to find out what repressed memories or impulses have led to the creation of new personalities for this person. (p. 560)

Doctor 3 is seeing a depressed person (Patient D). Learned helplessness may lead to depression, which is why this doctor is trying to help this person realize that she does indeed have control over her life. (p. 561)

Doctor 4 is seeing a person with bipolar disorder (also called manic depression) (Patient B). Genetic factors seem to play a large role in this affective disorder, which is why the doctor is trying to trace the family history. (p. 564)

Doctor 5 is treating a social phobia, which is characterized by the fear of being negatively evaluated by others (Patient C). She is trying to find out what learning experience has caused this person to be afraid of saying the year 1952 in public. (p. 556)

No. 3 The Causes of Mental Disorders

Doctor 1 is checking on a neurotransmitter level. He believes that there is a physical problem causing the schizophrenia. This conforms to the medical model. (p. 569)

Doctor 2 is a psychodynamically-oriented psychologist. She believes that undesirable impulses or memories are at the root of her patient's problems. (p. 560)

Doctor 3 is a cognitive-behavior therapist. He wants his patient to learn that she has control over her life and behavior. (p. 564)

Doctor 4 is trying to trace the genetic components of bipolar disorder. The medical model views genetic factors as important in the causes of mental disorders. (p. 565)

Doctor 5 believes that a learning experience is at the root of the social phobia that her patient is experiencing. This view is associated with the behavioral approach. (p. 557)

MULTIPLE CHOICE QUESTIONS

Facts and Definitions

1. From a statistical point of view, behavior would be considered abnormal if
   a. it caused discomfort.
   b. a very small percentage of the population displayed it.
   c. it were bizarre, but appropriate to the situation in which it was displayed.
   d. a person's ability to meet the demands of everyday life were impaired.

2. Encouraging conformity is associated with which approach to defining normality?
   a. Psychopathological
   b. Valuative
   c. Statistical
   d. Practical

3. The dysfunction criterion is most associated with which approach to defining abnormality?
   a. Statistical
   b. Psychopathological
   c. Valuative
   d. Practical

4. Supernatural explanations of abnormal behavior form the basis of what model?
   a. Behavioral
   b. Phenomenological

c. Biological

d. Demonological

5. According to the _____ model, behavior disorders are evidence of an obstruction in the self-actualization process.

a. phenomenological

b. demonological

c. psychopathological

d. perceptual

6. DSM-III-R is unlike most of its predecessors because it

a. explains the causes of each disorder on Axis I.

b. provides criteria that must be met before a person can be given a diagnostic label.

c. does not consider a person's medical history.

d. describes each disorder from a psychodynamic viewpoint.

7. The increase in inter-rater reliability associated with the use of DSM-III-R has been attributed to what feature?

a. The inclusion of neurotic and psychotic categories

b. Listing the causes of all disorders

c. Listing criteria to be used prior to assigning a diagnostic label

d. The validity of DSM-III-R

8. A conversion disorder is characterized by

a. functional impairment of a limb or sensory ability with no apparent physical cause.

b. severe pain with no apparent cause.

c. a constant fear of becoming seriously ill.

d. frequent vague complaints of physical symptoms.

9. Massive repression of unwanted impulses or memories is responsible for dissociative disorders. Who would say this?

a. A behavioral theorist

b. A phenomenological theorist

c. A psychodynamic theorist

d. A humanistic theorist

10. Behavioral theorists would probably say that people who _____ are or could become depressed.

a. exaggerate the dark side of events

b. blame themselves when things go wrong

c. jump to overly generalized pessimistic conclusions

d. All of the above.

11. Which type of schizophrenia is the most common?

a. Thought disordered

b. Paranoid

c. Catatonic

d. Disorganized

12. Alcoholics tend to be

a. wealthy, educated, and male.

b. poor, elderly, and educated.

c. divorced, male, over sixty-five, and lonely.

d. distributed throughout the population.

13. Cocaine is a

a. barbiturate.

b. hallucinogen.

c. depressant.

d. stimulant.

14. What type of personality disorder would you expect to find among people in jail for fraud?

a. Narcissistic

b. Depressive

c. Anti-social

d. Affective

15. People with Alzheimer's disease have problems with learning and memory, judgment and impulse control, and also have poor personal hygiene. This is called

a. delirium.

b. dementia.

c. conversion disorder.

d. inorganic mental disorder.

MULTIPLE CHOICE QUESTIONS

Application of Concepts

1. Mary Sue, a brilliant neurosurgeon, visits the local animal shelter every morning and lectures the animals on the dangers of ingesting poisonous microbes. Although her behavior is considered a bit strange, the shelter's workers like having someone lavish attention on the animals. Afterward Mary Sue goes to work and starts her day on time. Her behavior would be considered abnormal according to which approach?

   a. Statistical

   b. Psychopathological

   c. Logical

   d. Practical

2. Stephen drinks so much every weekend that he is barely able to function on Monday. His behavior would be considered abnormal according to which approach?

   a. Statistical

   b. Practical

   c. Psychopathological

   d. Logical

3. Zelda is depressed. She is sitting in her cell after being condemned as a witch according to the criteria set by the church. What century is she living in and what model of abnormal behavior do her prosecutors believe in?

   a. Twentieth, demonological

   b. Twentieth, medical

   c. Fifteenth, demonological

   d. Fifteenth, phenomenological

4. Sergio, a psychiatric intern, has just completed an evaluation of his new patient by using DSM-III-R. Read his evaluation and find what is missing: the patient is experiencing major depression, has a dependent personality, has had very minor stress in the past few months, and is in good physical health.

   a. Axis I

   b. Axis II

   c. Axis IV

   d. Axis V

5. Vivian, a graduate student in psychology, has dropped out of school. She cannot attend class because the thought of leaving her apartment leaves her feeling nauseated, anxious, and faint. Her symptoms suggest that she

   a. suffers from agoraphobia.

   b. has a phobia of classrooms.

   c. has a somatoform disorder.

   d. has test anxiety.

6. Joe is a psychotherapist. One of his patients, Regina, complained of being very shy and lonely. She also said that she had a very intense need to repeatedly touch all four walls of any room she has never been in before. Joe told her that she had learned this compulsive behavior so that she could delay immediate social contact with anyone in the room, thereby avoiding the anxiety caused by her extreme shyness. Joe adheres to the _____ model of abnormal behavior.

   a. psychodynamic

   b. phenomenological

   c. behavioral

   d. biological

7. Tom has been suffering from severe chest pain for the past few weeks. His doctor has run extensive tests, but can find no physical problem. Tom

   a. may have a somatoform pain disorder.

   b. is a hypochondriac.

   c. is paranoid.

   d. suffers from a phobia of lung cancer.

8. Hans, a police officer, was working the night shift when he came upon a young man who claimed that he could not remember his name, where he

lived or worked, or anything else about himself. Most likely the mystery person displays

    a. dissociative disorder.
    b. antisocial personality disorder.
    c. multiple personality.
    d. schizophrenia.

9. For the past 3 months, Beth has been sleeping twelve to sixteen hours a day and has gained thirty pounds. Gail, on the other hand, can barely sleep at all and has lost fifteen pounds without trying; she just does not want to eat. Both women could be suffering from

    a. obsessive-compulsive disorder.
    b. major depression.
    c. hyperchondriasis.
    d. hypochondriasis.

10. Philip displays bipolar disorder. Which statement would best describe him?

    a. He is sometimes very depressed and sometimes in a pleasant mood.
    b. He is alternately depressed and wildly elated.
    c. He has sudden onsets of depression that last for a few hours and then he feels fine.
    d. His disorder is a very common one.

11. Richard has just brought home a dog from the pound. He was told that the dog's previous owners had kept it on a leash and beat it daily for no reason. Richard notices that when the neighborhood kids bother the dog it does not even try to run away. If we could examine the dog's brain we would probably find

    a. an excess of dopamine.
    b. an abnormally low level of norepinephrine.
    c. deterioration of the frontal lobes.
    d. enlarged ventricles.

12. Robert has been diagnosed as schizophrenic. He is positive that all the students sitting around him during a test are cheating by reading his thoughts. This describes what type of thought disorder?

    a. Thought blocking
    b. Thought withdrawal
    c. Thought insertion
    d. Thought broadcasting

13. While visiting a psychiatric ward, you overhear the following monologue by one of the patients. "Thereby the obfuscation incipient to redundant and undeniably factual parapsychosis is left in a state transcendental to the issue of man's inhumanity to buildings and federal income tax." This type of communication is called

    a. word salad.
    b. clang associations.
    c. insertions.
    d. attention association.

14. During your first semester at college you had a difficult time living with your roommate. He was basically insecure, but bragged about his accomplishments both in the classroom and out. He used all of your things as though he had a right to them, and he always had to be the center of attention at every party. Your roommate would be diagnosed as having

    a. an antisocial personality disorder.
    b. a narcissistic personality disorder.
    c. a process disorder.
    d. a sociopathic personality disorder.

15. Frank is so afraid of getting sick at the dinner table and being humiliated that he will not eat at a restaurant. Frank has

    a. a simple phobia.
    b. agoraphobia.
    c. a social phobia.
    d. an obsessive-compulsive disorder.

ANSWERS TO MULTIPLE CHOICE QUESTIONS

Facts and Definitions

1. *b* is the answer. The statistical approach says that a behavior is normal if many people in a given population display it; if few people display the behavior, it is considered abnormal. (p. 546)

a. The practical approach, in evaluating behavioral content, considers the discomfort a particular behavior causes as a factor for defining abnormality.

c. Content and when and where a behavior takes place are evaluated by the practical approach to defining abnormality.

d. Meeting the demands of everyday life is part of the dysfunctional criterion, an important feature of behavioral content evaluation in the practical approach.

2. *c* is the answer. To conform, one follows the practices of the majority. Statistically, behaviors that are displayed by the majority of people are normal. This is a problem because some of the world's unique (nonconforming) people might thus be considered abnormal. (p. 546)

a. Psychopathology is another name for mental disorder. It is not an approach to defining abnormality.

b. According to the valuative approach, behaviors that society designates as valued are normal. The problem when using this approach is not conformity, but, rather, deciding just who determines what is valued.

d. According to the practical approach, normal behavior can be unique (not seen frequently in other people) as long as the demands of everyday life are met, and the behavior is situationally appropriate or is approved of by others in that situation.

3. *d* is the answer. The dysfunction criterion, part of the practical approach, asks whether or not a person can display the behavior in question and still meet the demands of everyday life. (p. 547)

a. & c. The dysfunction criterion is not part of the statistical approach or the valuative approach.

b. Psychopathology, another word for mental illness, is not an approach to defining abnormality.

4. *d* is the answer. According to the demonological model, demons, gods, and witches were thought to cause abnormal behavior. (p. 548)

a. According to the behavioral model, abnormal behavior is learned, usually in a social context.

b. According to the phenomenological model, distorted perceptions of the world cause abnormal behavior.

c. According to the biological model, physical problems cause abnormal behavior.

5. *a* is the answer. According to the phenomenological model, failure to be in touch with and express one's own true feelings causes an obstruction in the self-actualization process. When this happens, the person distorts his or her perceptions of reality, which causes behavior disorders. (p. 550)

b. According to the demonological model, supernatural beings cause abnormal behavior.

c. Psychopathology is another word for mental illness, not an approach to defining abnormal behavior.

d. A person's perception of reality is a cause of abnormal behavior according to the phenomenological model, but perception is not a synonym for the name of this model.

6. *b* is the answer. Systems used prior to DSM-III-R provided inadequate guidelines or criteria for psychodiagnosis, causing low inter-rater reliability. The new, stricter guidelines of DSM-III-R have proved useful. (p. 552)

a. Older versions of DSM accepted the psychodynamic explanations of abnormal behavior. The newest version (III-R) describes the features of each disorder but does not provide causal explanations.

c. Axis III of DSM-III-R is devoted to physical problems.

d. DSM-III-R does not take any particular causal viewpoint of abnormal behavior. It simply describes the behavior.

7. *c* is the answer. The criteria for diagnosis have improved interrater reliability. (p. 554)

a. DSM-III-R has eliminated neurosis and psychosis from the list of major disorders.

b. DSM-III-R does not attempt to give causes for abnormal behaviors; it simply describes them.

d. The validity of DSM-III-R is still in question.

8. *a* is the answer. Typical conversion disorders involve functional impairment, such as blindness, paralysis, or deafness, with no apparent physical cause. (p. 559)

b. Somatoform pain is characterized by severe pain with no apparent cause.

c. Hypochondriacs constantly fear becoming seriously ill.

d. Hypochondriacs have a tendency to complain of vague symptoms.

9. *c* is the answer. Dissociative disorders involve some degree of disruption in memory, consciousness, or personal identity. According to the psychodynamic model, behavioral disorders are caused by unresolved *unconscious* psychological conflicts. When they threaten to become conscious and cause anxiety, the individual finds a way to keep them in the unconscious. To accomplish this, some people forget not only unconscious material but also who they are or any of the personal bits of information that identify them. (p. 560)

a. A behavioral theorist would say that an individual has learned wildly discrepant behaviors.

b. & d. A humanistic (phenomenological) theorist would say that an individual's multiple personalities actually represent the overt expression of dramatically conflicting perceptions of the world.

10. *d* is the answer. A cognitive social-learning theorist would say that our thinking, positive or negative, or blaming ourselves instead of the environment, can lead to depression. (p. 564)

11. *b* is the answer. Paranoid schizophrenia accounts for up to 50 percent of all diagnoses. (p. 568)

a. Thought disorders are symptoms, not a type of schizophrenia.

c. Catatonic schizophrenics account for 8 percent of the schizophrenic diagnoses.

d. Disorganized schizophrenics account for 5 percent of the schizophrenic diagnoses.

12. *d* is the answer. Alcoholics do not fall into any one demographic category (age, income, sex, and education), although the percentage of women and teenagers is increasing. (p. 572)

13. *d* is the answer. Cocaine is a stimulant, causing a feeling of self-confidence, well-being, and optimism. Extensive use may produce paranoid thinking and hallucinations, among other problems. (p. 574)

14. *c* is the answer. People in this category, also called psychopaths or sociopaths, display a long-term, persistent pattern of impulsive, selfish, unscrupulous, and even criminal behavior. (p. 575)

a. The main characteristic of narcissistic personality disorder is an exaggerated sense of self-importance. Although these people may be annoying in their constant quest for attention from the right people, they usually are not free of guilt, nor do they tend to commit crimes.

b. Depression is an affective disorder, not a personality disorder. It involves feelings of sadness, hopelessness, and loss of self-worth.

d. An affective disorder is not a personality disorder. Affective disorders, such as depression or mania, involve changes in emotions.

15. *b* is the answer. Alzheimer's disease is a severe brain disorder that produces dementia, a symptom of organic mental disorder. (p. 576)

a. Delirium is a different symptom of organic mental disorder, characterized by an inability to think clearly or concentrate on a particular subject for any length of time.

c. Conversion disorder involves physical symptoms, such as blindness or paralysis, for which there is no obvious physical cause.

d. There is no such thing as an inorganic mental disorder.

ANSWERS TO MULTIPLE CHOICE QUESTIONS

Application of Concepts

1. *a* is the answer. According to the statistical approach, behaviors not displayed by a large number of people are abnormal. Not many neurosurgeons lecture animals on the dangers of ingesting poisonous microbes. (p. 546)

b. There is no such thing as a psychopathological approach to abnormality.

c. There is no such thing as a logical approach to defining abnormal behavior.

d. The practical approach evaluates behavior content in the context of a situation. Mary Sue's behavior is not harmful and does not interfere with her everyday functioning, although it is a bit bizarre. However, this approach states that if everyone in the situation approves, even a bizarre behavior may not be considered abnormal. The shelter's workers like to see Mary giving the animals attention every day. Her behavior is not abnormal in this context.

2. *b* is the answer. Stephen's behavior prevents him from meeting the demands of his everyday life. Therefore, his behavior meets the dysfunctional criterion in the practical approach. (p. 547)

a. Many people drink heavily on the weekends and are unable to function on Mondays; from a strictly statistical view, therefore, Stephen's behavior may not be considered abnormal.

c. There is no such thing as a psychopathological approach.

d. There is no such thing as the logical approach to defining abnormal behavior.

3. *c* is the answer. From the fifth to the fifteenth century, supernatural explanations of behavior disorders dominated. Religious leaders played a large role in deciding who was a witch or a heretic. (p. 548)

a. & b. During the twentieth century, the medical model, which said that abnormal behavior is caused by physical problems, not sorcery, became established.

d. The phenomenological model had not been articulated in the fifteenth century.

4. *d* is the answer. Axis V evaluates the highest level of adaptive functioning over the previous year. This is not mentioned in Sergio's report. (p. 553)

a. Axis I lists descriptions of the major mental disorders. Sergio's patient is experiencing major depression.

b. Axis II lists childhood and personality disorders. Sergio's patient has a dependent personality.

c. Axis IV rates the level of stress experienced in the recent past. Sergio's patient has experienced very minor stress in the past few months.

5. *a* is the answer. Vivian becomes anxious when she thinks about leaving her home. This is a symptom of agoraphobia. (p. 556)

b. Being unable to attend class is a consequence of Vivian's fear of leaving her apartment, but it is not the object of her phobia.

c. Panic attacks are characterized by extreme terror, racing heartbeat, and, sometimes, the feeling of going crazy. Vivian did not experience any of these symptoms.

d. There is no mention of tests or test anxiety in the question. Vivian is afraid of leaving her apartment.

6. *c* is the answer. Behavioral theorists see compulsive behaviors as learned habits that allow a person to escape or avoid anxiety-provoking situations. For Regina, who is painfully shy, new social situations cause extreme anxiety. (p. 557)

a. A psychodynamic therapist would look for unconscious conflicts. Joe is focusing on the behavioral basis of Regina's problem.

b. A phenomenological therapist might suggest that Regina's behavior is a symbolic expression of her values or feelings.

d. Those who view abnormal behaviors as symptoms of biological or medical problems would look for physiological irregularities.

7. *a* is the answer. Severe pain in the chest, neck, or back with no apparent physical cause is a classic symptom of the somatoform disorder called somatoform pain. (p. 560)

b. A hypochondriac worries about being stricken with a serious disease and often reports vague symptoms. Severe pain is not a vague symptom.

c. A paranoid person usually worries about being persecuted by a particular person or group.

d. If Tom had a phobia about contracting lung cancer, then he would be a hypochondriac. See the explanation for response *b.*

8. *a* is the answer. A dissociative disorder is characterized by disruptions in memory, consciousness, or identity. (p. 560)

b. Someone with antisocial personality disorder usually displays a pattern of impulsive, selfish, and even criminal behavior. However, the symptoms associated with personality disorders do not usually include memory loss.

c. Symptoms of multiple personality may include blackouts or a loss of memory over a certain period of time when an alternate personality takes

over, but not a loss of personal information, such as one's name.

d. A schizophrenic experiencing thought blocking or withdrawal may feel as though he or she is being prevented from remembering his or her own name, job, or family, but there are no specific symptoms of memory loss typical of schizophrenics.

9. *b* is the answer. Weight loss or gain, as well as sleep changes, including oversleeping as well as insomnia, are typical of depression. (p. 561)

a. & d. Weight loss or gain and sleeping problems do not usually occur in obsessive-compulsive disorders.

c. There is no disorder known as hyperchondriasis.

10. *b* is the answer. A bipolar disorder belongs to the family of affective disorders because it involves changes in mood and, consequently, behavior. Bipolar means two poles, translated in this case to mean two extremes: depression and wild elation. (p. 564)

a. & c. A pleasant mood is normal, so there is only one symptom present in each answer: depression. Both mania and depression must be present before a bipolar disorder is suspected.

d. Bipolar disorders are very rare (1 out of 100) compared with depression (30 out of 100).

11. *b* is the answer. Richard's dog has learned helplessness; it has learned or come to believe that its actions—barking and growling—will not control its environment by scaring the children away. Learned helplessness is associated with low levels of norepinephrine. (p. 565)

a. An excess of dopamine is associated with schizophrenia.

c. Deterioration of the frontal lobes is associated with organic mental disorders; for example, Alzheimer's disease.

d. Enlarged ventricles are associated with schizophrenia.

12. *d* is the answer. Robert believes that other people can hear his thoughts. This is called thought broadcasting. (p. 567)

a. & b. The belief that a person's thoughts are being prevented or that thoughts are being "stolen" as soon as they appear is called thought blocking or thought withdrawal.

c. The belief that other people's thoughts are being put into a person's mind is called thought insertion.

13. *a* is the answer. Schizophrenics typically have disorders of thought, both in content and in form. Problems with form include word salad: communication that is just a jumble of words. (p. 567)

b. Clang associations are disorders of thought, but they usually involve words that rhyme or have double meanings.

c. Schizophrenics complaining of thought insertions, a thought content disorder, believe that other people are placing thoughts in their heads.

d. There is no such thing as attention association. You probably are confusing two symptoms of schizophrenia: loose associations and disorders of attention.

14. *b* is the answer. Your roommate sounds self-centered, arrogant, and thirsty for attention at all times. This combination of symptoms is typical of narcissistic personality disorders. (p. 575)

a. & d. Someone who coldly and calmly manipulates your feelings, time, or money would fit the description of an antisocial personality disorder.

c. There is no such thing as a process disorder.

15. *c* is the answer. Never displaying a behavior in public, such as eating or writing, for fear of humiliation is called a social phobia. Frank is afraid that he will embarrass himself by vomiting in public, so he refuses to eat at restaurants. (p. 556)

a. Simple phobias include fear of objects or situations, such as heights, dogs, or air travel.

b. Agoraphobia is a fear of leaving one's home and, sometimes, of being alone.

d. An obsessive-compulsive disorder is characterized by taking great pains to be organized, neat, clean, or particular about detail or by recurring, unpleasant thoughts.

Chapter 16

Treatment of Psychological Disorders

OUTLINE

I. INTRODUCTION (p. 584)

Psychotherapy is used by those who take a psychodynamic, phenomenological, or behavioral approach. It involves treating psychological disorders with psychological methods, such as analyzing problems, talking about possible solutions, and encouraging more adaptive ways of feeling, thinking, and acting.

II. GOALS, METHODS, AND FEATURES OF TREATMENT (pp. 586–591)

The goals of treatment are 1) helping clients understand problems, 2) reducing emotional discomfort, 3) encouraging expression of feelings, 4) providing new problem-solving methods, and 5) helping clients to think and to behave in new ways. This is accomplished through 1) providing psychological support, 2) eliminating troublesome behaviors and initiating new ones, and 3) promoting insight and self-exploration.

All methods of treatment share certain basic features, including

1. A suffering client or patient seeking relief from problems.
2. A person who is accepted as one who can help the client because of training or experience.
3. A theoretical explanation of the client's problems.
4. A set of procedures for dealing with the client's problems.
5. A special social relationship between client and therapist, which helps ease the client's problems.

III. PSYCHODYNAMIC PSYCHOTHERAPY (pp. 591–596)

A. The Beginnings of Psychoanalysis

As Freud began talking with patients, he discovered what he thought were unconscious memories and conflicts, which he came to believe were the cause of psychological problems.

B. The Goals of Psychoanalysis

Psychoanalysis attempts to help the patient gain insight about unconscious conflicts and wishes and to understand, or work through, their implications for everyday life.

C. Psychoanalytic Methods of Treatment

1. *Free Association.* This method consists of asking a client to verbalize *all* thoughts, feelings and memories that come to mind. The content and pattern of associations contain clues to unconscious material.

2. *The Interpretation of Dreams*. Patients report the <u>manifest content</u> (the surface story) of a dream and work to understand its <u>latent content</u> (the unconscious meaning) represented by the dream's symbols.

3. *The Analysis of Everyday Behavior*. Freudian slips (unintentional errors in speech) and lapses of memory may be related to unconscious material.

4. *Giving Interpretations*. The therapist's interpretations of free associations, dreams, and everyday behavior help the client understand and confront unconscious material.

5. *Analysis of Transference*. Psychoanalysts reveal nothing of themselves, hoping that the feelings, reactions, and conflict the client experiences toward others will be transferred onto the therapist. <u>Transference</u> may help clients reenact and gain insight into their problems.

C. Variations in Psychoanalysis

Psychoanalysis requires much time, money, verbal skill, and abstract thinking ability; these requirements limit its use. More broadly applicable variations on psychoanalytic treatments seek to help clients gain insight into their thoughts and feelings over a shorter period of time.

D. Some Comments on Psychodynamic Therapy

Critics argue that psychoanalytic concepts, such as defense mechanisms and the ego, id, and superego, are too difficult to scientifically measure. There is little research to document the superiority of psychoanalysis over any other form of treatment.

IV. PHENOMENOLOGICAL PSYCHOTHERAPY (pp. 596–600)

Treatment according to phenomenological approaches is based on the following assumptions: 1) treatment is a human encounter between equals, not a cure; 2) therapists provide an environment in which the patient can grow 3) an accepting and supportive relationship must be established if the person is to grow, and 4) clients are capable of choosing how to feel and think.

A. Person-Centered Therapy

Rogers's <u>person-centered therapy</u> is based on creating a relationship characterized by unconditional positive regard, <u>empathy,</u> and <u>congruence.</u>

1. *Unconditional Positive Regard*. The therapist must show that he or she genuinely cares about and accepts the client as a person and trusts the client's ability to change.

2. *Empathy*. The therapist must act as someone who wants to appreciate how the world looks from the client's point of view. Empathy is communicated through a technique called <u>reflection</u>.

3. *Congruence*. The way the therapist feels is consistent with the way he or she acts toward the client. The therapist's unconditional positive regard and empathy are real, not manufactured.

B. Gestalt Therapy

The goal of <u>Gestalt therapy</u> is to help clients become more self-aware and self-accepting so that they can begin growing again in their own unique, consciously guided directions. Gestalt therapists encourage clients to become aware of real feelings, which they have denied, and to discard foreign feelings, ideas, and values. Therapists are directive in helping clients focus on present, not past, feelings. Role play and a focus on body language are a part of therapy.

C. Comments on Phenomenological Therapy

Although this approach is seen as more positive in nature than psychoanalysis is, it does not have a concrete set of methods nor, except for Rogers's techniques, has it been scientifically evaluated.

V. BEHAVIOR THERAPY (pp. 600–608)

Therapists who use behavior therapy assume that problems are learned patterns of thinking and behaving that can be changed without looking for meaning behind them.

A. Basic Features of Behavior Therapy

Some of the most notable features of behavior therapy include:

1. developing a good client-therapist relationship

2. assessing behavior and setting specific goals

3. providing specific plans for changing behavior

4. continuously evaluating the effects of therapy

B. Methods of Behavior Therapy

1. *Systematic Desensitization.* During desensitization, a client practices progressive relaxation while imagining fear-provoking situations from an anxiety hierarchy. The combination of remaining calm while thinking about something feared weakens the learned association between anxiety and the feared object or situation.

2. *Modeling.* Through participant modeling, a client can learn or get comfortable displaying desirable behaviors. The therapist demonstrates desirable behaviors and the client gradually practices them.

3. *Assertiveness and Social Skills Training.* Clients can learn to express themselves appropriately and be more comfortable in social situations through assertiveness training and social skills training.

4. *Positive Reinforcement.* Therapists systematically use positive reinforcement to alter problematic behaviors. Receiving rewards or tokens is dependent upon a client's display of desirable or "target" behaviors. In institutions, behavior therapists sometimes establish a token economy.

5. *Methods Based on Extinction.* A procedure called flooding keeps patients in a feared but harmless situation. Once deprived of the normally rewarding escape pattern, a client has no reason for continued anxiety.

6. *Aversive Conditioning.* This technique uses classical conditioning to reduce undesirable behavior by associating it with some psychological or physical discomfort.

7. *Punishment.* To eliminate a dangerous or disruptive behavior, an unpleasant stimulus is presented after the behavior, which reduces its occurrence.

C. Cognitive Behavior Therapy

Cognitive behavior therapy can help people change the ways in which they think and behave. Rational emotive therapy (RET) tries to eliminate learned problem-causing thoughts. Cognitive restructuring and stress inoculation training can teach clients new and calming thoughts to help them cope with stressful or anxiety-provoking situations.

D. Some Comments on Behavior Therapy

Behavior therapy has been used to successfully alter many types of problematic behaviors. However, critics argue that punishment and aversive conditioning are dehumanizing, that not all problems are learned, and that changing behaviors or symptoms may not change the underlying problems.

VI. EVALUATING PSYCHOTHERAPY (pp. 608–611)

A. The Effects of Psychotherapy

Although there is still great controversy over the effectiveness of psychotherapy, it does seem to be beneficial. No specific therapy appears clearly better than any other type in dealing with all forms of disorder.

B. Differences Among Therapists

Many people with training ranging from none to doctoral degrees act as psychotherapists in some fashion. Several personal qualities make for particularly effective therapists. The therapist's skill at selecting and using a given method also contributes to the effectiveness of treatment.

VII. BIOLOGICAL TREATMENTS (pp. 611–615)

A. Electroconvulsive Therapy (ECT)

Electroconvulsive therapy (ECT), sending 70 to 150 volts of electricity through the brain, is now used to treat depression when other methods fail. Typically, patients are anesthetized, given a muscle relaxant, and have electric shock passed through the brain for about one-half second. Patients receive six to twelve treatments. ECT is one of the most controversial of the biological treatments.

B. Psychosurgery

Psychosurgical techniques, including prefrontal lobotomies, were once used to treat problems involving strong emotional responses. Today, psychosurgery is done only as a last resort and involves the destruction of only a tiny amount of brain tissue.

C. Drugs

1. *Antipsychotics.* Antipsychotic drugs are effective in reducing delusions, hallucinations, and other severe forms of disturbed behavior.

2. *Antidepressants.* Antidepressants can produce a gradual lifting of depression, allowing the person to return to normal life.

3. *Lithium.* Lithium is helpful in reducing and even preventing both the depression and mania associated with bipolar disorder.

4. *Tranquilizers* (antianxiety drugs). Tranquilizers are the most widely used of all legal drugs and relieve anxiety and tension. Some of them are potentially addictive.

VIII. COMMUNITY PSYCHOLOGY: FROM TREATMENT TO PREVENTION (pp. 615–619)

A. Community Mental Health Centers

Community mental health centers were developed following the advent of drug therapy, in an effort to treat clients in closer proximity to their families and communities. These centers provide long-term outpatient care, some short-term inpatient care, and other services.

B. Prevention

Community psychologists' primary prevention efforts include attempts to reduce difficulties with housing, job training, welfare, day-care facilities, and other related problems that can cause mental health problems. Efforts at secondary prevention include detecting psychological problems in their earliest stages and helping to keep them from becoming worse. Tertiary prevention efforts treat psychological disorders after they appear, with an emphasis on minimizing their long-term effects and keeping them from recurring.

C. An Evaluation

The goals of community-based programs have not yet been realized due to problems in effectively serving vast numbers of people and the refusal of treatment by many homeless patients.

KEY TERMS

1. **Psychotherapy** is the treatment of psychological disorders through psychological methods, such as analyzing problems, talking about possible solutions, and encouraging more adaptive ways of thinking and acting. (p. 584)

Example: Psychoanalysis, person-centered therapy, Gestalt therapy, rational-emotive therapy, and cognitive behavioral therapy are all examples of psychotherapy.

2. **Eclectic** refers to a philosophy of using treatment methods from different approaches depending on what treatment is most suitable for a particular problem, rather than adhering to one approach. (p. 584)

3. **Psychoanalysis**, a method of psychotherapy, seeks to help clients gain insight by recognizing, understanding, and dealing with unconscious thoughts and emotions presumed to cause their problems. Psychoanalysis also aims to help clients work through the many ways in which those unconscious causes appear in everyday behavior and social relationships. (p. 591)

4. **Free association** is a psychoanalytic method in which the client is asked to report *all* feelings, thoughts, memories, and images that come to mind. The content and, especially, the pattern of these mental processes should provide clues to unconscious activity. (p. 592)

REMEMBER: In free association, the pattern of thoughts is just as important as what is said. When clients stop talking or report that their minds have gone blank, Freud would say that they are trying to keep unconscious material from becoming conscious. He was most interested in the ideas just prior to these blank moments.

5. The **manifest content** is a dream's plot or story line, and often contains unimportant features and events from a person's day or reflects temporary needs. (p. 592)

Example: Gina was dreaming about rats fighting in a puddle of water.

6. The **latent content** is a dream's unconscious meaning, represented by the symbols in the dream. (p. 592)

Example: Gina was dreaming about rats fighting in a puddle of water (manifest content). According to psychoanalytic theory, rats might be dream symbols of our siblings and water might symbolize birth. The latent content of Gina's dream might have had something to do with the birth of her siblings.

7. **Transference** occurs when clients relate to the therapist based on their feelings, attitudes, reactions, and conflicts experienced in childhood toward parents, siblings, and other significant people in their lives. (p. 593)

Example: Ramona is complaining that she is tired of being under severe stress. Her therapist suggests that she join an exercise class. She immediately becomes defensive and sarcastic toward the therapist, saying, "Easy for you to say. You're thin and don't have to watch what you eat. Well, I hate exercising. God, you are as bad as my sister, always telling me how to improve myself." Ramona pauses for a moment and says, "I always wanted to be like her. My mother loved her so much and always paid more attention to her."

Notice that the anger and jealousy that Ramona originally directed toward the therapist is actually anger toward her sister. The therapist merely suggested that she join an exercise class to improve her energy level, not necessarily to improve her outward appearance.

8. **Group therapy** is psychotherapy conducted with groups of about five to ten people. The therapist can observe clients interacting with one another in real social situations; clients feel less alone when they

realize other people are struggling with problems; and clients can learn from one another. (p. 595)

9. **Family therapy** involves two or more individuals from the same family, one of whose problems make him or her the initially identified client, but the real client is the family. (p. 595)

10. **Person-centered (or client-centered) therapy**, developed by Carl Rogers, assumes that the client has a drive toward self-actualization and is based on a relationship between client and therapist, characterized by unconditional positive regard, empathy, and congruence. The therapist wants the client to learn to solve his or her own problems and is, therefore, nondirective and does not give advice. (p. 597)

Example: See examples for key terms 11, 12, and 13—empathy, reflection, and congruence— for specific therapeutic methods.

11. **Empathy**, an important feature of person-centered therapy, involves the therapist trying to see the world as the client sees it. The therapist may show the client that he or she understands not only by listening attentively, but also by reflecting what the client says. (p. 598)

Example: Yvonne came into therapy because she resented having to care for her younger sisters even though she knew that her mother was working three jobs. Yvonne's therapist must try to see the world from Yvonne's point of view and can accomplish this by understanding the constraints that Yvonne feels due to such tremendous responsibility.

12. **Reflection** is a method used in person-centered therapy. Therapists restate or paraphrase a client's responses in order to show the client that they are listening and to help the client be more in touch with his or her own feelings. (p. 598)

Example: Read the example for key term 11, *empathy.* The therapist might respond to Yvonne by saying, "You're tired of doing so much around the house with your sisters, which

prevents you from going out and doing what you want. You're angry at your mom." The therapist has reflected what Yvonne has said, which also demonstrates empathy.

13. **Congruence** (sometimes called genuineness) refers to a consistency in the therapist's feelings and behavior toward the client. The therapist's behavior toward the client must be a reflection of how he or she really feels; it cannot be an act. Ideally, the client will learn that openness and honesty can be the foundation of a human relationship. (p. 598)

Example: Read the examples for key terms 11 and 12, empathy and reflection. The therapist must genuinely feel empathy and unconditional positive regard for Yvonne. She cannot think to herself that Yvonne is spoiled and selfish. The therapist must actually accept Yvonne's feelings with unconditional positive regard for her worth as a person.

14. **Gestalt therapy** is a form of phenomenological treatment developed by Fritz Perls. Gestalt therapists take an active and directive role as they help clients to become aware of real feelings and impulses which they have denied, and to discard foreign feelings, ideas, and values. Also, the therapist helps the client to become more self-accepting. Methods used include dialogues with people, inanimate objects (even objects in dreams), and various body parts. (p. 599)

15. **Behavior therapy** uses the principles of learning to change behavior by helping or teaching clients to act and think differently. (p. 601)

Example: Rachel often becomes very angry with her children, only to feel guilty about her behavior later. A behavior therapist might help Rachel understand that she has learned to act this way in these situations and teach her new ways of behaving when interacting with her children.

16. An **anxiety hierarchy** is used in systematic desensitization, a behavioral therapy method. The

client, with the help of the therapist, constructs a set of increasingly fearful or anxiety-filled situations. While relaxing, the client imagines each situation on the hierarchy. The client works through the hierarchy gradually, imagining a more difficult scene only after being able to tolerate the previous one without feeling any distress. (p. 602)

17. **Modeling** is a behavioral therapy method in which a client can learn new behaviors by watching others do them. The client then practices these behaviors. (p. 602)

Example: Kip is afraid of snakes. Modeling therapy might include having him watch films of people handling snakes. Then he might be present in the same room while others are handling snakes. Finally, he can practice handling snakes himself.

18. **Assertiveness training** is a set of behavioral methods used to teach clients how to be more clear, direct, and expressive in social situations. (p. 603)

Example: Nan, a very shy woman, was constantly being taken advantage of despite her knowledge of auto mechanics. Every time she took her car to the mechanic, the garage overcharged her or did unnecessary work. She knew this, but just could not bring herself to say something about it until she had gone through assertiveness training.

REMEMBER: People are taught how to be assertive, not aggressive. Nan does not have to be aggressive in order to effectively express herself in the auto shop. Instead, she simply needs to be direct in her demand for fair service.

19. **Social skills training**, which teaches clients how to be more comfortable and effective in social situations, is a behavioral method of therapy. (p. 603)

Example: Because Margery felt so silly and uncomfortable during job interviews, she found it difficult to sell herself in these situations and rarely got the job despite her excellent qualifica-

tions. Through social skills training, she learned interviewing techniques that allowed her to be more comfortable, effective and hence, successful, in these types of encounters.

20. A **token economy**, based on principles of operant conditioning, is used by behavior therapists, mainly in institutional settings. A system is implemented in which clients must display certain behaviors in order to receive tokens. Tokens can be exchanged for extended privileges, such as snacks, movies, and field trips. (p. 603)

Example: Tony and his therapist have decided that he should be able to complete his daily homework and keep his room neat. For every completed homework assignment he receives two tokens. When he makes his bed, picks up his clothes, and keeps his dresser organized, he receives three tokens. Tony exchanges his tokens for field trips to local museums or going out to dinner in town.

REMEMBER: Eventually, social reinforcements, such as smiles of approval and encouragement, come to replace tokens.

21. **Flooding** is a behavioral technique used to treat phobias. The client is placed in a feared, but harmless, situation. Prevented from escaping, clients have the opportunity to realize that they have no reason to be afraid. (p. 604)

Example: Clinton was deathly afraid of riding on buses. He and his therapist rode a city bus for an hour. Clinton was very frightened at first, but calmed down, and eventually lost his fear.

22. **Aversive conditioning** is a behavioral technique based on classical conditioning. Negative behaviors often must be eliminated, at least partially, prior to learning new behaviors. Aversive conditioning associates the undesirable behavior with an unpleasant physical feeling. People will discontinue using behaviors that result in discomfort. (p. 604)

Example: In the movie *A Clockwork Orange,* the main character spends most of his time raping and beating women. Later he is forced to watch movies of these types of behaviors *while* experiencing the effects of a nausea-producing drug. After the treatment, the mere sight of a woman makes him violently ill.

23. **Cognitive behavior therapy** attempts to pinpoint thought patterns that lead to depression, anger, or anxiety. Once these thoughts are recognized, they can be eliminated and replaced with more constructive thought patterns. (p. 605)

24. **Rational emotive therapy** is a form of cognitive behavior therapy developed by Albert Ellis. Clients are taught to recognize self-defeating thought patterns and helped to replace them with more constructive thoughts. (p. 605)

Example: Brady is a personnel administrator and feels uncomfortable because he is often faced with disciplinary decisions that result in angry employees. His therapist has pointed out that it is unrealistic to think that everyone will like him and be happy with his decisions all of the time. Brady has learned to treat people fairly and not to expect them to always like his decisions.

25. **Cognitive restructuring**, a cognitive behavioral method of therapy, involves helping clients learn calming thoughts that they can use in stressful or anxiety-provoking situations. (p. 606)

Example: Hal was a straight-A student in high school and is very distressed that he might receive several B's this semester, his first at college. When he takes a test he becomes extremely nervous and uptight, which reduces his ability to do well. His therapist is teaching him specific thoughts to be used in these situations. For example, he can say to himself, "Just focus on taking the test and doing the best you can. Don't worry about being perfect or what other people will think if you don't get straight A's."

26. **Stress inoculation training**, a cognitive behavioral method of therapy, involves asking the client to imagine being in some stressful situation so that he or she can practice using new cognitive skills under controlled conditions. (p. 606)

27. **Psychiatrists** are medical doctors who complete special training in the treatment of mental disorder. (p. 610)

28. **SAUNA** is an acronym for the characteristics that are found in effective therapists. The letters stand for sensitive, active, unflappable, nonpunitive, and amoral (not imposing one's morals on a client). Together, these qualities allow a therapist to listen to clients with sensitivity and understanding, to make clients feel accepted, and to require the clients to assume responsibility for solving their problems. (p. 611)

29. **Psychologists** who do psychotherapy have completed a graduate program in clinical or counseling psychology, often followed by additional specialty training. (p. 610)

30. **Electroconvulsive therapy (ECT)** involves passing electric current through the brain for about one-half second. ECT is now used to treat depression when other treatments have failed. It is unclear why ECT is effective. It may be that the convulsions brought on by the shock alter the activity of neurotransmitters associated with depression. (p. 612)

31. **Psychosurgery** involves destroying a very small amount of brain tissue in order to alleviate psychological disorders. This treatment is used as a last resort in treating problems involving strong emotional reactions. (p. 613)

REMEMBER: Psychosurgery treats *psychological* problems through *surgical* techniques.

32. **Prefrontal lobotomy** is an early form of psychosurgery that involved drilling holes in the

skull, inserting a sharp instrument, and moving it from side to side to destroy brain tissue. (p. 613)

33. **Antipsychotic drugs**, used to treat severe psychopathology such as schizophrenia, block the action of dopamine. The use of the phenothiazines has been successful enough to allow many patients to be released from institutions. (p. 613)

34. **Antidepressants**, which increase the amount of serotonin or norepinephrine available at synapses, are useful in treating depression. (p. 614)

35. **Lithium**, used to treat depression and the mania associated with bipolar disorder, reduces the norepinephrine available at synapses. This drug must be given in high doses, requiring careful monitoring of the patient's blood. (p. 614)

36. **Tranquilizers (antianxiety drugs)** are used to reduce anxiety and tension and can become addictive. (p. 614)

37. **Community psychology** attempts to minimize or prevent psychological disorders. Community psychologists' efforts take two forms: primary and secondary prevention. Primary prevention involves trying to eliminate causative factors of underlying psychological problems (such as poverty and inadequate or crowded housing). The goals of secondary prevention efforts include early recognition of psychological problems and treatment designed to prevent problems from becoming worse. (pp. 615–616)

LEARNING OBJECTIVES

1. Define psychotherapy. Define eclectic. (p. 584)

2. Describe the goals of psychotherapy and the three general ways that treatments work toward achieving them. (pp. 586–587)

3. Discuss the five common features of all psychotherapies. (pp. 588–589)

4. Describe the history and goals of psychoanalysis. (pp. 591–592)

5. Define transference, free association, and manifest and latent content of dreams. Discuss the ways in which these methods of psychotherapy reveal clues about unconscious mental processes. (pp. 592–593)

6. Discuss the reasons underlying the variations on psychoanalysis, and describe some of the methods used. Discuss the criticisms of psychoanalysis. (pp. 594–596)

7. Describe the assumptions on which the phenomenological approach is based. (pp. 596–597)

8. Describe person-centered therapy. Discuss the importance of unconditional positive regard, empathy, congruence, and reflection in person-centered therapy. Know the reasoning behind them. (pp. 597–599)

9. Describe Gestalt therapy. Compare and contrast person centered therapy with Gestalt therapy. (pp. 599–600)

10. Define behavior therapy. Describe its basic features and the assumptions on which it is based. (pp. 600–601)

11. Define systematic desensitization, modeling, assertiveness and social skills training, token economy, flooding, aversive conditioning, and punishment as behavioral methods of therapy. Give an example of each term. (pp. 601–605)

12. Define cognitive behavior therapy. Compare it to and contrast it with behavior therapy. (p. 605)

13. Define rational-emotive therapy. Define cognitive restructuring and stress inoculation training. (pp. 605–607)

14. Discuss some criticisms of behavior therapy. (pp. 607–608)

15. Discuss the results of research that has attempted to evaluate psychotherapy's effectiveness. (pp. 608–610)

16. Describe the different types of psychotherapists. (pp. 610–611)

17. Discuss the assumption underlying biological therapies. (p. 611)

18. Describe the historical and present use of electroconvulsive therapy (ECT). (p. 612–613)

19. Describe the historical and present use of psychosurgery. (p. 613)

20. Describe the effects of antipsychotic, antidepressant, and antianxiety drugs. Know how each type of drug works within the nervous system. (pp. 613–614)

21. Define community psychology. Describe the types of work involved in community psychologists' attempts at primary and secondary prevention. (pp. 615–617)

22. Discuss the effectiveness of community psychologists' work. (pp. 618–619)

CONCEPTS AND EXERCISES

No. 1 Differentiating Approaches to Therapy

Completing this exercise should help you to achieve the following learning objectives.

(4) *Describe the history and goals of psychoanalysis. (pp. 591–592)*

(7) *Describe the assumptions on which the phenomenological approach is based. (pp. 596–597)*

(10) *Define behavior therapy. Describe its basic features and the assumptions on which it is based. (pp. 600–601)*

(12) *Define cognitive behavior therapy. Compare it to and contrast it with behavior therapy. (p. 605)*

(17) *Discuss the assumption underlying biological therapies. (p. 611)*

Several psychotherapists have met at a convention to have dinner. Over coffee they argue about the various causes of abnormal behavior and mental processes. Decide what type of therapy each therapist probably practices.

Patricia: Clearly, thoughts in the unconscious drive behavior. If unconscious thoughts are revealed, the client can understand and possibly change the problematic behavior. You, on the other hand, Sam, treat only the behavior and not the cause. _____

Sam: What does it matter if I treat only the behavior? My goal is to create new behaviors that allow people to function in their environment. If they are functional, they will probably be successful and receive positive reinforcement, making them feel good about themselves. _____

Miranda: She has a point, Sam. If you would try to alter conscious thought patterns as I do, replacing problematic ones with functional ones, then many behaviors associated with those thoughts might change as well. _____

Ida: I think you all are a bit on the manipulative side. We are therapists, but our clients have the ability to grow and change on their own. They just need to get in touch with their feelings. All we have to do is step back, accept them as people, and show them it's OK to accept themselves just as they are.

Lana: Pretty soon, you folks are going to be out of a job. When we understand how the brain works, we will be able to treat most psychological problems with drugs or corrective surgery. _____

No. 2 Identifying Methods of Therapy

Completing this exercise should help you to achieve the following learning objectives.

(5) *Define transference, free association, and manifest and latent content of dreams. Discuss the ways in which these methods of psychotherapy reveal clues about unconscious mental processes. (pp. 592–593)*

(8) *Describe person-centered therapy. Discuss the importance of unconditional positive regard, empathy, congruence, and reflection in person-centered therapy. Know the reasoning behind them. (pp. 597–599)*

(9) *Describe Gestalt therapy. Compare and contrast person-centered therapy with Gestalt therapy. (pp. 599–600)*

(11) *Define systematic desensitization, modeling, assertiveness and social skills training, token economy, flooding, aversive conditioning, and punishment as behavioral methods of therapy. Give an example of each term. (pp. 601–605)*

(13) *Define rational-emotive therapy. Define cognitive restructuring and stress inoculation training. (pp. 605–607)*

(18) *Describe the historical and present use of electroconvulsive shock therapy (ECT). (pp. 612–613)*

(19) *Describe the historical and present use of psychosurgery. (p. 613)*

(20) *Describe the effects of antipsychotic, antidepressant, and antianxiety drugs. Know how each type of drug works within the nervous system. (pp. 613–614)*

Following are several descriptions of treatments given to various clients. Give the name of each treatment.

1. Carol, a schizophrenic, takes a drug that blocks the action of dopamine in her brain. What type of drug is she taking? _____

2. Due to severe depression, Stephen takes a drug that increases the amount of serotonin and norepinephrine available at his brain synapses. What are the drugs that Stephen could be taking? _____

3. Betty is afraid of writing her name in public. Her therapist has taken her to a restaurant and asked her to write her name until she has covered several pieces of paper. What is this behavioral method? _____

4. Lucy is overweight. Her therapist has given her a drug that will make her nauseated as soon as she begins to feel the slightest bit full after eating. What is this behavioral method? _____

5. Flora received almost every treatment available for depression. Her doctor has suggested a drastic method as a last resort. What is this method of last resort? _____

6. Irene is painfully shy. Her teacher has devised a new system to prompt Irene to participate in group discussions at school. Every time Irene speaks she will receive ten points. At the end of the day she can cash in her points for special privileges, such as going to the library or choosing what book the teacher is going to read to the class. What behavioral method is her teacher using? _____

ANSWERS TO CONCEPTS AND EXERCISES

No. 1 Differentiating Approaches to Therapy

Patricia is a psychoanalyst. She believes that unconscious mental processes cause behavior. Methods such as free association, dream analysis, transference, and the analysis of everyday behaviors are designed to bring unconscious material into conscious awareness. (pp. 591–597)

Sam is a behavioral therapist. His goal is to change behavior, not mental processes. Methods such as token economies, flooding, and aversive conditioning are designed to change behavior. (pp. 600–605)

Miranda is a cognitive behavior therapist. She believes that behavior can be changed by altering harmful conscious thought patterns. Cognitive restructuring and rational-emotive therapy are methods designed to alter thought patterns. (pp. 605–607)

Ida is a phenomenological therapist. She believes that her clients have a natural tendency toward growth and change. Clients simply need to get in touch with their feelings. Empathy, reflection, congruence, and unconditional positive regard help the client achieve this goal. (pp. 596–600)

Lana is a biological therapist. She believes that altering the the nervous system's chemical activity will change behavior. (pp. 611–614)

No. 2 Identifying Methods of Therapy

1. Carol is probably taking a phenothiazine, which is used to treat severe disorders, such as schizophrenia. (p. 613)

2. Stephen is probably taking either a monoamine oxydase inhibitor or a tricyclic in order to combat depression. (p. 614)

3. Betty's therapist is using a method called flooding. Betty will be exposed to the object or event that she fears and not be allowed to escape. She will eventually realize that there is nothing to fear. (p. 604)

4. Lucy's therapist is using aversive conditioning. Lucy will come to associate the feeling of being full (conditioned stimulus) with nausea (unconditioned stimulus). (p. 604)

5. Flora's doctor will suggest that she receive electroconvulsive therapy (ECT), a last-resort treatment for depression. (p. 612)

6. Irene's teacher has set up a token economy. The points act as tokens, which can later be exchanged for the positive reinforcement of Irene's choice. (p. 603)

MULTIPLE CHOICE QUESTIONS

Facts and Definitions

1. The goals of any type of therapy would include
    a. providing psychological support.
    b. changing certain behaviors.
    c. promoting insight into personality and problems.
    d. All of the above.

2. The type of therapy to be used in a given case should depend on
    a. the nature of the client's problem.
    b. the time the client has available.
    c. the money the client has available.
    d. All of the above.

3. The focus of Freudian psychoanalysis is on
    a. replacing problematic behaviors with desirable behaviors.
    b. teaching the client new ways of thinking.
    c. getting the client in touch with his or her present feelings.
    d. helping the client gain insight into unconscious problems.

4. A _____ therapist would use rational-emotive therapy.
    a. psychoanalytic
    b. phenomenological
    c. cognitive behavior
    d. biological

5. In psychoanalysis, transference occurs when
    a. unconscious thoughts become conscious.
    b. clients transfer their feelings about a significant person in their life onto the therapist.
    c. the manifest content of a dream is translated into latent content.
    d. free association reveals unconscious conflicts.

6. Carl Rogers developed
   a. person-centered therapy.
   b. rational-emotive therapy.
   c. cognitive behavior therapy.
   d. object relations therapy.

7. Empathy in client-centered or person-centered therapy refers to
   a. perceiving the client's view of reality.
   b. restating or paraphrasing a client's words.
   c. unconditional positive regard.
   d. congruence between a therapist's words and actions.

8. In behavioral therapy, associating an unpleasant stimulus with the simultaneous occurrence of an undesirable behavior is called
   a. aversive conditioning.
   b. systematic desensitization.
   c. flooding.
   d. building an anxiety hierarchy.

9. Aversive conditioning is
   a. based on operant conditioning.
   b. based on classical conditioning.
   c. used to increase a behavior's occurrence.
   d. based on reward and punishment.

10. Group and family therapies were originally offered by _____ therapists.
    a. biological
    b. phenomenological
    c. behavioral
    d. psychoanalytical

11. Which of the following is not a problem encountered in research on psychotherapy's effectiveness?
    a. It is difficult to define success in psychotherapy.
    b. The results of most studies were fabricated.
    c. Research data indicating the success of psychotherapy has, at times, been ignored.

d. Therapists using different methods employ different measures of success.

12. In the past, memory loss, speech disorders, broken bones, and even death have been associated with which type of treatment?
    a. Psychosurgery
    b. Lithium
    c. Electroconvulsive therapy (ECT)
    d. Prefrontal lobotomy

13. Which of the following is *not* a criticism of drug therapy?
    a. Drugs may only treat symptoms and not the problem itself.
    b. Drug therapy may make patients depend on the drug, instead of on their own efforts, for improvement.
    c. Many drugs have unwanted side effects.
    d. Drug therapy is more expensive than any other kind of therapy.

14. In which scenario may a therapist *not* reveal confidential information?
    a. When discussing a case with a family member
    b. When defending oneself against a malpractice charge
    c. When the client requires hospitalization
    d. When the therapist feels the client may physically harm another person

15. Which of the following describes flooding?
    a. The client is gradually exposed to the feared stimulus.
    b. The client is placed in a fearful situation and not allowed to escape.
    c. The client learns not to let negative thoughts overwhelm or flood the mind.
    d. The client receives a negative stimulus following an undesirable behavior.

MULTIPLE CHOICE QUESTIONS

Application of Concepts

1. Last night Christi dreamed she was running around her backyard, dropping down into a well, and resurfacing through a hole in the ground, only to run back to the well and drop down again. This describes the

    a. manifest content of her dream.
    b. transference of her dream.
    c. latent content of her dream.
    d. free association within the dream.

2. Marion's therapist has asked her to talk to the dead fish that was in her dream. What kind of therapist is he or she?

    a. Psychoanalytic
    b. Behavioral
    c. Phenomenological
    d. Cognitive behavioral

3. Jill's therapist has recommended electroconvulsive therapy (ETC). Jill is probably experiencing

    a. schizophrenia.
    b. depression.
    c. hallucinations.
    d. anxiety.

4. Joe is a bartender with a high school education. He is sensitive to his customers' feelings, nothing shakes him, and he never tries to impose his own morals on them when asked for advice. Joe is probably

    a. a retired psychiatrist.
    b. a psychologist.
    c. a psychiatric social worker.
    d. a SAUNA.

5. Martha is a YAVIS. She would make

    a. a much better therapist than a SAUNA.
    b. a much better client than a HOUND.
    c. a much better therapist than a HOUND.
    d. All of the above.

6. Harvey is a psychotherapist. In treating his clients, he uses systematic desensitization and participant modeling in cases of phobia. What type of therapist is Harvey?

    a. Behavioral
    b. Psychoanalytic
    c. Phenomenological
    d. Biological

7. Belinda fears driving in the mountains. Her therapist has suggested that they take a ride into the mountains for several hours. What method is the therapist proposing?

    a. Aversive conditioning
    b. Modeling
    c. Punishment
    d. Flooding

8. Amy has been sent to a camp for children with behavior disorders. On her first day, she and her counselor decided what behaviors Amy would learn to do on a daily basis. These included playing cooperatively, speaking respectfully to the counselors, and helping clean the dining hall after dinner. Immediately following the successful display of a behavior, Amy will receive a pink piece of cardboard. Each day she can trade these for special activities and privileges. This is an example of

    a. aversive conditioning.
    b. flooding.
    c. token economy.
    d. cognitive restructuring.

9. Dan is a hyperactive child who continually injures himself. His doctors have tried everything they can think of to stop this behavior. What kind of therapeutic method would probably be best for Dan?

    a. Traditional psychoanalysis
    b. Flooding
    c. Punishment, followed by rewards for approved behavior
    d. Electroconvulsive therapy

10. Michael has spent the morning teaching pre-school teachers the early signs of psychological problems, hoping that children can be helped before their problems become severe. What level of prevention is this?

    a. Primary
    b. Secondary
    c. Tertiary
    d. None of the above.

11. Jacob has gone to see a therapist because he dislikes himself. He cannot seem to get perfect grades, and he is not the most popular person on his dorm floor. He feels depressed. What kind of therapy do you think would be best for Jacob?

    a. Antidepressant drugs
    b. Rational-emotive
    c. Aversive conditioning
    d. Token economy

12. Nina had been experiencing moods of extreme elation alternating with severe depression. What kind of drug will her doctor most likely prescribe?

    a. Tricyclics
    b. Phenothiazines
    c. Monoamine oxydase inhibitors
    d. Lithium

13. As part of Karla's therapy session, she spent an evening role-playing with other members of her group. Situations such as returning faulty merchandise, sending improperly prepared food back to the cook in a restaurant, and telling her roommate when she needs quiet in the room were the topics of the evening. Karla is experiencing

    a. depression.
    b. punishment.
    c. assertiveness training.
    d. aversive conditioning.

14. Robert has a dog phobia. He and his therapist go for a walk, and Robert watches from across the street as his therapist approaches people who are walking their dogs. The therapist asks the owner if the dog is friendly, lets the dog sniff his hand, and gently pats the dog. The therapist is using _____ to help Robert.

    a. token economies
    b. modeling
    c. flooding
    d. primary prevention

15. Vivian is tearfully telling a friend that she is depressed and does not even know why. Her friend says, "You seem to be so unhappy, a little confused, and maybe a bit scared too." Vivian's friend is using which method associated with person-centered therapy?

    a. Sympathy
    b. Empathy
    c. Reflection
    d. Both *b* and *c*.

ANSWERS TO MULTIPLE CHOICE QUESTIONS

Facts and Definitions

1. *d* is the answer. Although each therapist has his or her own methods and ideas regarding the causes of abnormal behavior, all therapies have common goals: providing psychological support, changing certain behaviors, and gaining insight into personality and problems. (p. 588)

2. *d* is the answer. Each method places varying constraints on the client's time and money. Further, some methods are better than others at correcting certain problems. For example, a businesswoman under a great deal of time pressure needs to reduce her fear of flying. She probably does not have the time for psychoanalysis, but could probably benefit from behavior therapy aimed specifically at reducing her fears. The choice of method will also depend on what the therapist's knowledge and experience suggest would be best. (p. 587)

3. *d* is the answer. The focus of psychoanalytic therapy is to reveal and to work through unconscious conflicts. (p. 591)

a. Behavior therapies usually focus on replacing undesirable behaviors with new ones.

b. Cognitive behavioral therapies focus on teaching the client new and more constructive ways of thinking.

c. Phenomenological therapists help clients to get in touch with and to express their present feelings.

4. *c* is the answer. Rational-emotive therapy is a cognitive behavioral therapy. Clients are taught to recognize damaging thoughts and to replace them with more positive and functional thoughts. (p. 605)

a. Psychoanalysts focus on revealing a person's unconscious thoughts and conflicts.

b. Phenomenological therapists focus on a person's feelings about themselves and their drive toward growth.

d. Biological methods are used either alone or in conjunction with other forms of therapy to cause changes in nervous system functioning.

5. *b* is the answer. Psychoanalysts believe that if they reveal nothing about themselves, clients will begin to transfer onto them many feelings and attitudes about conflicts experienced with significant people in their lives. (p. 593)

a. & d. Free association does help to reveal unconscious conflicts, making them conscious. This process is not called transference.

c. Interpreting a dream's manifest content in order to understand its symbolic or latent content is part of psychoanalytic treatment. This process is not called transference.

6. *a* is the answer. Carl Rogers developed the phenomenological methods called person-centered therapy, also called client-centered therapy. (p. 597)

b. Albert Ellis developed rational-emotive therapy.

c. Rational-emotive therapy is a type of cognitive behavioral therapy.

d. Object relations therapy is a variation of psychoanalysis.

7. *a* is the answer. A client-centered therapist must empathize, seeing or perceiving the world from the client's point of view. (p. 598)

b. Restating or paraphrasing a client's feelings is a way to demonstrate empathy.

c. Unconditional positive regard is necessary to let the client know that the therapist cares about and accepts the client as a person.

d. Congruence is the match between the therapist's words and actions toward a client. The therapist must actually experience, not just act out, unconditional positive regard and empathy for a client.

8. *a* is the answer. Aversive conditioning is used to decrease a behavior's occurrence. An unpleasant stimulus is experienced every time an undesirable behavior is displayed. (p. 604)

b. Systematic desensitization is used to decrease fears and anxiety. A client relaxes and thinks of increasingly fearful images. Eventually, the client can remain relaxed even while thinking about whatever previously caused him or her extreme anxiety.

c. Flooding is based on extinction. A client is exposed to the entire object, situation, or event that he or she fears. Since the client cannot escape, he or she has the chance to realize that the fear is unfounded.

d. Anxiety hierarchies are used in systematic desensitization.

9. *b* is the answer. Aversive conditioning is based on classical conditioning. For example, an alcoholic client wants to stop drinking. The client takes a drug that causes nausea whenever alcohol is consumed. The drink becomes a conditioned stimulus that signals the presence of nausea. Thereafter, the client will probably avoid the alcohol. (p. 604)

a. & d. Methods such as token economies and punishment are based on operant conditioning principles.

c. Aversive conditioning is used to *decrease* the occurrence of a specific behavior.

10. *d* is the answer. Psychoanalytic therapists were the first to offer group and family therapy. (p. 595)

a. Biological therapies are aimed at altering the functioning of the nervous system. Families may be informed as to how they can help an individual who is on medication, but this is not the focus of the therapy.

b. & c. Eventually, other types of therapists offered group and family therapy but psychoanalytical therapists were first.

11. *b* is the answer. Fabricated studies were not a problem mentioned in your text's discussion of the evaluative studies on psychotherapy. (p. 608)

a. & d. A behavioral therapist would probably define the success of a client differently than a psychoanalyst would, making it difficult to compare the effectiveness of different types of therapy.

c. Eysenck, who conducted one of the first large-scale comparisons of psychotherapy effects, was accused of ignoring evidence that therapy did indeed help clients.

12. *c* is the answer. In the past, ECT had serious side effects. Among them were broken bones, memory loss, speech disorders, and, in some cases, death. (p. 612)

a. & d. Psychosurgery also has serious side effects which include memory loss, but not broken bones.

b. Lithium is problematic to administer, but these side effects are not associated with this drug.

13. *d* is the answer. Drugs are not necessarily the most expensive form of therapy. Freudian psychoanalytic therapy, because it can take several years, is very expensive. (p. 614)

a., b., & c. These are all problems with drug therapy.

14. *a* is the answer. A therapist is bound by law to keep strictly confidential any information revealed by a client. He or she can only discuss a case with a client's family if the client gives permission. (p. 589)

b., c., & d. These are all situations in which the therapist may release information given by the client.

15. *b* is the answer. A client is exposed to the feared situation, object, or event and is not allowed to escape. For example, a client who fears elevators may spend quite a bit of time riding elevators with his or her therapist. Since the person cannot escape, he or she can come to realize there is nothing to fear. (p. 604)

a. Gradual exposure to a feared stimulus takes place in systematic desensitization or participant modeling.

c. Cognitive restructuring can teach a client to replace destructive thoughts with more effective or constructive thoughts.

d. Presenting an unpleasant stimulus after an undesirable behavior is called punishment.

ANSWERS TO MULTIPLE CHOICE QUESTIONS

Application of Concepts

1. *a* is the answer. A dream's plot or story line is called the manifest content. (p. 592)

b. Transference occurs when a client projects attitudes and feelings about a person in his or her life onto the therapist.

c. A dream's symbolic interpretation is called the latent content.

d. The method of free association does not occur within dreams. Clients may be asked to free associate about the content of their dreams.

2. *c* is the answer. A Gestalt therapist would be likely to have a client participate in a dialogue with inanimate objects in dreams. (Gestalt therapy is a phenomenological approach.) (pp. 599–600)

a. Psychoanalytic therapists use dream interpretation as a method of revealing unconscious conflicts. But role play or talking to objects in a dream is not part of psychoanalytic dream analysis.

b. A behavioral therapist probably would not be interested in a client's dreams.

d. A cognitive behavioral therapist probably would not use dream interpretation as a basic therapeutic method.

3. *b* is the answer. ECT is currently used to treat depression. (p. 612)

a. & *c*. ECT was once used to treat schizophrenia. Hallucinations are a symptom of schizophrenia and other serious psychopathologies.

d. Drugs are used to biologically treat anxiety.

4. *d* is the answer. Joe has many of the characteristics found in effective therapists. (p. 611)

a., *b*., & *c*. These alternatives all require academic degrees beyond high school.

5. *b* is the answer. A YAVIS is a young, attractive, verbal, intelligent, and successful client. A HOUND is a homely, old, unattractive, nonverbal, and dull client who probably will not do as well in therapy. (p. 622)

a. A SAUNA is sensitive, active, unflappable, nonpunishing, and amoral (does not impose his or her morals on a client). These characteristics are present in effective therapists.

c. The acronym YAVIS is used to describe a good client.

d. *b* is the answer.

6. *a* is the answer. Harvey is a behavioral therapist because he uses methods based on learning theory. (pp. 602–603)

b. A psychoanalyst would be far more likely to use free association, dream analysis, and other methods aimed at revealing unconscious material.

c. & *d*. A phenomenological or biological therapist would probably not use systematic desensitization.

7. *d* is the answer. To use the flooding method, a client is placed in a feared but harmless situation and not allowed to escape. The person soon realizes that he or she has nothing to fear. Exposing Belinda to the situation she fears and not allowing her to escape may help her overcome her fear of driving in the mountains. (p. 604)

a. Aversive conditioning is also used to decrease behavior. However, clients experience a negative stimulus when they engage in the undesirable behavior.

b. Modeling involves teaching a client desirable behaviors by demonstrating those behaviors and showing the client how to behave more calmly in feared situations. However, the client is not actually *in* the feared situation.

c. Punishment, a procedure used to decrease a behavior, involves presenting a negative stimulus following an undesirable behavior.

8. *c* is the answer. The camp has set up a type of economic system in which campers receive tokens when they display behaviors they have agreed to work on. The campers can exchange their tokens for various forms of positive reinforcement. In Amy's case, her tokens are exchanged for special activities and privileges. Token economies serve to increase the occurrence of desirable behaviors. (p. 603)

a. Aversive conditioning is used to decrease, not increase, a behavior's occurrence.

b. Flooding is used to decrease a behavior, usually avoidance.

d. Cognitive restructuring involves replacing negative and damaging thoughts with more constructive thoughts.

9. *c* is the answer. Self-injury is dangerous and needs to be corrected as soon as possible. Dan's doctors have tried many forms of therapy and each one failed. Punishment, used as a last resort, may help to decrease Dan's harmful behavior, allowing more adaptive behavior to be rewarded. (p. 605)

a. Freudian psychotherapy or psychoanalysis would be difficult for a child, who may not have adequate verbal skills or abstract thinking ability.

b. Flooding is used to decrease avoidance behavior due to a phobia. Dan does not appear to have a phobia. He is hyperactive.

d. Electroconvulsive therapy involves passing an electric current through one or both sides of the brain. It is used as a last resort to treat depression. Dan is hyperactive, not depressed.

10. *b* is the answer. Secondary prevention aims at recognizing and treating problems before they become severe. Michael can help the teachers learn to recognize psychological problems in their earliest stages. (p. 617)

a. Primary prevention attempts to remove the most general causes of psychological problems, such as overcrowded housing or unemployment.

c. Tertiary prevention attempts to treat psychological problems and to return patients to their community.

d. b is the answer.

11. *b* is the answer. Jacob's ideas about having everyone like him and being a perfect student are probably at the root of his depression. Rational-emotive therapy will help him to recognize and eliminate these unhealthy thoughts. (p. 605)

a. Jacob's depression might be alleviated by antidepressants. But, it is obvious that his thought patterns about being liked and perfect will continue to cause him problems. Changing his thinking should alleviate his depression on a long-term basis.

c. Aversive conditioning is used to decrease a specific behavior. Jacob needs to change his thought patterns, not a specific behavior.

d. Token economies are used to increase the occurrence of desired behaviors. Jacob needs to change his thought patterns, not his overt behavior.

12. *d* is the answer. Lithium is used to treat bipolar disorders. (p. 614)

a. & c. Tricyclics and MAO inhibitors are used to treat depression.

b. Phenothiazines are used to treat severe disorders, such as schizophrenia.

13. *c* is the answer. Karla is learning how to be assertive in social situations. Remember, assertive is not the same thing as aggressive. Karla can be assertive, get her food prepared the way she likes it, and not be aggressive about it. (p. 603)

a. Karla may be a little depressed that she cannot get what she wants in social situations. However, this depression is a symptom of not being assertive.

b. & d. Punishment and aversive conditioning are used to decrease undesirable behaviors. Karla is in therapy to learn new behaviors, not to decrease old, undesirable behaviors.

14. *b* is the answer. Modeling involves teaching a client desirable behaviors by demonstrating those behaviors and showing the client how to behave more calmly in feared situations. (p. 603)

a. Token economies involve receiving tokens for demonstrating desirable behaviors. The tokens can later be traded in for rewards or privileges. Robert is not performing any behaviors; he is watching how his therapist behaves with dogs.

c. Flooding involves placing the client in a feared but harmless situation. Once deprived of his or her normally rewarding escape pattern, the client has no reason for continued anxiety. If Robert and his therapist had shut themselves in a small room with a gentle, friendly dog, this would have been the answer.

d. The work of a community psychologist may involve primary prevention, removing the causes of psychological problems.

15. *d* is the answer. Paraphrasing what Vivian has said (reflection) expresses empathy; her friend seems to know just how she feels. (p. 598)

a. Sympathy involves expressing concern for someone else, but need not be based on empathy or involve reflection.

b. Both *b* and *c* are correct.

c. Both *b* and *c* are correct.

Chapter 17

The Individual in the Social World

OUTLINE

I. INTRODUCTION (p. 624)

Social psychology focuses on effects of the social world on the behavior and mental processes of individuals, pairs, and groups.

II. SOME BASIC SOURCES OF SOCIAL INFLUENCE (pp. 624–632)

A. Social Comparison

According to the theory of social comparison, people use other people as a basis of comparison for self-evaluation when there are no objective criteria.

1. *Reference Groups.* We use people who are similar to ourselves, or reference groups, for self-evaluation.

2. *Relative Deprivation.* As changes occur over the course of life, people change reference groups. People may, at first, find their self-

evaluations to be poor in comparison to others in the new group. Usually people do not compare themselves to others who are not in their immediate reference group. Chronic use of extreme reference groups can lead to depression and anxiety.

B. Social Facilitation and Social Interference

Social facilitation occurs when the mere presence of other people improves performance.

1. *Performance and Arousal.* The presence of other people tends to increase arousal or motivation. An increase in arousal increases performance on familiar or easy tasks, but decreases performance on unfamiliar or complex tasks.

2. *Sources of Arousal.* The presence of others may create arousal by making people apprehensive about being evaluated by others or by intensifying self-evaluation.

C. Social Norms

Norms are learned, socially based rules that prescribe correct and incorrect behaviors for various situations.

1. *The Reciprocity Norm.* People tend to behave reciprocally; they tend to treat others as they have been treated. People will concede, give in, or donate to an individual or group that has given them something.

2. *Differing Norms.* Norms vary with situations, cultures, and subcultures. When people move to a new reference group, they tend to adopt the new group's norms.

III. ATTITUDES, PERSUASION, AND ATTITUDE CHANGE (pp. 632–639)

A. The Nature of Attitudes

An attitude refers to cognitive (belief), emotional (positive or negative evaluation), and behavioral (way of acting) reactions to an object. These three components are not always strongly related. Attitudes are relatively stable, but can change.

B. Persuasive Communications

Persuasive communications can change attitudes depending on:

1. *Characteristics of the Communicator*. Maximum attitude change occurs when the communicator is perceived as credible, sincere, and similar to the listener.

2. *Nature of the Message*. A one-sided message is best when the audience agrees with the speaker's point of view. A two-sided message is best when the audience initially disagrees with the speaker. All messages should contain very clear conclusions. Fear appeals are more persuasive when they are not too frightening and include information about how the audience can avoid the fearful consequences.

3. *Characteristics of the Audience*. Individuals with low or high self-esteem are less susceptible to persuasive communications than individuals of moderate self-esteem.

C. Behavioral Influences on Attitudes

1. *Cognitive Dissonance Theory*. Most people prefer to have attitudes that are consistent with one another. When attitudes or beliefs are inconsistent, people tend to change one in order to make them consistent and reduce psychological dissonance.

2. *Self-Perception Theory*. People sometimes observe their own behavior in order to determine their attitudes.

IV. SOCIAL PERCEPTION (pp. 639–648)

Social perception is the way in which people perceive others and themselves.

A. First Impressions

1. *Schemas*. People often use schemas, which are coherent and organized sets of beliefs and expectations, to evaluate others, rather than using individual attributes.

2. *Forming Impressions*. People tend to give others the benefit of the doubt and form positive first impressions. However, negative information is given more weight than positive information.

3. *Lasting Impressions*. First impressions are difficult to change, because they shape our interpretations of new information about a person.

4. *Self-Fulfilling Prophecies*. An initial impression can create a self-fulfilling prophecy. The first impression elicits behavior that confirms the impression.

B. Group Stereotypes and Prejudice

Stereotypes are impressions or schemas of entire groups of people. They often lead to prejudice, a positive or negative attitude toward the group. The behavioral component of prejudice is often discrimination.

1. *Motivational Theories*. People with authoritarian personalities tend to obey anyone above them in social status and demand deference from anyone below them in social status. They need to identify the status of others in relation to themselves. People with authoritarian personalities may be predisposed to develop negative stereotypes of those perceived as occupying a lower status.

2. *Learning Theories*. Children often learn stereotypes from their parents, their peers, and others. The contact hypothesis states that stereotypes and prejudices about a group should be reduced as friendly contact between members of equal standing in the two groups is increased.

3. *Cognitive Theories*. Due to the complexity of the world, people tend to categorize others in

groups. Some of these groups represent stereotypes. People use distinctive characteristics, such as sex and age, as a basis for creating in-groups and out-groups.

C. Attribution Theory

We can attribute a person's behavior to the internal characteristics of a person or to the external characteristics of the situation.

1. *Criteria for Attributions*. How people go about making attributions depends on consensus, consistency, and distinctiveness. An internal attribution is made if *consensus* is low, *consistency* is high, and *distinctiveness* is low.

2. *Attributional Biases*. The egocentric bias is the tendency to assume that others act and believe just as you do. The ego-defensive bias is the tendency to take credit for success but to blame external causes for failure. Another attributional bias involves the *belief in a just world*. People tend to think that good things happen to good people and bad things happen to bad people. Attribution is also affected by the availability heuristic, which is the tendency to judge the frequency of an event by how easily the event comes to mind. People attribute behavior to causes that readily come to mind. The fundamental attribution error is the tendency to attribute our own behavior to external causes and other people's behavior to internal causes.

V. ATTRACTION (pp. 648–653)

A. Some Situational Determinants

1. *Propinquity and Familiarity*. The more often people interact the more they tend to like each other.

2. *The Circumstances of Contact*. If people meet others in positive circumstances, they are more likely to be attracted to each other.

B. Some Person-Related Determinants

1. *Similarity in Attitudes*. People tend to like others who have attitudes similar to their own.

2. *Physical Attractiveness*. People tend to like attractive people. Also, according to the matching hypothesis, people tend to be attracted to others who are about equally attractive.

C. Developing Intimate Relationships

1. *Self-Disclosure*. Self-disclosure is the revelation of a person's private world, background, fears, hopes, beliefs, weaknesses, and the like. The breadth and depth of the personal information disclosed and the acceptance of that information influences the development of a relationship.

2. *Long-Term Intimate Relationships*. Happily married couples report that their self-disclosure is extensive and that they love each other equally. Anger exists in both happy and unhappy marriages. In happy marriages, however, someone (usually the wife) breaks through the anger to discuss the problem at hand.

KEY TERMS

1. **Social psychology** focuses on the effects of the social world on the behavior and mental processes of individuals, pairs, and groups. (p. 624)

2. The theory of **social comparison** states that in the absence of objective criteria, people compare themselves to others for the purpose of self-evaluation. (p. 626)

Example: If you want to know how athletic you are, you might compare yourself to friends of the same sex.

3. **Reference groups** are the categories of people to which individuals see themselves as belonging and to which they habitually compare themselves. (p. 627)

Example: Jerome is a graduate student in psychology at a major university. He would probably consider his reference group to be other students his age. He would not consider people of his grandparents' age to be his reference group.

4. **Relative deprivation** occurs when people's relative standing in any dimension changes due to using a new reference group. People usually move from a high status position in one reference group to a low status position in a new reference group. (p. 627)

Example: Kent has just graduated with a Ph.D. in biology and taken a new job. At the university, he was considered one of the best students in his department. At his new job, he must start over and earn the respect of his superiors and peers. He has low status at the beginning of his new job in terms of pay and experience.

5. **Social facilitation** occurs when the presence of other people improves performance. Usually, the presence of others increases arousal because it indicates to performers that they will be evaluated. When the task is familiar, performance improves. But when the task is unfamiliar, performance often deteriorates. (p. 628)

6. **Norms** are learned, socially based rules that dictate correct and incorrect behavior for various situations. Norms vary with culture, subculture, and situation. (p. 630)

Example: Many of your daily behaviors follow the social norms present in our culture. Sometimes it is easier to understand norms by thinking about what would happen if these social rules were broken. Following are a few social norms:

You may not walk around to all the tables in a restaurant, sampling people's meals, in order to decide what you want.

You may not take a blanket, a pillow, and a portable television to the mattress section of a major department store and make yourself at home.

You may not go shopping in your underwear.

7. An **attitude** refers to cognitive, emotional, and behavioral reactions to an object. The cognitive component is made of beliefs; the emotional component is a positive or negative evaluation; and the behavioral reaction is an action of some kind. (p. 632)

8. The theory of **cognitive dissonance** states that people prefer that their many cognitions about themselves and the rest of the world be consistent with one another. When their cognitions are inconsistent, or dissonant, people feel uneasy and are motivated to make them more consistent. (p. 637)

Example: Joe is an advertising executive. He is working on a cigarette company's account, but he thinks that cigarettes should not be advertised to teenagers. His attitudes and behavior are inconsistent. He will have to change his attitude about cigarette advertising or change jobs in order to reduce his cognitive dissonance and the psychological tension it causes.

9. **Self-perception theory** states that we review our own behavior in order to determine what our attitudes are. (p. 638)

Example: To be initiated into his boyhood group of friends, John was required to eat a worm, a live goldfish, and the head of a bumble bee. After eating these, John liked the group even more than he did before. He inferred that he must like the group very much if he was able to overcome his loathing of worms, live fish, and bugs.

10. **Schemas** are organized, coherent sets of beliefs and expectations about objects, people, or events. Schemas help to shape our social perceptions of others. (p. 640)

Example: A new friend of yours has told you that her cousin is a big rock star. She invites you to meet him. You would be very surprised to find that her cousin is wearing a business suit, drives a V.W. bug, and has every Frank Sinatra tape ever made.

11. A **self-fulfilling prophecy** is the process by which an impression of a person, object, or event elicits behavior that confirms the impression. (p. 641)

Example: Joanna believed that she would never succeed in college, but to her surprise, got into a good university. However, during her first semester, she found that she had to study much harder than in high school. Joanna decided that her difficulties with her studies meant that she was stupid. She quit studying, thinking that it was of no use, and flunked out of school.

12. **Stereotypes** are impressions or schemas of entire groups of people. Stereotypes operate on the false assumption that all members of a group share the same characteristics. This can lead to prejudice. (p. 642)

Example: Joe is interviewing candidates for a position in his company. He has decided not to hire anyone having a Ph.D. He has been told by his peers that people who have their Ph.D.s are flaky, absent-minded, and lack social skills.

13. **Prejudice** is holding a preconceived positive or negative attitude about an entire group of people. These attitudes have cognitive, affective, and behavioral components. (p. 642)

Example: Isabelle, an American, went to study in Russia for a year. She met a child on the street one day who asked her why Americans wanted to destroy the world with nuclear bombs. The child had never been exposed to Americans before, but had prejudged them based on information from the press, her parents, and her peers.

14. **Discrimination** is the differential treatment of various groups that can result from the behavioral component of prejudice. (p. 642)

Example: Gabrielle has brought her date, a musician, to meet her parents. She is very embarrassed because her father will not even speak to him. Later, she asks her father to explain his extremely rude behavior. He remarks that all musicians are shiftless and no good and forbids her to see him again.

15. An **authoritarian personality** is characterized by viewing the world as a strict social hierarchy. These people feel they have the right to demand deference and cooperation from all those of perceived lower status. This perception sets the stage for the development of negative stereotypes, prejudices, and discrimination against those who are perceived as having lower status. (p. 643)

16. The **contact hypothesis** states that a person's prejudices and stereotypes about a group should be reduced with repeated friendly exposure (contact) to members of equal standing in that group. This provides an opportunity for prejudiced people to learn about members of the group as individuals. (p. 643)

Example: Anna grew up in the east. Her parents always told her that people who spoke with a southern accent were stupid and lazy. When Anna's company relocated her to Texas she was horrified, but eventually she came to enjoy interacting with her fellow employees and found them to be more than competent at their jobs.

17. **Attribution** is the process of explaining the causes of people's behavior, including one's own. Internal or external causes can account for people's behavior. (p. 645)

Example: How would you respond to an inquiry about the causes of your grades? Would you say that you are smart and work hard (internal causes) or that you are lucky and consistently end up with easy professors (external causes)?

18. **Consensus** is a criterion used to attribute someone's behavior to an internal or external cause. It is the degree to which someone's behavior is similar to other people's behavior. (p. 645)

Example: See example for key term 20, distinctiveness.

19. **Consistency** is a criterion used to attribute someone's behavior to an internal or external cause. It is the degree to which the behavior occurs repeatedly in a *particular* situation. (p. 645)

Example: See example for key term 20, distinctiveness.

20. **Distinctiveness** is a criterion used to attribute someone's behavior to an internal or external cause. It is the predictability of the behavior in many *different* situations. (p. 645)

Example: Clara is in the hospital for a tonsillectomy. One of the nurses, who came into her room to take her temperature, was very mean to her. Clara is trying to decide the cause of the nurse's behavior. She decides to see if the other nurses are any nicer than the first one. To her relief, the others are very nice (low consensus). After a few days, she realizes this particular nurse is always nasty to her (high consistency). Finally, she walks around the floor and notices that the nurse is mean to her fellow nurses and to the other patients (low distinctiveness). Based on these observations, Clara attributes the nurse's grouchiness to her personality (internal cause).

21. **Attributional bias** is a tendency to distort one's view of behavior. (p. 646)

Example: See examples for key terms 22, 23, and 24, egocentric bias, ego-defensive bias, and fundamental attribution error, for examples of various types of attributional biases.

22. The **egocentric bias** is the tendency to assume that others believe and act just as you do. (p. 646)

Example: Tom, a professor of consumer behavior, was surprised when his prize student decided not to get a Ph.D. Instead, the student decided to get a job. Tom had always assumed that his student shared his belief that being an academic was the only fulfilling job one could have.

23. The **ego-defensive bias** is the tendency to take credit for success but to blame external causes for failure. (p. 646)

Example: Jerry has noticed that whenever his company wins a big account with a new client, each person claims responsibility for the success. However, when a company decides to take its business elsewhere, everyone denies responsibility for the decisions that led to problems. People like to take credit for success but do not like to take the blame for problems.

24. The **fundamental attribution error** occurs when people tend to be more aware of the influence of situational factors on their own behavior than on the behavior of others. (p. 647)

Example: Latanya has flunked a botany exam. She tells her friend that the test was unfair, the teacher is a hard grader, and many people in the class cheated. She is angry that these situational factors prevented her from getting a better grade. The next day her brother calls and tells her that he has just flunked an algebra exam. Before he can speak another word, Latanya is telling him that he is either lazy or stupid or both. She thinks that her brother's behavior, not situational factors, caused him to flunk his algebra test.

25. The **matching hypothesis** states that a person is more likely to be attracted to others who are similar in physical attractiveness than to those who are notably more or less attractive. (p. 650)

Example: As you walk around your campus or neighborhood, look at the couples you see. They will often be about equally attractive.

LEARNING OBJECTIVES

1. State the definition of social psychology. (p. 624)

2. Discuss the theory of social comparison. Describe the relationship of reference groups to the process of self-evaluation. Define relative deprivation. (pp. 624–628)

3. Define social facilitation. Describe the influence of arousal on performance. Explain why the presence of others increases arousal. (pp. 628–630)

4. Define norms. Describe the influence of norms on behavior. Define the reciprocity norm and give an example of it. (p. 630)

5. Describe how culture, subculture, and situations determine norms. (pp. 631–632)

6. Define attitudes. Describe the cognitive, affective, and behavioral components of attitudes. Give an example of each. Discuss the sources of change in attitudes. (pp. 632–633)

7. Describe the characteristics of the communicator, message, and audience that create an effective persuasive communication. (pp. 633–636)

8. Describe the most effective use of fear appeals in persuasive messages. (p. 635)

9. Define cognitive dissonance. Describe the process of reducing cognitive dissonance. (pp. 637–638)

10. Define self-perception. Describe the influence of past behavior on attitudes according to the self-perception theory. (pp. 638–639)

11. Describe the influences, including schemas, on impression formation. Explain why impressions are difficult to change. (pp. 640–641)

12. Define self-fulfilling prophecies. Discuss the relationship between self-fulfilling prophecies and impressions. (pp. 641–642)

13. Define stereotype, prejudice and discrimination. Define the authoritarian personality. (pp. 642–643)

14. Describe the motivational theory of stereotypes and prejudice. (p. 643)

15. Describe the learning theory of stereotypes and prejudice. Define the contact hypothesis. (p. 643)

16. Describe cognitive theories of stereotypes and prejudice. (pp. 643–644)

17. Define attribution. Describe the criteria used in making attributions: consensus, consistency, and distinctiveness. (pp. 644–646)

18. Define the egocentric bias and the ego-defensive bias and give examples of each. Describe the influence of the availability heuristic on attribution. Define the fundamental attribution error and give an example of it. (pp. 646–647)

19. Describe the influence of familiarity, proximity, and contact on attraction. (pp. 648–649)

20. Describe the influence of similar attitudes and physical attractiveness on attraction. Discuss the matching hypothesis. (pp. 649–650)

21. Describe the factors that motivate people to maintain long-term, intimate relationships. (pp. 650–653)

CONCEPTS AND EXERCISES

No. 1 Identifying Reference Groups

Completing this exercise should help you to achieve the following learning objective.

(2) *Discuss the theory of social comparison. Describe the relationship of reference groups to the process of self-evaluation. Define relative deprivation. (pp. 624–628)*

Think about the answers to the following questions. You will probably find that you will compare yourself to others in order to answer the question.

The individuals or groups of people that you compare yourself to are your reference groups.

1. Are you attractive?

2. Are you extremely intelligent?

3. Do you dress well?

4. Are you well educated?

After you have answered the questions and identified your reference groups, think about where you will be in ten years. How could your reference groups change? In what situations could you experience relative deprivation?

No. 2 Persuasive Advertising

Completing this exercise should help you to achieve the following learning objectives.

(6) *Define attitudes. Describe the cognitive, affective, and behavioral components of attitudes. Give an example of each. Discuss the sources of change in attitudes. (pp. 632–633)*

(7) *Describe the characteristics of the communicator, message, and audience that create an effective persuasive communication. (pp. 633–636)*

1. Richard Nixon spent 21 million dollars on promotion and advertising during his presidential campaign. Following are some of the methods he used. State why each resulted in an effective and persuasive communication.

   a. Many famous Americans made commercial spots for Nixon. His spokesman in the South was John Wayne, and Jackie Gleason endorsed him in the East.

   b. Nixon made a series of one-hour question-and-answer television shows to be aired in various states. The questioners were picked to represent most of the groups in each state's population.

2. All the advertisements or marketing methods described below are attempting to increase the effectiveness of their persuasion with the same general method. See if you can spot the similarities.

   a. Many advertisements of household products show two women having a conversation instead of having one woman talk to the television audience.

   b. One automobile company gave models of a new car to several students on campus, hoping that the car's merits would be communicated by word of mouth among the students.

   c. Many companies leave samples of detergent on doorsteps and hope that the detergent's virtues will be talked about among the people in the neighborhood.

No. 3 Matchmaker, Matchmaker, Make Me a Match

Completing this exercise should help you to achieve the following learning objectives.

(19) *Describe the influence of familiarity, proximity, and contact on attraction. (pp. 648–649)*

(20) *Describe the influence of similar attitudes and physical attractiveness on attraction. Discuss the matching hypothesis. (pp. 649–650)*

(21) *Describe the factors that motivate people to maintain long-term, intimate relationships. (pp. 650–653)*

Clarence is the doorman at a high-rise apartment building in downtown Chicago. He is a notorious matchmaker. Read Clarence's plans for getting people together and choose the basis for his schemes from the following list of determinants of attraction.

proximity

self-disclosure

similar attitudes

physical attractiveness

1. Pat is always talking about the next antinuclear demonstration that she is going to attend. George works for the Environmental Protection Agency. Clarence decides to introduce them.

2. Clarence is not too interested in fashion but he notices that Trudie and Mark are always carrying bags from the same expensive stores. Both seem to take a great deal of pride in looking their best. Clarence thinks they would make a handsome couple.

3. Clarence, being a bit nosy, asks Pamela how her dates went on the weekend. Pamela complains that men just do not know how to open up and talk about themselves. Richard always says that he is tired of dating women who are more interested in his paycheck than in his personality. Clarence guesses that these two would get along well.

4. Adele has just moved into apartment 3D. Clarence knows that Stephen, a bachelor, lives in apartment 3E. He smiles to himself and plans their meeting.

ANSWERS TO CONCEPTS AND EXERCISES

No. 1 Identifying Reference Groups

There are no right or wrong answers to this exercise. It is designed to help you think about who your reference groups are.

1. You would probably compare yourself to your friends in order to determine how attractive you are. You should not use extreme reference groups and compare yourself to, for example, a movie star or a model from a fashion magazine.

2. To assess your intelligence you would probably compare yourself to your fellow students. Your reference groups probably changed as you left high school and entered college. In high school you were one of the best students, but college students are made up of the best high school stu-

dents. You may have initially experienced relative deprivation as you went from being one of the best to being average.

3. Again, you would probably compare yourself to your friends instead of comparing yourself to members of the upper-upper class.

4. You may consider your education average since most of your friends are probably also students. However, consider what would happen to your relative standing if you were to use people who had grown up during the Depression. For example, one of the author's grandparents did not have the opportunity to complete grade school. In comparison, your education is clearly superior.

No. 2 Persuasive Advertising

1. (p. 633)

a. Different celebrities were chosen to support Nixon in different areas of the country because they were considered credible and similar to the population in that area.

b. The members of the panels were selected because they were similar to the people living in the state in which the show was to be aired.

2. All of these promotional methods have one thing in common: they try to make the audience believe it has heard a sincere communication. (p. 633)

a. Overheard conversations appear to an audience to be more sincere than presentations that are obviously meant to persuade. Viewing two women talking to each other about a household product on television is similar to overhearing a conversation.

b. You would probably consider the word of a friend to be more sincere than an advertisement for a car.

c. Again, you would probably consider the word of a friend to be more sincere than an advertisement for a detergent.

No. 3 Matchmaker, Matchmaker, Make Me a Match

1. Pat and George probably have *similar attitudes* and interests about preserving the environment. (p. 649)

2. Trudie and Mark are probably both very attractive. People are usually attracted to people who are similar to them in *physical attractiveness.* (p. 650)

3. Pamela and Richard are both interested in finding someone they can talk to about themselves; they want to exchange information about their goals, preferences, and philosophies. *Self-disclosure* fosters intimacy. (p. 651)

4. Adele and Stephen live next door to each other. Clarence knows that they will come into contact with each other quite a bit. In general, we tend to like those people with whom we have a lot of contact (*proximity*). (p. 648)

MULTIPLE CHOICE QUESTIONS

Facts and Definitions

1. Norms are influenced by
   a. the surrounding culture.
   b. the surrounding subculture.
   c. the context of the situation.
   d. All of the above.

2. _____ are sets of people that we compare ourselves to during self-evaluation.
   a. Reference groups
   b. Relative groups
   c. Social facilitators
   d. Out-groups

3. Discrepancies between attitudes lead to
   a. prejudice.
   b. cognitive dissonance.
   c. the fundamental attribution error.
   d. relative deprivation.

4. A one-sided message should be presented when
   a. the audience is in agreement with the message before they hear it.
   b. the message is complex.
   c. the communicator is similar to the audience.
   d. the audience has never met the communicator before.

5. Reactance occurs when
   a. a message is very loud and emotional.
   b. the audience is ordered to adopt proposed attitudes.
   c. a communicator is not credible.
   d. a communicator is insincere.

6. Attributing behavior to an external cause requires _____ consistency, _____ distinctiveness, and _____ consensus.
   a. high, low, low
   b. high, high, low
   c. high, low, high
   d. low, high, high

7. Which of the following is a good predictor of the success of a relationship?
   a. Similar attitudes
   b. Similar degrees of attractiveness
   c. Equal self-disclosure
   d. All of the above.

8. Social facilitation improves performance most when
   a. the task is difficult.
   b. the task is time-consuming.
   c. the task is easy or familiar.
   d. the task is unfamiliar.

9. According to the reciprocity norm, we will behave toward others as

    a. we want them to behave toward us.

    b. they have behaved toward us.

    c. they have behaved toward other people.

    d. None of the above.

10. According to the fundamental attribution error

    a. we always attribute our behavior to internal causes.

    b. we always make an internal attribution for our successes.

    c. we expect others to behave as we do.

    d. we usually attribute others' behavior to internal causes.

11. Individuals with a _____ level of self-esteem are the most susceptible to persuasive messages.

    a. low

    b. high

    c. moderate

    d. impossible to determine

12. Cognitive dissonance and the self-perception theory differ in that

    a. cognitive dissonance involves attitudes and self-perception involves attribution.

    b. cognitive dissonance involves attitude change and self-perception involves social facilitation.

    c. cognitive dissonance involves the reduction of internal tension and self-perception does not.

    d. None of the above.

13. According to the _____ we assume that others think and behave as we do.

    a. egocentric bias

    b. ego-defensive bias

    c. fundamental attribution error

    d. authoritarian personality bias

14. The availability heuristic influences

    a. attributions.

    b. social facilitation.

    c. attraction.

    d. cognitive dissonance.

15. In-groups are similar to

    a. reference groups.

    b. relative deprivation groups.

    c. social facilitators.

    d. None of the above.

MULTIPLE CHOICE QUESTIONS

Application of Concepts

1. Social facilitation would probably hinder performance in which of the following situations?

    a. The university symphony giving a performance after practicing all semester

    b. Contestants on trivia game shows answering questions they have never heard before

    c. An athletic competition

    d. A seasoned instructor lecturing on her favorite topic

2. Jack is depressed. He took a job in the city after completing graduate school on a scholarship and graduating with honors. Now that he is in the city, it seems that everyone is older, richer, and wiser than he is. Jack is experiencing

    a. cognitive dissonance.

    b. relative deprivation.

    c. social facilitation.

    d. a self-fulfilling prophecy.

3. Norma loves to put cold cream on her face because she believes that it prevents wrinkles. She buys new cold cream about every two weeks. What is the affective component of her attitude toward cold cream?

    a. She buys a large quantity of cold cream.

    b. She loves cold cream.

c. She believes that cold cream will prevent wrinkles.

d. She puts cold cream on her face.

4. An ad campaign against drug use shows the bodies of several overdose victims. The narrator describes the deaths of each person. Why will this campaign be ineffective?

a. The ad is too frightening.

b. The ad does not mention how to avoid the problem or how to get help if a problem already exists.

c. The cognitive component of the attitude toward drugs is addressed but the behavioral component is not.

d. All of the above.

5. Georgette is trying to persuade her superiors in a large corporation to let her research division market a new device. She has heard through the grapevine that they already like her idea. What kind of presentation should she make?

a. Her message should be one-sided.

b. Her message should be two-sided.

c. One- and two-sided messages will be equally effective.

d. None of the above.

6. Sam is a conservationist. He has just found out that his company, which pays him very well, is going to be dumping toxic waste into the environment of a nearby community. He will probably

a. quit his job.

b. hold demonstrations on the company's doorstep.

c. remind himself of how well he is getting paid.

d. attempt to reverse the decision to dump toxic waste.

7. Every Christmas people are willing to dress up as Santa Claus, stand in a public place, ring a bell, and ask for donations for a charity. According to the reciprocity norm, more money will be donated if

a. passers-by are given candy canes before they are asked for money.

b. Santa Claus holds a large sign stating the name of the charity.

c. more than one Santa Claus stands in the same place.

d. Santa Claus clearly states the reason the money is needed.

8. Carol goes to a party to meet people. While there she is introduced to Larry, an attractive man about her age. During their conversation, Larry is rude several times. Based on what you know about impression formation, choose the best alternative.

a. Carol will assume that Larry is rude because he had a bad day.

b. Carol will assume that Larry is a rude person.

c. Carol is experiencing a self-fulfilling prophecy.

d. Carol will assume that Larry is similar to her and form a positive impression.

9. Gena had a terrible first day at work. Her boss was short-tempered and gruff with her. From then on she was constantly prepared for more nasty comments. When she received her six-month review, she was surprised at her negative evaluation. Her boss had said that she was constantly defensive. This was the result of

a. a stereotype.

b. prejudice.

c. a self-fulfilling prophecy.

d. discrimination.

10. A foreman at a manufacturing plant is having problems with racial relations among his employees. The blacks, Hispanics, and whites just do not get along. The foreman decides to reorganize his staff so that each work group, made up of people of equal rank, will have one person from each race. The foreman agrees with the _____ theory of stereotypes and prejudice.

a. motivational
b. cognitive
c. authoritarian
d. learning

11. Felicia's first novel has sold over one million copies. Her family thinks her success is due to her creativity and talent, but Felicia thinks it is due to luck. Felicia's explanation of the cause of her success demonstrates

a. the fundamental attribution error.
b. social facilitation.
c. the self-perception theory.
d. the ego-defense bias.

12. Clarissa is talking to a friend about her daughter Nicole. She says, "I have taught Nicole to be considerate, thoughtful and moral, but Nicole's father is responsible for her inability to manage her money." This is an illustration of

a. the fundamental attribution error.
b. the ego-defensive bias.
c. the egocentric bias.
d. reactance.

13. Julia is proud to be dating Vernon, since he is thoughtful and considerate to everyone. He always sends her flowers and is willing to help his friends. Julia's friends are envious; none of their boyfriends are as considerate as Vernon. Vernon's behavior demonstrates _____ consensus, _____ consistency, and _____ distinctiveness. Julia will attribute his behavior to an _____ cause.

a. high, high, high, external
b. high, low, high, internal
c. low, high, low, internal
d. high, high, low, external

14. Susan has just moved into a new dormitory. She will most likely become good friends with the girls

a. on the floor above hers.
b. in the dorm next door.

c. in the room next door.
d. at the other end of the hall.

15. With whom would you be most likely to fall in love at first sight?

a. Your tour guide in the Mojave desert in August
b. The person who fills your gas tank when you are in a hurry
c. The person you bump into on the quad on a beautiful spring day
d. There is an equal probability that you would fall in love with any of the above.

ANSWERS TO MULTIPLE CHOICE QUESTIONS

Facts and Definitions

1. *d* is the answer. Norms are influenced by culture, subculture, and individual situations. (p. 630)

2. *a* is the answer. The groups of people that we think of ourselves as belonging to and to which we compare ourselves are called reference groups. (p. 626)

   b. Our relatives may form a reference group. But we are members of many groups and compare ourselves to many groups besides our relatives.

   c. There is no such thing as a social facilitator. Social facilitation is improvement in performance due to the presence of other people.

   d. An out-group is any group which you do not consider yourself a member of.

3. *b* is the answer. Cognitive dissonance is internal tension or uneasiness due to the existence of conflicting attitudes or cognitions. (p. 637)

   a. Prejudice is a preformed negative or positive attitude toward an entire group of people. Stereotypes can lead to prejudice.

   c. The fundamental attribution error refers to mistakes made in explaining the causes of behavior.

d. Relative deprivation occurs when, as a new member of a reference group, a person's standing in comparison to others is low.

4. *a* is the answer. If an audience is already sympathetic to the communicator, a one-sided message should be presented. A two-sided message would only sow seeds of doubt. (p. 634)

b. The complexity of a message does not determine whether a one- or two-sided message will be more persuasive.

c. A communicator who is similar to an audience is more effective in persuasive communication. However, presenting a one- or two-sided message is not necessarily more or less effective in this situation.

d. There are many cases in which the communicator is not known to the audience prior to the presentation of the message. In these cases communicators should attempt to be sincere, relatively attractive, and credible. However, presenting a one- or two-sided message is not necessarily more or less effective in this situation.

5. *b* is the answer. When listeners are ordered to adopt new attitudes, they may react by taking an opposite point of view. (p. 636)

a. A message can be emotional without requiring the adoption of new attitudes.

c. A communicator who is not credible will not be very persuasive. But this is not what is meant by reactance.

d. An insincere communicator will not be very persuasive. But this is not what is meant by reactance.

6. *d* is the answer. Low consistency, high consensus, and high distinctiveness would lead to an external attribution. (p. 645)

a., b., & c. High consistency means that a person always behaves in a similar manner. Low consensus means that not many people display a particular behavior. Low distinctiveness means the behavior occurs in many situations. These features

would lead one to attribute someone's behavior to an internal cause; that person often displays the behavior in many situations whereas other people do not. The behavior is probably due to a characteristic of the person, and not to an external cause.

7. *d* is the answer. Frequent contact, similar attitudes, and sharing of thoughts and ideas are determinants of liking. (pp. 648–651)

8. *c* is the answer. The presence of others improves performance when a task is easy and familiar. (p. 629)

a. For difficult tasks, the presence of others increases arousal, which reduces the ability to perform.

b. The amount of time a task takes does not determine whether or not social faciliation takes place. The determining factor is the difficulty of the task.

d. The presence of others increases arousal. When people are aroused, familiar or best-learned responses appear and interfere with their ability to perform unfamiliar tasks.

9. *b* is the answer. The way other people have behaved towards us will determine our behavior towards them. If someone gives us something, we feel compelled to give something back. (p. 630)

a. Treating others as you wish to be treated is not described by the reciprocity norm.

c. Treating others as they have treated other people is not described by the reciprocity norm.

d. b is the answer.

10. *d* is the answer. According to the fundamental attribution error, we usually attribute others' behavior to internal causes. (p. 647)

a. According to the fundamental attribution error, we usually attribute our behavior to external, not internal, causes.

b. According to the ego-defensive bias, we attribute our successes to internal causes.

c. According to the egocentric bias, we expect others to think and behave as we do.

11. *c* is the answer. All else being equal, people with moderate levels of self-esteem are most susceptible to persuasive communications. (p. 636)

a. Those with low self-esteem pay little attention to and therefore are not as susceptible to persuasive communication.

b. Those with high self-esteem are confident of their own opinions and are not as susceptible to persuasive communications.

d. c is the answer.

12. *c* is the answer. Cognitive dissonance, unlike self-perception, involves internal tension caused by discrepant or conflicting attitudes. According to self-perception theory, people who are unsure about their attitudes examine their past behavior to determine them. This does not involve any uneasiness or internal tension. (p. 638)

a. Cognitive dissonance and self-perception theory both involve attitudes.

b. Self-perception does not involve social facilitation.

d. c is the answer.

13. *a* is the answer. The egocentric bias is the belief that other people act and think as we do. (p. 646)

b. The ego-defensive bias is the belief that our behavior is responsible for our successes but not for our failures.

c. According to the fundamental attribution error, we are more likely to attribute our own behavior to external causes, but we attribute other people's behavior to internal causes.

d. There is no such thing as the authoritarian bias. People with authoritarian personalities tend to identify other people's status in relation to their own. This creates a social hierarchy that may encourage the development of stereotypes.

14. *a* is the answer. The availability heuristic is the tendency to judge the frequency of an event by how easily an example of the event comes to mind. We attribute behavior to the cause that most readily comes to mind. (p. 647)

b. Social facilitation occurs when the presence of other people improves performance. This has nothing to do with what we remember best or what most readily comes to mind.

c. The factors which affect attraction are proximity, familiarity, similarity of attitudes, and equal self-disclosure.

d. Cognitive dissonance is the presence of internal tension due to conflicting cognitions. This has nothing to do with what we remember best or what most readily comes to mind.

15. *a* is the answer. An ingroup is any category of people of which we consider ourselves a member. (p. 644)

b. There is no such thing as a relative deprivation group. Relative deprivation occurs when our standing, in comparison to members of a new reference group, is low.

c. There is no such thing as a social facilitator. Social facilitation occurs when the presence of other people improves performance.

d. a is the answer.

ANSWERS TO MULTIPLE CHOICE QUESTIONS

Application of Concepts

1. *b* is the answer. Social facilitation impairs performance of unfamiliar tasks. (p. 629)

a., c., & d. Performing rehearsed music, competing in athletic events, and giving a favorite lecture all involve well-practiced and familiar activities.

2. *b* is the answer. Jack had a lot of status in his old reference group of students. Now that he is a member of a new group, it will take time to improve his standing in comparison to the other group members.

His low status at present is making him depressed. (p. 627)

a. Cognitive dissonance is the product of conflicting attitudes.

c. Social facilitation occurs when the presence of other people improves performance.

d. A self-fulfilling prophecy is an impression that elicits behavior confirming the impression. Jack's impressions are not making him depressed. His standing in comparison to others in his new reference group is making him unhappy.

3. *b* is the answer. The affective component of an attitude is a positive or negative evaluation of an object, person, event or situation. Norma loves (has a positive evaluation of) cold cream. (p. 632)

a. Buying cold cream is the behavioral component of Norma's attitude.

c. Norma's belief that cold cream will reduce wrinkles is the cognitive component of her attitude.

d. Putting cold cream on her face is part of the behavioral component of Norma's attitude.

4. *d* is the answer. Fear appeals that are too frightening and that do not tell the audience what behavior to adopt to avoid the fearful situation are not effective. (p. 635)

5. *a* is the answer. Georgette knows that her superiors like her idea. Therefore, she should present only the information that supports her division's new work. If she presents information that might suggest she not begin work, she may cause her superiors to have doubts about the project's merits. (p. 634)

b. & c. A two-sided message should not be given to an audience already sympathetic to the message. Presenting contrary evidence could cause the audience to become doubtful about its original sympathetic view.

d. a is the answer.

6. *c* is the answer. Sam does have conflicting attitudes. However, Sam can justify his job choice be- cause he gets paid a lot of money. Therefore, he will not experience cognitive dissonance. (p. 637)

a., b., & d. All of these alternatives would be correct if Sam did not have an external factor (high pay) which prevented cognitive dissonance from occurring.

7. *a* is the answer. According to the reciprocity norm, we tend to behave toward others as they have behaved toward us. People will feel more obliged to give money if they have been given something—in this case, a candy cane. (p. 630)

b. & d. Providing passers-by with more information concerning the charity may help to elicit donations, but is *not* related to the reciprocity norm.

c. Using a larger number of Santas in the same spot will not necessarily increase donations. Even if this did increase the amount of money given, it is *not* related to the reciprocity norm.

8. *b* is the answer. Negative acts such as being rude tend to heavily influence first impressions. Also, people assume that negative behavior reflects undesirable characteristics. Therefore, Carol will form a negative impression of Larry and probably assume that Larry is a rude person. (pp. 640–641)

a. In forming first impressions, people tend to assume that negative acts are due to some undesirable characteristic of the person being evaluated. Carol is likely to assume that Larry is rude, rather than believe his behavior is the result of a bad day.

c. A self-fulfilling prophecy occurs when an already-formed first impression of another person elicits behavior that confirms that impression. Carol had no impression of Larry prior to their conversation at the party.

d. All else being equal, we assume that others are similar to ourselves. Since we usually evaluate ourselves positively, we also evaluate others positively. However, all else is not equal in this situation. Larry is rude to Carol. Since negative acts usually carry a lot of weight and are assumed to reflect negative characteristics, Carol will form a negative impression of Larry.

9. *c* is the answer. Gena fulfilled her own prophecy. She was defensive because she expected her boss to be gruff. As a result he gave her a negative evaluation. (p. 641)

a. A stereotype is an impression of a group of people. Gena has formed a first impression about one person: her boss.

b. Prejudice is a preformed negative or positive judgment about a group of people. This would have been the correct answer only if Gena's first impression had led her to believe that all bosses were gruff and nasty.

d. Discrimination is the differential treatment of certain groups, not one person.

10. *d* is the answer. Learning theories of prejudice have led to the contact hypothesis, which states that stereotypes and prejudices about a group should be reduced as contact with that group increases. The foreman has arranged for contact between the races by placing one person of equal status from each race in each work group. (p. 643)

a. & c. The motivation theories of prejudice and stereotypes focus on the personality structure of the individual. People with authoritarian personalities view the world as a strict social hierarchy. These people know who they have to obey and from whom they can demand discipline. They often stereotype people of lower status.

b. The cognitive theories of stereotyping suggest that we categorize or stereotype people in order to simplify our complex world.

11. *a* is the answer. According to the fundamental attribution error, we attribute our own behavior to situational, external factors, such as luck. We attribute other people's behavior to internal factors, such as, in this case, creativity. (p. 647)

b. Social facilitation is the improvement of performance in the presence of others. The question is not concerned with Felicia's performance, but with her explanation for her performance.

c. Self-perception involves determining one's own attitudes. The question asks why Felicia attributes the success of her book to luck, not what her attitudes are.

d. The ego-defense bias predicts that Felicia would take personal credit for her success.

12. *b* is the answer. According to the ego-defense bias, we take credit for success but blame external causes for failure. Nicole's mother is taking credit for Nicole's good habits and qualities, but not for her bad ones. (p. 646)

a. According to the fundamental attribution error, Nicole's mother should attribute Nicole's behavior to internal characteristics. Instead, she believes that the causes of Nicole's behavior are her own and her husband's style of raising their daughter (characteristics that are external to Nicole).

c. The egocentric bias states that we believe other people think and behave as we do. Nicole's mother is not assuming that Nicole's behavior or thinking is like her own.

d. If Nicole had refused to manage her money in an effort to resist her parent's order to spend it in a certain way, then reactance would have been the correct alternative.

13. *c* is the answer. Vernon's behavior has a low degree of consensus because not everyone is considerate and thoughtful. His behavior has a high degree of consistency because *he* is always considerate and thoughtful. His behavior has a low degree of distinctiveness because he is considerate and thoughtful towards *all* his friends. This will lead Julia to attribute the cause of his behavior to internal characteristics instead of situational or external factors. (p. 645)

a., b., & d. Vernon's behavior could only be attributed to external factors if everyone were considerate and thoughtful (high consensus), if he were considerate only in specific situations (high distinctiveness), and if he were not consistently considerate (low consistency).

14. *c* is the answer. Research has shown that next-door neighbors are more likely to become good friends than people who live at opposite ends of the hall or farther away. (p. 648)

a., b., & d. People tend to like those with whom they have the most contact. Susan will probably have more contact with the girls living next door.

15. *c* is the answer. We are much more likely to be attracted to people if we meet them in a comfortable place. (p. 649)

a. You would be hot and sticky, not comfortable, on a tour of the Mojave desert in August.

b. When you were in a hurry, you would not have sufficient contact with a gas station attendant.

d. You would be more attracted to the person you met in comfortable physical conditions.

Chapter 18

Group Influences and Interpersonal Behavior

OUTLINE

I. INTRODUCTION (p. 656)

Social dilemmas are situations in which the short-term decisions of individuals become irrational in combination and create long-term, clearly predictable damage for a group.

II. CONFORMITY AND COMPLIANCE (pp. 656–665)

Conformity results from unspoken group pressure and compliance results from spoken group pressure.

A. The Role of Norms

Group norms tend to affect people's behavior even after they are no longer a member of that group.

B. Why Do People Conform?

Groups create norms; they decide what is right, wrong, and expected in a situation. Norms determine who will receive rewards and punishments in a given social situation.

C. When Do People Conform?

1. *Ambiguity of the Situation*. The more difficult it is to determine what is physical reality, the more people rely on the opinions of others.

2. *Unanimity and Size of the Majority*. Conformity is greatest when a group decision is unanimous. The more people in a group who make independent assessments, the higher the degree of conformity by an individual.

3. *Personal Characteristics*. People with high status are less likely to conform than those with low status. People are more likely to conform to a group when they like the group's members. Those with low self-esteem are more likely to conform, because of the desire for approval from attractive group members. People who are concerned with being liked or being perceived as correct are also likely to conform.

III. OBEDIENCE (pp. 665–671)

Obedience is a form of compliance in which people comply with a demand, rather than with a request, because they think they must or should do so.

A. Obedience in the Laboratory

1. Milgram created a procedure to measure obedience. He developed a situation in which subjects thought they were delivering shocks to a person. When confederates complained about the pain of the shock they were supposedly receiving, Milgram demanded that the subjects continue to deliver the shocks. Despite feeling stressed, 65 percent of the subjects delivered the full 450 volts of shock possible.

333

B. Factors Affecting Obedience

1. *Prestige.* When the status and legitimacy of the experimenter were removed from the situation, obedience decreased, but only from 65 to 48 percent.

2. *Proximity.* If the subject could not see the experimenter, obedience dropped from 65 to 20 percent. As the distance between the subject (teacher) and confederate (learner) decreased, the level of obedience decreased.

3. *Presence of Others Who Disobey.* The presence of others who disobey decreases obedience.

C. The Ethics and Value of Milgram's Studies

Some observers say the experiment was unethical, while Milgram argued that his debriefing procedure and continued contact with his subjects show that it was a positive experience. Ethical questions are difficult ones. Milgram's study would probably not be approved by today's ethics committees. History has supported Milgram's data. However, it has been suggested that the subjects' behavior was guided by their role and by their belief that they were not harming another person.

IV. AGGRESSION (pp. 671–679)

Aggression is an act intended to harm another person.

A. Approaches to Aggression

1. *The Psychoanalytic Approach.* According to Freud, aggression is an inborn instinct that can be channeled into socially appropriate activities that provide catharsis. Research does not support the existence of such an instinct. Evidence also shows that acting aggressively increases the occurrence of further aggression.

2. *The Ethological Approach.* Aggression is an instinct displayed in the presence of a releaser.

This approach is not based on human research and cannot account for the variety of aggressive acts humans have learned to display.

3. *The Role of Learning in Aggression.* People learn to be aggressive by watching others or by being reinforced for aggressive acts.

B. Emotional Factors in Aggression

1. *Frustration and Aggression.* According to the most recent version of the frustration-aggression hypothesis, frustration produces a readiness to respond aggressively; aggression will be displayed only if there are environmental cues that invite or are associated with an aggressive response.

2. *Generalized Arousal.* Transfer of excitation, an internal characteristic, and environmental conditions interact to produce aggression. Generalized arousal is most likely to produce aggression when the situation contains some reason, opportunity, or target for aggression.

C. Environmental Influences on Aggression

Hot weather, air pollution, noise, and crowding can all lead to increases in aggression.

V. ALTRUISM AND HELPING BEHAVIOR (pp. 679–683)

Helping behavior is any act that is intended to benefit another person. Altruism is a desire to help another person rather than benefit oneself.

A. Why Do People Help?

Helpfulness is seen in those who are more empathic and have internalized norms for helping behavior. People who are concerned with personal discomfort or about failing and who are less competent, adjusted, active, or assertive are less likely to be helpful.

B. When Are People Most Likely To Help?

Whether or not helping behavior is displayed depends on the interaction between the people involved and the situation in which they find themselves.

1. *Is the Need Recognized?* The need for help and why help is needed must be clearly understood.

2. *The Attractiveness of the Person in Need.* People are much more likely to provide help to those they find attractive or likable than to others.

3. *Familiarity with Surroundings.* People are more likely to offer help if they are in a familiar situation.

4. *The Presence of Others.* Diffusion of responsibility occurs in the presence of others and decreases helping behavior.

VI. COOPERATION AND COMPETITION (pp. 683–689)

Cooperation is any type of behavior in which several people work together to attain a goal. Competition exists whenever individuals try to attain a goal for themselves while denying that goal to others.

A. The Prisoner's Dilemma

Researchers have created a game in which cooperation guarantees the best mutual outcome, but in which there are incentives to compete. Players cannot be certain that their partners will cooperate. Research shows that people tend to respond competitively.

B. Factors Affecting Cooperation and Competition

Winning more than an opponent does seem to be rewarding. In addition, once competition begins, it tends to escalate.

1. *Direct Communication.* Cooperation increases when visual, auditory, nonthreatening, and relevant communication increases.

2. *Communicating a Strategy.* The reformed sinner strategy will increase cooperation. Behavior that is consistently cooperative can either increase cooperation or be viewed as an invitation to exploit. Playing tit-for-tat produces a high degree of overall cooperation.

VII. GROUP DECISION MAKING AND GROUP PERFORMANCE (pp. 686–689)

A. Decision Making in Groups

1. *Individual Opinions.* Despite group discussion, people making decisions within a group tend to stick with their original opinions.

2. *The Order of Discussion.* The first minimally acceptable solution that is offered usually survives as the group's decision.

3. *Group Polarization.* Group decisions are either riskier or more conservative than the average group member's decision. There are two mechanisms at work here. First, people tend to support the majority view, whether that view is risky or conservative. Second, as the group comes to favor a particular decision, a group norm forms, and members try to establish themselves as being the most committed to that norm. Individuals then begin to suggest extreme positions and polarization occurs. In small close-knit groups, decisions can reflect a process called groupthink, a pattern of thinking that, over time, renders members unable to evaluate decisions realistically.

B. Group Leadership

Leaders tend to score high on whatever skills are important to the group. They tend to have good social skills and be ambitious, enjoying their leadership positions. Leadership ability also depends on the situation and on the person's style of handling it. Both the task-oriented style and the socioemotional style of leadership are effective depending on the structure of the group's task and the time pressure the group is under.

KEY TERMS

1. **Social dilemmas** are situations in which the short-term decisions of individuals become irrational in combination and create long-term, clearly predictable damage for a group. (p. 656)

2. **Conformity** occurs when people change their behavior or beliefs as a result of real or imagined unspoken group pressure. (p. 656)

Example: Jill wears a suit to the office because all her coworkers wear suits.

3. **Compliance** occurs when people adjust their behavior because of the directly expressed wishes of a group. (p. 658)

Example: Carlotta, Cecelia, and Carmen are sisters. Their mother has told them that if they want to go swimming they must all clean their rooms. Carlotta and Cecelia hurry to straighten their rooms, but Carmen refuses, at first, to touch the mess in her bedroom. Carlotta and Cecelia keep after Carmen until she complies and cleans her room.

4. The **foot-in-the-door technique** is first making a small request and having it granted, then making larger requests until the asker's real request is granted. (p. 664)

5. The **door-in-the-face procedure** is first making a very large request and having it denied. The requester then admits that this was too large a request and instead makes a smaller one, which is what was wanted all along. (p. 664)

6. The **low-ball approach** is first asking for and getting a verbal commitment to grant a request. Then

the requester shows that only a larger version of the request will be effective, and asks the committed person to grant this larger request instead. (p. 664)

7. **Obedience** is a form of compliance in which people comply with a demand, rather than with a request, because they think they must or should do so. (p. 665)

Example: Carmen's mother tells her that she must clean her room and Carmen obeys.

8. **Aggression** is an act that is intended to harm another person. (pp. 671–672)

Example: Ned is feeling mean and nasty. He decides to play in the sand box at the playground. When he gets there, some of the children insult him. He retaliates by throwing sand in their faces with the express purpose of hurting them.

9. **Catharsis** is the release of pent-up impulses. According to psychoanalytic theory, socially acceptable activities can provide a substitute for overt aggression when accumulated aggressive impulses must be released. (p. 672)

Example: Psychoanalytic theory suggests that watching others act aggressively will have a cathartic effect. A person who is feeling aggressive could watch a violent movie, releasing the pent-up aggression. Note: research has shown that watching aggression tends to increase, not decrease, its occurrence.

10. A **releaser** initiates or sets off an instinctive behavior, according to ethologists. (p. 673)

Example: Newly hatched herring gulls will peck when they see the red spot on their mother's bill. The red spot is a releaser.

11. The **frustration-aggression hypothesis** (revised) suggests that frustration produces a readiness to respond aggressively, but that aggression will occur only if there are cues in the environment that

invite or are associated with an aggressive response. (pp. 675–676)

12. **Helping behavior** is any act that is intended to benefit another person. (p. 679)

Example: Mrs. Byrnes knows that one of her best friends is working extremely hard and has barely enough time to clean, cook, and do laundry. Mrs. Byrnes, an excellent cook, decides to prepare three weeks of dinners for her friend.

13. **Altruism** is a desire to help another person rather than to benefit oneself. (p. 679)

Example: People who sacrifice their own lives in order to save many others are acting altruistically.

14. The **diffusion of responsibility** is the tendency to deny any personal responsibility for responding to someone who needs help when others are present. (p. 683)

Example: A tour guide is escorting some tourists through the streets of Paris. Suddenly, a pedestrian falls and breaks her leg. Most of the people in the group just stand around watching and waiting for others to do something.

15. **Cooperation** is any type of behavior in which several people work together to attain a goal. (p. 683)

Example: Claudia and Missy are sisters. Until they were teenagers they could not stand one another. However, once they realized they were interested in breaking the same parental rules, they began to cooperate and cover for each other.

16. **Competition** exists whenever individuals try to attain a goal for themselves while denying that goal to others. (pp. 683–684)

Example: James is very intelligent. He knows that he can win a scholarship given to the highest ranking student at the end of the year. He decides on a competitive strategy and stops tutoring his classmates.

17. **Group polarization** is the tendency for groups to make decisions that represent a shift toward either riskiness or conservativeness. (p. 688)

18. **Groupthink** is the deterioration, over time, of a small, close-knit group's ability to realistically evaluate the options available and the decisions it has made. (p. 688)

19. A **task-oriented** style of leadership is characterized by providing close supervision, discouraging group discussion, and giving many directives. (p. 689)

20. A **socioemotional style** of leadership is characterized by providing loose supervision, asking for group members' ideas and opinions, and being concerned with subordinates' feelings. (p. 689)

LEARNING OBJECTIVES

1. Define social dilemma. (p. 656)
2. Define conformity and compliance. Describe the role of norms in conformity and compliance. (pp. 656–660)
3. Describe the factors that lead to conformity in groups. (pp. 660–663)
4. Define obedience. Describe Milgram's study and his findings on obedience. (pp. 665–668)
5. Name and describe the factors that influence obedience. (pp. 668–670)
6. Discuss the ethical considerations in carrying out an experiment like Milgram's. (pp. 670–671)
7. Define aggression. (pp. 671–672)
8. Describe the psychoanalytic approach to aggression. Define catharsis. (pp. 672–673)
9. Describe the ethological approach to aggression. Define releaser. (p. 673)

10. Describe the role of learning processes, including observational learning, in aggression. (pp. 674–675)

11. Describe the emotional factors that influence aggression. Define the frustration-aggression hypothesis. Describe the role of arousal and transfer of excitation in aggression. (pp. 675–678)

12. Describe the environmental influences on aggression. (pp. 678–679)

13. Define helping behavior and altruism. Describe the development of helping behavior. Describe the characteristics of helpful and unhelpful people. (pp. 679–680)

14. Describe the characteristics of situations in which people would and would not be likely to display helping behavior. Define diffusion of responsibility. (pp. 681–683)

15. Define cooperation and competition. Describe the research findings from experiments with prisoner's dilemma games. (pp. 683–685)

16. Describe the factors affecting cooperation and competition. Define the reformed sinner strategy and the tit-for-tat strategy. (pp. 685–686)

17. Discuss the influence of individual opinions and the order in which opinions are discussed on group decision making. Define group polarization and groupthink. (pp. 686–689)

18. Describe the three general characteristics of a good leader. Define the task-oriented and socioemotional styles of leadership. Describe the types of situations that call for the use of each style. (p. 689)

CONCEPTS AND EXERCISES

No. 1 Group Decision Making

Completing this exercise should help you to achieve the following learning objectives.

(17) *Discuss the influence of individual opinions and the order in which opinions are discussed on group decision making. Define group polarization and groupthink. (pp. 686–689)*

(18) *Describe the three general characteristics of a good leader. Define the task-oriented and socioemotional styles of leadership. Describe the types of situations that call for the use of each style. (p. 689)*

Charlotte is the president of a major corporation. She wants to give a problem to four different groups of her top management people. Match the descriptions of each group's interaction with the appropriate term from the following list.

Group polarization

Groupthink

Task-oriented leadership

Socioemotional leadership

Dominance of original opinion

Order of presentation

1. Group 1's members cannot seem to resolve their differences. Each member has his or her own idea as to how to solve the problem and refuses to give an inch. _____

2. Maria, who is leading Group 2, is frustrated. One member suggested a mediocre idea at the beginning of the meeting and it received some support. Four hours later, after some much better ideas have been generated, Maria cannot convince her group members to give up that first idea. _____

3. Group 3 has come up with a radical idea for the reorganization of the entire company. Charlotte cannot believe that the members would be in favor of such a risky idea. _____

4. Frank spent an hour at the beginning of the meeting gathering the opinions of all the group members. At the end of four hours the group has agreed on a plan of action that incorporates many of the members' opinions. _____

No. 2 The Elimination of Aggression

Completing this exercise should help you to achieve the following learning objectives.

(8) *Describe the psychoanalytic approach to aggression. Define catharsis. (pp. 672–673)*

(9) *Describe the ethological approach to aggression. Define releaser. (p. 673)*

(10) *Describe the role of learning processes, including observational learning, in aggression. (pp. 674–675)*

(11) *Describe the emotional factors that influence aggression. Define the frustration-aggression hypothesis. Describe the role of arousal and transfer of excitation in aggression. (pp. 675–678)*

Several politicians are discussing the possibility of eliminating war. Match their statements with the appropriate approach from the following list.

Ethological

Learning

Psychoanalytic

Emotional

1. *Politician 1:* Aggression is present in everyone. It cannot be eliminated. We can only hope to restrict individuals' and societies' displays of aggression by wiping out any stimulus that could trigger aggression or violence. _____

2. *Politician 2:* No, I disagree. I think war could be eliminated if violence were removed from television and other mass media. All of our teachers and all those with influence should be taught to present excellent role models for our children. _____

3. *Politician 3:* I agree with you, but we would also have to decrease the daily frustration that people experience. _____

4. *Politician 4:* If aggression is biological, then this predisposition cannot be eliminated. However, we could try to teach people how to channel aggressive energy into more productive activities. _____

ANSWERS TO CONCEPTS AND EXERCISES

No. 1 Group Decision Making

1. *Dominance of original opinion.* All members refuse to be persuaded to support any ideas but the ones they had when they walked into the meeting. (p. 686)

2. *Order of presentation.* The first idea to be presented and to gain positive support will usually be acted upon. This will occur even when later ideas are better than the first one. (p. 687)

3. *Polarization.* Groups tend to make polarized or extreme decisions. Extreme decisions can be either very risky or very conservative. (p. 687)

4. *Socioemotional leadership.* This group leader is asking for the opinions of all the members, a characteristic of this style of leadership. (p. 689)

No. 2 The Elimination of Aggression

1. *Ethological.* This politician believes that aggression is due to biological factors and is triggered by external stimuli. Aggression is similar to an instinctual behavior initiated by a releaser. (p. 673)

2. *Learning.* This politician believes that people learn how to be aggressive by watching others. (p. 674)

3. *Emotional.* This politician believes the revised version of the frustration-aggression hypothesis. (p. 676)

4. *Psychoanalytic.* This politician also believes that aggression is due to biological factors. However, he suggests that activities which would allow the rechanneling of aggressive energy would provide catharsis. (p. 672)

MULTIPLE CHOICE QUESTIONS

Facts and Definitions

1. Why do norms influence behavior to such a great degree?

    a. They allow us to predict the behavior of others.

    b. They let us know which behaviors will be rewarded.

    c. They let us know how to behave in new situations.

    d. All of the above.

2. Conformity is lowest in which type of person or situation?

    a. When the stimulus is ambiguous

    b. When the individual has high status

    c. When unanimity exists

    d. When an individual has low self-esteem

3. In the foot-in-the-door technique

    a. larger and larger requests are made.

    b. a straightforward request is made.

    c. a very large request is made, followed by a smaller one.

    d. the original commitment is devalued and a request is made for more.

4. Obedience is

    a. conforming to a command.

    b. private acceptance of a command.

    c. compliance with a command.

    d. usually in the form of aggressive behavior.

5. A releaser

    a. initiates an instinctual behavior.

    b. always causes aggression.

    c. causes a learned response.

    d. provides a cathartic effect.

6. Which of the following has been a major criticism of the ethological approach to aggression?

    a. Aggression does not provide a cathartic effect.

    b. This approach cannot account for the varied forms of aggression seen in humans.

    c. Eliminating models of aggression from the environment is too difficult.

    d. Frustration does not always lead to aggression.

7. Which is not true of the relationship between pornography and aggression?

    a. Aggressive pornography strongly influences men's attitudes toward rape.

    b. Men are more aggressive toward women but not toward men after viewing aggressive pornography.

    c. Some rapists become aroused after viewing aggressive pornography.

    d. All of the above are true.

8. Which of the following environmental factors has been associated with aggression?

    a. Weather

    b. Air pollution

    c. Noise

    d. All of the above.

9. Diffusion of responsibility occurs when

    a. many people are present and someone needs help.

    b. groups try to make decisions.

    c. a leader divides work equally among his or her staff.

    d. people do not take responsibility for aggressive acts.

10. The tit-for-tat strategy involves being competitive

    a. in response to competition.

    b. in response to cooperation.

    c. after being cooperative.

    d. after being competitive.

11. Groups tend to make

   a. risky decisions.
   b. conservative decisions.
   c. competitive decisions.
   d. extreme decisions.

12. Group polarization occurs when

   a. the last idea presented is approved.
   b. the first idea presented is approved.
   c. an extreme decision is made.
   d. a risky decision is made.

13. The phenomenon of poor decision making in close-knit groups is called

   a. group polarization.
   b. groupthink.
   c. catharsis.
   d. None of the above.

14. A task-oriented leadership style is useful when the job to be done

   a. is structured.
   b. is unstructured.
   c. does not need to be completed rapidly.
   d. is well understood by employees.

15. Which of the following summarizes the sociobiological view of helping behavior?

   a. People feel good when they help others.
   b. People display helping behaviors to protect the gene pool.
   c. People are helpful to protect other individuals.
   d. People learn to be helpful.

MULTIPLE CHOICE QUESTIONS

Application of Concepts

1. Perry is traveling in France. As he walks into his hotel, he notices everyone handing ten francs to the doorman. Perry also hands the doorman ten francs. This is an example of

   a. conformity.
   b. compliance.
   c. obedience.
   d. private acceptance.

2. Ethan has just joined a new group of friends. They want to go and break windows at the back of the school building for fun. Ethan protests, but the ridicule of his peers is too much for him. He finally decides to go along with the group. This is an example of

   a. conformity.
   b. compliance.
   c. obedience.
   d. private acceptance.

3. Lori has spent the afternoon with her bridesmaids, who are trying on various styles of dresses. The bridesmaids liked the pink backless dress, but Lori did not. She decides, even though no one actually asked her to concede, to go along with the crowd, and agrees to choose that dress. This is an example of

   a. conformity.
   b. compliance.
   c. consensus.
   d. None of the above.

4. Myron wants his secretary to stay late. He gets her to agree and then tells her that it will not do him any good unless she stays until 10 P.M. This is called

   a. the foot-in-the-door technique.
   b. the door-in-the-face technique.
   c. the low-ball technique.
   d. the reformed sinner technique.

5. Ken knows that because of politics he has to fire one of his employees. He wants to get one of his subordinates, Stan, to do the dirty work. In which situation will Stan be least likely to obey Ken?

a. If Ken is present when Stan fires the other employee

b. If Ken lets Stan think that the employee has not done a good job

c. If Ken calls Stan on the phone and tells him to fire the other employee

d. If Stan has to call the employee and fire him

6. Agatha is moving to a big city to begin her career. She wants to find a very safe apartment to live in. Which of the following areas should she choose?

    a. Near the airport, since her job requires her to travel quite a bit

    b. In an area that has zoning laws restricting the number of occupants per building

    c. In a high-rise apartment building

    d. Near the plant where she works, despite the smell

7. Patty has just broken her leg. In which situation will she receive the most help?

    a. On the quad during a rally

    b. In the auditorium where new students are signing up for classes

    c. On her way home for a shower after a workout

    d. If she screams that she needs help to whomever is near

8. Tim and Jill are both medical students at a very difficult school. At the beginning of the semester, Tim will not let Jill borrow his notes or help her prepare for exams. Before the midterm exam, he calls her and offers his notes and assistance. Before the final exam, Tim calls Jill and asks to borrow her notes. Tim is employing which strategy?

    a. Tit-for-tat

    b. Low-ball

    c. Reformed sinner

    d. Foot-in-the-door

9. Bernadette is a task-oriented leader. She would be most suited to lead in which type of job?

a. Generating ideas for long-term company growth

b. Getting a report out to the boss—yesterday

c. Managing people who are not familiar with their jobs

d. All of the above.

10. Sherry is in a jam. She needs a place to stay in New York while she looks for a job. Several weeks before her trip, she calls a friend and asks her to pick her up at the airport and let her stay for a night. Later, at the airport, she asks her friend if she can stay for several days. On the second day, she asks her friend if she can stay for an entire week. Sherry is employing which method of compliance?

    a. Reformed sinner strategy

    b. Tit-for-tat strategy

    c. The low-ball technique

    d. The foot-in-the-door technique

11. Donna is angry at her two sons. She finds them in their room having a laser fight way past their bedtime. They are using their toothbrushes as laser guns. She decides not to let them watch any more violent cartoons. Donna's decision is in agreement with which approach to aggression?

    a. Ethological

    b. Psychoanalytic

    c. Learning

    d. Frustration-aggression hypothesis

12. Amelia was strolling down the streets of Chicago. She noticed someone sprawled on the ground in a doorway. The person did not say anything and nobody else on the street seemed to notice he was there. Amelia decided she would just keep on walking. This is an example of

    a. diffusion of responsibility.

    b. the influence of norms on helping behavior.

    c. disobedience.

    d. compliance.

13. Karen is the coordinator of all the psychology teachers. She asks for opinions and suggestions from

all the teachers regarding any task the group must accomplish. What style of leadership is she using?

    a. Tit-for-tat
    b. Socioemotional
    c. Task-oriented
    d. Autocratic

14. Sally is excited about an idea that she is to present at her next sorority meeting. In order to increase the probability of convincing others that her idea is good, she should

    a. save it until the end of the meeting so people will remember it clearly.
    b. present it during the middle of the meeting to liven things up a bit.
    c. present it at the beginning of the meeting.
    d. None of the above.

15. Naomi has decided to run an experiment on obedience. She has asked her confederates to stop people on the sidewalk and order them to put money in an empty parking meter close by. Which confederate will produce the highest obedience rate?

    a. An old man dressed in tattered clothes.
    b. A man dressed in tennis shorts and carrying a racket.
    c. A man dressed in a white air force uniform.
    d. A man dressed in a construction worker's clothes.

ANSWERS TO MULTIPLE CHOICE QUESTIONS

Facts and Definitions

1. *d* is the answer. Norms tell us which behaviors are appropriate and which will be rewarded in a given situation. We can also learn how to behave in new cultures by learning the norms of that society. (p. 660)

2. *b* is the answer. Those who have high status do not conform as often as those with low status. (p. 663)
    a. As the ambiguity of a stimulus increases, so does conformity.
    c. Conformity increases greatly when a person is presented with a unanimous decision.
    d. Individuals with low self-esteem tend to conform in order to gain approval from attractive group members.

3. *a* is the answer. Making larger and larger requests is called the foot-in-the-door technique. (p. 664)
    b. Asking for exactly what you want is simply a request.
    c. The door-in-the-face technique is making a large request, having it denied, and then making a smaller request.
    d. The low-ball technique is devaluing the original commitment made and asking for more.

4. *c* is the answer. Obedience is a form of compliance in which people comply with a demand rather than a request because they think they must or should do so. (p. 665)
    a. Conformity results from real or imagined unspoken group pressure.
    b. Many of the subjects in Milgram's study did not privately accept or condone delivering an electric shock to people, but they did it anyway.
    d. Obedience and aggression are not always present together. Many people follow orders without the threat of aggression for disobedience hanging over them.

5. *a* is the answer. A releaser initiates an instinctual behavior. (p. 673)
    b. Releasers do not always cause aggression. In many species, releasers are found to initiate courtship and mating rituals.
    c. Releasers initiate stereotyped or instinctive behaviors. These types of behaviors are innate, not learned.

d. Catharsis is a psychoanalytic, not an ethological, concept. Freud thought that channeling aggressive energy into socially acceptable activities would allow it to be released in a harmless fashion.

6. *b* is the answer. Ethologists assume that aggression is innate. However, labeling aggression as instinctual cannot account for the many forms of human aggression. Learning must play a role in at least the expression of aggression. (p. 673)

a. The psychoanalytic approach to aggression has been criticized because viewing aggressive acts does not seem to provide a cathartic effect. Indeed, in some cases it has led to an increase in aggression.

c. According to the learning approach, in order to reduce aggression all models of aggression should be removed from the environment. This would be impossible.

d. The revised frustration-aggression hypothesis, an emotional approach to aggression, states that frustration predisposes us to aggression. Aggression will occur if there are aggressive cues in the environment.

7. *d* is the answer. Aggressive pornography does alter men's attitudes toward rape, does arouse some rapists, and does cause an increase in men's aggression toward women but not other men. (pp. 677–678)

8. *d* is the answer. Hot weather, air pollution (ozone or cigarette smoke), and unwanted noise are associated with higher crime rates and aggression. (p. 678)

9. *a* is the answer. When many people are present, diffusion of responsibility occurs and helping behavior is reduced. (p. 683)

b. You may be thinking of groupthink, the inability of a small close-knit group to realistically evaluate the decisions it makes.

c. You may be thinking of leadership styles. Diffusion of responsibility is only related to helping behavior.

d. Diffusion of responsibility is related to helping behavior, not to aggression.

10. *a* is the answer. When the tit-for-tat strategy is used, presumably to increase cooperation, competitive maneuvers are punished with competitive maneuvers. (p. 686)

b. If cooperative moves are punished with competitive moves, cooperation will decrease.

c. & d. All the strategies mentioned in your text involve responses to the other player's move. There are no strategies based on a pattern of cooperation or competition on the part of just one player.

11. *d* is the answer. Groups tend to make polarized, or extremely risky or conservative, decisions. (p. 688)

a. & b. Groups tend to make polarized decisions at either extreme: risky or conservative.

c. Groups may make a competitive decision with regard to another group; however, it is impossible to tell whether this decision is risky or conservative without more information.

12. *c* is the answer. Groups tend to make polarized, extremely risky or conservative, decisions. (p. 688)

a. & b. Groups tend to go with the first idea presented that gained even moderate approval.

d. Groups tend to make extreme or polarized decisions. These can be either extremely risky *or* extremely conservative.

13. *b* is the answer. Small close-knit groups tend to lose the ability to realistically evaluate their decisions. (p. 688)

a. Group polarization is the tendency of groups to make extreme decisions, either very risky or very conservative.

c. Catharsis is the release of aggressive tendencies by channeling that energy into socially approved activities.

d. b is the answer.

14. *b* is the answer. A task-oriented leadership style is useful when the job is unstructured or on a tight time schedule, or when employees are not very familiar with their jobs. (p. 689)

    a., *c.*, & *d.* A socioemotional style is useful when the job is structured, on a relaxed time schedule, and when employees are very familiar with their jobs.

15. *b* is the answer. Sociobiologists believe that helping behavior increases the chances of survival. Consequently, the chance of one's own genes being passed on increases. (p. 680)

    a. & *d.* A learning theorist would say that people learn helping behaviors because they are rewarded for them.

    c. According to sociobiology, people do not help others for the sake of the individual, but rather to increase the chances of passing on their own genes.

ANSWERS TO MULTIPLE CHOICE QUESTIONS

Application of Concepts

1. *a* is the answer. Perry, as a result of unspoken pressure, is conforming. (p. 656)

    b. If someone had suggested that he give the doorman ten francs, this would have been the correct alternative.

    c. If someone had demanded that he give the doorman ten francs, this would have been the correct alternative.

    d. If Perry had decided that he really should be giving the doorman ten francs, this would have been the correct alternative.

2. *b* is the answer. Ethan is changing his behavior in response to expressed (spoken) social influence. (p. 658)

    a. Conformity occurs when people change their behavior in response to real or imagined *unspoken* peer pressure.

    c. Ethan's friends did not demand that he go along with them; they just applied social pressure.

    d. Private acceptance would mean that Ethan has changed his mind about breaking windows. He changed his behavior due to peer pressure, but he did not change his opinion of the behavior.

3. *a* is the answer. Conformity occurs when people, in the face of unspoken peer pressure, change their behavior to match that of other group members. (p. 656)

    b. Compliance occurs when people change their behavior because of expressed social influence.

    c. When your behavior is based on your beliefs and happens to match that of other people, consensus exists.

    d. a is the answer.

4. *c* is the answer. Myron first got his secretary to agree to stay late. Then he devalued that commitment, saying it would not do him any good unless she stayed very late—until 10 P.M. (pp. 664–665)

    a. The foot-in-the-door technique involves starting out with a small request and then making larger and larger ones.

    b. The door-in-the-face technique involves originally making a very large request, usually being refused, and then making a smaller request. The smaller request is usually granted.

    d. The reformed sinner technique is a competitive strategy. Myron is not competing with his secretary.

5. *c* is the answer. As the physical distance between Stan and Ken increases, the likelihood of Stan obeying Ken decreases. This is similar to Milgram's experiment. When the proximity of the experimenter to the subject decreased, the obedience of the subject decreased as well. (p. 669)

    a. The level of obedience increases when an authority figure gives the directions while in close proximity. If Ken is in the room, Stan will be much more likely to obey.

b. If Ken can convince Stan that the employee is responsible for getting himself fired, the likelihood of Stan obeying will increase.

d. According to Milgram's experimental results, as the physical distance between the teacher (subject who is shocking the victim) and the learner (confederate) increases, the level of obedience increases. Therefore, as the physical distance between Stan and the employee increases, Stan is more likely to obey Ken. If Stan has to fire the employee over the phone (a greater distance than firing him in person) he will be more likely to obey Ken.

6. *b* is the answer. As crowding increases, so does aggression. Living in an area where zoning laws limit crowding would be safer than any of the other alternatives. (p. 679)

a. Living near the airport will increase the noise in Agatha's neighborhood. Unwanted noise has been associated with increases in aggression.

c. People who live in high-rises are more likely to act aggressively.

d. Air pollution raises levels of aggression.

7. *d* is the answer. Patty's screams will communicate that she does in fact need help. Research has demonstrated that when people clearly understand that a person is in need of aid, the incidence of helping behavior increases. (p. 682)

a. A rally is usually well attended. When many people are present, diffusion of responsibility occurs and helping behavior is less likely.

b. People who are unfamiliar with their surroundings are usually less likely to help. New students are probably unfamiliar with their surroundings.

c. If you are attractive and well-dressed you are much more likely to be helped. Patty probably doesn't look too attractive just after her workout.

8. *c* is the answer. The reformed sinner strategy involves being competitive at first and switching to cooperative behavior later. (p. 685)

a. The tit-for-tat strategy is punishing competitive moves with competition and rewarding cooperative moves with cooperation.

b. The low-ball technique is used to increase compliance by first getting a commitment and then devaluing that commitment and making an even larger request.

d. The foot-in-the-door technique is making gradually larger and larger requests.

9. *d* is the answer. The task-oriented style of leadership works best when time is short, when the task is unstructured, or when workers are unfamiliar with their jobs. (p. 689)

10. *d* is the answer. Sherry is gradually making larger and larger requests, which is the foot-in-the-door technique. (p. 664)

a. & b. The tit-for-tat and reformed sinner strategies are competitive strategies. Sherry is not competing with her friend.

c. The low-ball technique involves getting an original commitment, devaluing that commitment, and asking for more (what you really wanted in the first place). Instead, Sherry is gradually asking for more and more after her girlfriend has complied with previous requests.

11. *c* is the answer. According to the learning approach, we can learn aggression by watching others' aggressive behavior. The boys may have learned their aggressive behavior from watching violent cartoons. (p. 674)

a. From the ethological viewpoint, aggression is a biologically generated instinct.

b. According to the psychoanalytic viewpoint, aggression is innate, not learned.

d. According to the frustration-aggression hypothesis, aggression will be displayed if a person is frustrated and there are aggressive cues in the environment.

12. *a* is the answer. Helping behavior tends to decrease when many people are present and the need

for help is not clearly communicated. This is called diffusion of responsibility. (p. 683)

b. In our culture, norms would call for Amelia to help the person in the doorway.

c. Amelia had not been ordered by anyone to help; therefore, she was not disobeying.

d. Compliance occurs when people change their behavior in response to direct or expressed social influence. Nobody suggested to Amelia that she help the person in the doorway.

13. *b* is the answer. The socioemotional style is characterized by asking group members for their opinions. (p. 689)

a. The tit-for-tat method is a competitive strategy, not a leadership style.

c. A task-oriented style is characterized by giving directives without input from the group.

d. There is no such thing as an autocratic style of leadership.

14. *c* is the answer. The first idea that gains a positive response in a group decision-making session usually wins the support of the group. (p. 687)

a. & b. Sally should present her idea at the beginning of the meeting, not at the end or in the middle. The first idea to gain a positive response from the group usually is chosen over later ideas.

d. c is the answer.

15. *c* is the answer. The uniform will communicate a prestigious and authoritative presence. Obedience increases as the prestige and authority of the person giving the orders increases. (pp. 668–669)

a., b., & d. None of these types of clothing communicate prestige or authority.

Appendix

Statistics in Psychological Research

OUTLINE

I. INTRODUCTION (p. 695)

Statistics are visual and mathematical methods for describing and drawing conclusions from large amounts of data.

II. DESCRIBING DATA (pp. 695–701)

A. Frequency Histograms

Frequency histograms, graphic descriptions of data, are useful for visualizing and better understanding the "shape" of research data.

B. Descriptive Statistics

The numbers that summarize a pool of data are called descriptive statistics.

1. *N*. The easiest statistic to compute is N, the number of observations in the data set.

2. *Measures of Central Tendency*. There are three statistical measures that describe the typical value of a data set. The mode is the score that occurs most often in the data set. The median is the halfway point in a set of data; half of the scores fall above it and half fall below it. The mean is the arithmetic average of all the scores. All the scores in a data set are used to calculate the mean.

3. *Measures of Variablity*. There are two statistical measures that indicate the dispersion of scores in a data set, or measure variability. The range describes the distance between the highest and lowest score. The standard deviation measures the average difference between each score and the mean of the data set.

4. *The Normal Distribution*. When most of the scores in a data set fall in the middle of a distribution, with few extreme scores, the data resemble a bell-shaped curve called the normal distribution. The mean, median, and mode all have the same value. The normal distribution is the basis for percentiles and standard scores. A percentile indicates the percentage of subjects or observations that fall below a given score. A standard score expresses distance in standard deviations from the mean.

5. *Correlation*. The relationship between two variables is described by a *correlation*. The statistical measures that represent this relationship are called correlation coefficients.

III. INFERENTIAL STATISTICS (pp. 701–704)

Inferential statistics provide a measure of confidence or probability that conducting the same experiment again would yield similar results.

1. *Differences Between Means: The t test*. The t test, a type of inferential statistic, assesses whether differences between two means occurred by chance or as the effect of an inde-

pendent variable. Results that show a low probability of chance effects are statistically significant. Performing a *t* test requires using (1) the difference between the means, (2) the standard deviation, and (3) the number of observations or subjects. The researcher also takes the degrees of freedom and *p* value into account.

2. *Beyond the t test*. Other statistical tests are used to analyze data from experiments that are more complex than comparisons between two groups. Analysis of variance analyzes the effects of more than one independent variable on a dependent variable.

KEY TERMS

1. A **frequency histogram** is a graphic display of data in the form of bars that tells how often different data values occur. (p. 695)

REMEMBER: Frequency means how often. This graph tells you how often various scores occurred.

2. **Descriptive statistics** are mathematical methods of summarizing and presenting data. These include *N,* measures of central tendency, measures of variability, and correlation coefficients. (p. 696)

REMEMBER: Descriptive statistics describe data.

3. The measures of **central tendency,** the mean, mode, and median, are descriptive statistics. Each measure is a single number that represents the typical value of a data set. (p. 696)

Example: One teacher asks a second teacher, "How did your students do on their test?" The second teacher probably does not carry a graph (a frequency histogram) of her students' scores with her nor can she recite all of the scores from memory. But she can tell the first teacher that the scores had a *tendency* to *center* around a given number. That number will be the mean, the median, or the mode.

4. The **mode,** a measure of central tendency, is the most frequently occurring score in a data set. (p. 696)

Example: In the data set 2, 12, 15, 19, 20, 23, 23, 23, 27, 29, 30, the mode is 23.

5. The **median** is the score that divides a data set in half; half of the scores are higher than the median and half of the scores are lower than the median. The median is a measure of central tendency. (p. 696)

REMEMBER: The definition of median is *the score in the middle*. In statistics the median is the middle score; the score that divides the data set in half.

6. The **mean** is the arithmetic average. To compute the mean, add the numerical values of all the scores in a data set and divide that sum by the number of scores (N). This measure of central tendency takes into account all of the values of the scores in a data set. Therefore, even one extreme score can change the mean radically, possibly making it less representative of the data. (p. 697)

Example: For the data set 1, 2, 3, 4, 5, 5, 5, 6, 7, 8, 9, the mean is equal to $1 + 2 + 3 + 4 + 5 + 5 + 5 + 6 + 7 + 8 + 9/11 = 55/11 = 5$.

7. Measures of **variability** are mathematical representations of the dispersion or spread of scores in a data set. These include the range and the standard deviation. The larger the variability, the larger the dispersion of scores. (p. 697)

REMEMBER: Disperse means to scatter. Measures of variability will tell you if the scores in a data set are very different from each other (scattered) or if they cluster together around the mean.

8. The **range** is a measure of variability. To compute the range, subtract the lowest score from the highest score in a data set. The range is affected by extreme scores. (pp. 697–698)

Example: In the data set 2, 3, 4, 5, 5, 5, 6, 7, 8, 100, the range is $100 - 2 = 98$. If the extreme score, 100, is dropped, the range is $8 - 2 = 6$.

9. The **standard deviation** is a measure of variability, computed by the formula:

$$\sqrt{\frac{\Sigma D^2}{N}}$$

It measures the average distance between each score and the mean of a data set. The standard deviation will tell you how scattered the scores are around the mean. (p. 698)

Example:

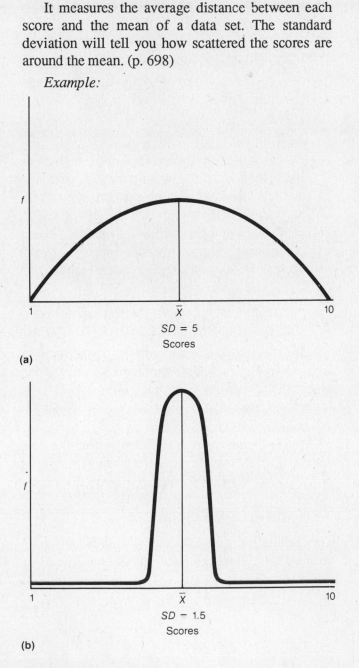

$SD = 5$
Scores

(a)

$SD - 1.5$
Scores

(b)

If the standard deviation is large, as in graph A, then the average distance between the scores and the mean is large. If the standard deviation is small, as in graph B, the average distance between the scores and the mean is small.

10. The **normal distribution** describes a data set in which the scores fall symmetrically around the mean, and is represented by a bell-shaped curve. The scores are scattered so that half are above the mean and half are below the mean. The mean, the median, and the mode are always equal in a normal distribution. (pp. 698–699)

REMEMBER: If you are having problems understanding what a normal distribution is, be sure to do the exercise "A Statistical Report Card."

11. **Percentile scores** indicate the percentage of people or observations that fall below a given score in a normal distribution. (p. 699)

Example: If your psychology exam score is at the 95th percentile, you know that you did better than 95 percent of all the people who took the test. It *does not* mean that you answered 95 percent of the questions correctly.

12. **Standard scores** express the value of a score by indicating its distance in standard deviations from the mean. (p. 700)

Example: A standard score of +1.5 means that the score is 1.5 standard deviations above the mean of the distribution.

13. **Correlation coefficients** are descriptions of the relationship between two variables. The formula is:

$$r = \frac{\Sigma\,(x - M_x)\,(y - M_y)}{\sqrt{\Sigma\,(x - M_x)^2\,\Sigma\,(y - M_y)^2}}$$

(p. 700)

14. **Inferential statistics** provide mathematical values of the probability that running the same experiment again would yield similar results. (p. 701)

15. The *t* **test** is one inferential statistical method used to analyze data. The outcome of this test indicates whether the differences found between two means are the result of chance factors or changes in the dependent variable produced by the independent variable. A *t* value is computed by the following formula:

$$t = \frac{M_1 - M_2}{\sqrt{\dfrac{(N_1 - 1) S_1^2 + (N_2 - 1) S_2^2}{N_1 + N_2 - 2}}}$$

(pp. 701–702)

16. **Statistical significance** occurs when the outcome of an inferential statistical method indicates that the probability of results being due to chance is so low (usually 1 to 5 percent) that the results can be confidently attributed to the action of the independent variable. (p. 701)

17. **Degrees of freedom** are numbers calculated for use in interpreting *t* values (and other inferential statistics procedures). (p. 703)

18. *p* **values** indicate the probability that differences in the data occurred by chance. (p. 703)

Example: If experimental results are significant at *p* less than .05, then the probability that the differences in the data occurred by chance are no greater than 5 percent or 5 out of 100.

19. **Analysis of variance** is an inferential statistical procedure used when the experimental design includes more than two experimental groups or more than one independent variable. (p. 703)

Example: The size of a group (the independent variable) may affect the speed (dependent variable) of that group's decision making. However, the type of decision to be made (another independent variable) may also affect the decision-making speed. If an experiment were designed to test the separate effects of both independent variables, as well as any possible interaction be-

tween them, analysis of variance could be used to analyze the data.

LEARNING OBJECTIVES

1. Know the differences between descriptive and inferential statistics. (pp. 696, 701)
2. Define frequency histogram. Know why it is used. (pp. 695–696)
3. Define measure of central tendency. State the names and definitions of the three measures of central tendency. Discuss the advantages and disadvantages of each measure. (pp. 696–697)
4. Know how to calculate the mean, median, and mode for a given data set. (pp. 696–697)
5. Define measure of variability. State the names and definitions of the two measures discussed in the text. Discuss the advantages and disadvantages of each measure. (pp. 697–698)
6. Know how to calculate the range and standard deviation of a given set of data. (pp. 697–698)
7. Discuss the features of a normal distribution. (pp. 698–700)
8. Define correlation. Know the formula for computing a correlation coefficient. (pp. 700–701)
9. Define *t* test. Know the formula for calculating a *t* value as well as the procedures for interpreting it. (pp. 701–703)
10. Define analysis of variance. Know when this statistic is used. (p. 703)

CONCEPTS AND EXERCISES

No. 1 Statistics and the Consumer

Completing this exercise should help you to achieve the following learning objectives.

(3) *Define measure of central tendency. State the names and definitions of the three measures of*

central tendency. Discuss the advantages and disadvantages of each measure. (pp. 696–697)

(5) *Define measure of variability. State the names and definitions of the two measures discussed in the text. Discuss the advantages and disadvantages of each measure. (pp. 697–698)*

Richard has just won the lottery. He has hired you to help him spend his money. He has given you a stack of statistical documentation on the qualities of all the brand name items he wants to buy. Richard knows nothing about statistics. Based on this statistical information, you must choose the best brand for the money.

1. Richard wants a sports car and cares only about its maximum speed. Your information says that the mean maximum speed of car A is 180 mph; the standard deviation for all the speed trials is 32 mph. The mean maximum speed of car B is 173 mph, with a standard deviation of 5 mph. Which car should Richard buy?

2. Richard wants to buy and sell property to make a profit. Therefore, he needs to know what areas contain properties that will increase quickly in value. In the last five years, Brentwood Oaks has had a mean increase in value of 15 percent and a standard deviation of 2 percent. Redwood Estates has had a mean increase of 18 percent and a standard deviation of .5 percent. In which area should Richard buy?

3. Richard has been overweight for most of his life and wants to get in shape. Clients at the Body Beautiful Fitness Center have achieved a mean loss of thirty-five pounds with a standard deviation of twenty pounds. Clients at the Bare Bones Fitness Center have achieved a mean loss of twenty-five pounds with a standard deviation of four pounds. At which center can Richard be more sure of losing twenty to twenty-five pounds?

4. Richard and one of his new friends want to bet on the season performance of various football teams. Each man will pick a team that he thinks has a chance of scoring the most points in the upcoming season. Whoever picks the highest-scoring team will win. Team A has a mean point total of 355 for the past 5 seasons with a standard deviation of 15 points, and team B has a mean point total of 370 for the past 5 seasons and a standard deviation of 5 points. Which team should Richard pick?

No. 2 Choosing the Correct Statistical Method

Completing this exercise should help you to achieve the following learning objectives.

(8) *Define correlation. Know the formula for computing a correlation coefficient. (pp. 700–701)*

(9) *Define t test. Know the formula for calculating a t value as well as the procedure for interpreting it. (pp. 701–703)*

(10) *Define analysis of variance. Know when this statistic is used. (p. 703)*

Pick the most appropriate statistical method for analyzing the data from the following three experiments.

A. A psychologist believes that the environment affects the development of connections among nerve cells in the brain. She raises two groups of rats: rats in one group (Group 1) live together in a cage filled with toys; rats in the other group (Group 2) are housed in separate steel cages with no toys. After several months, the psychologist examines the brains of the rats to see if there are differences between the two groups in the number of nerve cell connections.

B. Some psychologists believe that genetic factors determine intelligence. Others believe that environmental factors, such as educational opportunities, nutrition, and the quality of care received during childhood, determine intelligence. To test this hypothesis, a psychologist decides to compare the intelligence of children who have grown up in orphanages with that of children who have grown up in wealthy families.

C. A psychologist believes that the different types of therapy used to treat abnormal behavior are not really different from each other. To test this, he chooses three different therapies and divides his group of subjects, all of whom are suffering from severe depression, into three groups. Each group receives one type of therapy. After all the subjects have been treated for six months, their level of depression is measured.

No. 3 A Statistical Report Card

Completing this exercise should help you to achieve the following learning objective.

(7) *Discuss the features of a normal distribution.* *(pp. 698–700)*

You have just started attending a progressive high school. Instead of grades, your report card contains a normal distribution indicating where your performance falls in relation to everyone else's. Your parents, somewhat perplexed, ask you to interpret your report card.

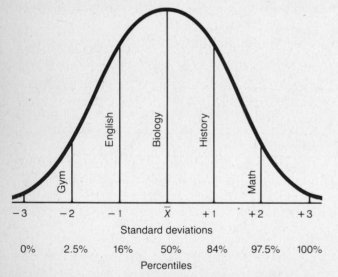

The graph represents a normal distribution. The top 10 percent of the class received As. The top 16 percent of the class received either As or Bs. 68 percent of the students received Cs. The bottom 16

percent of the class received Ds. *The bottom 2.5 percent received Ds and* Fs.

1. What grade did you get in history?
2. What percentage of the students in history did better than you?
3. In what course did you perform both better and worse than 50 percent of the class?
4. What percentage of the class did better than your performance in gym?
5. What grade did you get in math?
6. You scored higher than what percentage of your class in math?
7. In what course is your grade equal to the median?
8. In what course is your grade equal to the mode?

ANSWERS TO CONCEPTS AND EXERCISES

No. 1 Statistics and the Consumer

1. Richard wants to buy a car that is consistently fast. Car A has a higher mean speed than car B over all the time trials. However, the standard deviation is very large. This tells you that car A is fast, but not consistently fast; there was much variation in the data from the time trials. Car B's speed is 7 miles slower than car A's, but the variation is low. Therefore, Richard should buy car B, since he can depend on it to be more consistently fast.

2. To make money quickly but with very low risk, Richard must buy property that will increase in value consistently and at a fairly fast rate. Redwood Estates has a higher mean increase in property value and has a small standard deviation, which indicates that the mean is a good description of the increase in the property's value. Richard should buy land in Redwood Estates. Brentwood Oaks not only has a lower

mean value increase, but also has shown much variability in the increase.

3. If Richard wants to be sure to lose weight, he should go to the Bare Bones Fitness Center. Even though the mean weight loss there is lower by ten pounds, the variability is low, which tells you that most people who have gone there have lost close to twenty-five pounds. The Body Beautiful Fitness Center has a higher mean weight loss, but also a higher variability, which tells you that some people have lost a lot of weight there, but some have lost very little.

4. Team B has consistently scored close to 370 points for the past 5 years. Team A has a mean of 355 points, but they have not been consistent. This means that some years they scored well above 355 points and some years they scored well below 355 points. Team B's mean point total of 370 is higher and more consistent than team A's mean point total. Therefore, Richard should bet on team B.

No. 2 Choosing the Correct Statistical Method

A. This psychologist is going to compare the mean number of nerve cell connections in rats from Group 1 to the mean number of nerve cell connections in rats from Group 2. She will use a *t test*, which will tell her how likely it is that the differences between means of the two groups are due to the effects of the different environments or due to chance. If her results are significant, then she can conclude that the housing conditions did indeed cause changes in the number of nerve cell connections in the brains of the rats.

B. This psychologist is looking at the relationship between two variables: level of intelligence and environmental conditions. Therefore, he will find the *correlation coefficient* that represents this relationship. Remember, even if the correlation is very high, the psychologist can only conclude that these variables are related. He cannot conclude that environmental conditions cause changes in the level of intelligence. Correlation does not imply causation.

C. This psychologist is interested in the effect of therapy (independent variable) on depression (dependent variable). He wants to know if there are any differences between the effectiveness of *three* different types of therapy. Therefore there are three levels of the independent variable. These data require an *analysis of variance*.

No. 3 A Statistical Report Card

1. Your grade in history is a *B*. The top 16 percent of your class received either *A*s or *B*s. Only the top 10 percent received *A*s. Your history grade falls at the 84th percentile ($100 - 16 = 84$), not in the upper 10 percent. Therefore, you received a *B*.

2. Your history grade falls at the first, or +1, standard deviation, which is also the 84th percentile. Therefore you did better than 84 percent of the history students, and 16 percent did better than you ($100 - 84 = 16$).

3. In a normal distribution 50 percent of the scores fall above the mean and 50 percent fall below the mean. Your biology grade is at the mean. You performed better that 50 percent of your biology class and 50 percent of the class did better than you.

4. Your gym grade falls at –2 standard deviations. The percentile at –2 standard deviations is 2.5. You did better than 2.5 percent of the class. 97.5 percent of the class did better than you ($100 - 2.5 = 97.5$).

5. Your grade in math falls at the 97.5 percentile. The upper 10 percent of your class got *A*s. You are in the upper 2.5 percent ($100 - 97.5 = 2.5$) and therefore you received an *A*.

6. Your math grade falls at +2 standard deviations, which is also the 97.5th percentile. Therefore you did better than 97.5 percent of the class.

7. & 8. In a normal distribution the mean, median, and mode are equal. Your biology grade falls at the mean of the distribution; hence, your biology grade is equal to the median and the mode.

MULTIPLE CHOICE QUESTIONS

Facts and Definitions

1. N is equal to
   a. the number of subjects in an experiment.
   b. the number of observations in a data set.
   c. the number of independent variables in the experiment.
   d. the number of dependent variables in the data set.

2. The _____, a measure of central tendency, is affected by wild, extreme or unrepresentative scores.
   a. mean
   b. median
   c. standard deviation
   d. range

3. Researchers use _____ statistical methods to summarize and present their data.
   a. descriptive
   b. significant
   c. inferential
   d. standard

4. If a visual presentation of data is required you use a
   a. frequency histogram.
   b. normal distribution.
   c. measure of central tendency.
   d. measure of variability.

5. The mean is a poor descriptive measure of central tendency when
   a. the standard deviation is very small.
   b. it is very large.
   c. the range is very small.

d. there are extreme or unrepresentative scores in the data set.

6. A higher t value will be obtained if
   a. the N is large.
   b. the standard deviation is small.
   c. the difference between two means is quite large.
   d. All of the above will increase the t value.

7. Which of the following data sets would best fit the definition of a normal distribution?
   a. 1, 1, 2, 4, 6, 7, 8, 23
   b. 1, 6, 6, 12, 100, 100, 200
   c. 1, 2, 3, 4, 5, 5, 5, 6, 7, 8, 9
   d. 2, 4, 6, 8, 10, 10, 11

MULTIPLE CHOICE QUESTIONS

Application of Concepts

1. Chris has done an experiment that involves two independent variables. Which inferential statistical measure should she use to analyze her data?
   a. Mean
   b. Standard deviation
   c. t test
   d. Analysis of variance

2. Pierre has been computing t values for statistical analysis of his data. He has discovered a mistake in his calculation of the standard deviations for his data groups. They are much higher than he originally thought. The recalculated t values will be
   a. higher, thereby increasing his chances of getting statistically significant results.
   b. higher, thereby decreasing his chances of getting statistically significant results.
   c. lower, thereby increasing his chances of getting statistically significant results.
   d. lower, thereby decreasing his chances of getting statistically significant results.

3. You have decided to buy a certain kind of car because you have heard it gets great gas mileage. According to a consumer magazine, the mean gas mileage obtained during testing was 30, the median was 26, and the mode was 25. This tells you that

    a. if you buy the car you can expect to get 30 miles per gallon.

    b. the gas mileage will vary from 20 to 40 miles per gallon.

    c. the gas mileage is probably lower than 30 miles per gallon.

    d. if you buy the car you can expect to get 28 miles per gallon.

Mr. King is a high school football coach. He has kept track of the number of touchdowns his players have made for every game. Using the data that he has collected, answer the next three questions.

    Data: 1, 2, 3, 3, 8, 10, 7, 6, 5

4. What is the mode?

    a. 3
    b. 4
    c. 5
    d. 6

5. What is the median?

    a. 3
    b. 4
    c. 5
    d. 6

6. What is the mean?

    a. 3
    b. 4
    c. 5
    d. 6

7. Maxine found that she scored at the ninety-third percentile on her calculus exam. This means that

    a. she got 93 percent of the problems correct.

    b. seven other people in the class scored higher than Maxine.

    c. she scored higher than 93 percent of the calculus class on the test.

d. she did 93 problems correctly.

ANSWERS TO MULTIPLE CHOICE QUESTIONS

Facts and Definitions

1. *b* is the answer. Observations or scores are numerical representations of the measurement of the dependent variable. The total number of observations is called N. (p. 696)

    a. If each subject gives two responses or answers in an experiment then the total number of observations, N, will be equal to twice the size of the sample. Therefore, counting the number of subjects will not always give the value of N.

    c. The number of independent variables will not tell you how many observations a data set has.

    d. If we use the incentive experiment discussed in the text as an example, then we have one dependent variable: problem solving. This will not tell us the value of N.

2. *a* is the answer. To calculate the mean, the values of all the scores in a data set are used. Therefore, if one or more of the scores differs greatly from the rest, the value of the mean changes, making it a less accurate description of central tendency. (p. 697)

    b. The calculation of the median considers all of the scores but not their values, so that each score carries the same weight. The median is always the score that splits the data in half. Therefore, scores with extremely high or low values will not affect the median.

    c. The standard deviation is a measure of variability, not a measure of central tendency.

    d. The range is a measure of variability, not a measure of central tendency.

3. *a* is the answer. Descriptive statistics, such as the measures of central tendency, summarize the data set. For example, the mean summarizes all the numerical scores in a data set. (p. 696)

b. There is no such thing as a statistically significant method. Researchers use inferential statistics to conclude from data that experimental results are statistically significant.

c. Inferential statistics are the mathematical procedures psychologists use to *draw conclusions* from data and make inferences about what they mean.

d. There is no such thing as a standard statistic.

4. *a* is the answer. A frequency histogram is a pictorial representation of how often each score occurred. (p. 695)

b. A normal distribution describes a certain type of data set. It is not used to present data.

c. Measures of central tendency are numerical, not visual, descriptions of data.

d. Measures of variability are numerical, not visual, descriptions of data.

5. *d* is the answer. The mean is an average of the values of all the scores in a data set. Extremely low or high scores can have a huge effect on the value of the mean and it will not provide an accurate description of where most of the scores tend to fall. (p. 697)

a. If the standard deviation is small, most of the scores in the data set cluster around the mean and the mean accurately represents the central tendency of the data.

b. The size of the mean does not make it a better or worse measure of central tendency. A large mean could accurately indicate a predominance of large scores in the data set, or the presence of very large unrepresentative scores.

c. If the range is small there may not be much variability in the data. The less variability there is, the more accurate the mean is in conveying where the scores had a tendency to center.

6. *d* is the answer. The formula for a *t* value is

$$t = \frac{M_1 - M_2}{\sqrt{\frac{(N_1 - 1) S_1^2 + (N_2 - 1) S_2^2}{N_1 + N_2 - 2}}}$$

Mathematical reasoning shows that any of the answers will increase the value of *t*. This conclusion can also be reached by considering the purpose of a *t* test. *t* tests are conducted to determine if the obtained difference between two means is due to chance or the real effect of an independent variable. (p. 701)

a. As the sample gets larger, any random factors that are present should be cancelled out by the majority.

b. If the standard deviation is small, the means are more accurate descriptions of the activity in a data set. Therefore, any differences are more likely to be real and not a chance occurrence due to the presence of unrepresentative scores.

c. In the very worst situation the difference between two means could be due to bad samples, or extreme scores. However, if the means are large, there will still be a difference after all these effects are adjusted for.

7. *c* is the answer. The mean, median, and mode are equal in a normal distribution. (p. 699)

a., b., & d. None of these data sets have means, medians, and modes that are equal.

ANSWERS TO MULTIPLE CHOICE QUESTIONS

Application of Concepts

1. *d* is the answer. In an experiment with two or more independent variables, the results may be due to either of the independent variables or to the interaction between them. Analysis of variance can measure the size and source of these effects. (p. 703)

a. & b. The mean and standard deviation are necessary to compute inferential statistics (such as the *t* test and analysis of variance), but they are descriptive statistics.

c. A *t* test is an inferential statistic, but it is used to test the difference between two means in an experiment that uses only one independent variable.

2. *d* is the answer. If you look at the formula for a *t* test in your text, you will see that increasing the standard deviation will decrease the overall value of the equation or *t*. The lower the value of *t* the more likely it is to be smaller than the *t* values listed in a *t* table, and hence not statistically significant. (p. 702)

a. & b. A larger standard deviation will result in a smaller *t* value.

c. A larger standard deviation will result in a smaller *t* value. The obtained *t* value must be equal to or larger than the *t* values listed in a *t* table for the data to be considered statistically significant.

3. *c* is the answer. Since the mode and median are both below thirty, you should suspect that the mean has been artificially inflated by a few extreme, unrepresentative scores. Therefore, the gas mileage will probably be lower than thirty miles per gallon. (pp. 696–697)

a., b., & d. The mean has been inflated due to a few extreme unrepresentative scores. The car's mileage will be lower than thirty miles per gallon. However, you cannot predict on the basis of the data given just how much lower it will be, nor can you predict what the range of performance will be.

4. *a* is the answer. The mode is the most frequently occurring score, which is 3. (p. 696)

5. *c* is the answer. To find the median, rearrange the scores from lowest to highest and then find the score that splits the data in half. The data from lowest to highest: 1, 2, 3, 3, 5, 6, 7, 8, 10. There are nine scores, so the fifth score will split the set such that half the scores (four) are below it and half (four) of them are above it. The value of the fifth score is 5. (p. 696)

6. *c* is the answer. The mean is 5. It is calculated by adding all of the scores and then dividing by the number of scores. The sum of all the scores is 45, which divided by 9 (the total number of scores) is 5. (p. 697)

7. *c* is the answer. A percentile score indicates the percentage of people or observations that fall below a given score in a normal distribution. Therefore 93 percent of Maxine's calculus class received scores that were lower than hers. (p. 699)

a. A percentile does not show how many problems Maxine answered correctly. It does show how well Maxine did relative to the other people in her class.

b. You cannot calculate how many people did better or worse than Maxine unless you know how many people are in her class.

d. A percentile is not related to the number of problems on the test. There may have been only fifty questions on the test. She still could have scored at the 93rd percentile, indicating that of all the people who took that fifty-question test, Maxine did better than 93 percent.